D1458466

*Finally-a definitive, contemporary biography on Robert Murray M'Cheyne abounding with historical detail, sterling illustrations, and spiritual warmth. Fresh light is thrown on the Moderates and Evangelicals of M'Cheyne's day. The influence of Thomas Chalmers, Edward Irving, the Bonars, James Hamilton, Alexander Moody Stuart, William Burns, and other contemporaries is ably set forth. M'Cheyne himself is judiciously quoted in the context of his personal and pastoral joys and struggles. His conversion, faithful ministry, and journey to Palestine are covered in great depth and with sympathy, yet without resorting to hagiography. This book is a fascinating and compelling read, and will supplant every other biography on M'Cheyne, with the exception of Andrew Bonar's. May God graciously grant its readers the passion for Christ and holiness that M'Cheyne possessed!*

**Dr. Joel R. Beeke**
President of Puritan Reformed Theological Seminary,
Pastor of Heritage Reformed Congregation,
Grand Rapids, Michigan

*Murray M'Cheyne was not yet thirty when he died, just before the Disruption, but his half-dozen years of zealous hardworking holiness in his Dundee pastorate set standards that shaped ministry in the Free Church of Scotland for half a century. He was an outstanding man of God, and his life story, here told in fullest detail and with fullest sympathy, should on no account be missed.*

**Dr. J. I. Packer**
Professor of Systematic and Historical Theology,
Regent College, Vancouver

*For many years the Christian Church has been crying out for a decent, well researched and historically accurate biography of McCheyne. Leen van Valen's excellent Dutch work 'Gedreven door Zijn liefde' (driven by his love) goes a long way towards meeting that need. Now translated into English it will prove to be a useful source of information and a stimulus to all who have a love for the Lord's work in Dundee, the rest of Scotland's cities and indeed far beyond Scottish shores. McCheyne has much to teach us about how to reach the cities of the modern industrialised world for Jesus Christ. Read and learn.*

**Rev David Robertson**
St Peter's Free Church, Dundee

Cover:
McCheyne was an incredible man, a man deeply aware of Christ's love for him and for all people. He knew that this love was secure, a love which would not let him go. Even when, amid a sea of infirmity, McCheyne was aware of his own present struggle to 'decrease', he felt compelled and kept by Christ's love.

The rusty key symbolises some aspects of the security found in this love. The key was allowed to rust because, once it was used to lock securely, it was never required again. In the same way, once a believer is secure in Christ's love, Christ does not let the beloved slip from His grasp, but holds them firmly throughout eternity.

Christian Focus

ISBN 1 85792 793 1



Published in 2002 by
Christian Focus Publications, Geanies House,
Fearn, Tain, Ross-shire, IV20 1TW, Scotland.

www.christianfocus.com

Cover design by Alister MacInnes

Translated from Dutch edition © 1993,
by Laurence R. Nicolson.

Printed and bound by
WS Bookwell, Finland

# Contents

Yours in Carissimis Vinculis
Robt. Murray M'Cheyne.

Robert Murray M'Cheyne

# Preface

Nearly ten years after the first Dutch edition of my biography of Robert Murray M'Cheyne was published, it is a pleasant task to write a preface in a new English publication of my book. It is also a pleasant thought to know that the name of M'Cheyne has not been forgotten in the English speaking Christian world. The man and his work are a rare example of holiness and zeal in the Kingdom of Christ. I remember the preparations and research before finishing it, that I sometimes was so overwhelmed by the graciousness of this Scottish saint that I could not withdraw from weeping.

It is not my intention to write such a long preface as I did in the Dutch edition. I mentioned some names of persons who helped me to realize this great work. Two exceptions I will make: The first is Rev. William Macknight, retired minister of the Free Church of Scotland in Leith, now living in Northern Ireland, who inspired and helped me, especially with scarce information on M'Cheyne and his friends. I remember his and his wife's hospitality in their home in Edinburgh! Secondly I like to mention the translator of this book, Laurence Nicolson, who learned both English and Dutch in South Africa. How big a task it was for him and for his wife who both finished the translation about eight years ago.

The life of M'Cheyne is a rich ornament of the Lord's grace in a sinful being, or is it more? Is it not ashamed for us Christians in this postmodern age, where likely there is more of Laodicea's lukewarmness than of Pauline zeal. It is now almost one hundred years ago that the last great revival in Wales stirred up many minds. We need a new revival of the christian church in Western Europe! Happily I perceive some stirrings of revival spirit among young people in the Netherlands. Many among reformed young men and women are seeking peace for their heart and many had already found the Saviour. This may be an encouragement for our brothers and sisters in Britain to beseech the Lord for His powerful operations of His Spirit in their denominations.

Leen J. van Valen
October 2002

# Chapter 1

# 'I ONCE WAS A STRANGER TO GRACE...'

**On the threshold of a new era**

The year 1813 proved to be a turning-point in world history. Napoleon's fall signalled the advent of a new era. French imperialism had been brought to a halt. Eight years earlier, the Battle of Trafalgar, which exalted the English admiral Nelson to the status of a national hero, was the initial step toward victory. The planned invasion of the British Isles by the French emperor had been averted at that time. Wellington brought even more glory to the mighty British empire by his crushing defeat of Napoleon at the Battle of Waterloo.

At the threshold of this new era, Robert Murray M'Cheyne was born. Though the French quest for power and world dominion had been dealt a deathblow, yet the spirit of revolution had not been extinguished. The age of the Enlightenment gradually changed into an era in which liberalism would increasingly set the tone. The nineteenth century presented itself as the century when great changes would take place.

The desire for freedom and independence was indeed the dominant social current which was to control both Europe and Britain. Happily, however, there was an undercurrent as well. The Enlightenment, having wreaked havoc in the ecclesiastical realm and having exerted a paralysing influence upon spiritual life, proved to be incapable of extinguishing the fire of God's Spirit. With the onset of a new century, signs of a spiritual revival became evident in several European countries. The lukewarm spirit of superficial morality and the deification of art and culture set the stage for a renewed interest in the biblical themes of sin and grace.

M'Cheyne was born in Edinburgh on 21 May 1813. Andrew Bonar describes the year in which M'Cheyne was born as a time when 'the Great Head had a purpose of blessing for the Church of Scotland'. 'The Cross was lifted up boldly in the midst of church courts which had long been ashamed of the Gospel of Christ.'

M'Cheyne's home was located in the upper storey of 14 Dublin Street, in New Town, Edinburgh. The ancient capital city could boast not only of an illustrious history, but could rightly be adorned with the name 'Jerusalem of the West'. Dating back to the days of the great Reformer, John Knox, the gospel trumpet had struck a chord in many hearts. Unfortunately, the Enlightenment had also gained a foothold in the city. Human virtues, as they especially came to the foreground in education, art and science, were placed on a pedestal. Furthermore, the wealthy segment of society proved to be a fertile breeding ground for the philosophical ideas of men like David Hume.

Edinburgh's prosperity particularly manifested itself in New Town. The tall, majestic houses, built in Georgian style and situated along spaciously arranged streets (St Andrew's Square and Charlotte Square being the central points), were occupied by the middle and upper classes. The expansion of the city was initiated in 1756. Soon thereafter the rows of houses constituting George Street and Queen Street began to appear, followed by the side streets, to which Dublin Street belonged. On the south side the contours of Princes Street became visible. The adjacent North Loch, the body of water demarcating the border with the more elevated older city, was gradually entirely drained by means of the soil which became available from digging the foundations of the new homes. The North Bridge spanned the green valley which had come into existence as a result of this, and formed the connection with the Old Town. The Old Town surrounding the St Giles' Church, to which the medieval castle was adjacent, remained the centre of activity. High Street, being the main artery of the city, was the most important link in the Royal Mile which connected the Castle and Holyrood Palace. However, the contrast between the new and the old cities became increasingly greater. There was a glaring disparity between the comfortable homes of New Town, and the slums of the wynds of the Canongate and of Cowgate districts in the old portion of the city.

### The M'Cheyne Family

Adam M'Cheyne, the father of Robert, was employed in the legal profession, and belonged to the well-to-do class. Shortly after his marriage, Adam established residence in the capital city. Even after its union with England in 1707, Scotland retained its own judicial system. The capital city was the seat of the Supreme Court of Justice, the highest court of the land. Adam was not a lawyer, but a member of the Writers to the Signet, an old judicial board whose task it was to draft charters and ordinances for the Court of Session, the highest judicial body of Scotland. From 1814, he was a member of the illustrious Society of Writers to His Majesty's Signet, a prominent group of legal scholars who were considered to belong to the most wealthy class of the city.

Adam M'Cheyne hailed from the small town of Thornhill in Dumfriesshire. In 1802 he married Lockhart Murray

!4 Dublin Street, Edinburgh, birthplace of M'Cheyne.

Registration of baptism of Robert, dated 11th July 1813. His uncle Robert Dickson, minister of South Leith, administrated the Sacrament.

evd Thomas Gillespie, and Mrs Elizabeth Hunter his Spouse, St Cuthberts Parish
on Born 5th Jany last, named John Hunter. Baptised by Revd Dr Andrew Brown, Edinr
dam M'Cheyne, Writer, and Mrs Lockhart Murray Dickson his Spouse, St
drew Parish, a Son Born 21st May last, named Robert, Bapd by Revd Dr Dickson, South Leith
12th
ugh Peacock, Ayr Militia, and Mary Peacock his Spouse, St Cuthberts Parish
Son Born 30th May last, named John. Baptised by Revd Mr Crauford.

Dickson, who lived in the same region, in Ruthwell. Adam's family belonged to the working class, whereas his wife's family was more well-to-do. Her father, David Dickson, owned the Nether Locharwood estate, which was the most renowned property of Ruthwell. A most promising future lay ahead of the young couple.

Since the inception of the industrial revolution in 1780, prosperity had come to the nation. Ever since the invention of the steam engine by James Watt, a new world had opened up. Cotton factories sprang up everywhere, equipped with machines which were driven by this new source of power. Many thousands moved from rural regions to Glasgow and Edinburgh to earn a living in either trade or industry. This not only signalled the emergence of a new class of capitalists, but also a more sharply defined contrast between the upper and lower classes. The population of Edinburgh doubled within fifty years and consisted of more than one hundred thousand inhabitants around the turn of the century.

Before long, Adam M'Cheyne felt at home in the large city which pulsated with activity. His home at Dublin Street, and later at Queen Street and Hill Street (also located in New Town), was a place visited by prominent figures such as Henry Cockburn and Dr Henry Duncan. The latter, in addition to being the Church of Scotland minister of Ruthwell, was the founder of the savings banks, a man who was concerned with the social needs of his fellow man. Adam intermingled with ease in the upper echelons of society and was involved in the cultural life of the city. He was a faithful member of the Church of Scotland, but his religious life manifested little depth and earnestness.

The M'Cheyne family consisted of five children. The oldest was David Thomas, who, just as his father, chose to pursue the study of law. He was followed by Elizabeth Mary, who later proved to be an invaluable support for her brother Robert. The third child was William Oswald Hunter, who, after studying medicine, departed for India. The second daughter, Isabella, died only four months after her birth. Robert Murray, the youngest child of the family, was named after one of his relatives.

**Robert's Youth**

Robert was a compliant child. His father recounts that 'he was always a boy of the most amiable, I may even say noble, disposition. I never found him guilty of a lie or any mean or unworthy action; and he had a great contempt for such things in others.' Although Adam M'Cheyne was not a man who spared the rod, he could not remember ever having spanked his youngest son.

Aside from his gentle and tender nature, it was the boy's keen intellect which caught people's attention. When the father would review the school lessons with his brothers, it became apparent at an early stage that Robert was interested in classical languages. 'I recollect during his recovery from measles or scarlet fever when about four years old, he learned, as an amusement, the whole of the Greek alphabet, and was able even to form the letters in a rude way upon a slate.'

When Robert was six years old, the family moved to Queen Street, which was located in the immediate vicinity. Number 56 was a more spacious home than the one in Dublin Street. For sixteen years this was the residence of the M'Cheyne family. They were subsequently forced to leave this spacious dwelling, as the landlord omitted to perform a number of repairs.

In the meantime, Robert made rapid progress in the English school, where he was under the tutorship of George Knight. His inclination toward poetry and public speaking soon became evident. His resonant voice was noteworthy, and the feeling with which he would recite poems and verses from the Psalms was moving. He possessed great talents, though one would not call him extraordinarily gifted. Upon graduating from school, he was given a secondary rather than the highest award which had been bestowed upon his brother David and his sister.

In October 1821, Robert transferred to the Old High School. It was not the impressive building patterned after an Athenian

Princes Street Edinburgh; St John's Episcopal Church on the left, and St Cuthbert's Church of Scotland on the right.

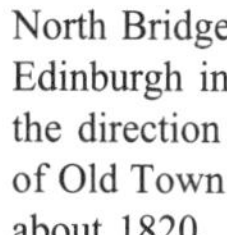

North Bridge Edinburgh in the direction of Old Town about 1820.

Edinburgh Old Town; St Giles and Old Parliament House about 1850.

Edinburgh Old Town, Liberton Wynd, one of the many slums.

temple which had been erected at the foot of Calton Hill, but rather the older school at Infirmary Street. Whereas the new academy was more oriented toward the wealthy citizenry, it was characteristic of the Old High School that its population consisted of a diverse mix of rich and poor. It was a most unique circumstance that during a period of great differences between classes, sons of the *bourgeoisie* of the New Town could associate with students from the slums of the Cowgate. Daily, the studious, youthful Robert would cross the North Bridge connecting the Old and New Town. During the winter, when it soon became dark, he may very well have gazed at the gaslights which, since 1818, illuminated the stores located on the adjoining South Bridge. There was also the theatre at the northeastern corner of the North Bridge which, in spite of protests, had opened its doors in 1769.

Thus it was that Robert continued his literary studies at the High School for a period of four years, immersing himself in the treasures of Greek and Roman classical literature. With auspicious success, he progressed from grade to grade, receiving numerous awards in doing so. He was intrigued by Virgil, Horatio, Ovid and Tibullus, and he even attempted to imitate the old poets. He also translated Latin verse; these being his first feeble attempts on the road to mastery of poetry. His first poem was entitled 'This Greece, but living Greece no more!' The heroism of the old Greeks appealed to the young M'Cheyne. His enthusiasm and ambition were stimulated by the ancient poets. His aversion for deceit and base conduct could, however, also be detected in his poems. His character was adorned with good qualities; his impeccable conduct was noteworthy. His entire deportment emanated activity and enthusiasm, whereas his lanky frame revealed that he was both lithe and strong. He observed his own virtues in the works of the classical writers; however, beyond this he did not progress. Outwardly he appeared to be both religious and pious, but this was essentially due to a natural disposition toward moral virtue, rather than proceeding from a heart that had been renewed by God's Spirit.

## A close-knit family

There was a good relationship between the members of the M'Cheyne family. The mother was rather more pensive of nature. Both parents, however, carried their children upon their hearts, supporting them in word and deed. Father M'Cheyne followed the progress of his children in school with great interest. He copied a few samples of Robert's poetry and prose and included them among the family memorabilia. The letters which he would occasionally write to his sons evidence a warm friendship. He was strict in raising them – however, not so as to alienate himself from them, but rather to build a relationship of trust. In so doing, he trained them to be independent at an early age, an independence based upon a healthy sense of self esteem.

The love and appreciation of the children for their parents were evidenced by the odes which they composed for them on the occasion of their birthdays. Initially, it was David who adhered to this custom, subsequently to be continued by Robert. In the ode which he composed in 1833, he reminded his father of the happy years of their home life. At that time his brother David had already died, and Robert had been converted. He reminisced on the hours which they had spent sitting around the fireplace. 'The flower of the flock,' David, had indeed been taken away, but 'the smaller home's circle, the closer we'll cling.' Subsequent to Robert's conversion, there continued to be a close tie with his family members. We shall soon observe that it was precisely in times of sorrow that the love of Christ drew them closer together, resulting in a more intimate bond of fellowship.

However, matters had not yet progressed this far. Initially, the care of the parents pertained more to the temporal future of their sons than to the salvation of their souls. It was Robert, the youngest son, in particular, who was placed upon a pedestal. Father M'Cheyne also relates that David was 'the greatest use to his two youngest brothers'. They could play games together for hours. They practised, each in their own way, writing the

Edinburgh New Town, Moray Place.

Edinburgh New Town, George Square.

Front of High School, Infirmary Street (1992).

various forms of poetry which flowed from their pens. Particularly when they became older, they were concerned about their mutual welfare. After William had concluded his medical studies and had moved to India, the entire family wrote lengthy letters to him. Thus, cheerfulness and a cosy atmosphere prevailed in the M'Cheyne family home.

At school Robert especially associated with Alexander Somerville, who became a lifelong friend. Robert enjoyed life and especially relished having a good time with others. In addition to his love for poetry, his interests included various forms of art, and already at an early age he began drawing landscapes. His athletic inclination found satisfaction in the pursuit of gymnastics. His school friend, Charles Dent Bell, would later remember Robert 'as a tall, slender lad, with a sweet pleasant face, bright yet grave, fond of play, and of a blameless life. I remember to this day his tartan trousers, which excited my admiration and my envy.' In every respect, Robert was a balanced person; he did not overact. In both his study and the management of his time he was orderly and neat. The notebooks and letters from his youth, which have been preserved, reveal a uniform style of handwriting which is easy to read. His notes are interspersed with illustrations. Initially he would tend more to tracing, for example, in copying the signature of King George III and the drawings of angels and priests from the old family Bible. As a high school student, however, he would make drawings of old castles and old churches in particular.

M'Cheyne would later reflect upon this period as one devoid of God. His life was everything to him, and he enjoyed it. He completely immersed himself in the things of this world, but was kept from excessive indulgence in sin. He was a 'stranger to grace and to God'. Externally he was a moral and virtuous man. During family and public worship he was both serious and devout, so that to some he appeared to manifest genuine piety. In reality, he was oblivious to the truth about his existence before God. At best he was a Pharisee who did not know his

Lockhart Murray Dickson (1772-1854). M'Cheyne's mother.

56 Queen Street.

20 Hill Street.

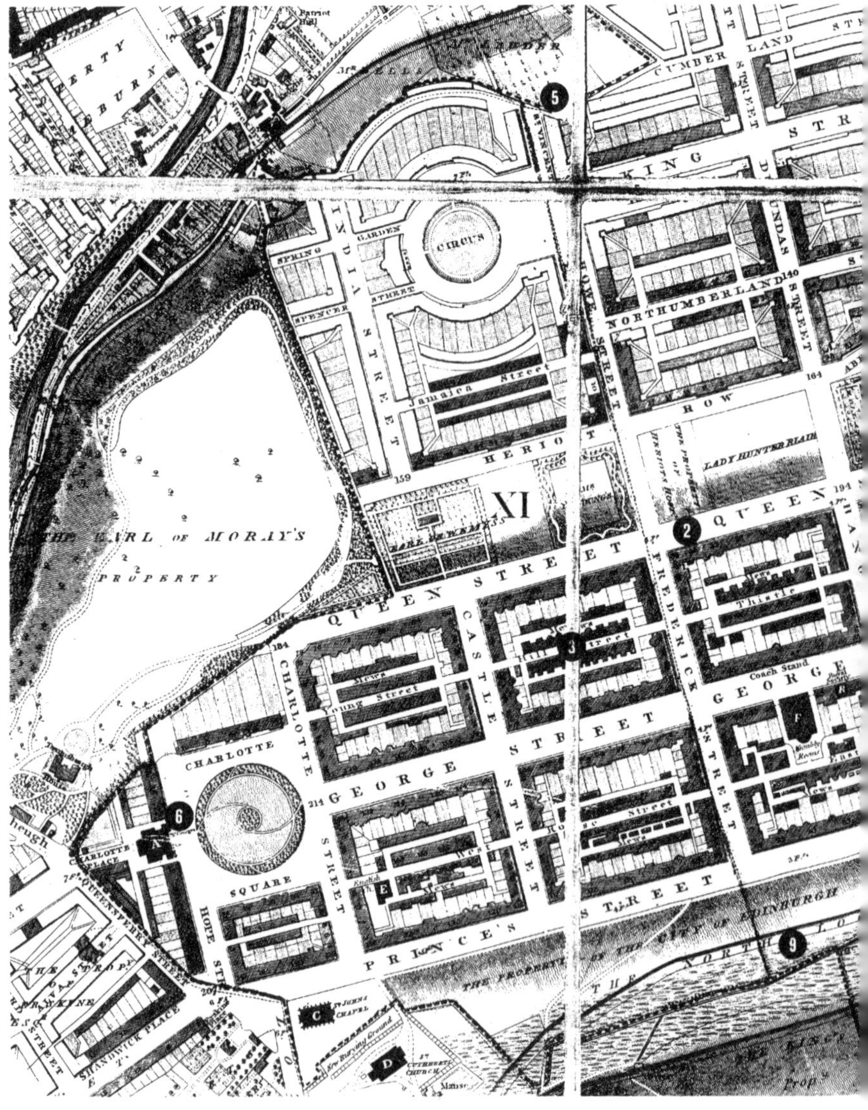


Edinburgh, New Town and part of Old Town. A part of the Plan of the City of Edinburgh and its environs, 1817. The parental homes in Dublin Street (1), Queen Street (2) and Hill Street (3) are all in New Town. The North Bridge (4) was the most important connection of New Town with Old Town. St. Stephen's Church (5) was not yet built. St. George's (6), St. Andrew's (7) Churches are to be seen. The Tron Church (8) was

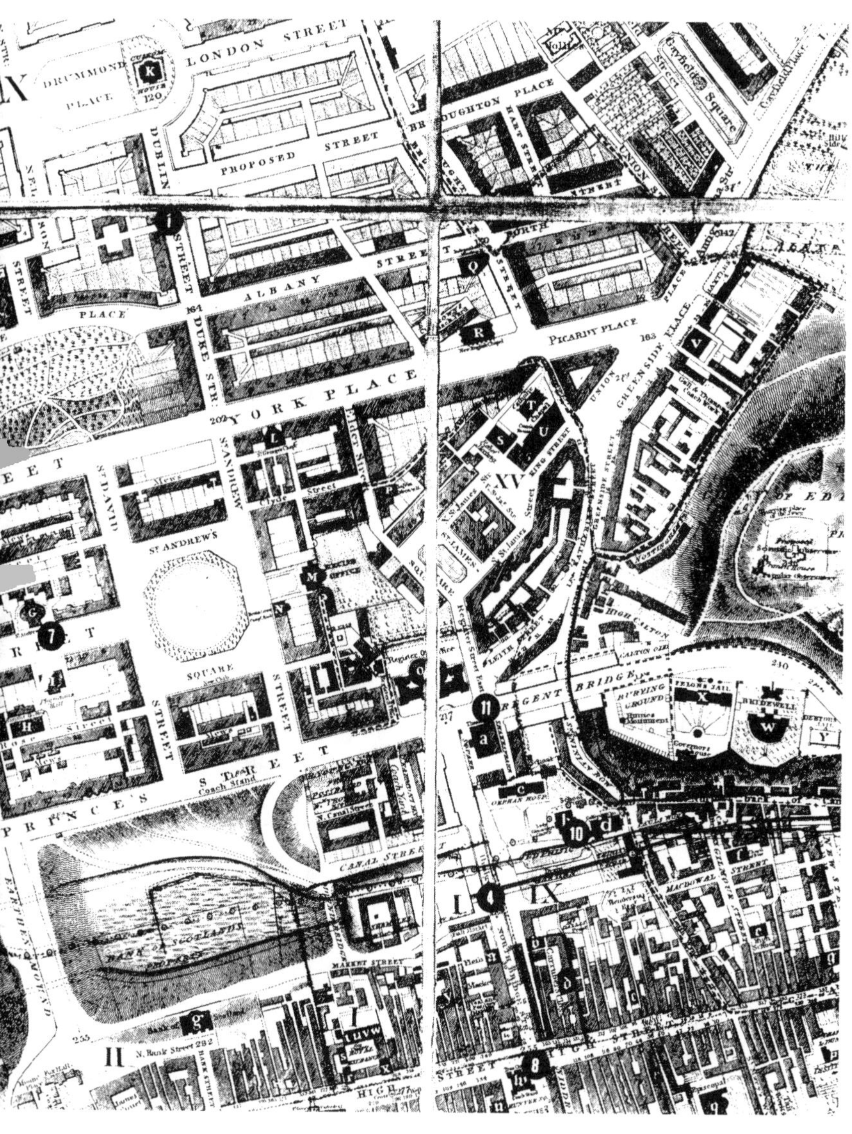


on the way from the parental home to High Street and Edinburgh University. The North Loch (9) was not yet filled up and Lady Glenorchy's Church (10) was not yet demolished for the coming of Waverley Railway Station. The Theatre (11) was a eyesore to the Evangelicals, but an attraction to them, who did not know of a contradiction between religion and worldly amusements.

own heart and relied upon an impeccable life. Outwardly he was able to control his youthful passions, but inwardly his heart was filled with self-righteousness. Robert, as well as his parents, had been moulded by the Enlightenment thinking, which dominated religious life at that time. Sin was considered to be a mere mistake, rather than constituting one guilty before God. Both the tranquillity of the domestic sphere and his carefree youth were, in reality, impediments as far as a true seeking after God was concerned. A false, inner peace kept his soul and conscience in the bonds of a tenacious sleep which, in God's time, would come to an end.

Robert had an aversion for idleness. He always rose early. An essay composed on this subject, entitled 'Early Rising', is a doxology upon beginning the day at an early hour. Sleep is necessary for infants and young children, but the time prior to sunrise and dew is 'the best and the most useful part of his life'. First, he praises the Creator who gives sleep for the acquisition of new strength, after which he includes a lengthy quote from John Locke. Furthermore, 'when we are more advanced on the stage of life, when we begin to put away childish things and to assume the man; it is then we may with safety and with profit cut off a few hours from our slumbers.' Early

Some drawings from the young Robert. Probably a church (opposite page) and the ruin of a castle in Dumfriesshire.

Essay

On Early-Rising.

Of all the bountiful provisions of Nature for the comfort and happiness of mankind, none is more wonderful, none more agreeable and necessary than the regular return of sleep.— When the frame of Man is jaded and fatigued by the labours of the bye-gone day, when his mind is borne down by grief, or harassed by some turn of fickle Fortune, it is then he feels, that sleep alone can "knit up the ravelled sleeve of care"— that sleep is "The death of each day's life, sore labour's bath

Balm of hurt minds, great nature's second course—

Chief nourisher in life's feast."—

In the tender years of Infancy, sleep seems to be still more neces.

Part of the first page of 'Early Rising', written by Robert.

rising does not only yield a wonderful opportunity to enjoy both the sunrise and nature, but it also renders a good opportunity for study. He then concludes his essay with a stanza from Shakespeare, in which the poet expresses what he experiences when observing nature – when the mist of the dew evaporates: 'When a thousand pearls the dewy lawns adorn.'

**Vacations in Ruthwell**

Even though M'Cheyne did not see many of those 'pearls' of nature in the urban setting, during his vacations he tried as far as possible to enjoy the beauty of the rural environment. The children would frequently stay with their mother's family in Ruthwell. James Dodds, a future study friend, who attended the academy in this locality, remembered the 'elegant, light hearted, yet promising lad'. Most often they would stay with an aunt in 'Clarence Cottage', a country residence located in the hamlet of Clarencefield, near Ruthwell. For his entire lifetime, Robert retained the memories of his visits to this region. A few drawings of these surroundings decorate his notebooks.

He evidently kept his parents informed of his experiences. His first letters dating from 1827 were written from the 'Cottage'; they reveal how much he enjoyed life on the farm as well as in the fields. 'Aunty has got 7 stacks and 2 barns full; 3 swine, 2 sows; 7 pigs; 8 hens ... 1 canary; 4 cows ... 37 cart-loads of potatoes.' Particularly the horses were an attraction for this boy. This served him well later on in life when, riding his 'Tully', he performed his pastoral duties in Dundee.

During his times in Ruthwell, he was a frequent visitor to the manse. Since 1799 Henry Duncan had served as pastor there. 'Uncle Henry' loved children and young people. His qualities and interests differed little from Robert's. The minister loved nature, was proficient in geography, and was familiar with literature. His home was a meeting place for many renowned persons of both social and ecclesiastical spheres of life. The sprawling grounds were a visual delight and Duncan 'was a landscape gardener of the first order, and adorned his spacious glebe as well as the precincts of the manse with the greatest skill and care'. He also had compassion on those of lesser means. Motivated primarily by social concern, he founded the first savings bank in 1810 – the bank for the lower class. Initially Duncan subscribed to the thinking of the Enlightenment, until the Lord began to delve into his heart to bring him to a saving knowledge of Himself. His conversion, however, did not signal the end of his interest in nature and the fine arts; albeit they were now of subordinate importance. The young student felt thoroughly at home in the manse of Ruthwell. As a boy he played in the large garden and felt sad if the Duncan family was not at home. Thus he wrote to his parents on 31 August 1820: 'The Manse is very empty just now; the boys being all away.' He also described the evening get-togethers in the manse: 'There was singing and spouting and I don't know what all.'

During his time as a high school student, he frequently visited the Highlands. Together with his friends or with his brother David, he would make trips to this mountainous region. There he could enjoy the beauty of nature to the full. Robert loved to make adventurous journeys through this rugged countryside. For his entire lifetime he retained his desire to make extensive trips. He would walk for hours without tiring. There were no symptoms of the fragile health that would trouble him later on. One day, he and some friends were hiking in the area surrounding Dunkeld. Malcolm McGregor, the inseparable friend of his youth, was among them. Toward sundown, they were wending their way through the hills in the direction of Strathardle, when they were overtaken by a dense fog. They lost their way and had to spend the night on the surface of the wet and chilly moor. For young Robert it was a frightening experience to be surrounded by the quietness and solitude of nature, without seeing any light. Even though they were overcome with great fear, the boys fell asleep at last – until the screeching of birds awoke them.

Prior to transferring from the High School to the university

Clarence Cottage 20th Octr
1827.

My Dear Father and Mother,

Auntie's letter of yesterday would inform you of our actions respecting the unlucky parcel; but I hope before this reaches you that the affair will be entirely settled. It appears to me that Mr Clarke's saying it was at Carlisle and the guard that it was at Dumfries (being directed to the care of Mr Dow instead of Mr Beck) is just putting us off; but time will show.

The Country is now assuming a bleak and wintry appearance, and the weather is now very unsteady 'smiles and tears together'. The woods are beautifully variegated but the leaves are fast falling and are already nearly as thick as those that "strew the brook of Vallombrosa". Still the Cottage looks beautiful and green. Still its inmates are gay – 'ever dancing full of glee" though all around us most are dreary. Mary and I called at

A letter of young Robert from Ruthwell; he drew his 'guest house'.

in November 1827, Robert stayed for a few months in Ruthwell. It was an unforgettable vacation. When the autumn colours began to appear in the garden, he wrote: 'Still the Cottage looks beautiful and green.' A sketch of the house adorns his letter of 20 October. The end of his vacation was at hand. His notebook contains an 'Adieu' to Ruthwell: 'Farewell to the barn, to the stable and byre. To Jessie and Mollie, to the blood full of fire.' He had to bid farewell to the beauty of nature, for his studies were once again before him.

The Lord was, however, preparing him for a different task. The 'beautiful things' of life were not to be the preparation for the calling that awaited him. The battle arena was approaching more and more. His carefree youth would soon be disrupted. For Robert the value of life would become more than immersing himself in nature and culture. As yet he was a stranger to a personal relationship with his Creator. He did not realize that his relationship with a righteous and holy God had been severed by sin. 'I knew not my danger, and felt not my load,' was the discovery he then made – a discovery which opened the door to his conversion from a superficial lifestyle to a deep consciousness of the things of eternal life.

**Moderates and Evangelicals**

We have observed that Robert received a religious upbringing. However, to what extent did spiritual life play a role in the M'Cheyne family? They attended worship in the Tron Church in High Street – in Old Town. The building dates back to 1637. The wooden church tower had been replaced after the great fire of 1824, and the construction of the South Bridge had also drastically changed in appearance. Two ministers, Alexander Brunton and William Simpson, served this flock at that time. They both sympathized with the Moderates, the dominant movement within the State Church. They were moderately orthodox in their thinking, when compared to such a minister as Alexander Carlyle, who set the tone during the second half of the eighteenth century. 'Jupiter Carlyle' from Inveresk, a village near Edinburgh, was an outspoken adherent of the Enlightenment, a worshipper of natural reason, and a lover of art and feminine beauty. He found much delight in worldly entertainment and the pride of life, and had much contempt for the 'Highflyers', as he dubbed the strict Evangelicals.

The moderate movement actually had its origin in legalistic influences which, from the beginning of the eighteenth century, had set the tone in the Scottish Church. The gospel was obscured by the moral qualifications which were imposed upon the hearers. More and more the emphasis of the preaching gravitated toward the marks of a holy life. The offer of grace

Henry Duncan (1774-1846), minister and philanthropist. Minister of Ruthwell from 1799, founder of the Savings Bank, the first savings-bank in history. First location of it in 1810 in Ruthwell, now worldwide in eighty countries as the International Savings Banks Institute.

The Manse of Henry Duncan in Ruthwell

was watered down and made to be contingent upon being penitent and fit. In the course of time these marks were transformed into a description of virtuousness; consequently, Christ was preached more as an example rather than a substitute. Enlightened thinking, which particularly found very fertile soil in England, was compatible with this. Ministers permeated their sermons with quotes from Socrates and Plato. Francis Hutcheson, the father of Scottish moderatism, laid the foundation for an enlightened theology by placing strong emphasis upon virtue and reason. Due to these developments, the majority of ministers were no longer interested in the fundamental truths of the Bible. Human talents were worshipped, and virtuous and civilized conduct were glorified.

M'Cheyne was born during a period when the Moderates were still setting the tone. Most areas in the country had been infected with the lukewarm religion of the Moderates. The glorification of reason and virtue did, however, have the opposite effect. Immorality, crime and social discontent had become more pronounced around the turn of the century. The severe poverty among the lower classes promoted a withdrawal from the church. The prosperity which accompanied the industrial revolution was narrow in scope, and for the working class no more than an illusion. The superficial sermons of the majority of the ministers only served to fire discontent. However, the Laodicean spirit which prevailed in the church was exposed before many. It was especially the work of lay preachers, such as James and Robert Haldane, which was the means whereby the eyes of many were opened to the spirit of superficiality. Therefore, when the Haldanes opened a Tabernacle in Edinburgh in 1801, there was much interest. The old themes of the gospel of free grace began to appeal to the people once again.

The ministers of the Tron Church were, however, not the worst. Sermons by Brunton which have been preserved, testify to a great earnestness. The matters of eternity were bound upon the heart; and yet something was seriously lacking. His call to repentance and to depart from sinful ways was only conditional. Near the end of the sermons only a few sentences were devoted to the forgiveness of sins, and the person of Christ came to the foreground briefly as the capstone of the message. Forgiveness and salvation were only offered to those who diligently strove to do good works. Sin and the inability of man to do any good were not denied, but they were watered down. To the ministers of the Tron Church, the cross of Calvary was not the focal point of their ministry.

Father M'Cheyne took his children to church at an early age. His reason for not attending St Andrews Church at George Street, not far from Dublin Street, is unknown. On the Sabbath, the children would remain at the church between services for catechetical instruction. 'I recollect,' so Adam M'Cheyne writes, 'that on these occasions the members of the congregation who remained to hear used to be struck with their peculiarly clear and harmonious recitations of the hymns and other exercises.'

After some time there was a new depth in the religion of the parents. The stimulus for this change was not so much a matter of inner conviction as it was the spiritual development of some of their children. Moderatism no longer had any appeal for them. Shortly after St Stephen's Church was opened in New Town in 1828, they joined the new congregation. The minister was William Muir, a man with evangelical principles. At this time, Robert became a member of the church. It was not done out of a matter of tradition but with a measure of sincerity. He listened to the sermons on the Sabbath with great interest, and participated in the weekly meetings in the kirk session room, affording the minister an opportunity to become well acquainted with him. Muir spoke highly of this young man and gave a good testimony of him.

In spite of his evangelical disposition, Muir was more a man of the middle way. His sermons were not fully Christocentric; he did not follow the line of the Marrowmen of the eighteenth century, as did his colleague, John Colquhoun, from nearby

Leith. At a later date, Robert opted for the preaching of John Bruce of New North Church, one of the divisions of the St Giles congregation, which worshipped in the Methodist Chapel at Nicolson Square from 1829-1835. During this period the evangelicals gained an ever stronger foothold in the old capital city. In the brand-new St George's Church – the impressive building at Charlotte Square which, from 1814, had Andrew Thomson as its minister – warm gospel tones were to be heard. Thomson was a worthy successor of Dr Erskine, the leader of the evangelical movement which increasingly gained influence. In the High Church congregation of St Giles', which temporarily worshipped at Hope Street, the talented Robert Gordon preached weekly; and since 1777, one could hear the old, familiar sounds of sin and grace in the 'Quoad Sacra Chapel' of Lady Glenorchy. There was also Thomas Randall, the worthy successor of Alexander Webster, who ministered with blessing in the Tolbooth Church, whilst also counselling the young men who were being trained for the ministry. Among the seceding churches, it was particularly Thomas M'Crie, the biographer of John Knox, who was a man of renown. The dry, moralistic sermons of the Moderates of the eighteenth century increasingly had to yield to the gospel message of men who, filled with zeal, made Christ the very centre of their message.

**His student years**

How did Robert fare at university? The old main building at the South Bridge Street was in the immediate vicinity of the High School. It was a rectangular building with a dignified, classic facade, which supported a round tower, making the building even more impressive. The famous architects, Adams and Playfair, were the designers of this famous complex, built between 1789 and 1834. Through these gates Robert entered in November 1827 to complete his education within a period of eight sessions.

During the first years he concentrated on furthering his classical education. George Dunbar instructed him in the Greek

Churches which were attended in Robert's youth:

- Tron Church, High Street/South Bridge, built in 1637. At first called Christ's Church, but as it was close to the weighing-house it received its present name. In this church the General Assembly of the established Church held their meetings in 1830-1840.

- St Stephen's Church, at the end of St Vincent Street. Built in 1826/1827 with 1,600 seats.

- St Andrew's Church, built in 1785 with 973 seats. Here began the Disruption in 1843.

- St George's Church, Charlotte Square, built in 1811 and opened in 1814, After a design of Robert Reid. It is now West Register House.

language, and David Ritchie, the minister of St Andrew's Church, in logic. His programme of study was comprehensive. The professors exerting the most influence on him were James Pillans and John Wilson, the latter teaching the subject of Moral Philosophy. He also took lessons in French, gymnastics and elocution. It was not clear what degree he was pursuing. A good preparation was essential for the study of theology; it is not known, however, whether Robert intended from the very outset to become a minister. In any event, there was no essential change in his spiritual thinking until 1831. More and more he became wrapped up in his studies, and his appetite for the acquisition of knowledge was insatiable. His academic training undergirded the moulding and development of his character in a most meaningful way.

His literary talents in particular blossomed more and more during the first years of this study period. His father writes the following concerning this: 'He turned his attention to elocution and poetry and the pleasures of society rather more perhaps than was altogether consistent with prudence. His power of singing and reciting were at that time very great, and his company was courted on that account more than was favourable to graver pursuits.' Thus the engaging Robert was the centre of attention among his friends. On the one hand, he was a refined and well-mannered young man. 'Everything he did seemed to bear the stamp of early culture and native refinement.' On the other hand, he was also capable of fascinating his audience with his humour and antics. Nevertheless, he always remained within the boundaries of decency and common courtesy. He had an aversion for students who imbibed an immoral lifestyle. 'He was by no means frivolous or conceited.' Although he enjoyed dancing and athletic activities, and was involved in the things of the world, he was able to exercise self-control. He pursued a carefree life, and his first years as a university student transpired without disappointments. It seemed as if a brilliant future lay in store for him. M'Cheyne was, according to Dr Chalmers's judgment of his friend, 'a fine specimen of the natural man.'

James Dodds remarks that Robert was 'full of that pride of heart and love of the world which afterwards, under the power of grace, he confessed and deplored'.

On the title page of his scrapbook – which contains the essays for his Greek and Latin professors, his addresses given to the Academic Society, and a large number of poems – M'Cheyne later wrote the significant phrase: *Dum relego scripsisse pudet*, that is: 'When I read again its contents, I am ashamed that ever I wrote them.' At a later date, he depicted his youth in a poem entitled 'Response,' written on 14 February 1832. He writes: 'When the wild march of life I first began, ('Tis not so long ago) my earliest plan was just precisely what you now advise, To eat, drink, laugh, sleep, wake, and thus grow wise. From morn till eve, from eve till merry morn ....' Thoughts of death and eternity did not occupy him at all, although he was not entirely without impressions. 'I kissed the rose nor thought about the thorn.' And thus he tried to silence the disturbing voice of his conscience. It was as if he were intoxicated with a desire for 'paradise lost'.

His passion for popularity seemed to be limitless. His interest was directed toward the female sex. This was more than the normal orientation toward the opposite sex which had awakened during his puberty. To this natural development was conjoined a more definitive love for charm and beauty. He had an eye for romance and feminine charm. 'On other objects soon my eyes were turned, and youth's romance within my bosom burned.' Valentine's Day, 14 February, was the opportunity *par excellence* for Robert to give expression to his lyrical effusions. He would compose his love songs, or canzonettes, according to the custom of the day. The majority of these poems date from the period of 1829 and 1830. He wrote ten poems for Susannah Hawkins. To Caroline, who would depart for England, he wrote a poem on 14 February 1830, entitled *Una Canzoneta,* and to Emily he addressed the farewell greeting: 'Forget me not....' He preserved a piece of hair from Constance Bullen very carefully with a poem which had more content than the others. It was a canzonet he wrote on 14 February 1832 subsequent to his conversion. Between the lines we can perceive a higher love that filled him: 'As sailors when peril of shipwreck is over, delight in the haven of rest. So hearts that have once loved can never love more. But seek for a heaven in the breast.'

It is difficult to determine from his poems whether his interest in girls of his age bore a deeper significance. In his conduct he was not yet mature; he was still somewhat boyish and as yet inexperienced in seeking out the proper direction for his life. Was he perhaps seeking for a life partner with whom he could share both joy and sorrow? He certainly had a great need for companionship and love. Even though Robert lived a carefree life, he was far from superficial. There were also times that the ephemeral nature of earthly things was impressed upon him. In 1830 he suddenly became seriously ill, which brought him face to face with reality. During this period he had contact with Mondego Mary Macgregor, an older sister of his school comrade Malcolm. She belonged to a Scottish family which had emigrated to Bogota in South America. She had been assigned the task of supervising her brother during his school years. In Robert's heart, feelings began to develop for her which were more than friendly sentiments. Mondego gave him a notebook consisting of pages of her writings and concluding with, 'Remember M.M.' Robert filled the remaining pages with poetry. For several years he would remember her birthday by writing a poem for that occasion. However, at a given moment she disappeared from the scene. Many years later, while on his way to Palestine, he visited her in London, and realized that she had not found true happiness yet.

## His religious life

And thus the first years as a student in Edinburgh passed. His recreational activities were not at all detrimental to his studies. In all of his classes he attained the highest honours. His favourite instructor was Professor Wilson, the famous author of *Noctes*

Robert Murray M'Cheyne. Self-portrait, a charcoal drawing made on 1st April 1830. Then he was 17 years old.

*Ambrosianae.* He lectured in Moral Philosophy, a subject that was very appealing to the young Robert. When the professor entered the lecture hall, he would be greeted with loud applause – proof of his great popularity. It was a climax for the vain student when Wilson awarded him first prize for a poem, 'The Covenanters'. In this poem, Robert vividly depicted the forbidden field meetings of the persecuted Presbyterians in the hills of the Pentlands – all of this against the background of the tragic defeat the Covenanters suffered there in 1666. He relates how the minister came from his hiding place to preach, and how the soldiers interrupted the service soon after, took him prisoner, and put him to death. It is as if the young poet had witnessed all this with his own eyes. The conclusion of the poem is very moving indeed. It contains the last words of the persecuted preacher, who ascends the scaffold and speaks to the gathered crowd: 'Ye faithful ones, Let not the horrors of my cruel death, Disturb your heavenward race, For if with Christ We suffer, then with Him we shall exalt.'

It is as if the poet is swept along in spirit when he concludes: 'Who died for me! Welcome, Thou Lamb of God, Thou joy and portion of my weary soul, Which shall endure through all eternity.' On 20 March he recited the long poem in Wilson's class. 'Thus the martyr died – And what shall we who live in peaceful days...?' It is as if the poet senses his own hesitation. Was he willing to sacrifice everything for Christ? Was he prepared to suffer shame for His Name? Or was the motive of his life his own honour – also with this poem?

M'Cheyne's religion was in essence Pelagian. His moralistic view of man was in reality a denial of original sin. Man is capable of attaining a certain measure of virtue, albeit not without divine assistance. He must be careful and watch over the issues of the heart. It is certain that everything here on earth remains imperfect and polluted with sin. It is for this reason that the believer pursues a heavenly goal. This diligence will ultimately be rewarded. 'Up, up, let us handle the plough while we may ...,' was the motto of his life.

The most difficult task for Robert was probably his striving to control his passions. His emotions and youthful zeal were subject to sinful desires coming from his heart. To the eye, a Pharisaical virtuousness, as a facade, can conceal the inner man as far as possible. He made a study also of these inclinations. His idols, such as Cicero and other philosophers, had preceded him in this. For Robert they were better examples than the apostle Paul. In January 1829 he completed his essay entitled, 'On the government of the passions.' This essay was born out of experience, not that of God's children in their continual battle between spirit and flesh, but rather the conflict between virtuousness and morality, and contrary feelings. M'Cheyne begins with the Creation and Fall in Paradise. There is the origin of the 'long train of unruly passions'. He even speaks of how 'a crowd of wild thoughts and turbulent passions make him continually an enemy of his own nature. Such a combination of good and evil is man.' He then proceeds to quote Paul relative to his battle against 'the law of sin'. However, this conflict is described more as a battle between one's religious and moral sense, and the unnatural passions. It is no wonder that he seeks to align himself with Socrates and Cato, who had become far advanced in self-knowledge, yet without ever having perceived in the least measure the extent of the pollution of sin. The issue for M'Cheyne is the victory over self, and this victory 'is far more than to compensate for the difficulties and all the dangers of the battle'. 'If we have not the power of commanding our passions,' we are slaves 'in the very truest sense of the word'.

This brilliant student must, however, come to the realization that it is impossible to be completely free from sinful passions. But there appears to be hope and a sense of victory when he concludes: 'Let us then be convinced that true happiness is only to be found in a well-regulated mind where passions never enter in to blast and to destroy.' Here the blindness of an unrenewed heart comes to the foreground – a heart reassures itself with the meagre comfort of an unfounded idealism. It is the expression of a heart which does not understand the reason for Christ's coming into the world – a heart that only yearns for peace and happiness, and has an aversion to being truly emptied as a result of the work of God's Spirit. The 'strong man armed' kept the heart of the promising Robert at peace. He grew up in a protected environment without concerning himself about his external salvation. He did not perceive himself as being ungodly to the very core of his being, and therefore he had no need of a Saviour. The religion of the Moderates confirmed him in his delusion, causing him to remain impervious to grace. It was necessary that the building of virtue and moralism which he had constructed collapse as a pack of cards. The moment decreed by God to open his eyes to this was near. M'Cheyne had to learn what he later expressed in poetry: 'Because I cannot move a limb until He say, "Unbind him."'

### The conversion of Chalmers

At the beginning of this chapter a turning-point in world history was mentioned. More significant than the victory over

Napoleon and his mighty empire were the first stirrings of a religious awakening which would soon become evident everywhere. Thomas Chalmers' conversion in 1811 signified a turning-point in the history of the Church of Scotland, which as yet was groaning under the bondage of the Moderates. Initially, Chalmers had also promoted the same ideals and views as Robert. When, in 1803, he became a minister in Kilmany, he was a Moderate. His sermons were permeated with moral theology, in which the virtues of man were the focal point. He accepted the Scriptures as the Word of God, but he did not understand what free grace was. He taught his people that 'the rewards of heaven are attached to the exercise of our virtuous affections'. As the capstone of his sermons he pointed to Christ. He taught that 'by the death of Christ there is hope to the sincere and humble penitent who wishes to forsake the evil of his ways'.

A turning-point in Chalmer's life was preceded by several deaths in his family circle, which brought him face to face with death and judgment. More and more he began to discover that there was a great vacuum within. He did indeed wrestle earnestly to rid himself of his sinful passions, but it was a striving in his own strength. The system of the Moderates constituting a religion of 'Do this, and thou shalt live,' proved to be a pernicious pathway. His eyes were opened to the gospel of God's grace. The only foundation of salvation was revealed to his soul: Christ and His finished work. Later he wrote: 'It is, believe in the Lord Jesus Christ, and thou shalt be saved. When this belief enters the heart, joy and confidence enter along with it. The righteousness which we try to work out for ourselves eludes our impotent grasp, and never can a soul arrive at true or permanent rest in the pursuit of this object. The righteousness which, by faith, we put on, secures our acceptance with God, and secures our interest in His promises, and gives us a part in those sanctifying influences by which we are enabled to do with aid from on high what we never can do without it. We look to God in a new light – we see Him as a reconciled Father.'

Thus the light arose in the dark soul of Chalmers. He went his way in uncertainty and doubt, until he saw at last that the Saviour had already accomplished everything.

Chalmers' conversion bore much resemblance to that of one of his pupils, Robert Murray M'Cheyne. The turning-point for Robert was no longer far away. In 1828 Chalmers was appointed as professor of theology at the University of Edinburgh. On a snowy day, 10 November 1828, Chalmers delivered his inaugural lecture in the presence of a large crowd. A new era had dawned for the theological class. The Lord led this master in His kingdom to the old capital city to train a generation of future ministers. He was an inspiring personality who brought the university to life again. The spotlight would once again be upon the central doctrines of the Reformers.

When Chalmers took up office for the first time in Edinburgh, M'Cheyne's direction in life had not as yet been determined. The Lord knew from eternity the way He would take with 'His chosen vessel'. Chalmers' lectures caused many students to reflect on their eternal state and brought many to repentance. His lectures on systematic theology impressed a stamp upon those who were preparing themselves for the sacred ministry. M'Cheyne had not yet arrived at this point. Upon the arrival of this professor, his heart was, as yet, still in darkness. Soon the light of God's grace would arise in his soul. Andrew Bonar remarks: 'For the same event that awakened his soul to a true sense of sin and misery, led him to the ministry.' The Lord would equip him for the ministry of the Word of God, and Thomas Chalmers would be instrumental in expounding to him 'the way of God more perfectly'.

# Chapter 2

# THE FIRE OF LOVE REKINDLED

## Conversion of David

The year 1831 was a turning-point in the life of Robert. His quiet and self-sufficient lifestyle was disturbed. The refined appearance and noble traits disappeared. Superficially he demonstrated in his religion a certain gravity and commitment, but that was nothing more than a veneer to hide the reality of his existence before God. Andrew Bonar admits that he had, 'at that time, a relish for no higher joy than the refined gaieties of society, and for such pleasures as the song and the dance could yield. He himself regarded these as days of ungodliness, days wherein he cherished a pure morality, but lived in heart a Pharisee. I have heard him say that there was a correctness and propriety in his demeanour at times of devotion, and in public worship, which some, who knew not his heart, were ready to put to the account of real feelings. And this experience of his own heart made him look with jealousy on the mere outward signs of devotion in dealing with souls. He had learned in his own case how much a soul, unawakened to a sense of guilt,

David Thomas M'Cheyne (1804-1831).

may have satisfaction in performing, from the proud consciousness of integrity towards man, and a sentimental allegiance of mind that chastens the feelings without changing the heart.'

His studies at the university progressed successfully. Soon these would be terminated and he would make further plans for the future. His parents were proud of their gifted son's love of studying, as indeed they were of his elder brothers, William and David. William had completed his medical studies and had departed for India in April. As a result of an appointment with the East India Company, he was assigned as medical doctor to the 54th Regiment. In those days it was quite an undertaking to make such a long journey. Neither was it easy for the household of 56 Queen Street to bid him farewell. It was as if the protection which the family offered was disturbed. His departure, with all its accompanying dangers, left those remaining behind with a sense of insecurity.

Both brothers were 'rare examples' for Robert; 'they were well conducted lads of the greatest promise,' at least that was the opinion of their father M'Cheyne. David, nine years older than Robert, was a second father who lovingly cared for him. His father mentioned with pride his many talents and his love of studying. At the high school as well as at college, he excelled with distinction. He surpassed Robert and William in his knowledge of the classical languages and ancient history. Like his father before him, he chose to study law, and after some time as an assistant in Queen Street, he was posted to the same college of 'The Writers to the Signet'.

David possessed much in common with his youngest brother. He had a captivating personality and therefore demonstrated a particular aversion for hypocrisy. He was irritated by exaggeration or a false impression of things. He related to the people around him with caution and sincerity and took much trouble to ensure that others understood him correctly, so that his words gave no occasion for misunderstanding or dishonesty. Various talents lent further import to his personality. He developed a keen interest in the art of poetry, as did his youngest brother, and it was no wonder that he helped Robert to write his first lines of verse.

With apprehension, he noticed that Robert made advances in worldly matters, especially during his first years at university. David had learned to strive after nobler things than vain pleasure. A few years later a dull look appeared in his eyes. It was not only a physical ailment that caused his melancholy state but a deep realization of eternal matters. He saw the relativity of all earthly things in the light of eternity. It was no wonder that he was sad when he saw how Robert was taken up with the world. He prayed many sincere prayers for him and earnestly warned him to seek eternal life. His serious-mindedness filled the other occupants of the house with awe. Due to his influence, the religious well-being of the family was gradually transformed. David was viewed as the pride of the house and he left a void whenever he was absent. His father missed him most of all.

The feeling of loss became even greater when an end came to the young and promising life of David. A dejected mood began to control him more and more until his strength was sapped. 'Many weary months did he spend in awful gloom, till the trouble of his soul wasted away his body.' A vacation trip to England didn't improve matters. When he wandered through the beautiful Lake District and climbed the mountains of Cumberland and Westmoreland he caught a chill. His weakened constitution couldn't offer resistance to this seemingly innocent cold, resulting in his contracting a high temperature. In this state David returned home. The members of his family surrounded his bed with great sadness and helplessly beheld as the end approached. However, they also noticed that the melancholy features vanished from his face. 'Joy from the face of a fully reconciled Father above lighted up his face.' In full peace and assurance of faith in his Saviour, David passed away on 8 July 1831.

**The effect of David's death on Robert**

Robert felt perplexed and dismayed seeing his beloved brother passing away. He had lost his great means of support and his stand-by. His heart was overcome with grief. David had been more than a brother to him; he had been an adviser who not only helped him with his studies, but also directed him to nobler pursuits. 'He gave me a Bible, and persuaded me to read it; he tried to train me as a gardener trains the apple tree upon the wall; but all in vain. I thought myself far wiser than he and would always take my own way. Many a time, I well remember, I have seen him reading his Bible, or shutting his closet door to pray, when I have been dressing to go to some frolic or some dance of folly.' Now it was all over. Never again would he see his brother, no more would he be able to discuss with him the Saviour of his soul. The image of his brother appeared to be deeply printed in his memory, an image which persisted in following him and, in fact, always remained with him. In the days of mourning and sorrow, he penned a 'Miniature Likeness' of his brother in poetic form:

Alas! not perfect yet – another touch,
And still another, and another still,
Till those dull lips breathe life, and yonder eye
Loses its lack lustre hue, and be lit up
With the warm glance of living feeling. No –
It never can be! Ah, poor, powerless art!

David's portrait was indelibly printed in his memory, but there was more. His poem remained incomplete as though he couldn't find the concluding verse. His thoughts remained fixed on the shining face of his dying brother. This visible foretaste of heavenly glory preoccupied Robert's thoughts. Furthermore, the look on his face depicting a longing for fellowship with the God of salvation, failed to let him go.

And oh! recall the look of faith sincere
With which the eye would scrutinize the page
That tells us of offended God appeased
By awful sacrifice upon the cross
Of Calvary – that bids us leave the world
Immersed in darkness and in death, and seek
A better country. And! how oft that eye
Would turn on me, with pity's tenderest look,
And, only half-upbraiding, bid me flee
From the vain idols of my boyish heart!

Here his writing stopped. It was as though his thoughts couldn't proceed further. He was deeply moved. David had something that he lacked. The attraction of the world couldn't give him what his brother had received by grace. David was now eternally happy and he extremely unhappy. The look on his dying brother's face bored like an awl into his conscience. Years later he wrote concerning the day his brother died: 'This day, eleven years ago, I lost my loved and loving brother, and began to seek a Brother who cannot die.' Robert didn't continue to mourn his deep loss; he realized, at that time, that he was without God. The Lord called out to him, in his loneliness, to put an end to his meaningless existence. One year later he wrote in his diary concerning the memorable day his brother died: 'On this morning last year came the first overwhelming blow to my worldliness; how blessed to me, Thou O God, only knowest, who hast made it so.' The seed his brother had sown began to bear fruit. From this day on the poems Robert wrote about his brother gradually began to come true:

He sought not now
To wreathe his brow
With laurel bough.
He sought no more
To gather store
Of earthly lore,
Nor vainly strove
To share the love
Of heaven above,
With ought below
That earth can show.
The smile forsook
His cheek his look
Was cold and sad;
And even the glad
Return of morn,
When the ripe corn
Waves o'er the plains,
And simple swains
With joy prepare
The toil to share
Of harvest brought
No lively thought
To him.

Robert was eighteen years old when his brother died. He never forgot that year. Bonar didn't know whether Robert could say with certainty that it was the year of his conversion but it was at least the year 'when the first streaks of dawn appeared in his soul'. For him the world had lost its lustre. His life of

Some family portraits drawn by Robert in 1830-1832, copied by A.L. Struthers.

ease was over. As with Christian in Bunyan's *Pilgrim's Progress*, he was likewise compelled to search for eternal life. He would not rest until he had found 'The Pearl of great price'. David was the central figure to direct his paths to Christ. A few years later he wrote to his brother William: 'Oh, Willie, when the world looks enticing and we are well-nigh giving up Christ and salvation for some pitiful pleasure that perishes in the using; if all heavenly arguments fail, a dying Saviour, a beseeching God, then may this earthly one have power to save us: even the remembrance of that gentle and most Christian brother whose kindness we too little esteemed while he lived, and who so often and in so many ways tried to save us from a world lying in wickedness.'

A transformation occurred in Robert's life subsequent to his brother's death. His father described the details later: 'The holy example and the happy death of his brother David seem by the blessing of God to have given a new impulse to his mind in the right direction.' 'Whether these events were under the blessing of God, the means of producing a saving change on his heart', his father could not say with certainty. Robert himself later stated, 'There was nothing sudden in his case, and that he was led to Christ through deep and ever-abiding, but not awful or distracting, convictions.' His conscience, however, was awakened to a realization of his lost and sinful state before God. It wasn't customary during those times to share such feelings with a minister of the gospel. However, he had a desperate need to confess them. He missed his brother, to whom he surely would have poured out his whole heart. In spite of his many contacts, he was overcome by extreme loneliness. He wrote later: 'This dear friend and brother died and though his death made a greater impression upon me than ever his life had done, still I found the misery of being friendless. I do not mean that I had no relations and worldly friends, for I had many; but I had no friend who cared for my soul. I had none to direct me to the Saviour, none to awaken my slumbering conscience, none to tell me about the blood of Jesus washing away all my sin, none to tell me of the Spirit who is willing to change the heart and give victory over passions. I had no minister to take me by the hand, and say, "Come with me, and we will do thee good."'

**The light breaks through**

The Lord began to sanctify the young man more and more. He became deeply convicted of his own sinfulness. David's words in Psalm 51 became his personal adage: 'Against Thee, Thee only, have I sinned, and done this evil in thy sight.' The revelatory light slowly dawned on his soul. However, the world continued its struggle with him. The prince of darkness didn't easily wish to let go of his prey. His conscience pricked him in his inmost being whenever he gave in to the inclinations of his heart. In December he wrote in his diary: 'A thorn in my side – much torment.' A few months later we read: 'I hope never to play cards again.' Then again: 'Never visit on a Sunday evening again' and 'Absented myself from the dance; upbraidings ill to bear. But I must try to bear the cross.' The people of the neighbourhood noticed that his behaviour had changed. He lost his fascination for the world, but the way to Christ remained hidden. He walked along, groping, falling and clambering up again. He read the Word of God and Christian literature. He talked with his friend, Alexander Somerville, about eternal matters. Together they studied the Greek Septuagint and the Hebrew text. They prayed much and tried to support each other in their endeavours to discover the truth.

Besides experiencing his own personal problems with the way of salvation, he occupied himself with theological issues. Thus he undertook an examination of the doctrine of eternal election and the free grace of God. Was he merely attempting to rationalize his personal involvement in God's sovereignty, or was he searching for a closely-reasoned argument by means of logic? In the meantime, he had applied to study theology. The Presbytery of Edinburgh granted him permission to attend Dr Thomas Chalmers and Dr David Welsh's lectures. Could he lead others to salvation in Christ if he himself had not reflected on these matters? What precisely moved him to study in order to pursue this marvellous calling? Bonar knew no answer to this; he asked himself: 'Could he say, like Robert Bruce, "I was first called to grace, before I obeyed my calling to the ministry"?' God's ways were not always consistently clear to him. It was an inner desire that urged him towards this decision, a desire that he himself possibly couldn't explain, because his heart was still so full of darkness. The Lord drew him continually from the refuge of his sinful existence, and the mists of unbelief and obstinacy gradually had to yield to the rays of the Sun of Righteousness.

### The *Sum of Saving Knowledge*

It was a simple and old writing that brought him into contact with 'the way of acceptance with God'. In March 1832 he began to read the *Sum of Saving Knowledge*. That work dated back to the mid-seventeenth century and was probably composed by the famous Scottish authors, David Dickson and James Durham. M'Cheyne describes the book that, in his day, was a supplement to the Westminster Confession of Faith and the Larger and Shorter Catechism, as 'the work which I think first of all wrought a saving change in me'. In a practical way the study of God's grace was explained and tersely applied. The point of departure in this work is John 6:37: 'All that the Father giveth me shall come to me; and Him that cometh to Me I will in no wise cast out.' It is divided into four sections: first: 'Our woeful condition by nature, through breaking the covenant of works'; followed by 'The remedy provided in Christ Jesus for the elect by the covenant of grace'; then 'The outward means appointed to make the elect partakers of this covenant'; and finally 'The blessings which are effectually conveyed.' The principal section is followed by 'The practical use of saving knowledge', 'Warrants to believe' and 'The evidences of true faith'. In beginning with the second to the last section, the free offer of grace would surpass all conditions and objections to its nature. There is talk of 'an open offer of Christ and His grace, by proclaiming of a free and gracious market of righteousness and salvation, to be had through Christ to every soul, without exception.' Furthermore, there comes to our notice the urgency of accepting Christ as He is presented in the gospel without delay: 'This is his commandment, that we should believe on the name of his Son Jesus Christ' (1 John 3:23).

The real essence of the writing constitutes 'the practical use', the way in which the sinner is introduced to the covenant of grace and becomes a partaker of Christ and His covenant benefits. This occurs by means of conviction and persuasion. The writers hereby distinguish between the conviction of sin, righteousness and judgment, 'partly by the law or covenant of works' and 'partly by the gospel or covenant of grace.' The law opens the door to the operation of the Spirit of God in one's conscience to effect a knowledge of sin and depravity. The gospel reveals the sin of unbelief, the rejection of the offer, which is the chief sin, and it points to the necessity of a genuine faith, whereby the soul is united with Christ. The Spirit continues to convict the soul as to the righteousness of Christ which is the only ground for reconciliation with God. Thus the convicted sinner comes to the true Saviour, who is presented to him in the gospel. 'Seeing thou sayest, "seek ye my face; my soul answereth unto Thee," "Thy face, Lord, will I seek." I have hearkened unto the offer of an everlasting Covenant of all saving mercies to be had in Christ, and I do heartily embrace Thy offer. Lord, let it be a bargain; "Lord, I believe; help my unbelief...."'

Thus the young M'Cheyne was brought into contact with the heart of the gospel. Thus he learned to embrace the Saviour by faith. He relied not on his own penitence nor his convictions, but only on the imputed righteousness of Christ. This simple writing brought him face to face with the Biblical relationship between the law and the gospel. He viewed it as a snare to seek rest outside of Christ in the works of the law. His awareness of his own sinfulness made him restless and compelled him to seek reconciliation with God. Andrew Bonar describes the way in which the Lord guided Robert to receive forgiveness of sins: 'The nature of his experience, however, we have some means of knowing. On one occasion, a few of us who had studied together were reviewing the Lord's dealings with our souls, and how He had brought us to Himself, all very nearly at the same time, though without any special instrumentality. He stated that there was nothing sudden in his case, and that he was led to Christ through deep and ever-abiding, but not awful or distracting, convictions. In this we see the Lord's sovereignty. In bringing a soul to the Saviour, the Holy Spirit invariably leads it to very deep consciousness of sin; but then He causes this consciousness of sin to be more distressing and intolerable to some than to others. But in one point does the experience of all believing sinners agree in this matter, namely their soul, presented to their view as nothing but an abyss of sin, when the grace of God that bringeth salvation appeared.'

## The essence of the law and the gospel

It is noticeable that precisely the crucial points of the *Sum of Saving Knowledge* became the themes for most of M'Cheyne's sermons. Thus he described better than any contemporary or friend could the condition of the soul which comes to the realization of his own lost state before God. In a series of sermons on John 16:8 he emphasized that the knowledge of misery alone could not save the sinner. It is necessary that he be convicted of the righteousness of Christ: 'Remember, anxiety for the soul does not save the soul. Sailors in a shipwreck are very anxious. They cry much to God in prayer and tears; and yet, though they are anxious men, they are not saved, the vessel goes to pieces and all are drowned.' '... So you are much afraid of the wrath of God, and it may be God has, in mercy, stirred up these anxieties in your bosom; but you are not yet saved – unless you come to Christ all will be in vain. Many are now in hell who were once as anxious to escape as you.' Rightly Bonar observes that M'Cheyne never reckoned his soul saved, notwithstanding 'all his convictions and views of sin, until he really went into the holiest of all on the warrant of the Redeemer's work; for assuredly a sinner is still under wrath until he has actually availed himself of the way to the Father opened up by Jesus. All knowledge of his sinfulness, and all his sad feelings of his own need and danger, cannot place him one step farther off the lake of fire. It is "he that comes to Christ" that is saved.'

The feeling of his guilt was no qualification for his acceptance before Christ, but served only as a means to cast himself upon Him. However, he was not without this conviction. He acknowledged his own condemnation and God's righteousness, so that he was silenced. Thus he received insight into 'the preparing operations through the law', concerning which he writes as follows: 'Had this evening a more complete understanding of that self-emptying and abasement with which it is necessary to come to Christ, a denying of self, trampling it under foot, a recognizing of the complete righteousness and justice of God, that could do nothing else with us but condemn us utterly, and thrust us down to lowest hell, a feeling that, even in hell, we should rejoice in His sovereignty, and say that all was rightly done.' In the acknowledgement of his deserving judgment, the Lord opened a way through Another who provided a complete acquittal according to His own merit.

**The change becomes known**

The great change in Robert's life didn't go unnoticed. Perhaps some were surprised because they viewed him as a genuine believer. The complacent and popular student now appeared to everyone as a humble Christian who was deeply aware of his own sinfulness. In times past he had relied on his own self-righteousness, on his own moral sense. The circumstances of his conversion bore a striking resemblance to those of Dr Chalmers. The latter, before his conversion, also fancied himself to be an upright Christian and made much of his virtues and responsibilities. As in his case, Robert's ideals were overthrown and he learned how, as a lost sinner, to find refuge in Christ and His completed work. His friends were amazed at his intense and well-meant fear of God. He even urged them to pursue the same things. The contents of his poems also changed. It was above all noticeable in his romantic poems. Instead of seeking to charm his female acquaintances, he demonstrated the necessity of accepting Christ. Thus he warned Constance Bullen of the dangers of pursuing popularity. He also pointed this out to Mondego Mary Macgregor, for whom he especially interceded:

> To the home that a Saviour bought by His death,
> To Him who no sinner will shun.

M'Cheyne's family experienced difficulty in assimilating all the changes. First, there was the departure of William, then the death of David, and now the conversion of Robert. In addition, the pride of their family chose the Christian ministry. The rank of preachers, in contrast to previous centuries, had waned in popularity. A lawyer's career bore more significance

Henry Martyn (1781-1812)

Legh Richmond A.M. (1772-1827)

than a servant of God's Word. There were a few preachers in the family. His uncle, Robert Dickson, was minister of South Leith parish church and his nephew, William M'Cheyne, served the Relief Church in Kelso. Of all the leaders in the Church of Scotland, Henry Duncan from Ruthwell was probably the one he knew best. No wonder that Robert went south to seek Uncle Harry's advice. It was Robert's desire to spend his life on behalf of his new Master. For many years he had grieved Him by his godless and worldly living; now he wished nothing more than to grasp the staff of the Supreme Shepherd. With this motive, he was enrolled as a student at the Divinity Hall of Edinburgh University in November 1831.

**The first struggle**

The recently converted Robert didn't easily take his first unsteady and hesitant steps on the way to life. He yearned for the company of more exercised saints, whom he dearly missed. He felt one with those who were totally committed to God and lived in a close relationship with the Saviour. During this time, M'Cheyne read the biographies of Legh Richmond and Henry Martyn. The *Memoirs* of Richmond, who died in 1827, were first published in 1828 in a biography, written by Grimshaw. He was a man who, after his conversion from a religion of legalism while he was a vicar in the Church of England, became a blessing to many. On the Isle of Wight, he was the means of the conversion of 'The Dairyman's Daughter', about whom he wrote a pathetic deathbed account. The story became world-renowned, as did the conversion history of 'Jane, the Cottager'. How insignificant Robert felt, as he read the life story of Richmond, who fervently longed for the extension of God's kingdom and in his life clearly demonstrated the fragrance of Jesus. 'Deep penitence, not unmixed with tears,' he wrote in his diary on 4 December 1831. 'I never before saw myself so vile, so useless, so poor, and above all, so ungrateful. May these tears be the pledges of my self-dedication!' Shortly before, he had read the commemorative writings of Henry

Martyn, who worked as a missionary in India and Persia. Martyn's diary testified to a self-sacrificial love for his Master. In 1812 he breathed his last. M'Cheyne sketched the details about him: 'Would I could imitate him, giving father, mother, country, house, health, life, all for Christ. And yet, what hinders? Lord, purify me, and give me strength to dedicate myself, my all, to Thee!' Most striking of all to him were the words of Martyn concerning his unworthiness, unproductiveness and anxiety over his work. What impressed him furthermore was his resignation to God's will and a premonition of his premature death.

The somewhat rationalistic preaching of William Muir in St Stephen's couldn't hold Robert's interest any longer. He loved to go and listen to John Bruce in the New North Church and also to James Martin, who from 1831 was the successor of Dr Andrew Thomson. In October, Martin was inducted in St George's, where he preached the gospel for three years until his premature death. He was a God-fearing man. After hearing one of his sermons, Robert related: 'Oh, how humble, yet how diligent, how lowly, yet how watchful, how prayerful night and day it becomes me to be, when I see such men! Help, Father, Son and Spirit.' Martin was a worthy successor to Dr Thomson, who died in front of his house in February 1831. M'Cheyne gives an account of the widespread grief that took control of the entire city when Thomson's sudden death was announced. He added: 'Pleasing to see so much public feeling excited on the decease of so worthy a man.' Now Thomson was not just anybody, because since the death of John Erskine he was the leader of the Evangelicals. His friend, Thomas Chalmers, would soon follow in his footsteps in the struggle on the church front. M'Cheyne viewed these men with great respect. Concerning their preaching, he was encouraged greatly in his soul by John Bruce, and while attending preaching he was most often in the company of his friend, Alexander Somerville. His friend grew up in St Andrew's Church, where Sabbath by Sabbath he sat under the preaching of the full-blooded Moderates, Andrew

John Bruce D.D. (1794-1856), minister of New North Church Edinburgh.

Grant and David Ritchie. 'I could never gather that any of my friends had ever got any good under the preaching. All had the uniformity and stillness of death.'

The more the light of the gospel of Christ shone into M'Cheyne's soul, the more the world lost its fascination. Having seen Jesus and having followed after the Lamb of God, he took leave of sin and the world. When he heard of a friend that 'she was determined to keep by the world', he was motivated to write a few verses, one of which reads:

For the human heart
Can ne'er conceive
What joys are the part
Of them who believe;
Nor can justly think
Of the cup of death
Which all must drink
Who despise the faith.

It was Constance Bullen who succumbed to the vanities of life. He couldn't neglect in poetic terms to point her yet again to eternal life. In this respect, he likened her to a day-butterfly's wing, which is adorned with beautiful colours and flutters in the sun. Similarly, the vain flower endures but a season!

He became still more practised in the work of Christ as Surety. Without Him he could not continue to live. After he had experienced many a shaking in his heart, he surrendered himself to Him. In Him alone he found peace. 'I have found much rest in Him who bore all our burdens for us.' He had the liberty to go to Him no matter how bad and hard he felt. 'But perhaps my old sins are too fearful, and my unbelief too glaring? Nay; I come to Christ, not although I am a sinner, but just because I am a sinner, even the chief.' Although his feelings fought against it, he knew no other way but to go to Him. 'And though sentiment and constitutional enthusiasm may have a great effect on me, still I believe that my soul in sincerity is desirous and earnest about having all its concerns at rest with God and Christ; that His kingdom occupies the most part of all my thoughts and even of my long-polluted affections. Not unto me, not unto me, be the shadow of praise or of merit ascribed, but let all glory be given to Thy most holy Name!' Jesus, Jesus alone was the subject of his love and affection.

I come to Christ, because I know
The very worst are called to go;
And when in faith I find Him,
I'll walk in Him, and lean on Him,
Because I cannot move a limb
Until He say, 'Unbind him.'

### Partaking of the Lord's Supper

After his conversion, it was his desire to commemorate the death of his Saviour. In this way, he intended also to testify to the hope that was in him. It was not customary in Scotland to give an open testimony of faith before the congregation; the table of the Lord stood open only for those who had confessed their faith before the kirk session. It was in May, 1832 that he partook for the second time. One year earlier, he had also made use of the holy communion, but 'he was then living at ease and saw not the solemn nature of the step he took'. On the one hand, his heart's desire was to partake of the sacrament, but on the other hand, he was forced to undergo a strict self-examination, whereby he reviewed his past life.

'What a mass of corruption have I been! How great a portion of my life have I spent wholly without God in the world, given up to sense and the perishing things around me! Naturally of a feeling and sentimental disposition, how much of my religion has been, and to this day is, tinged with these colours of earth! Restrained from open vice by educational views and the fear of man, how much ungodliness has reigned within me! How often has it broken through all restraints, and come out in the shape of lust and anger, mad ambitions, and unhallowed words! Though my vice was always refined, yet how subtle and how awfully prevalent it was!' M'Cheyne had no single reason for taking a pride in himself. He earnestly humbled himself before the Lord in the dust. It was God alone who awakened him out of his sinful stupor. M'Cheyne partook of holy communion not as a righteous person but as a sinner, who expected his help and salvation to come from God in Christ alone. The Lord demonstrated His goodness at the table. The next day he wrote: 'How much more was the creature loved than the Creator! O great God that didst suffer me to live whilst I so dishonoured Thee, Thou knowest the whole; and it was Thy hand alone that could awaken me from the death in which I was, and was contented to be. Gladly would I have escaped from the Shepherd who sought me as I strayed but He took me up in His arms and carried me back; and yet He took me not for anything that was in me. I was no more fit for His service than the Australian, and no more worthy to be called and chosen.'

M'Cheyne didn't partake of the Lord's Supper as a righteous

man but as a sinner, who expected his salvation and help only from God in Christ. He received some blessing at the table of the Lord, about which he wrote: 'I well remembered when I was an enemy and especially abhorred this ordinance as binding me down but if I be bound to Christ in heart, I shall not dread any bands that can draw me close to Him. Evening: Much peace. Look back, my soul, and view the mind that belonged to thee but twelve months ago. My soul, thy place is in the dust!'

**A craving for holiness**

The craving to live a holy life went hand in hand with a deep sense of his own depravity. 'Much carelessness, sin, and sorrow. "O wretched man that I am! who shall deliver me from this body of sin and death?" Enter thou, my soul, into the rock, and hide thee in the dust for fear of the Lord and the glory of His majesty. What change is there in the heart! Wild, earthly affections there are here; strong, coarse passions; bands both of iron and silk. But I thank Thee, O my God, that they make me cry, "O wretched man!" Bodily weakness, too, depresses me.' He noticed that sins were a reality. His worldly heart tried to draw him away from the Lord. 'This last bitter root of worldliness that has so often betrayed me has this night so grossly carried me away, that I cannot but regard it as God's chosen way to make me loathe and forsake it forever. I would vow; but it is much more like a weakly worm to pray. Sit in the dust, O my soul!' The craving after the world was sometimes so strong that he knew not how to resist it, but in the course of time grace triumphed.

Sometimes the pride in his heart welled up. So he wrote: 'Oh for true, unfeigned humility! I know I have cause to be humble; and yet I do not know one half of that cause. I know I am proud; and yet I do not know the half of that pride.' He earnestly sought God's presence in prayer daily. He quickly took to the practice of fasting. But it didn't come easily for him to practise his religion. At one stage he confessed, 'Mind quite unfitted for devotion. Ineffectual prayer.' How he struggled to bring forth the fruit of his conversion! His soul also thirsted after God to live a holy life before Him. Robert, however, realized that within him he possessed no power to overcome the multitude of sins. Diligently, he examined himself to see if there were a reason for his withdrawal from his Lord. Was it not the neglect of his God-given talents that caused his unproductiveness? He wrote thus: 'somewhat overcome. Let me see that there is a creeping defect here. Humble, purpose-like reading of the Word omitted. What plant can be unwatered and not wither?'

M'Cheyne maintained a lively awareness of his sinfulness, not only prior to his conversion but also thereafter. Precisely this conviction motivated him to find refuge in Calvary's cross. 'Clear conviction of sin is the only true origin of dependence on Another's righteousness and therefore (strange to say!) of the Christian's peace of mind and cheerfulness.' However, he didn't continue to bemoan his own sins or revert to introspection, but he continually set his course heavenward. He didn't concern himself with a superficial and sentimental sense of his own failings. Thus he wrote in a letter to someone who, he feared, was only sentimental, and not really under a sense of sin: 'Is it possible, think you, for a person to be conceited of his miseries? May there not be a deep leaven of pride lurking in us telling how desolate and how unfeeling we are in brooding over our unearthly pains, in our being excluded from the unsympathetic world, in our being the invalids of Christ's hospital?' He questioned a conviction of sin that did not end in genuine repentance, as a fruit of faith in Christ as he is offered in the gospel. Bonar observes in this connection: 'He had himself been taught by the Spirit that it is more humbling for us to take what grace offers than to bewail our wants and worthlessness.'

**Hours of silent prayer**

His times of private devotion were intended as a means of

humbling himself before the Lord, similar to a training school in the way of holiness. The habit of rising early, just as he had advocated before his conversion, was to continue for the rest of his life. 'Rose early to seek God and found Him whom my soul loveth. Who would not rise early to meet such company? The rains are over and gone. They that sow in tears shall reap in joy.' Rightly he could give assent to the expression: the early bird catches the worm. In the glimmer of dawn before the sun arose, he could often rejoice in the rays of the Sun of Righteousness. These were the best hours for his soul. It was here that his thoughts were directed heavenward; here he knew especially of the Elims in the wilderness of life which were a foretaste of heavenly glory. During these times he was also made aware of how strongly he clung to the earthly and his own nature. 'Reading Adam's *Private Thoughts*. Oh, for his heartsearching humility! Ah me! on what mountains of pride must I be wandering, when all I do is tinctured with the very sins this man so deplores; yet where are my wailings, where my tears, over my love of praise?'

It was not easy to hold fast to that which he had received in solitude. 'Private meditation exchanged for conversation. Here is the root of evil: Forsake God, and He forsakes us.' In his relationships with others it was necessary to preserve his fellowship with God. He wished to be holy as his Saviour was. How could he guard his thoughts and control his passions? Could his *Essay on the government of the passions* provide a guiding principle in this respect? In this work he had prescribed many guidelines to help channel his feelings in a wholesome direction. In his own strength he could not achieve anything. He was totally dependent on help from above. He was well aware that passivity and slovenliness could only lead him further away from God. It was necessary to exercise himself in watchfulness but then not in his own strength. Only through the power of Christ's blood could he overcome; only through faith could 'the walls of Jericho' of his idolatrous heart be pulled down. Above all, the trials were necessary to draw him still closer to Christ. 'If nothing else will do to sever me from my sins, Lord, send me such sore and trying calamities as shall awake me from earthly slumbers. It must always be best to be alive to Thee, whatever be the quickening instrument. I tremble as I write, for oh! on every hand do I see too likely occasions for sore afflictions.'

Trials were there also for his body. His lithe, handsome form was often struck by ailments which would remain with him his whole life. He often suffered from fevers, which necessitated his staying in bed. In November 1834 he received an attack which didn't last too long. He then wrote in his diary: 'Bless the Lord, O my soul, and forget not all His benefits. Learned more and more of the value of Jehovah Tsidkenu.' A few days later he took up his pen to write a poem. From his life's experience he wrote:

He tenderly binds up the broken in heart,
The soul bowed down He will raise:
For mourning, the ointment of joy will impart:
For heaviness, garments of praise.

And then followed the characteristic conclusion:

Each heart has by great tribulation been torn,
Each voice turned from wailing to praise.

His thoughts were often determined by his deceased brother. David's death spurred him on to seek God. His brother's last few years were an example of a life that was dead to the world. In him he saw a true glimpse of the heavenly life, in consideration of which the world's desires faded away. On 14 August 1834, he commemorated the birthday of David: 'Partial fast, and seeking God's face by prayer. This day thirty years ago my dear brother, now passed away, was born. Oh, for more love, and then will come more peace.' The same day, he wrote his well-known poem on 'The Barren Fig Tree'. He saw in this an image of himself. How many times had he ignored God's call? How much fertility was there around his life's tree? How often had his own brother directed him to heavenly concerns? Could he bear fruit to the glory of God? It was his deep longing henceforth to consecrate his life to his Master.

Learn, O my soul, what God demands
Is not a faith like barren sands,
But fruit of heavenly hue.
By this we prove that Christ we know,
If in His holy steps we go;
Faith works by love, if true.

**Jehovah – Tsidkenu**

In the same year, to be precise, on 18 November 1834, M'Cheyne wrote his famous love song, *Jehovah-Tsidkenu* (The Lord our Righteousness). It was written after another attack of fever, which was a violent one. He feared that death would swallow up his life. Would he die? Had he a Surety for his guilt? He found, once more, his only refuge to be in the covering of Christ's righteousness. The imputed righteousness of Christ was once 'the Watchword of the Reformers'. The Lord had not only given him a deep insight into the doctrine of justification of the ungodly, but more than that, he received comfort from it in his heart. He experienced and tasted the favour of his heavenly Father in His forgiving grace. The righteousness of his Beloved Surety was the only resting place for his heart, in both life and death. Now the Lord led him back and gave him a view too of the river of death. He recorded the experience of his soul in verse so that others too would receive comfort from it.

First, the poet gives a retrospective glimpse of his life, a life outside of God's love and estranged from his reconciling blood:

I once was a stranger to grace and to God,
I knew not my danger, and felt not my load;
Though friends spoke in rapture of Christ on the tree,
Jehovah Tsidkenu was nothing to me.

He once went his way without any knowledge of his sinful and lost state before God. With a false sense of peace, he journeyed on the road to eternity. The Lord awakened him from his sinful sleep:

When free grace awoke me, by light from on high,
Then legal fears shook me, I trembled to die;
No refuge, no safety in self could I see
Jehovah Tsidkenu my Saviour must be.

The law pricked his conscience: 'But when the commandment came, sin revived, and I died.' M'Cheyne learned to bow his heart before God. He embraced his Saviour as his only Deliverer:

My terrors all vanished before the sweet Name;
My guilty fears banished, with boldness I came
To drink at the fountain, life giving and free
Jehovah Tsidkenu is all things to me.

Now, the law could condemn him no longer. Christ had removed the curse of eternal death from him. Robert laid his sins on the Lamb and His complete righteousness became his portion. He sang, because of the assurance of sins forgiven:

Jehovah Tsidkenu! my treasure and boast,
Jehovah Tsidkenu! I ne'er can be lost;
In thee I shall conquer by flood and by field –
My cable, my anchor, my breastplate and shield!

The retrospection ended at Calvary's cross. Here he found his justification through faith in the crucified Saviour. That was the only foundation. Although turbulent fevers might snatch him away from this life, and the sins of his inner depravity assail him, his anchor remained steadfast.

His end was not yet. The Lord had much work for him to do. He equipped him for heavenly service, but that was not all. He endowed him with courage and strength to bear the trials and weaknesses of his life. These were necessary to keep him humble, and to assist him to die to all that was outside of Christ, so that he might yearn after the heavenly Canaan. This was the conclusion of his pilgrim's song:

> Even treading the valley, the shadow of death,
> This 'watchword' shall rally my faltering breath;
> For while from life's fever my God sets me free,
> Jehovah Tsidkenu my death-song shall be.

# Chapter 3

# EQUIPPED FOR THE HEAVENLY SERVICE

## Light and guidance in the studies

It was M'Cheyne's heart's desire to consecrate his life to God. 'What right have I to steal and abuse my Master's time? "Redeem it", He is crying to me.' He wrote these words in his diary on 18 December 1831. A month prior to this, he had enrolled as a student at the faculty of theology. He had meanwhile completed his studies in arts with good results. Now he no longer allowed himself to be motivated by an excessive love of studying in order to satisfy his desire for knowledge. He was aware, subsequent to his conversion, that he should use his talents in the service of God. He no longer continued to build on his education in the classics, but instead used these as an aid to further study. The light of the ancient philosophers was to a certain extent enlightening, but at the same time dangerous. 'Beware of the atmosphere of the classics,' he wrote later. 'It is pernicious indeed; and you need much of the south wind breathing over the Scriptures to counteract it. True, we ought

Thomas Chalmers D.D. (1780-1847)

Jonathan Edwards (1703-1758)

Alexander Duff D.D. (1806-1878)

to know them; but only as chemists handle poisons to discover their qualities, not to infect their blood with them.'

The young student knew the true value of theological studies. These were nothing more than an aid in equipping him to be a servant of the Word of God. It was of the greatest importance to him to be taught by God's Spirit, to examine the Word and prayerfully occupy himself with his heavenly Father's business. He knew moderation in all things, so as to prevent all his time being swallowed up in studying. Thus, from experience, he could write to a student: 'Do get on with your studies. Remember you are now forming the character of your future ministry in great measure, if God spare you. If you acquire slovenly or sleepy habits of study now, you will never get the better of it. Do everything in its own time. Do everything in earnest; if it is worth doing, then do it with all your might. Above all, keep much in the presence of God. Never see the face of man till you have seen His face who is our life, our all.'

The value of his studies depended not only on his talents but also on his prayer life. 'I feel it far better to begin with God, to seek His face first, and to get my soul near Him before it is near another.' With Paul it was his daily request: 'Lord, what wilt Thou have me to do?' And with Isaiah: 'Here am I; send me!' He had received a burning desire in his heart to proclaim God's Word. But what did God want him to do? Preferably, he wished to become a missionary to the heathen. He was envious of Alexander Duff, who in August 1829 was inducted as the first missionary of the Church of Scotland in St George's of Edinburgh. Dr Chalmers conducted the service, after which he departed for India. Robert thought that God had also predestined him to become a missionary. He shared this longing with his study-fellow, Alexander Somerville. 'If I am to go to the heathen to speak of the unsearchable riches of Christ, this one thing must be given me, to be out of the reach of the baneful influence of esteem or contempt. If worldly motives go with me, I shall never convert a soul, and shall lose my own in the labour.'

David Welsh D.D. (1793-1845)

Main building of the University of Edinburgh, South Bridge.

Was his ingrained pride still getting the better of him? Was it possibly his fear that he would be controlled by a secret longing for fame that motivated him to choose missions to the heathen, because there he would receive no honour? Did the biography of David Brainerd impress him in this regard? Brainerd had been a missionary to the Indians of North America a century before. His diary testifies of a great deal of self-denial and sacrifice for the sake of Christ. 'Most wonderful man!,' wrote M'Cheyne on 29 June 1832. 'What conflicts, what depressions, desertions, strength, advancement, victories, within thy torn bosom! I cannot express what I think of thee. Tonight, more set upon missionary enterprise than ever.' 'Oh, for Brainerd's humility and sin-loathing dispositions!'

It was partly because of his poor health that his wish to go to the mission field was never realized. He never lost this desire even when the ministry lay open before him. When Duff returned to Scotland on leave, a few years later, M'Cheyne was among his audience. 'He spoke with greater warmth and energy than ever. He kindles as he goes. Felt almost constrained to go the whole length of his system with him ... I am now made willing, if God shall open the way, to go to India,' he wrote. Soon afterwards he became a member of the Missionary Association, an institution for the promotion of missions to the heathen.

Bonar pointed to the fact that this desire had to do with a selfless surrender to his Master. It was precisely his egoistical nature and desire for ease that were to be subjected to God's will. The work of a servant of the Word was nothing more than a task of self-denial. 'Must there not be somewhat of this missionary tendency in all true ministers? Is any one truly the Lord's messenger who is not quite willing to go when and where the Lord calls?'

The preparation for the task of a servant of the gospel meant more to M'Cheyne than study alone; it meant also years of testing, and seeking God's will and way for his life. Was he moved by the spiritual need of souls? Was God's honour really at stake? And if he wished to devote himself to missionary work, what was his underlying motive? 'Why is a missionary life so often an object of my thoughts? Is it simply for the love I bear to souls? Then, why do I not show it more where I am? Souls are as precious here as in Burma. Does the romance of the business not weigh anything with me? The interest and esteem I would carry with me? The nice journals and letters I should write and receive? Why would I so much rather go to the East than to the West Indies? Am I wholly deceiving my own heart, and have I not a spark of true missionary zeal? Lord, give me to understand and imitate the spirit of those unearthly words of Thy dear Son: "It is enough for the disciple that he be as his Master, and the servant as his Lord." "He that loveth father or mother more than Me, is not worthy of me."' 'Gloria in excelsis Deo!'

**A stern self-examination**

Robert's life was one of continual training. He guarded against reckless thoughts and feelings. His enthusiasm was continually tempered by self-examination, but he didn't give himself over to endless self-analysis. However, his tendency towards discovery and personal heart-knowledge caused him to grow in holiness. He yearned after uniformity with Christ, but he found so much in himself that was nothing more than selfishness. Precisely the subtle feelings of his heart made him vigilant. He tried his best to be honest with himself but, at the same time, he was afraid. Thus he wrote in his diary: 'Too much engrossed, and too little devotional. Preparation for a fall. Warning. We may be too engrossed with the shell even of heavenly things.'

He not only exemplified the Word in his life, but he eagerly read biographies of the great men of God's kingdom in order to further his self-examination. We have seen already how he took note of the lives of Legh Richmond and Henry Martyn. He discovered the biography of David Brainerd in the works of Jonathan Edwards, which he procured in June 1832. Chalmers had probably drawn his attention to this eighteenth-century American theologian. Thanks in particular to his books, he made the acquaintance of theological and philosophical thinking. Edwards understood much of the depth of the knowledge of God; he had an intense awareness of his own sinfulness and God's eternal majesty. By reading these writings, M'Cheyne dedicated himself to a greater extent to the struggle against superficiality, which he perceived in himself. Why had the Lord directed His love at him? Was he better than others? 'Truly, there was nothing in me that should have induced Him to choose me. I was but as the other brands upon whom the fire is already kindled, which shall burn for evermore!' He thought himself dirt in God's eyes. This realization made him feel small and humbled him. It roused him to higher aspirations instead of to the vain pleasures of the world. A servant of the gospel should detest all that is idle: 'How apt are we to lose our hours in the vainest babblings, as the world! How can this be with those chosen for the mighty office?... Alas, alas! my soul, where shalt thou appear? O Lord God, I am a little child! But Thou wilt send an angel with a live coal from off the altar, and touch my unclean lips, and put a tongue within my dry mouth so that I shall say with Isaiah, "Here am I, send me."'

**His professors**

The divinity hall of the University of Edinburgh was well-known during this time. The character of the lectures was determined by three men, namely, Alexander Brunton, David Welsh and Thomas Chalmers. Brunton taught Hebrew; Robert knew him from Tron Church, where he was the minister. His educational methods impressed him greatly and thus he made good progress. Before he began his theological studies, he had immersed himself in the biblical languages. In due course, he could read the Hebrew text as easily as he could the Greek New Testament. It was his daily habit to go through twenty-five Bible verses. It was of great assistance to his understanding of God's Word that he could read the original text. The treasures

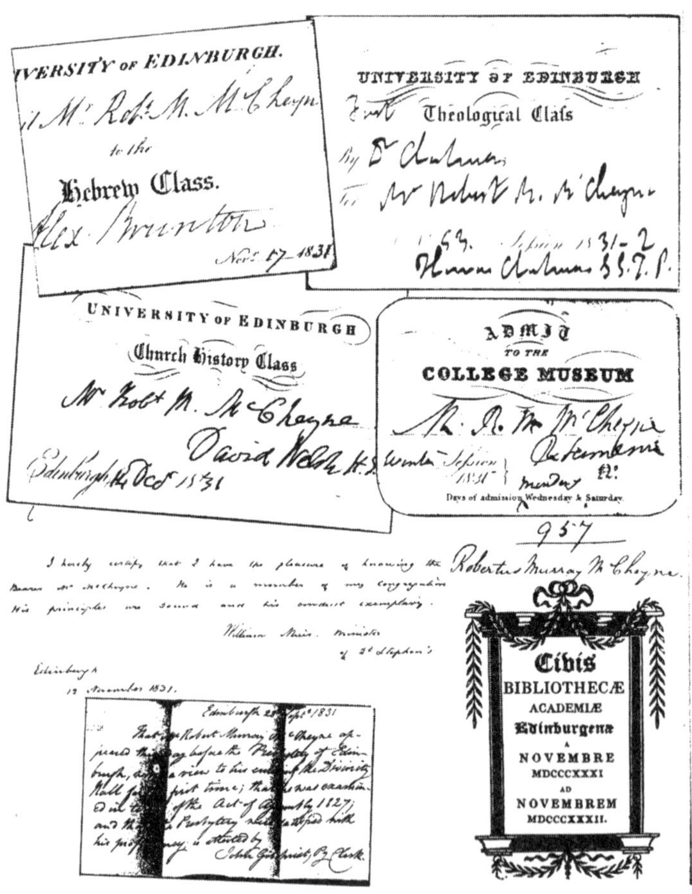


University Class cards of Robert: Hebrew Class of Alexander Brunton, Theological Class of Thomas Chalmers, and Church History Class of David Welsh. Library tickets and a ticket of the College Museum. An attestation of William Muir, his minister of St Stephen's, and a declaration of the presbytery of Edinburgh that he was admitted to the Divinity Hall.

of the Bible became even more real to him. Brunton's lectures were engaging and enriching. A note from his diary illustrates his love of studying: 'Wild wind and rain all day long. Hebrew class – Psalms. New beauty in the original text every time I read.'

David Welsh commenced with his duties at the University during the year 1831, when M'Cheyne began his theological studies. Welsh lectured in church history. After he had been a minister in Kirkcudbright and Glasgow, he received a welcome appointment as professor. He found himself better suited to teaching than to pastoral work. In contrast to Brunton, who continued to serve his congregation, Welsh applied himself wholeheartedly to his new task. He played a significant role in the battle against the influence of the Moderates. He was a God-fearing man with a humble spirit, who knew his own shortcomings. He was far from aloof in his relationships: he invited his students to visit him at home. Frequently he asked himself what the purpose of his lectures was, and whether these were relevant to his students. He confessed his own weakness and need: 'Lord I am vile. Pardon my sin, and let not my transgression be laid to the charge of those who fail in consequence of my neglect.' It was a struggle for him to guide his students in all simplicity. 'Enable me to cultivate simplicity and godly sincerity' was his prayer while he was still a minister. Thus, he wished to lecture with absolute dependence on the Great Teacher of Righteousness. Every Saturday, he set aside an hour to pray for his students and daily he sought the presence of the Lord to see if he was faithful in fulfilling his duties.

Welsh meant a great deal to M'Cheyne. He dealt with his subject in a systematic and orderly way, dividing the history of the church into three periods, the final one comprising the effect of the Reformation on Europe. His strength lay not so much in his original way of thinking, but more in his knowledge of the facts, which he articulated in a lively manner. His teaching methods agreed with Robert. In addition, he could offer valuable advice outside the range of his subject, which was invaluable to the young student. Welsh's scope of knowledge was wide and yet his instruction was clear. Besides the period of the Reformation, he felt at home with the history of the early church, an example of which is to be found in a short note in Robert's diary: 'Dr. Welsh lecture on Pliny's letter concerning the Christians in Bithynia.'

### The influence of Thomas Chalmers

Thomas Chalmers exercised the greatest influence on M'Cheyne. Seldom had a professor enjoyed such popularity among his students. After his appointment in 1827, the College Hall became totally full. An additional gallery was built to house the crowd of students and interested persons. Chalmers was endowed with many gifts. He felt truly at home, however, in the pulpit. He endeared himself to the hearts of his first congregation, Kilmany in Fife, who reluctantly allowed him to leave. When he became a preacher in Glasgow, people would throng outside the church building even before the service began. The contents of his sermons were nothing other than the time-honoured gospel, although he also preached a series on other topics. His *Astronomical Sermons* and *Commercial Sermons,* which he preached in Glasgow, gained him a greater reputation still. After a short while as professor at St Andrew's University, he left for the capital city. A new task awaited him there. He still had feelings of homesickness towards his first congregation, where he had found the Lord and had been able to work with such blessing. Years before he moved to Edinburgh, he had stood on Calton Hill, which is situated on the eastern side of New Town. He had looked intently in the direction of Fife and it was as if he observed his pastorate behind the hill of Normanlaw. 'I was gazing with a most eager direction of my heart to that dear vale which stretches eastward from its base. Oh! with what vivid remembrance can I wander in thought over all its farms and all its families, and dwell on the kind and simple affection of the people, till the contemplation becomes too bitter for my endurance.'

Did his eye catch sight of the southern side of the Calton Hill, where it beheld the proud monument of Nelson? He noticed then, surely, the dome-shaped tower of the university complex near the North Bridge, and the underprivileged quarters of Canongate and Cowgate. Both of the old city quarters later impressed him. Chalmers was not a man to limit his gaze to the four walls of the lecture hall, but he was aware also of what happened within the confined space of the wynds. His deep compassion for society remained with him for the rest of his life. He was not only a servant of the church, but of the nation as well. In this capacity, he followed in the footsteps of his great predecessor, John Knox.

It is not the purpose of this book to give a complete description of the versatile Thomas Chalmers. He was 'the chief propelling power of a new spiritual movement', the leader of the Scottish revival. He moulded the lives of many students, not merely within his own country, but also from other parts of Europe and the rest of the world. 'It was impossible to be in his classroom without feeling the influence of the spiritual and intellectual atmosphere that pervaded it,' was how James Dodds characterized the lessons of the man he so admired. Although his line of thinking wasn't as profound as that of men such as Rutherford and Owen, yet, in his own right, he was an original theologian. The strength of his philosophy lay more in simplicity than in the complex domain of metaphysics. The basis for his theology was in fact formed in Kilmany, at a time when he observed the purpose and power of the gospel. The essence of his study on grace was: reconciliation made possible through the blood of Christ and faith as the instrument to appropriate His righteousness.

The penetrating way in which he conveyed his knowledge to the students was expressed by Horatius Bonar: 'Dr. Chalmers, in a very different strain, one day startled his students. He had been dwelling on the simplicities that make up the gospel of Christ: a theme on which he loved above all things to dwell. He "expatiated" on the "good news" as that which, when simply believed, brings peace to the tossed spirit. He then came to speak of those who mystified faith and held it up as one of the most complex acts of the human mind, consisting of no small number of separate emotions which required to be gone through, tested, and approved of by the conscience, ere the sinner could take rest or be entitled to extract peace from the thing believed.' He aimed at the inclination to possess the characteristics of inner grace, rather than simply resting on the promises of Christ which are 'yes and amen' in Him. Thus Chalmers exposed his students to the heart of the gospel.

It was God's guidance to expose M'Cheyne and many other prospective evangelists to the teaching on grace which was preached from many pulpits in Scotland during the period before the Moderates. Subsequent to his inner transformation, Chalmers received a profound insight into the teaching of the justification of the ungodly through the merits of Christ. The book, *The Marrow of Modern Divinity* by Edward Fisher, especially impressed him. God's grace founded on the sin-offering of Christ was the central theme of his theology. Besides practical English authors like William Romaine and James Hervey, he was inspired by Jonathan Edwards, who had also impressed M'Cheyne. In consideration of the gospel, he was of the opinion that its offer could never be too generous. He pointed out, however, that the elect were the only beneficiaries of the work on the cross of Calvary and its fulfilment, but he also valued the point of view of men such as Baxter and Amyrauld.

Chalmers was a moderate Calvinist, and yet the teaching on predestination held no great significance for him. In spite of his appreciation of the Westminster Confession, his doctrine of the Christian faith possessed a totally different sequence. If the teaching of Westminster was strongly systematic and established on eternal decrees, with Chalmers we find an entirely different approach. In his *Institutes of Theology,* a systematic theology resembling closely the methods he used in his lectures, he followed the historical approach. He didn't begin his lectures with teaching on God and the eternal decrees,

Class notes about the Assurance of Faith and of Experience.

but instead followed the course of man from the time of Creation. His point of departure was 'Natural theology', the inherent knowledge of God, 'Evidences of Christianity', and 'of the Disease for which the Gospel Remedy is provided'. Beginning with the fall of man, including all its consequences, he directed his students to the remedy. Thus he went to work on the great act of salvation effected at Calvary. He spoke with emphasis on the power of the blood of Christ and His atoning work. Instead of a dry presentation of the facts, he tried to penetrate through to the riches of God's free grace, demonstrated to a lost mankind through the Mediator's offer. His theology was built on these basic assumptions: Christ, as the Saviour of the world, was reaching out to justify and sanctify those who believed in Him; faith is no more than a complete reliance on God's Son, as the gospel teaches us. Thus the *extent*, the full extent, of the atonement received a deeper dimension, according to Chalmers. He didn't wish to undermine the teaching on election, but he would not allow it to dominate his thinking.

## Chalmers's lectures

What kind of reference books did Chalmers use in his lectures on systematic religion? It is noticeable that he gave the *Lectures in Divinity* by his own teacher, Professor George Hill of St Andrew's University, a significant place on the list, while Butler's *Analogy* and Paley's *Evidences* also appeared. Thus Chalmers pointed out the dry and uninteresting teaching of the Moderate Hill in contrast to Edwards, whose theology, on the whole, was orthodox. But Chalmers brought life to Hill's systematic theology, and knew how to convey his dogmas in a gripping manner. The motto of his teaching on grace was: 'All is of grace, that all may be to the glory of God.' On this foundation he established his philosophy which imitated Calvin's. M'Cheyne's character was also moulded in this way. It was precisely this practical method that impressed him so much. The teachings of both Chalmers and Welsh were an adequate foundation in preparation for the holy ministry. It deepened M'Cheyne's insight into the grace of God, it sharpened his view on the teaching of Christ's all-sufficient righteousness and enlightened his presentation of the gospel. Chalmers's lectures also resulted in a deepening of his life of faith. His professor's stress on the need for assurance of salvation contributed to a strengthening of his faith, which had endured many temptations and would always find its rest in the finished work on the cross.

M'Cheyne's dictated notes, which have been preserved, give us a glimpse into Chalmers' treasure-room. Above all, the practical advice must have appealed to him, which is evident from his neat, selective notes which he copied out in final draft. The subjects were mostly pastoral, illustrated from the experience of the life of faith: 'Assurance of Faith and of Experience', 'Salvation only by atonement', 'Relation of the Law to the Gospel', 'The Hope of Faith and the Hope of Experience', 'The true Ground of Assurance', etc. The Christ centred approach attracts one's attention.

Chalmers had a clear insight into the promises of God's

Word. According to him, the differences between the assurance of faith and of experience were not contradictory. In the first place, assurance rests on God's witness beyond man's control; secondly, it depends on the witness of God's Spirit in man. He was apprehensive of a move to the one extreme, especially when it concerned basing one's assurance on feelings. He referred to a self-examination without faith in the promises of the Word: the glimpses into the dark room of the heart alone give no good prospect, 'Any more than if you ought to strain your eyes in the dark room, than take help from the windows. Open the shutters and admit the sun. So if you wish to look well inwardly. Look well out.... This is the very way to quicken it. Throw widely open the portals of faith and in this every light will be admitted into the chambers of experience. The true way to facilitate self-examination is to look believingly outwardly.' In this way there is no contradiction between experience and faith, but instead they go hand in hand. It is characteristic of M'Cheyne that he underlined the last conclusion. In this manner, perhaps he found that, for him, the area of tension was removed.

Observations on the doctrine of reconciliation through the completed and substitutionary work of Christ must surely have appealed to Robert. Chalmers states that in reconciliation 'mercy and righteousness meet together in fullest harmony'. 'You cannot too frequently insist upon this,' he suggested to his attentive audience. 'It is the right instrument for the conversion of the people. You may tell your people that if they refuse the mercy of God in this way, they will find it in no other, which includes that they will never find Him while seeking Him in a general way.' Hereby Chalmers aimed at teaching on reconciliation based on God's universal goodness, which began to gain ground during his time.

### Relationship between law and gospel

Chalmers also possessed a clear insight into the relationship between the law and the gospel. 'That righteousness by faith is the "shibboleth" of evangelical preaching, for Christ is the end of the law for righteousness.' The law should not be seen as a condition for preaching the gospel. 'You need not fear to preach the gospel as freely as possible.' Christ and his reconciling work is the only content of the gospel. A mixture of the law and the gospel opposes free grace and leads to an oppressive legalism, something which the Reformers warned against. M'Cheyne sought by imitation of his professor to find the precise balance. He knew that the pitfall of self-righteousness could put the sinner to sleep. One quotation from the exposition of the *Epistle to the Galatians*, written by Luther, interrupted his lecture notes. It dealt with the difference between the law and the gospel. The great Reformer pointed out the dangers of 'the white devil' and 'the black devil'. The latter led to the 'fleshly sins' of the world; the first fostered the 'spiritual sins' of self-righteousness. Robert learned here by convicting grace how cunning the heart is and that the poison of self-righteousness is no more than a denial of the completed work of Christ.

Chalmers' method was both concise and simple, also with respect to a person's introduction to Christ. No single condition, be it penitence or repentance, should be an impediment to a person in coming to Him. He found himself in good company with John Bunyan, who tried in his books to refute all supposed objections with regard to the simple faith. M'Cheyne couldn't resist using a quotation from one of the many books of the English tinker-preacher. He probably borrowed the quotation from *The Jerusalem Sinner Saved.* His contact with souls who were seeking salvation clearly occupied his time. Many of those who didn't understand the difference between the cooperation of both works and grace, and who exchanged the gospel for a new law, were prevented from coming to the cross. They could only believe if they felt good about themselves. 'The spirit of the law still ruleth in such a soul,' was the conclusion of Bunyan, with which M'Cheyne could heartily agree.

The various aspects of the study in the doctrines of grace

attracted the interest of the student and the sympathy of Chalmers. The themes of sin and grace were later to become central to Robert's preaching and pastoral work. Christ was the basis of his life of faith, and not his experiences. He found his Saviour revealed on every page of the Word of God. One particular category of texts according to a subject, which are among his notes, revealed that the Person of Christ is mentioned in various ways, as for example: 'Preciousness of Christ', 'Confessing Christ', 'Seeking after Christ'. He also enumerated texts concerning sin and self-righteousness. He wrote that 'Salvation is only by the free grace of God in Christ Jesus our Lord.' As Chalmers had done, he maintained the Bible sequence in the study on grace as appeared in the *Institutes* of his professor: 'On the disease for which the Gospel remedy is provided, the essence of the Biblical remedy, and the extent of it.' However, the heart of his theological thinking was the pre-eminence afforded the work of the Son of God. M'Cheyne could heartily agree with that which Chalmers wrote after reading *The Marrow of Modern Divinity*: 'I feel a growing delight in the fullness and sufficiency of Christ. O my God, bring me nearer and nearer to Him.'

Partiality was foreign to Chalmers. He kept his eyes open for topics of the times in which he lived. Much of his thinking on philosophical, theological, but also, for example, on a political level were collected by M'Cheyne in a section of his notebook, which he entitled, 'Miscellaneous'. We find here too Chalmers' viewpoint on entanglements in the church. Chalmers knew very well with whom he crossed swords. He didn't avoid the struggle and turned out to be the most powerful leader the evangelicals had known in any century. He knew too how to refute the pernicious ideas of the Scottish Philosophical School. One of M'Cheyne's observations, concerning a lecture, speaks volumes: 'Dr. Chalmers grappling with Hume's arguments.' If David Hume had been alive, he would have found in Chalmers a formidable opponent.

The versatility which characterized Chalmers, was

something the student Robert shared in common with him. Both showed a great interest in geology and biology. The wonder of God's creation was a subject of study and meditation for M'Cheyne. According to Bonar, he was convinced that even the treasures of Egypt should be spent in the service of Christ. 'He was indeed "an earnest student", unconsciously elevated, as it were, above most of his contemporaries by a zeal in the pursuit of sacred learning that seemed to know no bounds.' Thus passed the years of study in Edinburgh. Subsequent to the completion of his lectures, his life's journey was directed towards New Town. The M'Cheyne family remained in the Queen Street home until the conclusion of his studies. In 1835, they moved to 20 Hill Street, a bigger home in a somewhat narrower street. His evenings were taken up with rewriting of lecture notes and preparation for the following day. He tried as far as possible to maintain a daily routine. Of course, he observed his times of fasting and solitude for prayer and meditation.

**Study-fellows**

Who were his fellow students? Frequently, we come across Alexander Neil Somerville. Somerville and M'Cheyne knew each other from high school days in Infirmary Street. He was born during the same year as Robert, and lived in Northumberland Street. Ever since they could remember these two young men were close friends. James Dodds gives us a bird's-eye view of their friendship. 'These two students seemed literally inseparable. Along with many others, I was often amused at the closeness of their companionship. They sat beside each other in the classroom; they came and went together; they were usually seen walking side by side in the street.' Thus one was the shadow of the other and no one could break the bond. 'The fact was that they loved each other dearly in the Lord.' That was actually the secret of their friendship. They spent much time in prayer and talking on spiritual matters. They were examples of godliness and commitment to God's service.

In the first year of his theological studies, Robert also befriended the Bonar brothers, Andrew and Horatius. They belonged to a godly family that had produced many preachers. In contrast to M'Cheyne's parents, the Bonars, who didn't live far away, held a fundamental evangelical belief. They were members of the Lady Glenorchy's Chapel, a church building erected in 1774 between the Old and New Town, not far from North Bridge. The Bonars treasured good memories of the preacher, Thomas Jones. Robert associated much with Andrew, who was two years his senior. The three, Robert, Alexander and Andrew, used often to wander near Duddingston Loch, a small lake close to Holyrood Palace and the hill, Arthur's Seat, and on the hills around Edinburgh. They spoke not only about the wonders of God's grace but also addressed a multitude of problems and subjects. Sometimes they would sing and bow the knee in the stillness of nature around them in order to pour out their hearts to God. Andrew Bonar wrote concerning this in his diary on 30 May 1835: 'We sang together, sitting upon a fallen oak-tree, one of the Psalms.'

These three could be likened to the three disciples of Christ, Peter, James and John. Robert was the disciple whom Jesus loved, Alexander Somerville was Peter, and Andrew Bonar, James. Their characteristics were fairly well matched: who would dare to deny that Robert loved his Saviour dearly; that Alexander was 'fervidly earnest always, sometimes impetuous, and even impatient'? It could, however, be said of Somerville that during his pilgrimage of sixty years he never once denied his Master. Thus continued Andrew Bonar: 'I sometimes think that we three at that time were like the three disciples you read of – Peter, James, and John before the day of Pentecost.' 'Christ took these three into the chamber of Jairus' daughter, and taught them how to raise dead souls. He taught us from the very first to put no stress upon human appliances, but to keep to the gospel word. He took us to the transfiguration hill, and showed us His person from time to time. He taught us to delight in His person, and to behold in a glass the glory of the Lord, and

Lady Glenorchy's Chapel, built in 1774, near the North Bridge.

Duddingston Loch, a loch behind Arthur's Seat in Holyrood Park.

be changed into the same image. He took us to Gethsemane at communion times, and showed us the cup that the Father gave Him to drink, and which He drank, leaving no dregs behind.'

**Edward Irving**

During the summer holidays, the three friends met together of a morning once a week to speak about a theological question or to expand their knowledge of Greek and Hebrew. Thus they discussed, during one whole vacation, a topical subject during this time: unfulfilled prophecy.

Edward Irving, who had earlier been Chalmers' assistant at St John's Church in Glasgow, started them thinking on this topic. In 1829, he delivered a number of lectures before a large audience in St Cuthbert's Church and later in the Hope Park Chapel. It was during the month that the General Assembly met. From seven o'clock every morning, he spoke on prophetic subjects. 'Like the voice of Elijah raised from the dead, he thrilled the spirits of many thousands.' He was a fiery advocate of premillennialism, a thousand years reign of peace, preceded by the return of Christ, who would then personally reign on the earth. This signalled a breakthrough, for most old Scottish theologians adhered to a traditional postmillennialism. The resistance to these 'new-fashioned ideas' was so great that Irving was prevented from continuing in some churches. He was later dismissed, not on account of his ideas on Bible prophecy, but due to his defence of the gifts of the Spirit, such as speaking in tongues, which he had tried to introduce into his own congregation. M'Cheyne also was inspired by his premillennialistic standpoint, although to a lesser degree than were Horatius and Andrew Bonar. He preserved the notes of every lecture carefully.

Despite Irving's extreme views, he held him in high esteem. It came as a shock to him when he heard of his death on 9 November 1834. He wrote: 'I look back upon him with awe, as on the saints and martyrs of old. A holy man, in spite of all his delusions and errors. He is now with his God and Saviour,

We the Undersigned members of the Exegetical Society hereby declare our intention to read during the course of next year the Books of Isaiah and Jeremiah or one or other of them in Hebrew - and one of the books of the New Testament in Greek.

Henry Moncreiff.
Andrew A. Bonar
Robt Kinnear
Thos Brown
Walter Wood
John Thomson
Alexander N. Somerville
George Smeaton
Robt. Murray McCheyne.

Edinburgh
24. May 1838.

Brotherly Agreement of the members of the Exegetical Society, written by Robert and signed on 24th May 1838

Edward Irving (1792-1834)

whom he wronged so much, yet, I am persuaded, loved so sincerely. How we should lean for wisdom, not on ourselves, but on the God of all grace.' A similar tolerance towards the thinking of others always remained with M'Cheyne. This liberality also characterized his friendships, which he would never have broken off for reasons of secondary importance.

A group called the Exegetical Society was of great significance to Robert M'Cheyne's circle of friends. This was formed on the advice of Chalmers, prior to the Bonars and M'Cheyne embarking on theological study. It was a select party that met at 5:30 every Saturday morning in the vestry of St Stephen's. Their goal was the exegetical study of God's Word. This examination was to be undertaken in the widest sense. It concerned not only the exegesis of sections of the Scriptures, but also dealt with the literature and geographical aspects. During the time when M'Cheyne became a member, the group consisted of eighteen members. Careful notes were taken of every meeting and the contributions of the students were bound together in thick leather foolscap volumes. Besides the Bonar brothers, Somerville and M'Cheyne, young men, who would later fulfil a leading role in church life, were also members. Thus we come across names like Thomas Brown, George Smeaton and William Wilson, the latter of whom became preacher at the Seaman's Chapel in Dundee. When M'Cheyne became a preacher, the Society still met, but shortly afterwards it was disbanded. As secretary, M'Cheyne arranged a 'Brotherly Agreement' for 24 May 1838, when the members bound themselves, among other projects, to study the Bible books of Isaiah and Jeremiah in the original language. At that time M'Cheyne was already minister of St Peter's in Dundee.

### Evangelization in the slum quarters

The great motivation behind the bustling activities of the student life was without doubt Thomas Chalmers. Besides his lectures, another reason for this collective diligence was his informal contacts. Regularly he invited his students for a meal

St John's Close, a slum in Canongate in 1867.

at his home, where he proved himself an excellent host. Of course, his wife and daughter were amongst the group. He also organized a discussion group for theological students of which M'Cheyne and his friends were also members. James Dodds, who also studied at that time in Edinburgh and already knew M'Cheyne from Ruthwell, remembered one of his lectures that was 'full of fine fancy and Hebrew learning'. In the past his way of speaking was 'florid and ornate', but gradually it became plainer. When he became a preacher his vocabulary possessed the 'severe simplicity and spiritual beauty' which characterized his later writings. For the character formation of his students, Chalmers envisaged something which extended beyond the walls of the university. He wanted to demonstrate to his students something of the reality of a fallen world. Not that he encouraged them to visit places of pleasure, but he wanted them to get in touch with the dire spiritual need of mankind without God. He had compassion on the poor. Already, in Glasgow, he had been touched by the lot of the poorer classes. He noticed with sadness that especially the poverty-stricken quarters of town were still deprived of the gospel. There was a great shortage of church buildings to care properly for the spiritual needs of the people. The same need he found in the capital city. The narrow, dark wynds around Canongate and Cowgate with the high staircases, hid not only an alarming poverty but also an unlimited ignorance. Many were totally alienated from God and His law. Immorality and crime abounded and the children were brought up to ultimately meet their end at the gallows. The Moderates among the clergymen gave more attention to the educated forms and culture than to the fate of these poor unfortunates. Secularization was on the increase. In 1836, there were no less than 36,000 people who never attended a church service.

When Chalmers arrived in Edinburgh in 1827, he made the acquaintance of Lady Grace Douglas, who was touched by the lot of the families in the slums. She planned to finance an evangelist at her own expense, who could work in these areas. Chalmers thought immediately about one of his first converts in Kilmany, Alexander Paterson. Although he had not studied and only knew how to handle horse and plough, this young man had a heart that not only loved his Saviour fervently, but was moved by the spiritual fate of his neighbour. So Paterson moved from the little, peaceful village in Fife to Canongate, the district that had fallen deepest into godlessness. He told his friend, Robert Edie, of all the things that he had experienced: 'This is a wonderful field in which the Lord hath cast my lot.' He wrote in 1828: 'Amidst all the gospel-light that is now shining, thousands are living in gross darkness, and walking in darkness, and dying as they live! Oh, my soul is pained within me at times. I still meet with many who confess that they know not Jesus. There are hundreds of families that cannot read one word. They are just bringing up their children in the same way.' The evangelist worked for twenty-five years in these surroundings. He witnessed here the love of the Saviour for those lost in sin. Was it he, perhaps, whom M'Cheyne heard once preaching on the street of whom he made mention: 'Heard a street-preacher, foreign voice. Seems really in earnest. He quoted the striking passage, "The Spirit and the bride say, Come, and let him that hears say, Come!" From this he seems to derive his authority. Let me learn from this man to be in earnest for the truth, and to despise the scoffing of the world.'

The work of Paterson was merely a drop in the ocean. Soon the idea came to Chalmers to get the students involved in evangelization work. With this in view he established the Visiting Society. M'Cheyne and his friends eagerly joined this group. Earlier, he and Andrew visited the neighbourhood of Castle Hill, and the impression these slums left on him was astonishing: 'Such scenes I never before dreamed of. Ah! why am I such a stranger to the poor of my native town? I have passed their doors thousands of times; I have admired the huge black piles of building, with their lofty chimneys breaking the sun's rays. Why have I never ventured within? How dwelleth the love of God in me? How cordial is the welcome even of the poorest and most loathsome to the voice of Christian sympathy! What embedded masses of human beings are huddled together, unvisited by friend or minister! "No man careth for our souls" is written over every forehead. Awake, my soul! Why should I give hours and days any longer to the vain world, when there is such a world of misery at my very door? Lord, put Thine own strength in me; confirm every good resolution; forgive my past long life of uselessness and folly.' From that moment on, he became one of the most ardent members of the evangelization committee. Every Saturday the group met in Chalmers' home, after which time, each went his own way. Somerville and M'Cheyne worked in a part of Canongate, where 346 people lived in forty-seven houses. It was the district of 'Seaton's Close, No. 265, to Mid Common close, including

Riddlc's Close, being partly in New Street Parish and partly in Leith Wynd Parish.' 'His experience there was fitted to give him insight into the sinner's depravity in all its forms,' wrote Bonar. Soon the two started a Sabbath School here. They visited all the houses and soon won the confidence of the ignorant people. On 24 March 1834 they visited the first address, about which Robert wrote: 'Visited two families with tolerable success. God grant a blessing may go with us! Began in fear and weakness, and in much trembling. May the power be of God.' Later on he wrote: 'Entered the house of .... Heard her swearing as I came up the stairs. Found her storming at three little grand-children, whom her daughter had left with her. She is a seared, hardhearted wretch. Read Ezekiel 33. Interrupted by the entrance of her second daughter, furiously demanding her marriage lines. Became more discreet. Promised to come back – never came. Her father-in-law entered, a hideous spectacle of an aged drunkard, demanding money. Left the house with warnings.' M'Cheyne and Somerville worked in the Canongate neighbourhood together with their pastor, John Bruce of the New North Church. Bruce organized, from within his own congregation, the evangelization work in this district. The fruit followed thereafter. Many a person's heart was touched and many began a new life with God. A few weeks before he started his work, he was encouraged to hear that he had been instrumental in awakening a soul from its sin. From the moment of his conversion it was his deepest desire to win souls for Christ. How he besought the Lord Himself in prayer to fulfil his desire! Now he could write with joy in his diary: 'The precious tidings that a soul has been melted down by the grace of the Saviour. How blessed an answer to prayer, if it be really so! "Can these dry bones live? Lord, Thou knowest." What a blessed thing it is to see the first grievings of the awakened spirit, when it cries, "I cannot see myself a sinner; I cannot pray, for my vile heart wanders!" It has refreshed me more than a thousand sermons. I know not how to thank and admire God sufficiently for this incipient work. Lord, perfect that which Thou hast begun!'

## Churchgoing in Edinburgh

The Lord lent support to His disciple in his training to become a servant of the gospel. He learned to forsake his own strength and put his trust in Him entirely. His way of life was: 'I will instruct thee ... in the way which thou shalt go; I will guide thee with mine eye' (Ps. 32:8). His study years were extremely beneficial to him. Quite apart from his lectures and evangelization work, the sermons of other servants of the Lord were indispensable to him. The ministry of evangelical pastors was consolidated in Edinburgh during those years. Clergymen in the pulpit everywhere proclaimed the gospel of reconciliation. He received much instruction from John Bruce, with whom he regularly kept in contact. Bruce preached before crowded audiences, particularly when, in 1837, he occupied the ancient preaching place of the Moderates in St Andrews. He was a lively preacher who knew how to captivate his listeners from beginning to end. M'Cheyne summarized his sermons every Sunday evening, until he found that the work required too much concentration and time. Therefore he wrote this note: 'Determined to be brief with these, for the sake of a more practical, meditative, resting, sabbatical evening.'

He regularly visited St George's. After Martin's death, the young Robert Smith Candlish took up his office here in 1834. He was a man not only renowned as a servant of the gospel, but also well known for his involvement in the Mission to the Jews. In 1835, a co-worker arrived, one by the name of Alexander Moody Stuart, who had received a command to establish a new church in the parish quarters of New Town. Regarding church extension, there were many new churches built during this time. A chapel was purchased in Young Street, which was an extension of Hill Street, where the M'Cheynes lived. Once the new congregation of St Luke's was established in May 1835, the M'Cheyne family eagerly attended the services there. The preaching of Moody Stuart expressed an experimental tone, with a stress on a personal knowledge of the Saviour by a living faith. He knew, in contrast to other evangelical pastors, like

John Bruce and Robert Candlish, how to plumb the depths of the human heart. His evangelical warmth as well as his deep compassion for the salvation of lost souls moved the young student.

When he heard Moody Stuart preaching, M'Cheyne didn't hesitate to offer his opinion: 'I have found the man.' Moody Stuart himself was attracted to Robert, who was four years his junior. His first impression was: 'It was to me a golden day when I first became acquainted with a young man so full of Christ.' An intimate friendship began to develop that day. Other students also gathered around the blessed ministry of this anointed pastor. A circle of interested persons was formed, and soon he invited the would-be pastors to visit the manse: 'We agreed to hold a weekly prayer meeting in order to pray for an hour.' M'Cheyne's father and mother also felt somehow drawn to him. They left St Stephen's and joined the new congregation.

**End of study period**

M'Cheyne's studies came to an end. In the spring of 1835, he appeared before the Presbytery of Edinburgh to be examined in order to receive his licence to preach. The day before this candidates' exam he wrote in his diary: 'Tomorrow I undergo my trials before the Presbytery. May God give me courage in the hour of need. What should I fear? If God see meet to put me into the ministry, who shall keep me back? If I be not meet, why should I be thrust forward? To Thy service I desire to dedicate myself over and over again.' It was a tense time for him. On 29 March he attended his last lecture. 'College finished on Friday last. My last appearance there. Life itself is vanishing fast. Make haste for eternity.' Trust as well as fear filled his heart. The exams caused the inevitable tensions. He informed his brother, William, that 'all heckling me like so many terriers on a rat'. His own pastor, John Bruce, was among the examiners. M'Cheyne also had to preach a trial sermon before his professors. Chalmers, in particular, gave the candidate cause for

Parish Church in Annan.

Popular Sermon

On Rom: V. 11

the joy in God

26. June 1835

1. Preached in Annan Church before Presbytery - 1 July 1835

No man

N

No man cometh

Oh that

No man

Oh Oh

Oh

Oh ye

'Popular Sermon', held in Annan before the presbytery. See his notes: 'Oh, oh..', and 'No man...'

apprehension. In spite of his trust in God, Robert was a human being of flesh and blood. Over-confidence and unrealistic enthusiasm were totally foreign to him. 'I would like better to preach to the world than to critics,' he wrote.

In April, he preached a trial sermon before Professor David Welsh. The theme of the lecture was 'The lost sheep and the lost penny' (Luke 15:1-10). He had learned much from Welsh, including how to subdivide a sermon into sections. 'I used,' said he later, 'to despise Dr. Welsh's rules at the time I heard him; but now I feel I must use them, for nothing is more needful for making a sermon memorable and impressive than a logical arrangement.' He wrote out the sermon in calligraphy. Was it the choice of his heart to speak about Him 'who is come to save that which was lost'? Did he not desire to lead souls to the true Shepherd? He portrayed man's depravity in a profound way: 'We all like lost sheep have gone astray.' 'There is none righteous, no, not one.' The good Shepherd 'stands stretching out His hands all the day', and calls lost sheep: 'Whosoever findeth me, findeth life and shall obtain favour of the Lord.' His invitation to sinners to come to Christ was emphatic: 'Take heed then, in embracing the Saviour that you take Him as a complete Saviour.' He is a perfect Redeemer for hopeless sinners. There is joy in heaven over one sinner that repents: 'And that there is joy in the presence of these angels of God over a sinner persuaded to cast all his care on the Saviour.' 'There is joy for none can pluck you out of the Saviour's hand.' Robert M'Cheyne then concluded with the words of Psalm 24, with the song that the heavenly chorus of angels sang: 'Lift up your heads, O ye gates; and be ye lifted up, ye everlasting doors; and the King of glory shall come in.' This 'Responsive Song' formed the conclusion to his sermon:

> Who is this King of glory?
> The Lord of Hosts
> He is the King of Glory!

Both Welsh and Chalmers were impressed with his examination results. Later on his father remembered well that 'we have heard that Dr. Chalmers was highly pleased, and all the other ministers'. Before he had finished the usual examination in front of the Presbytery, he received calls from several quarters to become a probationer. Thus John Bonar of Larbert asked him to become his assistant. Together with a few other fellow students, he appeared before the committee of the Edinburgh Presbytery for an inquiry. As sometimes occurred, he asked for the remaining trials to apply to the Presbytery of Annan. His own examiners were themselves so busy testing candidates that, in this way, he would be eligible to be stationed somewhere sooner. The parish of Ruthwell was situated within the district of Annan. It was thus probable that his spiritual friend and father, Henry Duncan, had been influential in this.

**Trial sermons before the Presbytery**

He had to deliver three trial sermons before the reverend fathers and brethren of the Presbytery of Annan. It was a difficult day for Robert. The 'Popular Sermon' dealt with Romans 5:11: 'And not only so, but we also joy in God through our Lord Jesus Christ, by whom we have now received the atonement.' A few abbreviated sentences remained on the front page of this preserved sermon: 'No man'; 'No'; 'Oh ye'. What made him write such notes? Was it the appalling thought that 'None that seek God'; that 'No man can come to Me, except the Father which hath sent Me draw him'? Was he deeply gripped by the lost state of man? It is not clear, but we do know, from the *Memoirs* of Andrew Bonar, of the feelings that inspired him at the end of the memorable first March of the year 1835: 'Preached three probationary discourses in Annan Church, and, after an examination in Hebrew, was solemnly licensed to preach the gospel by Mr. Monylaws, the moderator. "Bless the Lord, O my soul; and all that is within me, be stirred up to praise and magnify His holy Name!" What I have so long desired as the highest honour of man, Thou at length givest me – me who dare scarcely use the words of Paul: "Unto me who am less than the least of all saints is this grace given, that I should preach the unsearchable riches of Christ." Felt somewhat solemnized, though unable to feel my unworthiness as I ought. Be clothed with humility.'

The signing of the formula, which included his adherence to the Westminster Confession of Faith as the subordinate standard of the church, gave him the right 'to preach the gospel of our Lord and Saviour Jesus Christ as a probationer for the holy ministry'. The following Sabbath, he preached his first sermon in the church at Ruthwell. He dealt with the theme of the bathing-water at Bethesda in the morning service and the narrow gate in the evening. It was an unforgettable day. For the first time, he proclaimed the gospel to the people. He didn't preach to critical listeners, but before a variety of people. That evening he wrote: 'Found it a more awfully solemn thing than I had imagined to announce Christ authoritatively; yet a glorious privilege!' And he wrote to his brother: 'If I live, you see, I may soon be a preacher of the gospel – an honour to which I cannot name an equal under the sun.'

It was as if he felt that God was present. A difficult and impossible task awaited him. Without the Holy Spirit's equipping, he was powerless. His competence rested entirely on Him, who had called him out of darkness into His wonderful light. It was his strong conviction that 'to be in Christ before being in the ministry was a thing indispensable'. He often drew attention to the words of Jeremiah about false teachers: 'I have not sent these prophets, yet they ran; I have not spoken to them, yet they prophesied' (Jer. 23:21). He was well aware of his godly calling. Bonar notes: 'His soul was prepared for the awful work of the ministry by much prayer, and much study of the Word of God; by affliction in his person; by inward trials and sore temptations; by experience of the depth of corruption in his own heart, and by discoveries of the Saviour's fullness of grace.' The trials did come. Since his conversion four years ago he had passed through many waters.

'God's way is in the sea and in the great waters.' However, he was continually rescued from his fears, 'by the same divine hand that had drawn him out at the first; till at length, though still often violently tossed, the vessel was able steadily to keep the summit of the wave.'

It was precisely the trials that kindled the flame of his faith. Bonar compares him to Moses, who cleaved the rock by the power of God so that streams of water flowed forth. Did his power not lie in the Word of the One who commissioned him? An unknown path lay ahead of him, but like Moses 'he was under the guidance of the pillar cloud'. At that time he wrote a few poems on the following theme: 'They sing the song of Moses' (Rev. 15:3). M'Cheyne was only at the start of his desert journey, when he sang the song:

The night is dark, the storm is loud,
The path no human strength can tread;
Jesus, be Thou the pillar cloud,
Heaven's light upon our path to shed.

But in the midst of his night of guilt and trials he saw the heavenly pillar of fire which preceded him. It was, in fact, the great supreme Shepherd who led him to the green pastures of His testimony and the still waters of His love:

Yet would I lift my downcast eyes
On Thee, Thou brilliant tower of fire –
Thou dark cloud to mine enemies –
That hope may all my breast inspire.

John Archibald Bonar D.D. (1801-1863), minister of Larbert.

Larbert Parish Church, built in 1820.

# Chapter 4

# THE FIELDS OF LARBERT AND DUNIPACE

## Probationer

'I arrived here in safety about 7 o'clock on Saturday evening.' Thus the young probationer began his first letter, dated 9 November 1835, from the Larbert Manse of John Archibald Bonar, minister of the united parishes, Larbert and Dunipace. He had preached at several places after the memorable day on which he received licence to preach the Word. The time had arrived for him to assist Bonar for one year in the densely populated Carron valley, south of Stirling. He wrote: 'Yesterday I preached here to a large congregation on Isaiah 1, the same as I preached in Lady Glenorchy's and again on Ezekiel 33:10-11. I was very thankful when I got finished, for my preparation had been but slight.' His first sermons were more pronouncements: 'If our transgressions and our sins be upon us, and we pine away in them, how should we then live?' Or did he stress the following verse: 'As I live, saith the Lord God, I have no pleasure in the death of the wicked'?

Grave monument of Robert Bruce (1554-1631).

Larbert and Dunipace included together more or less seven hundred families. Since the establishment of the Carron ironworks there in 1759, the population had increased markedly. In 1790, only four hundred people lived in the area; in 1831, four thousand; and by the time M'Cheyne commenced his ministry, two thousand more were added. In the early days, the population consisted of farmers only, but now most of them found work in the industrial sector, such as the ironworks and coal mines. Many came from the large cities of England to find work here. The result was that Larbert developed into the largest industrial area of Scotland at this time. Dunipace maintained the ancient means of subsistence: agriculture. The consequence of this population increase goes without saying; the labourers were, on the whole, coarse people who didn't take Christian morals seriously. They were often found in the many tippling and beer houses, where they regularly over-indulged. Other social violations from the time of the industrial revolution were prevalent here. Children of eight or nine were working twelve hours a day making casting moulds at the scorching mouths of the Carron ironworks furnace, where accidents often occurred. These working conditions had a harmful effect on the people. The indifference and spiritual poverty were great. However, a considerable number visited the church on the Sabbaths. But the long working hours made the people tired, so that it wasn't as easy as one would think to stay awake during Bonar's long sermons.

**John Bonar**

John Archibald Bonar, just as Horatius and Andrew, was a descendant of John Bonar of Torpichen, a sympathizer and contemporary of the well-known Thomas Boston, who belonged to the so called *Marrow Men*. The minister of Larbert was a nephew of both Robert's friends. He was twelve years older than his recently acquired assistant and had worked there since 1826. It was an impossible task for one pastor to properly serve the densely populated and extensive parish. There were, besides the parish churches, three 'preaching stations' as two of which were at Carron and Kinnaird. He was grateful that he could regularly ask for help from candidates who had graduated for the ministry. William Hanna, a son-in-law of Thomas Chalmers, had worked with him for a while before Robert arrived.

The parish church of Larbert was built in 1820; it replaced a much smaller building. When M'Cheyne arrived in Dunipace, the church was still brand new; the newer building was completed in 1834. Before the Reformation, the little parish churches of Larbert and Dunipace were separate congregations belonging to the Church of St Ninians of Egglis. The Scottish parliament decreed in 1617 that both parishes should unite. Within the boundaries of Larbert was the Kinnaird property, which from early days belonged to the Bruces. This well-to-do family was not only well-known because of its involvement in the iron industry, but also because of devout Robert Bruce, who died here in 1631 after having been victim of years of exile and misunderstanding. His tombstone in the churchyard was a place of reflection for M'Cheyne. He was overjoyed to know that this great man in God's kingdom had worked and prayed here. Later he wrote from Palestine: 'May the Spirit be poured upon Larbert as in Bruce's days.' It was his heart's desire that the coarse people in the Carron valley be re-awakened, as in earlier days. Larbert had known more men of God, like Thomas Hog, who had carried the pastoral staff here with much blessing during the height of the Second Reformation. But the influence of the century of Enlightenment which followed did not exclude Larbert, although the Moderates knew how to rock the people to sleep with their boring sermons about virtue and good works. Bonar tried to break through their deep spiritual sleep. He preached with power on the subject of reconciliation through Christ alone. Until his death in 1863, his sermons were characterized by balance. His sermon on Proverbs 8:4 and 6 carried the significant title: 'Universal gospel Invitations Consistent with Total Depravity and Particular Redemption.'

**The first Sabbath**

M'Cheyne could totally agree with his 'bishop's' preaching when he heard him on the first Sabbath after his arrival at Carron's school. He preached 'with great effect and plain common-sense power for an hour and a half.' Did M'Cheyne mention the time duration because of his objection to long sermons? He thought it necessary to abbreviate his own sermons because the tired working people would soon lose their concentration. The people appreciated it very much that the new probationer limited himself to speaking for no longer than thirty-five minutes. Quality was of greater significance to M'Cheyne than quantity!

The first Sabbath was an eventful day. The autumn sun shone down on the valley when he preached the gospel message to the full church. After the service, a certain Mr Campbell 'of some place near Torwood' came up to him. He asked him to pay a visit to one of his small holders who was on his deathbed. On the way there, they were talking on topics of the papacy and the restoration of the Jewish nation, subjects that had always captivated the probationer. When they reached the farm in Carbrook, they heard that old Archibald, who feared the Lord, had just died. Fortunately, Bonar had visited him on the previous Saturday, but hadn't expected that his life would end so abruptly. The thoughts multiplied in the young probationer's mind, not only when he stood next to the deathbed, but also when he saw the house: 'The evening was deliciously fine, not a cloud over the whole sky. The wind was hushed; the trees all quite embrowned with autumn leaves; Ben Ledi and the distant hills were covered with sprinklings of snow. The sun had just set, and spread a mellow watery tinge over the scene. The little cottage was before us, and everything seemed congenial with the death of a Christian. The sun had entered its rest. The birds were going to their rest. The dead leaves were gone to their rest. It was the Sabbath day, when Christ entered into his rest. And it was Archibald Macleay's dying hour when he entered into the rest remaining for the people of God.' M'Cheyne spoke words of comfort to the grieving widow 'her daughter, two sons, and several neighbours' at Archibald's bedside. An hour later M'Cheyne was once again back at the manse. He then accompanied Bonar to Carron School. He was very tired when he arrived home, and went to bed at once.

**Pastoral work**

Robert assumed his task with enthusiasm. His 'good bishop' delegated to him the task of caring for the 'sheep' of the eastern part of his parish. Tully, his pony, became his faithful companion whenever he went on home visits in the fields of Kinnaird 'among the colliers' or to other places. On Monday, 16th November, he again drew up a report of his activities. The previous Sabbath he had preached in Dunipace and Kinnaird. Altogether, he had walked about twelve miles, but he was not yet tired. The weather was favourable. 'I never saw

Home of Robert's landlady, Mrs Graham, in Larbert, as drawn by himself.

such weather and such a country.' From the parish he looked out on to the river Carron, that divided into two streams. 'The sun rose most gloriously and the moon shone at the same time.' He praised the hospitality of Bonar, but also mentioned his fault: 'Secrecy.' But, fortunately, he opened up more to his assistant preacher, who wished to hide nothing from God and the people. Soon Robert would move to Mrs Graham's house, situated on the main road from Larbert to Carron. He asked his parents to send him some books, preferably by boat, because that was the cheapest. He also confided in them that he was comforted by reading Jeremiah One, finding in it a confirmation of his calling.

On 16th November he moved to the premises of his new landlady. A picture of his new residence was included in his next letter to Hill Street, Edinburgh. To the right of the newly erected building of Dr Mitchell stood Mrs. Graham's prominent house. The right-hand top window was Robert's room: the little window on the left was a 'light closet' in which he could store some books. The large room was full of furniture: 'it contains a bed, two chests of drawers, three tables, and six immense chairs; with my two trunks, locomotion is rather impeded.' Thus he kept his family in Edinburgh informed. The view from his window was splendid and panoramic. He viewed the estates of Carronvale, the little village of Campbellane, as well as a glimpse of Falkirk. At night he saw the fire-ovens lighting up the horizon. At seven o'clock he would arise and at night he went early to bed. Not only did he have food for his soul that the Lord gave him in abundance, but he experienced no food shortage at this time either. His breakfast consisted of porridge with enough milk. Tea, scarce at that time, was sent from Edinburgh. Good food was important to him, and he related to his caring mother that his diet consisted of everything from potatoes to apples!

It was his task as assistant minister to take turns in preaching at Larbert and Dunipace and during the week to visit as many people as possible. Immediately he observed the difference between the two churches. Larbert consisted of busy workers and Dunipace mainly of staid farmers. And not to forget 'the wilds' of Kinnaird, he mentioned the colliers, who showed little human emotion. Bonar and M'Cheyne's main goal was pastoral care. Both realized the full responsibility that weighed on their shoulders. Souls were created for eternity. It was their daily supplication to the Lord to open 'windows from heaven' over this area. M'Cheyne soon found himself attached to these people. When he lived in Dundee he still kept up contact with his first 'flock'. A letter to Bonar dated 1837, is a clear indication of his concern: 'What an interest I feel in Larbert and Dunipace! It is like the land of my birth. Will the Sun of Righteousness ever rise upon it, making its hills and valleys bright with the light of the knowledge of Christ!'

Daily he would set out on his pony, but not without preparation! Andrew Bonar explains that 'the forerunner of each day's visitations was a calm season of private devotion during morning hours. The walls of his chamber were witnesses of his prayerfulness, I believe of his tears as well as of his cries.' His landlady could hear his psalm singing every morning. She couldn't have noticed, however, that he was wrestling with God

Notes of his visitations in Larbert.

for the salvation of souls. Here he read and studied the Word of God; here he studied diligently Jonathan Edwards's books, which encouraged him greatly. Here he perused the letters of Rutherford that powerfully spread the fragrance of King Jesus. But the Bible was precious to him above all else. He spent much time scrupulously examining the Holy Scriptures. Herein he found treasures of grace and life. And the Holy Spirit enlightened his understanding to learn the mysteries of Christ. He saw the Word confirmed in his life: 'Bread out of the eater, and honey out of the lion.'

### House visitation

He thought pastoral guidance of great importance just as his 'bishop' did. The work of God's two messengers was characterized by diligence and compassion. It says a lot that the probationer wrote home: 'There is not a Carroner's wife who takes a pain in her head or foot but she has a minister at her door weekly till she gets well.' He thought it amusing that his visit was announced a day in advance by an elder, who advised the people: 'Their houses and barns are all as clean and shining as pennies new from the mint.' But the neatness of their houses was merely a veneer. The hearts of the people who lived there were impure. Very soon the young and acute candidate discovered that 'the hearts and faces are the same' as those that he met in the slums of Canongate in Edinburgh. What coarse people the mine-workers of Kinnaird were! Kinnaird was the most important area for his work. All the same, he related to these people better than he had expected. 'The people are savages for ignorance, but very amenable to kindness as all savages are.' He calls them: 'My sweet colliers.'

He discovered an example of ignorance in the form of an old woman. 'She was the most melancholy monument I ever saw,' he wrote in June 1836. 'She is so deaf that she says hardly anybody can make her hear. She is so blind that she cannot read. And she is so old that she will very soon die. I suspected that she made herself more deaf than she was in reality and, therefore, tried to make her hear. She knew that Jesus had shed His blood. But when I asked her why, she said that "really" her memory was so bad that she did not know.' It seemed as if he were in the jungles of Africa. How humiliating was this example, for himself too; he could hear and see, but was it to God's glory? Did he use his senses to try and discover what served eternal peace?

'He that winneth souls is wise.' These words in the book of Proverbs were applicable to M'Cheyne. But it distressed him that he saw so little fruit, so few workings of God's Spirit in the fields of Larbert and Dunipace. Where was the blessing on his work? For months on end, he was working entire days in this vineyard. It seemed rather like ploughing on the rocks than working on the well-prepared ground of his hearers who had reacted with faith to his preaching.

Despite this, the probationer continued with his work. He believed that through God's faithfulness, the fruit would be forthcoming.

We follow his daily routine during a few days in July as he worked in the mine-working village of Red Row. He diligently noted every visit down in his notebook. He wrote the text about which he spoke in purple ink. The little village had more or less fifty houses, and on one day he visited twelve. He rang the bell first at John Hunter's, number 22. We read: 'He, not at home. She, stout woman with sensible face. Spoke of her four bairns dead; three beside her.' Visit 14 July 1836. 'I stand at the door and knock. Altogether a decent woman. Husband to be at meeting.' Then the next house: Number 23, James Rankin's house. Death had struck here as well. 'Two children; three dead.' The child mortality rate was considerable at this time. Robert spoke on the 'story of sick child'. And so he continued down the street: Number 24: 'Red-haired man; honest, inquiring face.' He spoke here concerning: 'Suffer the children to come.'

A few days later he continued. The next address: 'Intelligent man'; he prayed here for 'the workers underground'. Then a woman with a 'wicked face' who, all the same, turned out better than he had expected. And then the last address: 'ill-looking man. Hard, hard woman. A large family of mocking lasses.' He addressed them with 'One thing needful, pardon and new heart.'

It was 21 July; the summer had begun a month previously, but the spiritual winter was not yet over. Darkness covered the mining area. M'Cheyne came into contact with hard hearts. 'Tried to break this northern iron,' thus he concluded his report.

The iron industry of Carron had once made the cannon-barrels for the battle of Waterloo. They were produced from the hardest steel, and murderous gunpowder came from the barrels to belch forth destruction over the almost invincible armies of Napoleon. But harder than the steel of the cannons were the hearts of the people of Larbert. M'Cheyne couldn't influence them; God's omnipotence alone was able to break these hearts. With this realization he visited the villages. He was permitted to sow, but it was God who gave the increase. Thus terminated his visits to Carronshore: 'Lord, bless the words of feebleness and make them words of power. Work Thou, and Thine be the praise.'

**Decline**

Thus M'Cheyne continued from strength to strength, until he came face to face with the valley of tribulation, 'the valley of Baca', and purification. From early morning until late at night he was busy. By the end of December he had a relapse. Pain in his chest and a worrying cough were warning signs to him not to continue on in this vein. His friends were afraid that his lungs were affected. There was no other recourse but to discontinue his work temporarily. He went to his parental home in order to recover. The doctor diagnosed the beginnings of tuberculosis. The tissue of the lungs was unaffected, but the right lung hardly functioned. Thoughts of fear and insecurity sprang into his mind. How could he continue? He didn't hesitate to inform Bonar immediately of the truth that was a grievous disappointment to him: 'If I am not recovered before the third Sabbath, I fear I shall not be able to bear upon my conscience the responsibility of leaving you any longer to labour alone, bearing unaided the burden of six thousand souls. No, my dear sir, I must read the will of God aright in His providence, and give way, when He bids me, to fresh and abler workmen.' He didn't mince matters; the work in Larbert had to continue, because the need was great. He certainly hoped to return recovered, as he said: 'With a heart tutored by sickness, to speak more and more as dying to dying.' The need of the souls in his parish weighed more heavily on him than his physical infirmities. He couldn't resist writing about a few sick people saying that he thought often about them. 'I can do no more for their good, except pray for them. Tell them that I do this without ceasing.'

We see here a new dimension in his prayer life. He prayed more for the needs of others than for himself. He wrote the following to the pastor of Larbert: 'I feel distinctly that the whole of my labour during this season of sickness and pain should be in the way of prayer and intercession.' By the latter, he meant that, just as Moses sought God face to face, so should he for his poor flock. He carried the sheep close to his heart, just as the high priest at one time carried the people of Israel on his breastplate. In this way, his entrance into the Holy of holies was assured. His fatigued and sick body could not prevent him from interceding for them continually. When it concerned himself, he would examine his own heart, declaring that his remaining depravity was of grievance to him. Thus he surrendered himself entirely to his Commissioner. God does only that which is good, although it is opposed to the rebellious nature of the human heart. 'Paul asked,' he wrote, "What wilt Thou have me to do?" And it was answered, "I will show him what great things he must suffer for my name's sake." Thus it may be with me. I have been too anxious to do great things. The lust of praise has ever been my besetting sin; and what more befitting school could be found for me than that of suffering alone, away from the eye and ear of man?'

No training is without a struggle. The learning school that the young and active candidate sought wasn't always comfortable. His heart wasn't as compliant as he wished. On the one hand he was prompted to pray continually, but on the other, his resistant heart kept him from praying. 'And yet, so strongly does Satan work in our deceitful hearts, I scarcely remember a season wherein I have been more averse to these duties.' Jude's words were a comfort to him: 'Building up yourselves on your most holy faith, praying in the Holy Ghost, keep yourselves in the love of God.' It was not only necessary to be encouraged by the love of God, but also to be kept in it. Sanctification is and remains God's work. In his own strength he could never make progress. He couldn't deny that the Lord had given him abundant grace, but in his flesh he had nothing to boast about. 'I cannot doubt that boldness is offered me to enter into the holiest of all.' And then follows the way of his soul in the sanctuary of God's love. Thus he was allowed to go 'by the new and bloody way', not only forgiven, but accepted in the Beloved. 'I cannot doubt that, when I do enter in, the Spirit is willing and ready to descend like a dove, to dwell in my bosom as a Spirit of prayer and peace, enabling me to "pray in the Holy Ghost".'

Christ's holiness was his holiness as well; this was the secret of his life. More and more he longed for fellowship with Christ and continually he was allowed to experience His presence. The oil of God's Spirit which was poured over him, spread the fragrance of Christ's garments. He sought refuge alone in the wounds of His Saviour, who 'is ready to rise up as my Intercessor with the Father, praying for me'. He couldn't deny that he was constrained by Christ's love and that He still heard his prayers. But still he sensed there was something lacking: 'I cannot doubt that thus to dwell in God is the true blessedness of my nature; and yet, strange unaccountable creature! I am too often unwilling to enter in. I go about and about the sanctuary, and I sometimes press in through the rent veil and see the blessedness of dwelling there to be far better than that of the tents of wickedness; yet it is certain that I do not dwell within.' Thus M'Cheyne moved on during these weeks of his sickness in the hard school, learning that 'He must increase, but I must decrease.'

**Continuation of preaching**

He returned once more to Larbert in January, 1836. A few weeks later he moved to a house in Carronvale that was offered to him 'free of rent'. Now that he lived close to his working area, his sister Eliza would come and assist him more often. Gradually he resumed work. It was a miracle that he could stand in front of his congregation once more. Revived and strengthened, he climbed the pulpit of the full church. He continued with his diary on the 21 February. It was Sabbath and twice he had preached on the righteousness of God, with reference to Romans 1:16, 'For I am not ashamed of the gospel of Christ.' The purpose of his diary 'ensures sober reflection on the events of the day as seen in God's eye'. The purpose he had in writing his daily experiences surpassed the harmful side of it, because he was afraid of 'making you assume feelings and express rather what you wish to be than what you are'. It was nonetheless good to remember the deeds of the Lord. Thus his diary became a reminder in God's presence. He blamed himself that he 'was more engaged in preparing the head than the heart' that Sabbath. This caused him to feel inferior in God's sight.

The next Sabbath he preached in Dunipace on Romans 5:10 with more emotion than ever. His heart was open to God's Spirit. It concerned reconciliation through the blood of Christ; and nothing speaks more to the heart of the believing soul than that which the Saviour has effected through His suffering and death. A week later, his heart was like an overflowing stream. This was also because he had avoided the mistake he had made on the 21 February. Head and heart were now in equilibrium and therefore 'the heart and the mouth were full'. The Lord gave room for speaking. 'How happy and strange is the feeling when God gives the soul composure to stand and plead for Him! Oh, that it were altogether for Him I plead, not for myself!'

Not only did he grow in grace, but there was also progress in his preaching. The ministry from within God's sanctuary was noticeable in his soul. Andrew Bonar notes: 'He gave out not merely living water, but living water drawn at the springs that he had himself drunk of; and is not this a true gospel ministry?' He imitated his heavenly Master in speaking words not of human wisdom, but 'in demonstration of the Spirit and of power'. His intellect was subservient to the anointing and enlightenment of God's Spirit. Heavenly sweetness spread, as it were, from the pulpits of Larbert and Dunipace. The learning process during his sickness caused him to be more dependent on the ministry from heaven. He didn't despise the studying, but it was subservient to the preparation of his heart which looked up to God in prayer. And, above all, his preaching revealed a deep compassion for souls. Rightly, his friend wrote: 'If we are ever to preach with compassion for the perishing, we must ourselves be moved by those same views of sin and righteousness which moved the human soul of Jesus.'

Thus weeks passed by. Conscientiously, the weak Robert applied himself to his task. His preaching became more spontaneous and eloquent. From the start, he disliked reading his sermons. He did keep an outline, though, that served as an aid to his memory, although he often didn't use it. On one particular Sabbath, he lost his sketch. As he rode on Tully to Dunipace, the paper slipped out of his pocket. He came to the realization that he could now preach without his outline. In future he left his paper at home. The result was he was more dependent on God in his preaching and more unconstrained in his approach. 'Man's extremity is God's opportunity,' he noted, which means that He helps those that are in dire need. He noticed that he mastered the language well and that his sentences were fluent. They were not the graceful sentences of an orator, but he spoke simply and tersely. 'One thing always fills the cup of my consolation, that God may work by the meanest and poorest words, as well as by the most polished and ornate, yea perhaps more readily, that the glory may be all His own.'

**Contents of his sermons**

He usually preached three times a Sabbath, stressing the practical issues. The contents consisted of subjects such as the rebellion and the fall of man, salvation by grace, the love of Christ and the wretchedness of the godless. It was especially his longing to apply the truth of God's Word to his listener's heart. The unbelievers in particular received much attention. With tears he admonished them to come to Christ. Thus he wrote on 16 March: 'Preached with some tenderness of heart. Oh, why should I not weep, as Jesus did over Jerusalem?' He conversed with his audience honestly. Once he spoke about 'The Parable of the Sower and the Seed', which elicited from Major Dundas of Carron Hall the pronouncement: 'I congratulate you, Mr. M'Cheyne, on being the only minister I have heard tell the people their faults.' The probationer couldn't appreciate this compliment. He didn't wish to be flattered by people.

The pitch determines the music, so the saying goes. M'Cheyne didn't wish to soften the potency of God's Word, but he discovered that he was sometimes too harsh and bold in his preaching. Even though the gospel is not the sort of message desired by men, yet it remains 'a gentle message, that should be spoken with angelic tenderness'. He discovered that harsh words, even while preaching, were not always spoken with sincerity or compassion. He once asked Andrew Bonar about the subject of his sermon. Bonar had preached on 'The wicked shall be turned into hell'. This dreadful verse elicited from M'Cheyne the next question: 'Were you able to preach it with tenderness?' Was this a reprimand? Most of the time preaching about hell doesn't result in much fruit. Often this leads to hardening and indifference. If harsh and cold words are recited in such sermons, the effect is still less. Bonar discovered that precisely the offer of grace in the lavish preaching of the gospel causes the greatest enmity, but at the same time, it is also the most effective: 'When we preach that the glad tidings were intended to impart immediate assurance of eternal life to every sinner that believes them, we strike deeper upon the proud enmity of the world to God, than when we show the eternal curse and the second death.'

'Eventful week; one year I have preached Jesus. Have I? or myself? I have often preached myself also, but Jesus I have preached.' This was the conclusion that M'Cheyne came to on the 3 July 1836, after having preached for one year. That day he spoke about the jailor 'with some glimpses of the genuine truth as it is in Jesus'. He noticed that many of his own experiences appeared in the sermons. Did he not preach too much about his own experiences? Was this not done at the expense of preaching on the subject of the cross? According to Andrew Bonar, he dwelt longer on the experiences of God's children than on 'the glad tidings'. Thus, not only important were the steps 'whereby the sinner might be brought to discover his guilt, but also the marks that would evidence a change'. This method of preaching was the result of his own deep knowledge of the human heart and of his life experience. But it didn't hinder the preaching of the gospel. 'Never did he preach other than a full salvation ready for the chief of sinners.' He disliked preaching that only highlighted the dogmatic side of the truth, without proclaiming the true life emanating from God. It was beside the point for him 'to speculate or to doctrinise about the gospel', but rather about the truth that is in Jesus. Rightly, Bonar observes: 'The glorious fact, "By this Man is preached unto you the forgiveness of sins", is the burden of every sermon.'

Despite the attention he afforded the way in which a sinner is brought to salvation in Christ, the cross of Calvary stood central. Thus he wrote on 12 June 1836: 'Today a sinner preached Jesus, the same Jesus who has done all things for him, and that so lately!' 'Evening. Somewhat helped to lay Jesus before little children in His beauty and excellency.' He also saw his own shortcomings. We read on 8 July: 'Today missed some fine opportunities of speaking a word for Christ. The Lord saw I would have spoken as much for my own honour as His, and therefore shut my mouth. I see a man cannot be a faithful minister until he preaches Christ for Christ's sake until he gives up striving to attract people to Himself and seeks only to attract them to Christ.'

His own imperfections were a hindrance to him in bringing the message in the full power of the Holy Spirit. His pride and desire for honour, especially, were still a part of him. It was a difficult struggle for him to die to himself. Regularly, we read in his diary, as on 12 June: 'A day ... of much temptation to flattery and pride.' It was precisely his sickness that was an instrument in God's hand to humble him. He wrote on 8 July: 'Since Tuesday, have been laid up with illness. Set by once more for a season to feel my unprofitableness and cure my pride. When shall this self-choosing temper be healed? "Lord, I will preach, run, visit, wrestle," said I. "No, thou shalt lie in thy bed and suffer," said the Lord.' M'Cheyne had to learn to totally surrender himself to God, so that He alone would receive all the glory. 'I fear Thou wilt not bless my preaching, until I am brought thus to hang on Thee.' This training in holiness gave him the expectation that soon streams of blessing would ensue.

**Contact with home**

Weekly he kept his father, mother and sister Eliza up to date with the details of his life in Larbert. He sympathized intensely with his family and thought about their salvation as well. Just before he was struck with illness, he urged them not to neglect the salvation of their soul: 'Keep yourselves all well, regular and earnest in seeking Christ.' It seemed that he was afraid that they didn't know Him as their refuge and Mediator. He wrote in the same letter 'that forgiveness of sins and acceptance with God become every day in my view more unspeakably precious'. The previous Sabbath he reflected on Psalm 23, the comforting Psalm intended for the sheep of the flock of Christ, who have entered the true door to the sheepfold. Could his parents say this as well? He urged them to go to Moody Stuart's church; he was a faithful ambassador of Christ, who rightly divided the Word.

He heard from his father that his brother William, in India, was seriously occupied with eternal things. 'I do hope that he will leave behind him good evidence that he hath found the Saviour,' for in seeking Him, one has not yet obtained salvation. It is necessary to belong to 'the justified people of the Saviour.' 'Oh dear Mamma, there is no other way of dying in peace than by being joined by the Lord Jesus.... It is not prayers and tears that will blot out sins, else all the world would be saved. It is only having Jesus in our arms that gives peace.' He reminded them of his brother David who, at the time, was the only one in the family who could die in a saving state. It was five years ago since he had passed away. In his diary, Robert also made a note of the following: 'This day my brother has been five years absent from the body and present with the Lord, and knows more and loves more than all earthly saints together. Till the day break and the shadows flee away, turn, my Beloved!'

The bond with home grew stronger only since he had become a probationer. It was an encouragement to him that his family prayed for him. On 1 February 1836, after he had spent time at his parental home because of sickness and then worked again for a few weeks, he sent a message to his mother that he had felt 'wonderfully well' the last Sabbath. 'There was deep snow on the ground but the day was mild.' Warmly dressed in a thick winter coat, he went to church. Eliza was with him. 'She has been a great comfort to me.' His appetite had improved so considerably that he ate two eggs at breakfast. In one of his letters, he asked for a receipt from the doctor and he hoped that his father and mother were looking after his pony. Tully wasn't too well, but later on, when his inseparable companion was with him again, he could write: 'Tully is really well, quite well, like a minister's pony now, so fat and sleek with little work.' The animal had shown symptoms of paralysis, but now it could carry its master once more across the wide fields of Larbert and Dunipace.

He received a cheerful but at the same time saddening report from his parents. It concerned his brother William. 'God mingles judgments and mercies,' he thus began his letter on 2 February. He was full of joy when he learned that his brother showed 'such manifest proof of a work of grace'. 'It is true God seems to be bringing him through deep waters, yet I do not believe that ever such an awakened soul perished, for it is written "When thou passest through the rivers, I will be with thee, and through the waters, they shall not overflow thee."' William's faith was very weak and he was 'under a cloud', and yet his spiritual life showed 'volumes of comfort'. M'Cheyne sensed that it was the truth about his brother, in spite of the deep waters he found himself in. The letter doesn't mention what afflictions he experienced, but we read between the lines that it was very difficult for him. He reasoned that it was good for

Painting of parish church and manse of Larbert. The manse was built in 1797 and pulled down in 1945.

Parish Church of Dunipace, built in 1834. Nowadays it is out of use.

Eliza to stay with her parents, in spite of the help he could have used after his sickness.

His father visited him regularly. On one occasion, he accompanied Eliza and the doctor to 'Mrs. Graham's home'. When his father and sister stayed overnight at his place, he would write an extra note to his mother, because she remained on her own behind! Thus, in the beginning of July, they came to Larbert. It was fair weather. His mother, who experienced little of the country life, had to know that 'the crops are looking full and beautiful'. The Lord was so good to them, as well as to nature's kingdom! M'Cheyne always spoke with reverence about God. Day by day He would shower them with blessings. He also listened to the call of the young ravens. Sometimes M'Cheyne felt the need to put his thoughts about his faithful God into poetic form. Thus on 13 May, he sent home, without much explanation, four verses with the title: 'Orphans Hymn'. This was in reference to Hosea 14:4, 'For in Thee the fatherless findeth mercy'. In the same way that the hungry ravens cry out for food and receive it, the hearts of the orphans are filled with good things. The Father of the orphans gives more than any 'a father, mother or friend' can give.

The mother may forget her child
She loved so well before
But if in Jesus reconciled
Shall lov'st be evermore.

When earthly bonds of love fail, the faithful Father in heaven, who never abandons his orphans will never fail. 'Charity never faileth.' He calls them: 'My children dear' and 'help us to say "Our God".'

**Association with people**

One of M'Cheyne's characteristics was that he so quickly became attached to people. In Larbert and Dunipace friendships were also formed. Some friendships were continued in the future, such as in the case of Campbell of Carbrook, whom he met on the first Sabbath. The youth of the congregation also found a place in his heart. He was in charge of the Sabbath School at Torwood School. One August evening he spoke about the lost sheep before a group of gypsies who were gathered around a fire. He soon began catechizings for young people, not then a customary practice in Scotland, at least not in separate classes for the young. The church tower room in Larbert was an excellent place for this purpose. In Dunipace too he set up separate boys, and girls, groups. In June of that year, he recorded an attendance, on the first evening, of twenty-two girls and he expected twenty-three boys to turn up the following evening. It was his strategy 'to entertain them to the utmost and at the same time to win their souls'. His artistic and musical talents helped to gain and hold their attention. He wrote with much enthusiasm about his youth meetings: 'I gather all sorts of interesting scraps to illustrate the catechism and try to entice them to know and to love the Lord Jesus.' It was heartening for him that a while later, especially among the girls in Dunipace, he noticed a more than unusual emotion. 'One of them seemed to be thoroughly awakened. Thanks be to Thee, Lord, for anything,' he wrote that evening in his diary. It was as if he saw a cloud, the size of a man's hand, and that gave him courage.

M'Cheyne associated with young and old alike in Carron valley, as if they all belonged to his own flock. Bonar observed that when visiting 'the sheep' he carried out the duty of a true shepherd 'to strengthen the diseased', 'to heal the sick', 'to bind that which was broken', 'to bring again that which was driven away' and 'to seek that which was lost' (Ezek. 34:4). The last mentioned applied to a young man who had fled from his parental home. M'Cheyne felt so much compassion for his welfare that he wrote him a long letter on 8 August. It is striking that M'Cheyne tried to identify with the young man's motivation in leaving. Was he any better a person? He wrote him an honest letter: '... It is so short a while since I was just like you, when I enjoyed the games which you now enjoy and read the books which you now read...' 'The same youthful blood flows in my veins that flows in yours, the same fancies and buoyant passions dance in my bosom as in yours.' Thus he placed himself alongside the runaway, because by nature he wasn't any better. Yet he also enjoyed the permissible things of life: 'I am not like a grey-headed grandfather, then you might answer all I say by telling me that you are a boy. No; I am almost as much a boy as you are; as fond of happiness and of life as you are; as fond of scampering over the hills, and seeing all that is to be seen, as you are.'

He next wrote from his own personal experience: that no one had pointed him to the Saviour, except for his own brother; how he had followed the desires of his own heart. At first his life was careless, without disappointments. 'I fancy few boys were ever happier in an unconverted state than I was. No sorrow clouded my brow; no tears filled my eyes, unless over some nice storybook.' He was unaware that he walked on the edge of a precipice. Yet, he was far from happy, and that he realized only when the Lord opened his eyes to see it. What was his message to the sheep that had strayed? M'Cheyne pointed him to the true happiness, in whose light everything else falls by comparison. 'Now, do you think it would not give you more happiness to be forgiven, to be able to put on Jesus, and say, "God's anger is turned away"?' The joy of God's people is the only real joy. He gave him guidelines for Bible reading and prayer. He pointed him towards Christ as the only way to salvation: 'Now, forgiveness may be yours now. It is not given to those who are good. It is not given to any because they are less wicked than others. It is given only to those who, feeling that their sins have brought a curse on them which they cannot lift off, "look unto Jesus", as bearing all away.'

**Farewell**

The time drew near for his task in Larbert to come to an end. The Lord guided him to the new flock he would take under his care. He was now twenty-three years of age. His birthday didn't pass unnoticed. He wrote in his diary: 'Blessed be my Rock. Though I am a child in knowledge of my Bible and of Thee, yet use me for what a child can do, or a child can suffer.' He spoke with modesty, although the world judged him differently.

Meanwhile, this young man with great gifts of heart and mind, had gained a reputation. It was especially Bruce, Welsh and Chalmers who watched out for him. They looked around to see if there was a congregation without a pastor where he could become the preacher. The friendship with Chalmers was especially 'quite moving' to him, thus he wrote to his father. But it was especially Robert Smith Candlish, the minister of St George's in Edinburgh, who brought him into the limelight. Besides giving him the chance to preach in his church on a number of occasions, he involved him in mission work and appointed him co-worker for *The Scottish Christian Herald*. One of the first articles he wrote for the church weekly newspaper dealt with 'Sudden Conversions'. Candlish was closely involved in the background when St Peter's Church in Dundee made a call on the young candidate. Before he could accept this call, John Bonar of Larbert gave him a laudatory testimonial on 6 April 1836. He called him a young man with 'excellent talents, solid study, sound principles and real piety'. 'He is greatly beloved and delighted in by my people and the longer they know him and the more they see of him, the better they loved him.' Bonar's influence on him should not be underestimated. According to his father's opinion, the example of Bonar had 'a most powerful influence in the formation of Robert's ministerial character if not in the style of his preaching. Indefatigable activity and perseverance appear to me to be perhaps the most striking characteristics of both.'

The time for farewell soon drew near. On 22 June he preached for the last time in Carronshore. Thus he wrote: 'My last. Some tears; yet I fear some like the messenger, not the message; and I fear I am so vain as to love that love. Lord, let it not be so. Perish my honour, but let Thine be exalted for ever.' The following Sabbath he preached with a full attendance. The preaching wasn't any more difficult for him, but he, nonetheless, asked himself if it were all the work of grace. 'I know that all was not of grace; the self-admiration, the vanity, the desire of honour.' All this in him was not yet put to death. There was also no room for praise, even though he didn't deny that the workings of grace were found in his preaching. It was a matter of treasure in earthen vessels, which he carried about in him. He was merely a tiny instrument in God's hands, and nothing more.

His final sermons to the congregations of Larbert and Dunipace dealt with Hosea 14:2: 'O Israel, return unto the Lord' and Jeremiah 8:20: 'The harvest is past.' A report which he sent to his parents, gave an impression of this event: 'I preached my farewell sermon at Dunipace last Sabbath day ... I never saw the church so full before ... It is very sad to leave them now and to leave them thus. What multitudes of houses I have never entered. So many I have only stood once on their hearthstone and prayed. In some few I have found my way so far into their affections but not so far as to lead them to Jesus. My classes are a little more anxious and awakened than they were, especially some of the young women; but permanent fruit, none is visible. Yet I leave them just as the farmer leaves the seed he has sown. It is not the farmer that can make it grow; he can only pray and wait for the latter rain.' The evening of that day he wrote: 'Lord, I feel bowed down because of the little I have done for them which Thou mightest have blessed! My bowels yearn over them, and all the more that I have done so little. Indeed, I might have done ten times as much as I have done. I might have been in every house; I might have spoken always as a minister. Lord, canst Thou bless partial, unequal efforts?'

The months in Larbert were a time of purification for M'Cheyne. In reality, his probation was a better training school for him than the years he had spent studying in Edinburgh. His friend, Andrew Bonar, wrote: 'He had been taught a minister's heart; he had been tried in the furnace; he had tasted deep personal sorrow, little of which has been recorded; he had felt the fiery darts of temptation; he had been exercised in self-examination and in much prayer; he had proved how flinty is the rock, and had learned that in lifting the rod by which it was to be smitten, success lay in Him alone who enabled him to lift it up.' Thus the Lord prepared his servant. Though He concealed the fruits from him, they were nonetheless there. The scattered seed would not return void. It was sown with tears of love. 'He that goeth forth and weeping, bearing precious seed, shall doubtless come again with rejoicing, bringing his sheaves with him' (Ps. 126:6). Despite the less productive side of his eleven month stay in Larbert, he remained optimistic, and at the time of his farewell he wrote the following to Bonar: 'But if at length the iron front of unbelief give way, if the hard faces become furrowed with the tears of anxiety and of faith, under whatever ministry, you will rejoice, and I will rejoice, and the angels, and the Father and God of angels, will rejoice.' In Carron valley bonds of friendship were established which were to remain strong. Later he wrote: 'Larbert and Dunipace are always on my heart, especially on the Saturday evenings, when I pray for a glorious Sabbath!' How thankful he was, that at his farewell, he could transfer his duties to his friend, Alexander Somerville, who was to become Bonar's assistant and his successor. He advised Alexander and mentioned everyone by name. He wrote: 'Take more heed to the saints than ever I did.'

A poem about Mungo Park dates back to his short stay in Larbert. He wrote this poem referring to a story about a traveller in the desert, who while wandering across the dreary, sandy plains and occupied with melancholic meditations, suddenly espied a tiny moss plant. In his observance of this delicate, yet beautiful little plant, his dull gaze was transformed and he received the courage to continue.

From gazing on the tender flower,
We lift our eyes to him Whose power

Hath all its beauty given;
Who, in this atmosphere of death,
Hath given it life, and form, and breath,
And brilliant hues of heaven.

Thus the scanty fruit that M'Cheyne came across on his pilgrim's journey, in the vineyard which included the fields of Larbert and Dunipace, was planted by his Commissioner. He encouraged M'Cheyne to continue following His way. According to the promise of Psalm 72, 'the fruit thereof shall shake like Lebanon' (Ps. 72:16).

# Chapter 5

# ST PETER'S CALLS!

## Dundee and surroundings

'I then went to Dundee, through the Carse of Gowrie, the most fruitful valley in the kingdom; and I observed a spirit of improvement prevails in Dundee, and all the country round about it. Handsome houses spring up on every side, trees are planted in abundance, wastes and commons are continually turned into meadows and fruitful fields. There lacks only a proportionable improvement in religion, and this will be one of the happiest countries in Europe.' John Wesley, the English Methodist, made these notes in his diary on 1 May 1784, when he visited the region surrounding Dundee once again. In days gone past, the area of the old harbour city overlooking the Firth of Tay together with the hinterland, the Carse of Gowrie, had received much blessing from the Lord. Adam Philip observes: 'The Carse has been the seedplot of harvest behind, and of harvests to be. Some of the great knights of the Christian Church are linked with its story ...' George Wishart, the spiritual father of John Knox, preached to the plague-sufferers

Dundee from the Firth of Tay.

Panorama of Dundee from Law hill. Between the many factories the Cross Church is visible.

at the city wall of the Cowgate in Dundee in approximately 1545. When he came to the little, old church of Invergowrie to the west of the city, he spoke these prophetic words about Scotland: 'This realm shall be illuminated with the light of Christ's apostles.' At these same ruins, which according to history go back to the year 431, M'Cheyne regularly bowed his knees to pray for his new congregation in Dundee.

M'Cheyne walked in the footsteps of one of his predecessors in Dundee, the saintly John Willison, who was a minister approximately a hundred years earlier. Willison was involved in the well-known revival of 1742 in Cambuslang and Kilsyth, and he had always longed for this work of God to sweep over his city too. He wrote to the English Methodist, George Whitefield, that he had shed many tears for the inhabitants. He was also happy when he observed the promptings of spiritual life. 'A good many of the young people in this place have joined meetings for prayer and repeating sermons.' When Whitefield came to the city to preach, the work grew. 'We see now great numbers of them awakened to seek the Lord and cry after Jesus.' Many, especially young people, were permitted to attend the Lord's Supper. There wasn't such a breakthrough as there had been in Cambuslang, but there were hopeful signs that encouraged Willison to continue to pray for a revival. The breakthrough failed to materialize and much of this city came under the influence of the Age of Reason.

Approximately 51,000 people lived in Dundee when M'Cheyne took pastoral responsibility there. Since the time that Wesley preached there the population had almost doubled. Besides being an important harbour city, it had also become an industrial centre. The development of steam machines had transformed the old mills into new factories, where linen, rope and, above all, jute were manufactured. The population growth was due principally to these forms of industry, which provided work and prosperity. However, women and children also sought work in the unhealthy factories. The city expanded beyond its old boundaries; new districts sprang up in no time; the harbour

## NEW NORTH-WEST CHAPEL, HAWKHILL.

A GENERAL movement having been made throughout the bounds of the Church of Scotland, for the purpose of securing sufficient pastoral superintendence, and proper church accommodation, to those quarters of the land which are now destitute of these advantages, it becomes especially incumbent on the religious inhabitants of Dundee to unite heartily in a scheme so well fitted to promote the best interests of their fellow citizens and countrymen. The manufactures and commerce of this town have prospered with unexampled rapidity, and have brought a vast accession to the community of those classes which stand most in need of the pulpit and household ministrations of an enlightened Christian adviser. Between the census of 1821 and 1831, about 15,000 were added to the population; since 1831, we may state the probable increase at 5000,—making a total increase to the population, in fourteen years, of 20,000 souls. For these rapidly increasing numbers, the only additional provision made within the pale of the Establishment, has been,—

| | |
|---|---|
| St David's Church, | about 3000 sittings. |
| Enlargement of Cross, | |
| Enlargement of Chapelshade, | |
| Accommodation by building Lochee Chapel, | |
| Accommodation by building Ferry Chapel, | |

Adding this to the actual accommodation in 1821, we have—total accommodation in all the Churches and Chapels 11,000, for a population of 51,000.

A part of the Minute Book of St Peter's Church, accounts of the meetings of the Managers. Here an account of 15th November 1837, in which we read of the new gas lighting. Peter Thomson said that the spire of the tower was finished and paid!

Minute of a Meeting of the Managers
of St Peters Church held in the Vestry on the
evening of Wednesday the 15th of Novemr 1837
at 7 Oclock—
Present Messrs David Brown
James Thomson Alexr Moncur
Alexr Ogilvy & Geo H Newall
David Brown Esq Chairman
The Treasurer informed the meeting that the
collections of the Seat-rents for the current half
year amounted to about the same sum as
that collected last half year, that the collections
at the church door also amounted to a sum
equal to that of last half year and that in

was also extended; new schools were built to accommodate the child population increase. The city throbbed with new life, but the true life from God threatened to ebb away. The 'Jute barons' had their luxurious villas, but the workmen usually lived in small, dirty houses, which were hastily erected. Districts such as Hilltown were a breeding ground for epidemics resulting from a shortage of sanitary facilities. The inhabitants had to draw water from the pools where the factories had dumped their cooling water. It was no wonder that cholera, typhus and other sicknesses prevailed there.

The population's moral standards didn't improve. The wages were higher than previously, but the money found its way to more than a hundred beer houses, where the young labourers, in particular, took to strong drink. The public houses formed a glaring contrast to the eleven bakeries of which the city boasted!

With the population increase came also a growth in non-churchgoers. Apart from that, the number of seats in the seven parish churches and the three Chapels of Ease totalled no more than seven thousand, while the churches of the seceders could hold only another seven thousand souls. The number of non-church-goers was estimated at nine thousand souls. There was thus a desperate need for more seating for church-attenders. Thomas Chalmers had foresight in his unveiling of the extension plans. The Chapels Act of 1834, after years of discussion in the General Assembly of the church, at last offered the possibility of erecting churches with equal rights to those of the parishes. The Moderates had long opposed this decision; apparently, they were afraid that their influence would decline due to the considerable increase in the number of candidates from among the Evangelicals. Now the building of new church buildings could be energetically effected.

## The building of St Peter's

St Peter's in Dundee was the first *Quoad Sacra Chapel* to be erected in the country according to the new rule. In 1835, John

St Peter's in Dundee, after an engraving in 'Additional Remains' of M'Cheyne.

Roxburgh, the minister of St John's, wrote a circular letter in which he requested funds for the construction of a new 'Chapel in the northwest quarter of the Hawkhill'. St John's parish forms part of the so-called City Churches, the great cruciform church in Nethergate. Most of the church buildings were close to each other in the city centre, far from the suburbs. The new church in the West End would have to be a sober building 'to secure at once quantity and cheapness of accommodation'. A strip of ground adjoining Perth Road, not far from Firth of Tay, was selected for this purpose. The introduction to the Minute Book of the Managers of St Peter's gives us a summary of the arguments favouring the construction of this 'North West Chapel, Hawkhill': 'Between the census of 1821 and 1831, about 15,000 were added to the population; since 1831, we may state the probable increase at 5,000, making a total increase to the population, in fourteen years, of 20,000 souls.' The expansion of seats in the existing church buildings could not possibly cater for this growth. The social predicament of the inhabitants was observed with concern. Chalmers's portrayal of the poorer classes was indeed applicable to Dundee: 'There is a fearful remainder of irreligion and practical heathenism ...'

The St John's parish circular letter had intentionally announced a delay in the implementation of the plans because the St Peter's cash-book recorded that, from November 1834 until the end of the same year, all subscriptions and free gifts totalled no less than £625. These included offerings made in all parts of the city as well as the surrounding areas. Roxburgh's letter was the means by which the funds streamed in to such a degree that, in the spring of 1835, work on the building could begin. On 11 July, the bricklayer was paid £100; on 7 August £150; while on 27 August each of the carpenters was paid £150.

The new church came into use on 15 May 1835. It was a sombre building that displayed no trimmings. The pulpit and the precentor's desk at the front of the church were the only decorative parts. The construction of the spire was to wait until 1839, when St Peter's, with its 1175 seats, would be completely finished. A churchyard formed the view from the road; the entrance beneath the tower took the churchgoers into the spacious hall, including an oval-shaped and spacious gallery. In the original plan, space for a school on the western side of the church was borne in mind, so 'that the blessings of religion and the benefits of knowledge may be imparted together'. The construction of the school came somewhat later, however. When a start with the latter was made in July 1835, some ladies sought to add one storey to the building for the purpose of 'the education of girls in sewing and other household arts'. The kirk session decided a year later to extend the school which had to provide for three hundred pupils.

**The call of a minister**

Now that the building was completed, the new congregation could be established. A kirk session was formed; managers for the oversight and maintenance of the building – nine persons in all – were, in the first instance, appointed by St John's and later by St Peter's itself: three members by the kirk session and six members directly by the congregation. The first session, consisting of ten elders, was appointed by St John's Church. Now the time was ripe to call a pastor. The St John's kirk session then made contact with Chalmers, Welsh and Candlish, prominent persons from the circle of Evangelicals. The minister to be called should be a 'pious, active, and efficient preacher'. Among the list of recommended candidates to be received from Edinburgh were the names of Andrew Bonar, Alexander Somerville and Robert Murray M'Cheyne, the latter receiving preference in Candlish's eyes. All candidates would come for an interview and, ultimately, the communion members of St. Peter's would make the final decision.

In Larbert, Robert waited the turn of events with growing excitement. He wrote to his parents: 'My two greatest intimates being made my rivals. I have no doubt we will contend with all humility in honour preferring one another. If the people have any sense, they will choose Andrew Bonar.' M'Cheyne preferred the country life to that of the city, but he was nonetheless prepared to go to Dundee, if that were God's will. What kind of man did the new congregation want? In a local newspaper, the *Dundee Advertiser* of 19 August 1836, there appeared lucidly: 'Not the man of controversy, but the man of prayer – not a loiterer, but a labourer in the vineyard, one who will be found more frequently in the chambers of the sick and the afflicted than amidst the gaieties of the drawing room.' When M'Cheyne preached his trial sermon in the brand new church building, the choice was soon decided. It wasn't necessary for the other candidates to turn up because the congregation was almost unanimous in their judgment that he was the most suited to take on the duty of pastor. Thus M'Cheyne was chosen in August 1836, by general consensus. Bonar observes: 'He accepted the call under an awful sense of the work that lay before him. He would rather, he said, have made choice for himself of such a rural parish as Dunipace; but the Lord seemed to desire it otherwise. "His ways are in the sea."' More than once, at a later stage, he would say: 'We might have thought that God would have sent a strong man to such a parish as mine, and not a feeble reed.'

The first time that he preached in St Peter's, he spoke on the parable of the sower and the seed. That was on the 14 August. During the morning he was not in the mood to preach, but that afternoon he spoke 'with more encouragement and help of the Spirit' on the voice of the Beloved in Song of Songs 2:8-17. And 'in the evening, with all my heart on Ruth. Lord, keep me humble.' He later heard that this sermon, about the choice Ruth made, had been a cause of blessing to two souls. The *Dundee Advertiser* of 2 September reported on the second time he preached: 'We have reason to believe, confirmed the favourable opinion formerly entertained of him. As a preacher he is earnest and persuasive rather than argumentative. His command of Scripture, imagery, and illustration is intensive; but some of his figures he pursued rather too far. His voice has considerable power; but it is deficient in flexibility. Upon the

Map of Dundee in 1832. The main church, Cross Church on the Nethergate (1) in the centre of the city. Perth Road (2) and Hawkhill (3) were the main streets of West-End. The harbour (4) was a centre of activities, but the port became more and more an industrial city.

whole, he promises to be an acceptable preacher; and we hope that, in the discharge of the other duties of a minister, which are not less important, the people will be not disappointed.'

**Ordination**

The day of his induction approached. With much anxiety of spirit he made his way to Dundee. He travelled by way of Perth and spent the night in the manse of his friend, James Grierson, in Errol, a town not far from Dundee. The next morning he was occupied by three Bible texts in particular. The first was Isaiah 26:3, 'Thou shalt keep him in perfect peace whose mind is stayed on Thee; because he trusteth in Thee.' 'This verse was seasonable; for, as he sat meditating on the solemn duties of the day, his heart trembled.' And: 'Meditate upon these things' (1 Tim. 4:15). It was his prayer that this word would take root in his heart. In conclusion: 'Here am I, send me'; this, Isaiah's prayer, was his also. It was unimportant where he was required to go, as long as the Lord sent him. Thus the candidate wrestled before the Lord. When he got up from his knees, it was in his heart: 'Lord, may Thy grace come with the laying of the hands of the Presbytery.'

It was 24 November 1836. The church of St Peter's was crammed full. John Roxburgh of St John's led the induction service. The laying on of hands and the reading of the formula formed a solemn culmination to the holy service. It was the next Sunday, 27 November, when M'Cheyne was introduced in the morning by John Bonar from Larbert and, in the afternoon, the new minister delivered his first sermon on Isaiah 61:1-3: 'The Spirit of the Lord God is upon Me; because the Lord hath anointed Me to preach good tidings unto the meek; He hath sent Me to bind up the brokenhearted, to proclaim liberty to the captives.' Here we find the mystery of his rich ministry. It was no daring self-confidence that ushered him to the pulpit to preach on these words. Yet he knew that he was anointed by the Holy Spirit and spoke with a rock-hard conviction, in deep and humble dependence on God. These prophetic words, once earnestly quoted by the Saviour in Nazareth, meant much to him. Each year, he recalled the text of his first sermon in St Peter's, and his summaries were stored away with his sermon collection.

It was this sermon that was the means whereby several souls were awakened from their sleep of spiritual death. In his sermon about the same text six years later, he observed: 'The anointing of the Holy Spirit makes a successful gospel minister.' So it was in Christ's ministry. 'The Spirit of the Lord God is upon Me.' So it is in every minister. 'The more anointing of the Holy Spirit, the more success will the minister have.' 'A faithful watchman preaches a free Saviour to all the world.' This was the great object of Christ's ministry: 'To proclaim the acceptable year of the Lord.' In this way, M'Cheyne set out on his task in Dundee. That Sabbath evening, John Bonar preached on 'These times of refreshing'. 'A noble sermon, showing the marks of such times. Ah! when shall we have them here? Lord, bless this word to help their coming! Put Thy blessing upon this day! Felt given over to God, as one bought with a price.' He came to this harbour city with a deep longing for a spiritual revival. When would dawn for Dundee 'the days of refreshing' by means of the living water from the kingdom of God?

The *Dundee Advertiser* devoted detailed attention to the arrival of the new leader. After the custom of the day, a dinner was held on the day of his induction. Sixty guests listened to the speeches and congratulations in Campbell Hall's hotel, but of greatest interest was the after-dinner speech of St Peter's sympathetic and prepossessing new minister. The master of ceremonies was the elder, Alexander Balfour, who was flanked by his fellow church officers, David Brown, David Martin and James Thompson. Mr Campbell, the hotel keeper, was the first to receive a compliment in the report. The toasts were enumerated; all were made to well-known persons, from the royal family to the Lord Lieutenant of the country, as well as to the Earl of Airlie. An attitude of joy and thanksgiving prevailed, which wasn't drowned out by the usual cheers and applause.

The reporter experienced more of the atmosphere of 'ecclesiastical sentiment'.

M'Cheyne's speech was the climax of the dinner. All eyes were concentrated on him when he first addressed the moderator, Mr Roxburgh, who had given such a striking summary of the necessary qualities of a minister, 'the best declaration he had ever listened'. 'He had stated that a minister should be "outwardly called and inwardly called" ere he was properly qualified for the pastoral office.' Now M'Cheyne found it difficult 'to say exactly what an inward call is'. This brought him to the point of comparing his situation to the call of Gideon. 'Gideon's was a message of judgment, theirs of mercy and peace. It was not necessary therefore, that it should be miraculous. It was only required that ministers should be taught of God; and his feeling had always been to do nothing on earth but to preach the gospel of Jesus.' Did he mean to say that he could identify no definite call to his office? But what was his mission other than to announce the good news? And when he impressed upon his attentive listeners 'with the utmost humility' that he desired nothing other than to preach 'Christ and Him crucified', there followed a resounding applause, according to the *Dundee Advertiser*.

But his speech wasn't finished yet. An anecdote came to mind, and with this he wished to conclude. He reminded his audience of Dr Muir of Glasgow, who once asked a colleague what was the 'extent of his church'. His colleague answered that 'its chief glory was that it was filled to the door'. Dr Muir wished to better this because it wasn't the quantity of listeners that determined the glory of a church, but 'the presence of the Lord is the true glory of every church'. Upon saying this M'Cheyne picked up his glass and directed a toast to 'the health of the communicants of the new parish of St Peter's'. This was the conclusion to this November day in Dundee. With the desire in his heart that the glory of the Lord should pervade St Peter's, M'Cheyne left for his new apartment on Strawberry Bank, a narrow side street off Perth Road. His sister Eliza

Ruin of the Church of Invergowrie, once consecrated to St Peter, the oldest known church north of the River Tay.

Old house on Hawkhill in West-End.

accompanied him, because she was provisionally appointed to take over her brother's housekeeping.

**First impressions**

On 30 November he wrote a report to his 'Papa, mamma and Willie' of his first impressions of Dundee. (His brother had arrived on leave from India.) Robert and Eliza felt immediately at home in their new lodgings. Thus he wrote, it is, 'really a very comfortable one, with the exception that it smokes a little. But Dundee is full of smoke and maybe that is the reason. Or possibly, the chimney needs cleaning out again.' It was not advantageous to his weak air passages. 'My pony is immediately opposite in a very comfortable stable.' Meanwhile he had consecrated his first bridal couple and presently many would follow. Next week, he hoped to get to know the church council better: 'The outward appearance of the elders is respectable. What they are inwardly I have to learn.' He set high standards for the position of elder, especially later when he had more insight into church discipline. He didn't have any high expectations of the city: 'I fear it is a very dark corner this ....' His first impression in his diary was: 'A city given to idolatry and hardness of heart. I fear there is much of what Isaiah speaks of: "The prophets prophesy lies, and the people love to have it so."'

From the start there was a good attendance at St Peter's. The population within the parochial boundaries totalled 3,400 souls, of which only a third could fit into the church building. People came from other parts of the city to listen to the new minister. Approximately seven hundred members had a fixed seat. The rent of these seats was considerably lower than those in the other churches. Sometimes M'Cheyne would have to make his way using elbows and knees in order to arrive at the pulpit. The people even sat on the steps of the pulpit and in all corners of the church. Chairs had to be added to the aisles and the galleries. Was it the compelling new minister's speech that attracted so many people? Was it the anointing of God's Spirit, which he demonstrated in such great measure? The light had come to the candlestick, but it was yet 'a dark church' and 'it only makes the darkness visible'.

The church services lasted much longer compared with those to which he was accustomed in Larbert. His father observed that 'he lost some friends and hearers' because the services went on so long, and he held three services every Sabbath; 'but I doubt not their places were filled by others.' In the long run, the long sermons didn't do his weak constitution any good. 'His voice, once melodious, soon became cracked and broken.' Despite this, he had a magnetic appeal for his listeners. This was no gift of eloquence, but it was his poetical talent that enhanced the warm tone of his sermons. Smellie stresses in a concise and powerful manner: 'There was pathos in it; there was winningness; there was fire.' In a melodious manner his voice formed the short sentences which he spoke to his attentive congregation. His greatest gift lay, not in the manner of his delivery, but in the simplicity with which he rendered the good news of salvation. St Peter's pulpit was filled with breath of the power of God's Spirit. Everyone felt that Christ's messenger had come into their midst, a man who was filled with compassion for lost souls.

Besides the three Sabbath services, the kirk session soon established a prayer meeting every Thursday evening. This was a new custom for the Dundee congregation, but their appetite was aroused. On an average, eight hundred people attended these gatherings, concerning which M'Cheyne observed: 'They will be remembered in eternity with songs and praise.' Later he wrote about these weekly services: 'Many were deeply affected during the preaching of this discourse; especially when that head [point] on being enemies of the cross was begun many sobbed aloud.'

Besides Bible study, prayer remained a central feature of these gatherings. He wrote concerning these to Bonar: 'I give my people a Scripture to be hidden in the heart, generally a promise of the Spirit or the wonderful effects of His outpouring.' There was ample time devoted to prayer before as well as after the Bible reading, and thereafter a reading often followed on a section of the history of revival. These gatherings were also attended by people from other parts of the city.

Due to the prevalence of ignorance, he found it necessary to hold separate catechism classes for the adults. He also didn't forget the work amongst the youth; in addition to the expanding Sabbath Schools, Bible classes were held for the older teenagers, which were attended on Tuesday evenings by 250 young people. He dealt with the Westminster Catechism and Bible topics at these classes. A blackboard served to explain the teaching by means of sketches, in which he was expert. He also gave opportunity for discussion around the topic, in order to get to know his students better. Here the foundation was laid for the Communicants' Class, for those who wished to partake in the Lord's Supper. The elders were also involved in this class and it wasn't difficult to find suitable teachers for the Sabbath School.

Apart from the Bible classes and Sabbath Schools the new pastor had concerns over the day and evening schools. The evening school was intended for girls who worked during the day in factories or did domestic work. At all schools, the Bible was read daily and the catechism was taught. The kirk session carefully appointed the teaching staff; they were not only to be qualified to teach, but it was also important that their hearts were 'touched by the Spirit of God'. Many visited the school in the following years, which was also recommended by the government. Characteristic is M'Cheyne's idea that 'the chief use of the school is to convert the souls of the children'. How necessary it was to bring the young heart into contact with the gospel! Although the religious upbringing should begin in the family, yet it was the task of the church to assist in this. The Sabbath Schools themselves were a cause for much interest; in 1839, about one hundred and fifty children attended. As well as the special children's morning service at eight o'clock, there was Sabbath School every evening between six and eight o'clock.

Yet, despite all this, he felt that too little was done for the children. He became jealous when he attended a youth gathering in the church of Blairgowrie in January 1837, where four hundred children, aged six to twenty-five years, listened attentively to stories told by the teachers and ministers. In a circular letter he reported on the events that had impressed him. 'I never did see so pleasant a sight. I do not remember ever spending a happier evening.' Tears of emotion splashed down his cheeks. 'I wish we could have something as good in Dundee.' Besides the Bible stories, there were, of course, the missionary narratives, which were of topical interest at that time. M'Cheyne also spoke to the young children for twenty minutes on the love of Jesus. Tea and cake were distributed and much attention was afforded to singing. How moving it was when many children's voices echoed through the church to the sound of Psalm 23: 'The Lord is my Shepherd.'

M'Cheyne loved singing a great deal and therefore attached much value to good congregational singing. He thought it was a shame that 'Christians did not endeavour to sing the praise of God well'. His musical ability played a role here. During the summer months he organized separate Song Evenings. He usually didn't use songs, but psalms and those 'Paraphrases' that were approved by the church; these were metrical versions of Bible texts. A great favourite was Paraphrase 54: 'Jesus my Lord, I know His name.' He was no supporter of choirs, and even less of organ playing during the worship. To the contrary, however, he was liberal in his use of hymns. Often he would lead the singing in the church himself, when his favourite tune, that of 'Newington', was chosen as the psalm to be sung. Later this tune became known as 'M'Cheyne's tune'.

M'Cheyne devoted himself completely to that which his hand found to do. He had too little time to do everything and his body wasn't always able to keep up the pace. In January 1837, he became sick once more, but fortunately he soon improved. 'The same God that raised up Hezekiah has raised me up,' he wrote in his diary. From now on he preached for the first time in his new 'silk gown'; he thought that he looked more like a bishop than a minister. Despite the fact that a 'deputation' had carefully taken his measurements, his official robe was far too large in front of the pulpit. His wish was: 'I hope it may be like the mantle of Elijah and bring with it a double portion of the Spirit from on high.' But in the long run he took off his gown and preached henceforth in his usual dress.

**His poor health**

M'Cheyne lived close to death not only because he had such an intimate relationship with Jesus, but also because he had such poor health. He continually drew his parents' attention to the brevity of life. It seemed very strange to him that his father wished him to take out a life insurance that should apply to his next of kin. He had no wife. Should he be concerned about the future? Was it permissible? His father could not convince him on this score; Christ's words were more important to M'Cheyne: 'Lay not up for yourselves treasures upon earth.' Worldly riches were sham in his eyes because, he esteemed the Pearl of great price higher than all else. The knowledge of God and enjoyment of Him forever, as the Westminster Catechism words it, give one true happiness.

He knew very well how to make proper use of the things of life which his heavenly Father gave to him. He wrote thus on 13 March 1837 to his family: '... Let us be glad in all that God gives us so richly to enjoy and use all for Him. If we are His children washed in the blood of His Son led by His Holy Spirit living a life of prayer and reading of the Word and growing in likeness and nearness to Him then we are happy now and shall be happier by far, when this world, with its scenes of loneliness and sin has passed away.'

Robert and Eliza weathered the first winter without many problems. During January, in particular, he had to make a way for himself through a thick layer of snow which blanketed the streets and alleys of Perth Road and surroundings. His sister was of great support to him. Together they decided how to

Manse of M'Cheyne, 16 Strawberry Bank (left house). An old photograph of about 1890. The house still exists.

furnish the manse. His parents wished to do their bit, but Robert thought the chairs given by his mother, costing twenty-seven shillings, and the large French bed, too extravagant and expensive. M'Cheyne didn't cling to earthly possessions, although he knew their proper use. His sister wasn't permitted to arrange the furnishing of his home on her own, although she undertook the greater share. Eliza described in detail the drawing room and dining room furniture, the curtains, the blinds for the windows, as well as the measurements of the apartment. Thus she wrote that her brother found 'our house very small and has too much furniture already in some places'.

More important to him was the view from the house on Strawberry Bank. The Firth of Tay, with the hills of Fife in the background offered a splendid view. He could also see Errol, the home of his friend, James Grierson. He enjoyed during spring 'the apple trees all in full blossom'. A walk along the shore of Tay bay past Magdalen Yards, nearby his house, gave him relief. The railway line which, in a few years time would determine the view and would later be linked up with a long column bridge, hadn't yet been constructed. The view of the water from the slope was still unobstructed. Thus he could look across the bay towards the horizon. The shimmering morning sun on the water was a sight that made him forget everything else. Everything, that is, except the thoughts about the Sun of Righteousness, who had poured His rays in such great abundance into his soul. It was then that he couldn't help writing to his father and mother and pointing out this Saviour to them: 'May He that makes it shine, shine into your hearts to give you the knowledge of the glory of Christ.'

'I feel more and more happy in Dundee,' he wrote on 3 February to his parents. 'No stipend or honour or home or anything could make up for that.' Nor could the letter from Lady Carmichael of Castle Craig, which offered him a manse in the little parish of Skirling. That was quite soon after a stay of a few months! She had made his acquaintance in Larbert and was full of praise for him. M'Cheyne, however, didn't allow himself to be persuaded by the proposition of a peaceful life in a country community of three hundred people. He replied to her resolutely in a long letter after first asking his father how he should address the noble lady. He wrote to her, 'Dear Madam, 'still, dear Madam, I am here. I did not bring myself here. I did not ask to be made a candidate for this place. I was hardly willing to be a candidate ... O no, I dare not leave this people.' His parents were in favour of his accepting the offer of the Lady, but Robert stood his ground. He wrote to his father: 'I dare not leave three or four thousand for three hundred people. Had it been offered me before, I would have seen it a direct intimation from God, and would heartily have embraced it.' 'But God has not so ordered it. He has set me down among the noisy mechanics and political weavers of this godless town.' 'Perhaps the Lord will make this wilderness of chimney-tops to be green and beautiful as the garden of the Lord, a field which the Lord hath blessed.' Nothing and no one, including the attractive calls he received from St Leonard's Church in Edinburgh as well as St Martin's in Perth, could tear him away from Dundee.

**Personal piety**

The enabling strength behind M'Cheyne's ministry originated from his communion with God. Alexander Moody Stuart observes that he heard him once saying: 'I cannot begin my work, for I have not yet seen the face of my God.' And in the *Christian Daily Companion* he himself wrote: 'Those only who have experienced the dawning of the Sun of Righteousness on their soul can know what it is "to wait for the Lord, more than they that watch for the morning".' As the sick person longs for 'the first gleam of morning light coming in at the window', even so, the tired Levite directed his gaze 'towards the east, to see if the day began to break over Mount Olivet'. Motivated by this desire, M'Cheyne rose at half past six every morning. The sun's wintry rays had not yet risen over the water of the bay when he had already sought the light of God's friendly countenance. First, he spent two hours in prayer and meditation, one hour of which was spent praying for the conversion of the Jews. He devoted the time from half-past eight until ten o'clock to family worship and breakfast, after which time he would saddle his pony to go out on his daily visits. On the Sabbath he followed a different schedule; he made use of seven periods, in total six hours, for studying the Scriptures and for prayer. He often sang a psalm or song to awaken his soul after he had arisen. He usually read three chapters of the Bible every morning. 'I love the Word of God, and find it sweetest nourishment to my soul.' Thus he used the early morning hours 'for the nourishment of his own soul; not, however, with the view of laying up a stock of grace for the rest of the day for manna will corrupt if laid by but rather with the view of giving the eye the habit of looking upward all the day, and drawing down gleams from the reconciled countenance'.

He often devoted the morning hours to an intensive study of God's Word, although he would sometimes do so after his daily work in the congregation. He was thus occupied, in April 1837, with a study of the epistle to the Hebrews. He received more light on the holy mysteries of this Bible book: 'Came to a more intelligent view of the first six chapters than ever before.' He also continued to read the works of Jonathan Edwards, as well as many devotional books. The *Reformed Pastor* by Richard Baxter, the Puritan, was a guide to him in relating to the members of his congregation. He was impressed by the fruit produced in Baxter's church in Kidderminster, which had undergone a complete transformation.

The environment of church and manse had a rural atmosphere during his time. M'Cheyne was often to be seen on his Tully at Blackness and Crescent. During the first few years, he rode to the ruins of the church of Invergowrie to spend an hour in solitude. Beneath the trees of the tumbled-down church garden, he often bowed the knee before God. Did he realize that here George Wishart, the Reformation martyr, had made his famous prediction that Scotland would see prosperous times? Wasn't it high time this prophecy was fulfilled? Dundee certainly needed a revival, and M'Cheyne was busy daily to bring this about!

He didn't merely keep to his times of personal devotion. Until the end of his life, he abided by a day of confession and fasting once a month. In order to do this, he used the guidelines written down in his notebook, the pages of which had become brown and worn out with the passing of time. Thus, he strove towards a daily routine, not to adhere to a legalistic system, but rather in order to spend the whole day in God's presence. A thorough self-examination determined once more his own shortcomings. Thus, he complained once: 'My prayers are scarcely to be called prayer.' We come across these complaints frequently during his time in Larbert, but wasn't he progressing in his sanctification? Bonar observes that 'there was a rapid growth in his soul, perceptible to all who knew him well, from this time'. During this time of his life, he exercised himself in vigilance, and yet he realized that his sanctification was incomplete and that only by appropriating the cleansing blood of Christ could it be effective in his life. During the first years after his conversion, the complaints in his diary were replaced more and more by notes such as: 'Much prayer and peace' and 'much peace and rest tonight. Much broken under a sense of my exceeding wickedness, which no eye can see but Thine. Much persuasion of the sufficiency of Christ, and of the constancy of His love. Oh, how sweet to work all day for God, and then to lie down at night under His smiles!'

**Firstfruits**

Although, on the one hand, he felt quite at home in Dundee, yet, on the other hand, the first few months of his stay there were very difficult. Many sick people were present in his congregation, some of whom were afflicted with contagious diseases. Consequently, this resulted in an increased risk for the already weak minister. He devoted the greatest part of his time to visiting the sick and the dying. He never refused a request to visit someone. He often stood at freshly-dug graves in St Peter's graveyard. He officiated at the first funeral in February. Such occasions required great effort. He used to ask himself if he was faithful in his relationships with these people. Thus he wrote subsequent to one funeral in September: 'Buried A.M. Felt bitterly the word, "If any man draw back," etc. Never had more bitter feelings at any funeral.'

Despite the disturbing events at the start of his ministry there, he was pleased with God's miraculous acts. During every sermon there were those whose hearts were struck and who called out: 'What must we do?' This gave the weak pastor renewed hope. He hadn't come across such fruit in Larbert and Dunipace. In the summer of 1837, during his struggle with the calling from St Martin's, he secretly brought it before the Lord, and he received a wonderful answer: 'I prayed that in order to settle my own mind completely about staying, He would awaken some of my people. I agreed that that should be a sign He would wish me to stay. The next morning I think, or at least the second morning, there came to me two young persons I had never seen before, in great distress.' To M'Cheyne it was a sign from heaven. He heard reports of other people who were convicted of their sin. It was his desire that his diary should report, not only the fruit that he had seen on his work in the Lord's vineyard, but also, the lack of it, if that were the case.

On 28 March 1837, he spoke on 'the first success among my people'. This occurred when he administered communion for the first time. From the first time that he conducted a service, some consciences were smitten. Did he mean by this that the Lord was completing His work by His Holy Spirit? His sermon on Ezekiel 22:14: 'Can thine heart endure,' etc. was blessed to awaken M.L. The one on Song of Songs 5:2, 'Open to me,' etc., the Sabbath after the sacrament, was the cause of blessing to another. These were happy days. M.D. was awakened by visiting the catechism classes for admittance to holy communion and another by the conversation at the tables. At the words, 'I know thee, Judas,' she trembled, and would have risen from the communion table. Years later, a woman could remember the incident clearly. She had spoken to the woman whom M'Cheyne had visited, who related to her that she had been greatly disturbed by her own soul. The minister's brief word was a timely one for her. These were glad days when one after another, souls were awakened. 'The people looked very stirred and anxious, every day coming to hear the words of eternal life.' It was God's Spirit that began to blow through St Peter's.

M'Cheyne associated cautiously with the people among whom the Spirit of God appeared to be working. He was apprehensive of his approaching task and of possible sentimental troubles. 'Now it appears to me there is much falling off; few seem awakened – few weep as they used to do.' He hoped that one woman would awaken to the truth because of the previous day's preaching, or preferably through God Himself. 'I do not know, however, whether grace is begun in her or not.' He didn't lay hands on anyone in haste. Eternity itself surely depended on it. He distinguished two groups regarding souls wherein God's Spirit was active. The first were those who were awakened to the realization of their own wretchedness. They had not yet experienced the rebirth and didn't know Christ. The second group consisted of those who had 'a believing heart'. They were enabled to see Christ beyond their own experience and 'the first look to Christ makes the sinner mourn'. Repentance and faith were, as far as he was concerned, two inseparable benefits, which may never be viewed as distinct from one another. True sorrow, according to M'Cheyne, is no condition for faith but instead is a fruit resulting from faith. In this respect, he followed closely in the footsteps of the Scottish theologians, who viewed repentance as a fruit of one's union with Christ.

**The problem of assurance**

M'Cheyne could not ascertain with certainty when a sinner was saved or not. He wasn't able to measure the depths and sincerity of the work of God's Spirit. The Saviour's saying, 'The wind bloweth where it listeth,' was applicable also to his flock in Dundee. He knew from his own experience that true faith could be accompanied by uncertainty. He knew, however, that there existed many misconceptions concerning the assurance of faith. It was his desire, by means of the compass of God's Word, to be careful in his contacts with people. A person who 'was awakened' by means of his preaching, asked him a few questions concerning conversion and the assurance of faith. He responded to these queries one by one. From this example, it can be concluded that he guided souls who wrestled with the question of eternal security. First of all, he established the fact that he didn't believe 'that there are many saints who live and die without a comfortable sense of forgiveness and acceptance with God'.

During the times in which he lived, it was too easy to be of the opinion that most of God's children don't arrive at an assurance of salvation. 'I fear this objection is generally made by those who are living in sin, and do not wish to know the dangerous road they are on.' He was also aware of the tendency of some, during his time, to trace the marks of grace in their lives, whereby they concluded their interest to Christ. As a result, he answered as his second point that 'a sense of forgiveness does not proceed from marks seen in yourself, but from a discovery of the beauty, worth, and freeness of Christ (Ps. 34:5). We look out for peace, not in.' M'Cheyne acknowledges that there is also an assurance which arises from 'what we see in ourselves; the seal of the Spirit, love to the brethren, etc., are the chief marks'.

It was an indisputable fact in M'Cheyne's mind that God was working in the hearts of His children in a diversity of ways. That which his 'sheep' had experienced in practice intensified this belief. He was of the opinion that no essential difference existed between those who had come into the faith during his ministry and those who were already converted before his arrival. He maintains, with sadness, that many of his converts 'are very unholy'. He never recorded what he based his thesis on. The power of godliness was more important to him than a story based on words. A holy life emanating from Christ is still the best characteristic of grace. This life is not demonstrated in great ups and downs, but in constantly embracing and following a loving heavenly Father, even during times of suffering and temptations. 'Still there are many good figs many of whom I am persuaded better things, and things that accompany salvation.' He found that in earlier times 'many used to be taken for Christians who had only a name to live, and were dead'. According to him, there was, at that time, more observable and discernable light in the lifeless preaching of the Moderates than before.

M'Cheyne didn't wish to go to the other extreme. There is gradual progress in assurance. A common mistake is that this clear conviction that Christ is mine is an attainment far on in the divine life, and that it springs from evidences seen in the heart. When one sees himself a new creature, Christ on the throne in the heart, love to the brethren, etc., it is often thought that he may begin to say, 'My Beloved is mine.' Yet by simply resting in Christ one has assurance, and such a person may say he is a child of God. 'I believe that many people keep themselves in darkness by expecting something more than this,' he observes. In the appropriation of faith there is security, but 'I do think it is inseparable from believing the record'. It has to do with God's promises, in the first place, and not an assurance from the experience of the heart *per se*. 'It is like opening the shutters of a dark room; the sun that moment shines in. So the eye that is opened to the testimony of God receives Christ that moment.' Here we are reminded of Thomas Chalmers' views which he tried to impress upon his students. According to his perspective, it was necessary for those who were touched by God's Spirit to be directed to the Lamb of God, who takes away the sin of the world. It was never his intention to thrust man back on his own resources, but instead to urge him towards faith in Christ.

**Commitment to the congregation**

The work of God by means of his labour soon became visible in St Peter's. His call was not in vain. The Lord placed His seal on his arrival and confirmed this with demonstrations of His grace. Preaching was the most prominent means whereby souls could be drawn into a commitment, but there was still more work to be done. M'Cheyne knew the importance of follow-up care. His pastoral visits took him not only to the sick and dying. The entire West End of Dundee was his area of ministry, and here too people who no longer attended church could be found. The sheep who, through faith in the crucified, had entered into the true sheepfold by means of the door of His blood, needed spiritual guidance. A prerequisite was to become intimately acquainted with them. Thus, for the first time, he met a great variety of people who feared the Lord. All this diversity in spiritual life was not the only means of engaging him, but it made him more vigilant and alert. In his dealings with his flock he tried to be honest, whether in disciplining or comforting them.

Thus, M'Cheyne continued wholeheartedly with his work among the indifferent people of Dundee. He was unafraid of routine or monotony. In many of his colleagues he noted that 'duty presses on the heels of duty in an endless circle'. Every day presented him with new opportunities. Where 'the Spirit is quickening both the pastor and his flock, then there is all the variety of life', Bonar observed. He had little time for those who sounded his praises. The Lord kept his feet close to earth to prevent him from becoming proud. 'Much affliction, also, was a thorn in the flesh to him.' In the pulpit he was often ministered to by the fullness of heavenly glory. But as soon as he made his way into the vestry, and from there homewards, he became aware of his weaknesses. He frequently writes about himself in the following way: as 'strong as a giant when in the church, but like a willow-wand when all was over'. But despite all his depression and feelings of helplessness, he remained rock-firm throughout the trials of his life. God's lovely face preceded him on his way. 'As yet I have been kept not only in the sight of His reconciled countenance, but very much under the guiding eye of our providing God.' This joyful assurance of His love didn't abandon him. His trust was that God's Spirit, dwelling within him, keeping him safe and steadfast, was the inspiration behind a life of holiness. In this way, his pride was forced to yield and eventually perish.

His holy life exerted an influence on his congregation. Although he was often the subject of mockery and scorn, as far as both the light-hearted Christians and the gross godless

Dundee Harbour about 1840.

were concerned, yet he gained the respect of many. His tenderness, patience and longsuffering were virtues that influenced both stubborn and inflexible characters alike. The sweet fragrance of Christ that he so richly spread made him not only hated but also noticed. In this way, he continued during the first years of his ministry in Dundee. Gradually, the Spirit of God began to blow through St Peter's and the people of Dundee became increasingly convinced of the fact that a true prophet was in their midst, one who had his eye on nothing other than their salvation.

# Chapter 6

# SHEPHERD OF SOULS IN A HARBOUR CITY

## Working conditions

M'Cheyne realized only too well what were the requirements of a pastor and teacher. In a list of twenty-five points, he summed up the conditions that such a person should fulfil. Naturally, 'He should be a voice to speak the gospel, an angel of glad tidings'. Then he made mention of the need 'to wrestle with God, and to wrestle with men'. Seeking God's honour and the salvation of souls were of absolute importance for a good and trustworthy heavenly messenger. In conduct undefiled, 'neither flattering words', nor the desire for honour and recognition were but a few characteristics. 'Laboriousness night and day' in the vineyard was characteristic of him, as well as the need to admonish everyone personally as well as from the pulpit.

It wasn't easy to be a pastor in a harbour and industrial city such as Dundee. The chilly spiritual climate required much wisdom and prudence in approaching people. A detached approach could only fail, while obtrusion could produce little fruit. The city life consisted of working from early morning until late at night. The factories, which sprang up everywhere and underwent expansion, offered work to young and old alike. Even children of nine years of age found jobs in the burgeoning jute industry, which had supplanted the flax warehouses. A certain John Myle mentions in his diary that he had to rise at five o'clock in the morning and work until half-past six in the evening. This kind of environment could lead to nothing else but all kinds of evil. This was how life continued in West End, the working environment of M'Cheyne where glaring contrasts among the population existed. There was a core of religious people who upheld the old traditions of Scottish spirituality, but there also lived many who totally ignored God and His law.

Despite the industrial prosperity of the city, the district of St Peter's was poverty stricken. It included not only a densely populated section, but also an extensive area of surrounding land. The houses in West End consisted mostly of small apartments, which often accommodated large families. Although the living conditions were better than in the city centre, such as in Hilltown and Cowgate, yet the factory labourers here lived under primitive conditions. The new pastor wished to become well acquainted with the inhabitants. This was impossible in Larbert due to the extent of the parish, but here he could carry out most of his visits in the vicinity of the manse. Here too he put into practice the visiting strategy that he had learned from Chalmers. He proceeded to work not from the addresses of his congregational members, for in fact the entire area within the boundaries of his parish was viewed by him as his sphere of work. In Larbert he had visited on an average twelve to fifteen families per day, but here he sometimes visited as many as twenty. He was often on the go for six hours during his visitation. He found by experience that the procedure he followed was efficient, and it supplemented in an effective way his work of preaching. In this way, he acquainted himself with his congregational members; according to M'Cheyne:

learning to know more of the families, 'of their circumstances, trade and providence, enables you to preach to their case.'

### House visitation

What constitutes the purpose of carrying out house-to-house visitation? Bonar notes the 'need of feeling as though God did visit every hearer.... Our object is not to get duty done, but to get souls saved.' This was indeed the pastor of St Peter's goal. 'Mr. M'Cheyne used to go forth in this spirit; and often, after visiting from house to house for several hours, he would return to some place in the evening, and preach to the gathered families.' He went systematically to work. He would announce his visit a day in advance. He made a neat drawing of the plan of the houses together with the names of their occupants. It was not possible, however, for him to visit all of the families, due to his many duties and his poor health. He began by surveying the church surroundings, which he included in his map, especially the streets between Perth Road and Hawkhill which converged a few hundred yards to the west of St Peter's. Thus he visited the houses of Duncan's land, the lane to the west of St Peter's, Church Lane, Stewart's Wynd and the many homes in both main streets of West End.

During the evenings he would record the notes made during his visits in his Visitation Book. He devoted a separate section to the sick. On the first page he wrote:

> Jesus: 'I was sick, and ye visited Me.'
> Believers: 'When saw we Thee sick or in prison?'
> Jesus: 'Verily, I say unto you, Inasmuch as ye have done it unto one of the least of these My
> brethren, ye have done it unto Me.'

It was a tiring and often thankless task to ring the door-bell at every house and to speak with the people about eternal matters. He wasn't acquainted with most of them, and thus their reaction remained a surprise to him. In this way, he gained

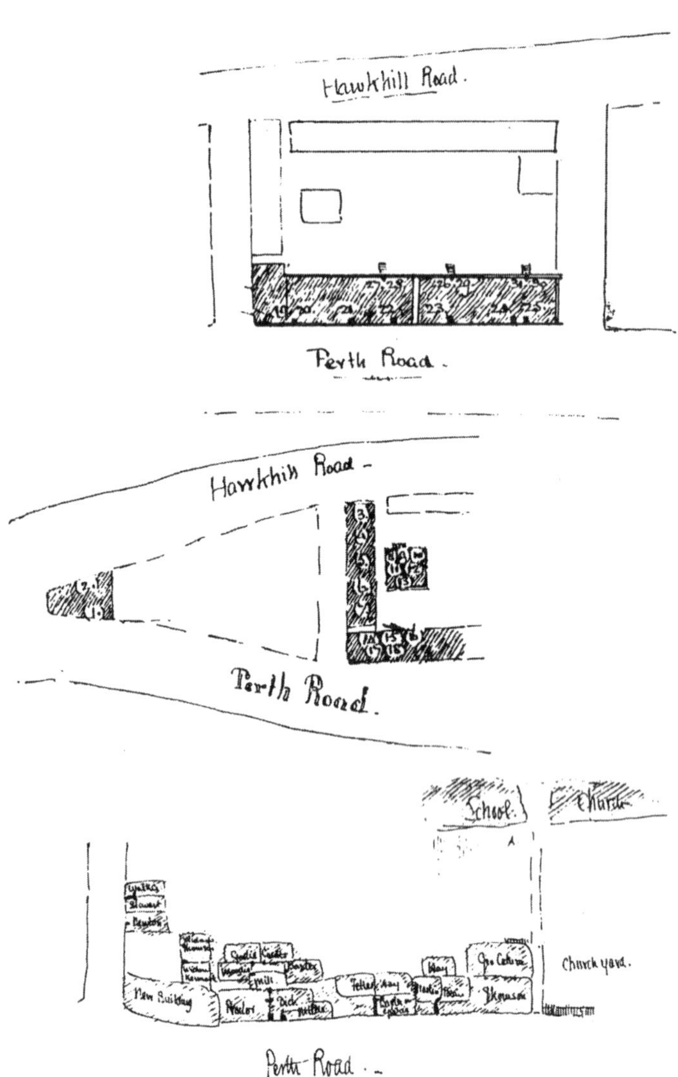


Maps of 'home visits' of McCheyne around St Peter's, between Hawkhill Road and Perth Road.

a good idea of who lived in the city area. He also met many of the Old Light Dissenters, members of the conservative Original Secession Church of the 'Aitken group'. Having entered he would first read a portion of Scripture, whereupon he would deliver a serious message in order to leave some kind of impression on the occupants' minds. He asked after the welfare of everyone, also of any possible domestic servants and guests, and invited them finally to attend a meeting which he had planned, weather permitting, to take place that evening on a lawn. These Cottage Sermons lasted approximately one and a half hours and were also attended by people from elsewhere.

Eagerly M'Cheyne made notes on his pastoral visits. He had a separate section of his notebook in which he noted down the physical condition of the sick whom he visited more frequently. He made a note, not only of the information, but also the Bible portion that he had discussed and the impressions he had received. In addition, unusual experiences received a place in his Visitation Book, such as: 'Singing canaries tried to beat me', and 'queer old hag of a woman yet her soul is precious as mine'. He named a ploughman by the name of a 'clod-pole', to which he added: 'Touch Thou his heart.' It was obvious that he couldn't do this work every day, because it would have been too tiring for him. It demanded a great deal of concentration and patience. Despite all the disappointments, he thought it a gratifying task. He gained a great knowledge of the character of people during his visits. There were also those days that he experienced the obvious blessing of God, such as on 26 September 1838: 'Good visiting day. Twelve families; many of them go nowhere. It is a great thing to be well-furnished by meditation and prayer before setting out; it makes you a far more full and faithful witness. Preached in A.F.'s house on Job: "I know my Redeemer liveth." Very sweet and precious to myself.'

We shall follow the pastor on his sick round as he visits the home of one of the occupants of Step Row. His name is Thomas Tyrie, who has been suffering from consumption for five years.

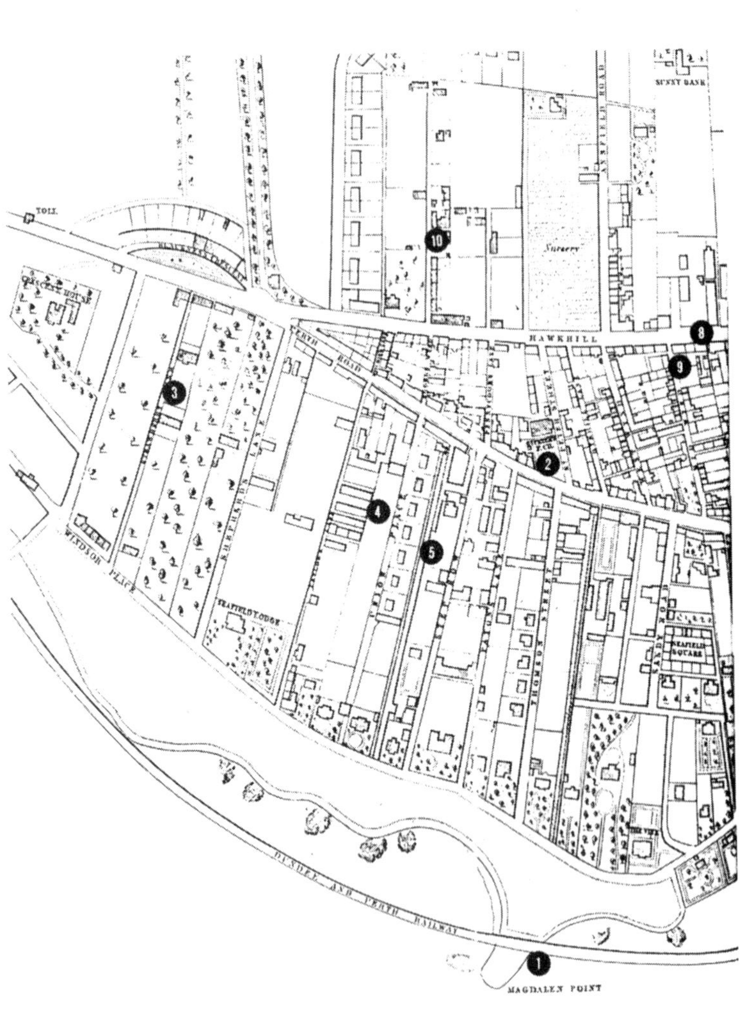


Part of the Map of Dundee in 1846. The West-End of the city with the 'Dundee and Perth Railway', built after 1843, that crossed Magdalen Point (1). St Peter's Church, now Free St Peter's (2) is not far from Strawberry Bank (3), in which the Manse of M'Cheyne was.

His second Manse was in Union Place (4). The rope factory (5) made the pulling down of that house necessary. In Miller's Wynd (6) James Laing lived and in Park Place (7) was the home of the family of Thain. Other known streets are Hawkhill (8), Mid Wynd (9) and Tait's Lane (10).

He is taking opium apparently as a painkiller. M'Cheyne's first visit to him was on 12 December 1836. He spoke on 'hell and annihilation'. As Scripture reading he chose the parable of the lost sheep. 'He attentive. Has read his Bible, rather to cavil at it. Neighbours in.' A week later he spoke to him about the 'lost piece'. 'He still attentive, and consent to the whole truth.' His condition began to deteriorate so much so that M'Cheyne visited him more frequently. The pastor was happy when he heard that a great transformation had taken place. 'He spoke of his peace within during these weeks.' The next time he spoke on 'Christ a Substitute'. 'Explained the whole gospel, and pressed it on him.' M'Cheyne, however, remained cautious because opium can seriously affect the thoughts and feelings of a person. 'Who knows but there may be some work of the Spirit here? He says that his views of his own heart and of Christ are both changed.' On 30 December the man died. 'Thus ends this short but interesting history. There was certainly wonderful change in the man. He took to his Bible, before unread; spoke with interest of his soul and of the Saviour; was glad of my visits, and squeezed my hand always with affection. But whether there was a work of grace the Day shall declare.'

In this manner, M'Cheyne went from house to house. He spoke to people irrespective of whom he met. After one such visitation day he wrote: 'Having warned thirteen families the night before, I girded myself for that combat and commenced. I met great kindness in every house, though there were only three or four belonged to my church. Most were Old Light dissenters, who have many truly godly people among them. One widow I came upon, who of children and grandchildren has twenty-five altogether; about a dozen were in the house. I went over all with great comfort, taking a rest in the middle. One woman offered me my dinner of "sowens", which she was preparing for her husband.' It was a typical Scottish meal consisting of starch mixed with the husks of oats. 'I was home before six, and was just sitting down to my meal of meat and tea, when in came a well-dressed gentleman.' He made the unexpected request that M'Cheyne should officiate at his daughter's marriage ceremony. It had to take place immediately, because the minister hadn't turned up. The latter's mistake was the reason M'Cheyne was asked to lead the service. The gathering went ahead unhindered; some were moved and much interest was shown in his speech. 'I was presented by the bridesmaid with a pair of long silk stockings, as large and massy as would serve a bishop.' During the evening he held the usual meeting for those whom he had visited during the day. Three rooms were filled with people listening attentively to the minister. One Roman Catholic was also present. M'Cheyne couldn't oversee his audience in the different rooms and according to him, his words were as shots fired from 'the Highlander's gun that fired round the corner'. Maybe, though, his words had struck home in the consciences of some of the sinners.

### Visitation of the sick

The sick found a special place in his heart. He conscientiously visited particularly the serious cases. Besides an alarming infant mortality rate there were also, regularly, epidemics between the years 1833 and 1839. During this time, approximately twelve thousand people in the city were struck by a contagious fever, one thousand two hundred of whom were carried to their graves. When the pastor had only just begun his ministry, many were troubled by flu. He was not only concerned about their spiritual welfare, but also their physical condition. Often he would take the pulse rate and sometimes dared even to diagnose the sickness. Thus, we read in his notes: 'Listened at her back and heart and heard work of death going on fearfully.' He also had an eye for psychical suffering; he found that doctors too often neglected this sickness. They should make a closer study of God's Word in order that they would better be able to encourage their patients. The neglect of tranquillity of mind exerted a contrary effect on the healing of a person's body. When he noticed that a patient was advised to take whisky, he prohibited it. The usual 'murderous lies' attached to the bed to conceal the real sickness shocked him. No wonder that the doctors, in general, were not fond of faithful ministers. In this respect, the following note by M'Cheyne is significant: 'Dr. Tennant has forbidden all disturbance from ministers. So the body doctor has thrust out the soul doctor.'

The elders assisted him in his visitation of the sick, especially during an epidemic, when it was impossible to give everyone equal attention. He was progressive in his attitude to the appointment of woman deacons, who especially visited the widows and lonely in order to help them in their oppression. With great compassion, M'Cheyne associated with the sufferers. Short notes sometimes speak volumes such as: 'Poor Alice, I shall never forget thee till judgment, then may I see thee a gathered jewel.' The following report was made with a sense of disappointment: 'Died, 8 June at 2. It is to be feared, as he lived. Oh, Lord, lay not this soul's blood to my charge. Truly I might have seen him oftener, and spoken plainer, and more affectionately, and less stiffly. Heard that he thought me hard upon him. Something about hell seems to have struck by him. His hard-hearted wife had reviled our often coming: "Are they gaun make him minister?"'

There were also other examples, such as occurred at one of his first sick visits or which was to a young woman from his congregation. She had suffered from cholera for four years, because of which she was struck dumb. There were some of God's children who read to her from the Bible and prayed with her. Then in 1836, the Lord loosed her tongue, and the first words that she uttered constituted praise and gratitude for what the Lord had accomplished for her soul. During the same period, M'Cheyne stood at the deathbed of a man who, until a short while previously, had denied the Creator's existence. But the Lord humbled him completely and offered him new hope for the life to come. These examples were of great comfort to the young minister and he could also pass on these testimonies to other sick people.

Was there progress with the dejected people of God he visited? He was sad with the sorrowful and stood alongside God's children who were sad, as well as those who lay rejected on their sickbeds. Reasonings of comfort flowed from his mouth, for he knew how to say the appropriate word at the right time. Bonar wrote: 'His voice, and his very eye, spoke tenderness.' Yet he received comfort in return when he gladly and quietly listened to how the Lord sanctified the ways of His people. He wrote to a friend thus: 'There is a sweet word in Exodus 3:7, which was pointed out to me the other day by a poor bereaved child of God: "I knoweth their sorrows." Study that; it fills the souls. Another word like it in Psalm 103:14, "He knoweth our frame." May your own soul and that of your friends, be fed by these things. A dark hour makes Jesus bright. Another sweet word: "They knew not that it was Jesus."'

**First funerals**

A short report on a sickbed that resulted in the first funeral at which M'Cheyne officiated at St Peter's churchyard still exists: 'January 25, 1837. Visited Mt. M'Bain, a young woman of twenty-four, long ill of decline. Better or worse these ten years past. Spoke of "The one thing needful" plainly. She sat quiet. February 14. Had heard she was better – found her near dying. Spoke plainly and tenderly to her, commending Christ. Used many texts. She put out her hand kindly on leaving. 15th. Still dying like; spoke as yesterday. She never opened her eyes. 16th. Showed her the dreadfulness of wrath: freeness of Christ; the majesty, justice, truth of God. Poor M. is fast going the way whence she shall not return. Many neighbours always gather in. 17th. Read Psalm 22; showed the sufferings of Christ; how sufficient an atonement; how feeling a High Priest. She breathed loud and groaned through pain. Died this evening at seven. I hardly ever heard her speak anything; and I will hope that thou art with Christ in glory, till I go and see.' Her funeral took place on 20 February. 'Prayed at her funeral. Saw her laid in St Peter's Churchyard, the first laid there, by her own desire,

Edward Cairds wife's grave in St Peter's Churchyard.

St Peter's Churchyard

in the fresh mould where never man was laid. May it be a token that she is with Him who was laid in a new tomb.'

During the same month another member of the congregation died, for whom he could find no legitimate reason for hope. It was certainly discouraging for him to watch people dying who didn't testify to the assurance of eternal life. During this time M'Cheyne met a woman who was worried about her state before God. When he spoke on Romans 8:1: 'There is therefore now no condemnation to them which are in Christ Jesus,' she asked him: 'But am I in Christ?' At the next visit she asked, 'What is to believe?' The words of the teacher offered her no comfort. Death came through the windows of her room. 'No smile; no sign of inward peace. Spoke of "Remember me".' Again he held out the gospel to her and tried to explain the message of grace and forgiveness in a simple manner. Sometimes she spoke. She felt at home with the Bible, but she couldn't find the key to open the door. Ten days before she actually died, she was more cheerful both in her appearance and speech. Had she received a small ray of hope? A few days later she was 'faintish and restless; no sign of peace'. The pastor spoke on: 'I am the Way' and read Psalm 25 to her. One day later: 'Still silent and little sign of anything.' He read Psalm 40, concerning 'the fearful pit', into which the woman had probably sunk. Was the Rock still far from her? Had she no tiny bit of faith whereby she could see Jesus? He could obtain no further word from her. She passed away on 1 February: 'No visible mark of light, or comfort, or hope. The day shall declare it.'

### Attendance to souls

M'Cheyne was honest in his association with others. If he should be forced to leave his flock and they perished without receiving assurance of their salvation, he would then refer judgment to the righteous Judge. It was a difficult task to offer advice, not only to those who lay at death's door, but especially those who were convicted by the Lord. How did he relate to those who were awakened to a realization of their own sinfulness before God? He understood that on the one hand, there was a great danger that they would secretly justify their faith by their conviction and humiliation. On the other hand, these people were vulnerable to despondency; often they desired a deeper conviction and humiliation so that, in this way, they would make themselves presentable to Christ. They hadn't yet understood correctly that rejection of Christ, as represented in the gospel, is a punitory evil, yes, that it can even be reckoned as the worst of sins. 'A knowledge of our guilt, and a sense of danger, will not,' so he spoke, 'of themselves keep us from falling; nay, these, if alone, may ... thrust us down the slippery places. We are truly secure only when our eye is on Jesus, and our hand locked in His hand. So that the history of backslidings, instead of leading us to doubt the reality of grace in believers, will only be found to teach us two great lessons, namely the vast importance of pressing immediate salvation on awakened souls, and the reasonableness of standing in doubt of all, however deep their convictions, who have not truly fled to the hope set before them.'

He attended to those awakened souls with tact and wisdom. He tried not to disguise the truth, but wished to come straight to the point. 'In dealing with souls,' thus wrote Bonar, 'he used to speak very plainly.' One came to him who assented to his statements of the gospel, and yet refused to be comforted, always looking upon coming to Christ as something in addition to really believing the record God has given of His Son. He took John 3:16-17: 'For God so loved the world ...', etc. The woman said that 'God did not care for her'. Upon this he at once convicted her of making God a liar; and, as she went away in deep distress, his prayer was, 'Lord, give her light!' Sometimes he could be harsh, especially when he noticed that the conviction of sinfulness was superficial and that there seemed to be no awareness of the need to be reconciled with God. In this connection, he met an anxious soul, who was struck during a sermon by the words: 'Unto whom coming as unto a living stone.' She felt that she 'knew nothing of this precious stone'.

She went to talk to him about this. 'I am surely not converted,' she continued. Her conviction, however, missed the deeper meaning and in this instance, M'Cheyne found it necessary to take a firm line with her: 'You are a poor, vile worm; it is a wonder the earth does not open and swallow you up.' Fortunately, these harsh words didn't degenerate into animosity, but the Lord used them to bring her into a deeper discovery of who she was. 'She came a second time with the arrows of the Almighty drinking up her spirit. For three months she remained in this state, till, having once more come to him for counsel, the living voice of Jesus gave life to her soul while he was speaking of Christ's words.'

M'Cheyne knew from experience how deceitful the human heart is; how impossible it is to talk a person out of the props and supports of his life or to a lost soul about seeking his salvation in Christ alone. He once related the following about an anxious person: 'Another: Very staid, intelligent-like person, with a steady kind of anxiety, but, I fear, no feeling of helplessness. Thought that sorrow and prayer would obtain forgiveness. Told her plainly what I thought of her case.' He didn't avoid the disease, neither did he whitewash over it. He didn't make out that it would be a bed of roses to follow Christ, neither did he make hollow promises of easy comforts. He also guarded himself against bringing people into despair, by denying them the cure. Instead he always suggested the remedy in association with the disease. He never tried to keep souls away from Christ by requiring more and deeper convictions or by a contemplation of symptoms of many kinds. He continued to point to Christ's work and faith as the only means whereby righteousness can be obtained. According to him, faith was no complicated matter, great transaction or extraordinary revelation. Instead it was no more than the empty hand which Christ takes in His and embraces as promised in the gospel.

Concerning this, we wish to quote the following: 'The more God opens your eyes, the more you will feel that you are lost in yourself. This is your disease. Now for the remedy. Look to

Christ; for the glorious Son of God so loved lost souls, that He took on Him a body and died for us, bore our curse, and obeyed the law in our place. Look to Him and live. You need no preparation, you need no endeavours, you need no duties, you need no strivings, you only need to look and live. Look at John 17:3. The way to be saved is to know God's heart and the heart of Jesus. To be awakened, you need to know your own heart. Look in at your own heart if you wish to know your lost condition. See the pollution that is there.... To be saved, you need to know the heart of God and of Christ. The four Gospels are a narrative of the heart of Christ. They show His compassion to sinners, and His glorious work in their stead.'

We saw in the previous chapter how M'Cheyne attached much value to a well-founded assurance of the salvation in Christ. The question comes to mind whether he included a word also for those who were immature in the faith. Now he knew assuredly that some of them made assurance the foundation of their salvation instead of Christ and His finished work. What he was concerned about was growth in the knowledge and grace of Christ. With this in mind, he advised and counselled those who were wavering. They couldn't live on solid food and therefore needed extra attention. The sucklings were to be gently led, the lambs needed support and the fainthearted needed the comfort of the gospel. He impressed the following admonition on the heart of one of his colleagues: 'Those who are already in Christ, seek for success among them. He gave some pastors and teachers for the perfecting of the saints. Never forget Christ's words: "Feed My sheep, feed My lambs." Be like Barnabas, a son of consolation. Exhort them to cleave to the Lord. Do not say, "They are safe, and I will let them alone." This is a great mistake. See how Paul laid out his strength in confirming the disciples.'

His pastoral task wasn't limited to the believers and convicted souls. As pastor he desired the salvation of his entire district. Therefore, he devoted much attention to those who never put a foot inside St Peter's or any other church building. He earnestly reprimanded public sinners, punished the self-righteous, pointing them to the wrath of God, but simultaneously he prescribed the only way of deliverance from their deserved fate. He didn't disguise the disease, neither did he withhold the cure. He certainly addressed sinners in a soul-stirring way. He associated with souls in a sincere manner. Take the following as an example: 'A young woman was with me tonight in great distress. She said, "I have a wicked heart within me that would sink a world." M'Cheyne said, 'I am thankful to hear you complain of your wicked heart, dear friend, it is unsearchably wicked. There is not a sin committed on earth or in hell but has its spring and fountain in your breast and mine. You are all sin, your nature is sin, your heart is sin, your past life is all sin, your prayers are all sin. Oh, that you would despair of being righteous in yourself! Then take the Lord Jesus for your righteousness. In Him is no sin. And He stood for us, and offers to be your shield, your way to the Father. You may be righteous in Christ with a perfect righteousness.'

**Caring for the young**

We saw earlier how he cared for the young in the congregation. His concern was not only for catechetical teaching, important though it was to him. He greatly appreciated unrestrained contact with the children. When he walked along the street, he couldn't help addressing boys and girls and pointing out eternal salvation to them. He wrote simple stories on behalf of the Sabbath School, stories such as 'Reasons why children should fly to Christ without delay.' It was on New Year's Day 1839, that he voiced these thoughts based on the realization of the transitoriness of life for young people. He tried as often as possible to speak to their imagination, and used an illustration of Dundee as a harbour city. 'You have seen a ship upon the river, when the sailors were all on board, the anchor heaved, and the sails spread to the wind, how it glided swiftly past, bounding over the billows; so is it with your days: "They are passed away as the swift ships."'

Life is not only short, but also uncertain. It is possible for children to die. 'Oh, if you had to stand as often as I have beside the dying bed of little children to see their wild looks and outstretched hands, and to hear their dying cries; you would see how needful it is to fly to Christ now. It may be your turn next. Are you prepared to die? Have you fled for refuge to Jesus? Have you found forgiveness?' One's youth is the best time to seek God. As their compassionate shepherd and teacher, he could speak from experience when he made known the fact that the world offers a certain kind of pleasure: 'The song and the dance, and the exciting game, are most engaging to your hearts. But ah! think a moment. Is it not an awful thing to be happy when you are unsaved?' He then demonstrated the true joy that is to be found in Christ. 'To be forgiven, to be at peace with God, to have Him for a father, to have Him loving us and smiling on us, to have the Holy Spirit coming into our hearts, and making us holy, this is worth a whole eternity of our pleasures.' Can eternal bliss be compared with the pleasure offered by the world? 'Who can tell the sweetness and the peace which Jesus gives in such an hour? One little girl that was early brought to Christ, felt this when long confined to a sickbed. "I am not weary of my bed," she said, "for my bed is green, and all that I meet with is perfumed with love to me. The time, night and day, is made sweet to me by the Lord. When it is evening, it is pleasant; and when it is morning, I am refreshed."'

Bonar observed that M'Cheyne's heart went out to the children. After a visit to a few Sabbath School classes, he wrote: 'Had considerable joy in teaching the children. Oh, for real heart-work among them!' He could indeed place himself in a child's soul; he earnestly tried to touch the tender stirrings of the youthful heart! A poem which he wrote at the beginning of a book for a young boy from the congregation, speaks volumes:

Peace be to thee, gentle boy!  
Many years of health and joy!

Love your Bible more than play,
Grow in wisdom every day...

Who is able to count the number of boys and girls that he might have led to Jesus? He imitated his Master in being a true friend to children. Sometimes he asked very simple questions, such as: 'Walter, do you love your soul?' The boy whom he had seen playing, walked on but the words sank deep into his young heart. Later, he confirmed that M'Cheyne's question moved him so that it ultimately resulted in his calling as a minister. M'Cheyne didn't impress upon them the fact that they were children of one Father, without mentioning one word about sin. His understanding was: 'The greatest want in the religion of children is generally sense of sin ...; we are so often deceived by promising appearance in childhood.' Thus it was also in his experience, in the first place; he was a virtuous boy, but he didn't know himself. He was able to observe the authenticity of the work of grace in the children's hearts by their awareness of sin. A heart that is unimpressionable and lives recklessly, is incapable of receiving God's grace. M'Cheyne, however, drew the attention of the youth not only to their wicked hearts; he introduced them to the Good Shepherd, who also calls young sheep to Himself. In a pamphlet written at a later date, with the expressive title, 'To the Lambs of the Flock', he began with an exhortation to seek Christ: 'Beloved children, Jesus is the Good Shepherd. His arm was stretched out on the cross, and His bosom is open to receive you.' He did not leave before he had impressed the following words of wisdom on their hearts: 'Will you wish to be gathered thus? Go now to some lonely place, kneel down, and call upon the Lord Jesus. Do not leave your knees until you find Him. Pray to be gathered with His arm and carried in His bosom. Take hold of the hem of His garment, and say, "I must – I dare, no – I will not let Thee go except Thou bless me".'

**Admission to the Lord's Table**

He spent unforgettable hours with his young communion candidates. During these times he descended into the depths of the heart. He was chiefly concerned about personal contact, especially so as to come to a knowledge of what went on inside them. These Communicants' Classes were the source of much blessing. It wasn't customary in Scotland to prepare the youth in this manner for holy communion. Even prior to the first time he administered this sacrament, he began with these classes. He was then with much liberty allowed to take on thirty-seven new candidates. 'This is the season, when a minister comes to know the fruit of his ministry,' he once observed. With great and fatherly care, he prepared the candidates for the momentous moment when they would either be permitted or refused admittance to the holy table.

Public admission was not an acceptable practice in the Scottish church. In M'Cheyne's day, candidates were admitted thoughtlessly. M'Cheyne set no age limit requirements; the single condition for participation in the sacraments was a knowledge of the Saviour. He admitted children of fourteen or fifteen years, if he perceived any openness to Christ in them. He diligently noted down the first impressions the candidates made on him. For this reason, he tried to form a picture of them in his mind during the catechism classes. He knew better than to rashly admit people who not only were ignorant of teaching, but also showed no single sign of true faith. Thus he refused admittance to those who were only aware of some awakenings or convictions in their hearts; according to him this was insufficient evidence of their possession of salvation. Whenever he actually observed a degree of faith, even though merely a spark encompassed by much unbelief, he showed himself to be a father who embraced his anxious child to his breast. When the moment arrived to present the 'token' for admittance to the Lord's Supper, then he found it difficult to control himself because of his emotion.

On the average he would accept half of the class. Many

names, including those who were refused admittance, decorated his notebook. Thus we read: 'M.K., sprightly and lightsome, yet sensible; she saw plainly that the converted alone should come to the table, but stumbled at the question, If she were converted? Yet she claimed being awakened and brought to Christ.' Another: 'Very staid and intelligent-like person, with a steady kind of anxiety, but I fear, no feeling of helplessness. Thought that sorrow and prayer would obtain forgiveness.' He couldn't accept her, and he explained to her what she was lacking. A few more examples were: 'Jane Graham – admitted under Mr. Jaffray when careless; now deeply awakened under my ministry and Jessy Small's words. Would not come forward in deep distress.' 'Thomas Ritchie, awakened under my ministry in St. Peter's ever since he came a twelve-month ago from Kilspindie. Fine clear knowledge and seemingly grasp of the truth. Admitted.' By the end of the year 1838, he could announce: 'Admitted about twenty-five young communicants; kept two back, and one or two stayed back. Some of them evidently brought to Christ. May the Lord be their God, their Comforter, their all! May the morrow bring still richer things to us, that we may say as of tonight, "Thou hast kept the good wine until now".'

M'Cheyne wished to preserve the holiness of the Sacraments. He enforced strict regulations with regard to both the communion, as well as the baptism of children. He observed their conduct closely, even more than the testimony of their lips. He didn't wish to condemn them; a simple confession of faith in Christ was sufficient, the confirmation of which should be demonstrated by the conduct of life.

It was his custom to ask if those who wished to use the Sacraments were saved. This direct and personal question alone was blessed to the hearts of many young people who used to come carelessly to holy communion and before his arrival had been admitted into the church. As time passed, he compiled a list of questions to ask. In addition, he wrote down a short explanation of the meaning of holy communion. The questions were intended for 'young communicants, to be answered in secret to God'. They were specifically aimed at probing, until this point in time, what had moved them to request admittance. 'Is it to please your father or mother, or any one on earth that you think of coming to the Lord's table?' thus rang the first question. The fourth was: 'What are your real motives for wishing to come to the Lord's table? Is it to thank God for saving your soul?' The eighth question was characteristic of M'Cheyne: 'Should those come who have deep concern about their soul, but are not come to Christ?' The ninth excluded any chance of subterfuge: 'Do you think you have been awakened by the Holy Spirit? brought to Christ? born again? What makes you think so?'

The procedure was the same with baptism. At every baptismal service, he would give an explanation of the meaning of the sacrament, at the same time emphasizing 'that it was only for believers and their children, and that the use of water was of no value to non-believers'. On one occasion, he refused to baptize a child that lay on the point of death. An indifferent father invited him to his house to baptize his child. No members of the family had ever set foot in the church. M'Cheyne immediately went to the poor dwelling where he came across the dying child. The people whom he met there were godless. He earnestly addressed all present concerning their godless and guilty state before God. He declared that under these circumstances the child should be denied baptism. He didn't try to avoid the reproach that came his way as a result. The parents asked him to carry out the baptism 'for the sake of the poor child'. It was heartless, wasn't it, to allow the child to die in this manner. He made it clear that baptism didn't save one, and that merely out of concern for the father and mother he would have to refuse their request. They raised their voices yet louder and called him a cruel man. M'Cheyne took a firm stand and pointed out that it was they 'who had been thus cruel to their child'. After once more having issued an urgent warning, he parted company.

## The importance of discipline

Discipline was an essential part of his pastoral work. In the beginning, he didn't think it necessary to come across as one who deals out punishment. He avoided acute confrontations, and even acknowledged in a sermon during the induction of elders, that he 'was exceedingly ignorant of the vast importance of church discipline'. 'I thought that my great and almost only work was to pray and to preach.' Disciplinary cases which came before the church council scared him off, and he handled these most reluctantly. However, as time passed, he realized that good church discipline could only be healthy. A new revelation came to him, and he saw clearly 'that if preaching be an ordinance of Christ, so is church discipline. I now feel very deeply persuaded that both are of God, that two keys are committed to us by Christ: the one the key of doctrine, by means of which we unlock the treasures of the Bible; the other the key of discipline, by which we open or shut the way to the sealing ordinances of the faith.' He experienced good co-operation with his elders. His first session consisted of ten elders, among whom were James Thompson, Peter Thompson, David Kay, William Gibson, Alexander Balfour and David Brown. Later we come across the banker, Peter Hunter Thoms, Edward Caird, James Wallace and John Matthewson, godly men who were of great support to him. It was a pity that the session's minutes were mislaid, so that little is known of the work of these office bearers.

M'Cheyne expected much of his elders. Apart from possessing a life of piety and dedication, they had to be capable of teaching and leading others. Each one was appointed to a district of the parish, for which he commanded the oversight. The elders were deeply involved in the Sabbath School work and carried out an exacting supervision of the daily teaching. In addition, they gave their attention to the work of evangelization. They bore in mind their leader's poor health and tried to relieve him as often as possible. The congregation also co-operated in every way together with their shepherd. St

Peter's flourished especially when more souls came to a saving faith. The congregation was not exclusively a gathering of people who met together every Sabbath to listen attentively to the gospel message, but it became known as an active church. In evangelization endeavours, tracts were distributed far and wide; there was much attention given to mission work; in short, everything which concerned the kingdom of God was of importance to many. St Peter's grew up into 'a city that is set on a hill' and 'a light on a candlestick'. The shepherd's love for his sheep radiated powerfully. No wonder then that they spoke of him with great appreciation. In a later declaration of the session, they could not fail to express their feelings towards their leader: 'We avail ourselves of this occasion to express our attachment to the ministry of our pastor... For his abundant and devoted labours amongst us, we feel deeply grateful. We have ourselves, we trust, profited by those labours; and we believe that the chief Shepherd has honoured him to gather out of the flock over which he has been placed many who shall be to him a crown of rejoicing in the day of the Lord.'

**Poor relief**

The material concerns of his congregation also received his attention. Care of the poor was badly neglected during the age of the Moderates. Evangelicals such as Thomas Chalmers and Henry Duncan of Ruthwell joined the struggle against social injustice, which began to take on even greater proportions. The industrial revolution was accompanied by enormous problems which didn't exclude Dundee. It wasn't easy for M'Cheyne also to take care of the poor effectively. Personal salvation was first and foremost, but it was still the task of the church to relieve the lot of the lower classes. Chalmers especially emphasized that this concern should not only be directed at 'the household of faith', but to the community at large. The Spirit of Christ moves one to help the poor, but where were the merciful Samaritans? In one sermon on Mark 16:15, M'Cheyne remarked: 'This is what we need in this town – a ministry that will go to seek the people.

We need men with the compassion of Christ who will leave home, friends, comforts all behind and go into the haunts of profligacy, the dens of the Cowgate, and with the love and life of Jesus persuade them to turn and not die.'

M'Cheyne proclaimed not only the gospel to the poor, but also supported them in their difficulty. Regular collections were taken up in St Peter's in order to actually tackle the need. It is not clear whether the concern was merely for the poor of the congregation, or whether the money was intended for the whole district. Yet M'Cheyne saw the poor rather as a God-inflicted problem. On 26 September 1838, he visited a woman with seven children, who were extremely poor. He spoke on 'God feeding the ravens and clothing the lilies,' but we don't read that he supported them financially. With concern he noticed that Dundee 'in special manner had been visited by commercial distress; poverty, one of the sorest curses that God sends, lies heavy on us'. He called people to humble themselves before God, so that His displeasure might be averted. Poverty was in his eyes a judgment of God upon sin. 'I have no confidence in poor laws or any change in our laws benefiting the poor, as long as we lie under God's displeasure.'

The sharp contrast between rich and poor in the extremely industrious city cast a slur on the social and moral life, and sowed the seeds of discontent. John MacPherson was a minister during this time in the Hilltown part of town, which was particularly poverty-stricken. He wrote 'A few wretchedly clad children are playing in the gutters.... The court is dark, for the windows are poorly lighted, the inhabitants in many cases being unable to afford gas.' The interior of the houses are even worse than the outside: 'Take a seat! Where? There is neither chair nor stool. The only seats are holes scooped out of the earthen floor in a semi-circle round the hearth. In these dirty holes we have seen father and mother sitting drunk, smoking or sleeping ...' This was the picture of the slums and alleys of Dundee. During this time, the church knew not by which just means the social evil of poverty should be tackled. In 1844 a concerning

George Lewis (1803-1879), minister of St David's Church from 1839. Other colleagues of M'Cheyne were John Baxter (1809-1893) of Hilltown Church, John Roxburgh (1806-1880) of St John's and Patrick Leslie Miller (1812-1866) of Wallacetown Church.

The 'Cross Church' on the Nethergate, after an engraving of the $18^{th}$ century. Originally consecrated to St Clement, the patron of the sailors; later on St Mary's, built in the twelveth century. Destroyed by fire in 1641, 1645 and 1841. The tower of 'The Steeple' is from medieval origin ($15^{th}$ century). The church was divided in 1788 in five parishes, to which in 1823 a sixth one was added, the known St David's which later on had its services in a large building on South Tay Street. St John's held services in the nave of St Mary's and became in 1835 an apart parish, not depended of the Cross Church, with a church of its own. The Hilltown Church, opened in 1838, and St Andrew's Church built in 1772, were Chapels of Ease, as was Wallacetown Church, which was opened in 1840.

the poor was passed, and men such as Chalmers of Scotland and Lord Shaftesbury of England did their utmost to implement a system of caring for the lower classes as stimulated by the church and government alike.

Although M'Cheyne saw poverty in the first place as a sign of God's punishment, he wasn't without a feeling of philanthropy. Together with his fellow ministers, he spoke regularly about the needs of the city population. John Roxburgh of St John's, with whom Chalmers was well acquainted, was a man who was moved by social concerns. George Lewis of St David's put the needs of the city-centre in order. M'Cheyne had good contact with both these men concerning the spiritual and material well-being of the expanding harbour city. Together they followed in the footsteps of John Willison, one of the most godly ministers of the eighteenth century, whose name still lived on in the minds of the people. He was also a man who could relate to the common person, and who was of great blessing to many due to his generous service. It was no wonder that M'Cheyne was called a 'Second Willison'. He took to heart the well-being of every fellow citizen. He devoted himself on behalf of the fear of God within the city of Dundee. The Word began to bear more and more fruit and the results became apparent in the city life. The question of a Sabbath day of rest was also honoured by the government. Even the local press, which was not much in favour of the Evangelicals, wrote with appreciation about the peace which emanated from church people, and about the fact that 'the old ladies went to church with their Bibles under one arm and a folding stool under the other'. The churches were overflowing, just as St Peter's was. The Cross Church in the city centre was also the church centre of Dundee, where M'Cheyne also officiated a few times. He also preached once more in St Andrew's Chapel, a Chapel of Ease, built in 1772, near Cowgate, where once George Wishart had proclaimed the gospel to those suffering from the plague. The city was suffering and in need, and only the great heavenly Healer could alleviate its distress.

St Andrew's Church Dundee.

Thus the first years in Dundee elapsed for M'Cheyne. Day and night he worked in the vineyard. His sister Eliza, whom he sorely needed, was a great support to him. She surrounded him with much love and was happy when his health flourished. He made no effort to look for a wife. Had he no need of a life partner? What was his opinion of marriage? These are questions that cannot be satisfactorily answered. His character was not averse to romance; this was apparent from his student years. His affection for Mondego Mary Macgregor and others was not hidden from the public eye. He must have evidenced an interest in marriage when he associated in Dundee with Miss Maxwell, the doctor's daughter. This occurred apparently during the years 1837 and 1838. His correspondence with his parents provides no information on this. Whether it reached a stage of engagement, history doesn't record, but it is certain that the courtship didn't last long. According to family members, her family had to bring the relationship to an end because they saw in his poor health no sound basis for a marriage to Mary. Thus he remained a bachelor, in contrast to all his friends.

**Physical weakness**

M'Cheyne continued tirelessly. At first he wrote regularly to his parents that his health was flourishing. It didn't remain this way. His work dealt a blow to his already weak constitution. He had been busy for two years in his congregation when he experienced another relapse. Towards the end of 1838, his heartbeat became violent and his weak lungs gave trouble. The doctors advised him to take a complete rest. For months he forced himself to continue; day and night he was at the beck and call of his sheep. This now cost him dearly. However, it was a joy to suffer in the service of his Master. The spiritual care of his sheep took precedence over everything. The manse door stood open to all, even overnight. Should a convicted sinner ring the bell to ask for advice, he would be filled with great joy. He allowed himself to be disturbed even on a Saturday, when he was busy with his study.

One day, he was very busy in his house on Strawberry Bank when someone made an appeal for help yet again. His spontaneous response was: 'Certainly, what do we live for otherwise?' Nothing was too much trouble for him, as long as his body agreed to play along. He felt absolutely committed to St Peter's. He saw no reason to leave Dundee. The Lord may well have had more work for him than in the harbour city alone, but He Himself would have to pave the way. As long as his message bore fruit, he could find no motive to leave his flock. His gospel possessed no uncertain note, as we shall learn from the following chapters. To him it was more than a sign from heaven to remain loyal to this congregation. Should he ask for a sign, if he were requested to take up a post elsewhere? He certainly continued to seek God's way, even though appeals from other quarters might come. Above all else, however, the Word was his guide, and he took heed to its effect on his congregation. In this respect he was unashamed, because the Lord of the harvest abundantly blessed his work. For him, this was a sufficient sign to remain in Dundee. In a poem about 'Gideon's Fleece', he gave expression to these feelings, concerning the possibility of leaving his flock:

> But when the message which we bring
> Is one to make the dumb man sing;
> To bid the blind man wash and see,
> The lame to leap with ecstasy;
> To raise the soul that's bowed down,
> To wipe away the tears and frown,
> To sprinkle all the heart within
> From the accusing voice of sin –
> Then, such a sign my call to prove,
> To preach my Saviour's dying love,
> I cannot, dare not, hope to find.

The most known portrait of Robert Murray M'Cheyne, which was inserted in the first and many subsequent editions of the 'Memoirs and Remains'. The original portrait is still kept in the Kirk Session room of Larbert Parish Church. It is a posthumous engraving of unknown hand. The basis of it was a self-portrait which after M'Cheyne death was lent to Andrew Bonar, the author of the 'Memoir', by M'Cheyne's father. He wrote to Bonar: 'I have a pencil drawing of his face, made by himself when he was about 21 years old.'

# Chapter 7

# THE SOUND OF THE TRUMPET

## Preach the Word

'The grand business of the minister, in which he is to lay out his strength of body and mind, is preaching.'

M'Cheyne spoke these words at the induction of his old school comrade, Patrick Leslie Miller, who on 16 December 1840 became minister of the new Quoad Sacra Chapel in Wallacetown, Dundee. For five years now M'Cheyne had laboured in the vineyard of the Lord. His top priority was preaching, without underestimating the importance of other pastoral duties. The chief content of his preaching of the Word was nothing other than 'Jesus Christ crucified'. Thus he wrote on 22 March 1837 to his family in Edinburgh: 'It is strange how sweet and precious it is to preach directly about Christ, compared with all other objects of preaching.' He preached first and foremost the living Jesus, and no dull topics were the subject of his sermons.

Sometimes it was as if his soul was overwhelmed by the love of Christ. Both in and out of the pulpit, this theme was

The interior of St Peter's, as it was in 1836. This photograph was made about 1870. The front was changed fundamentally in 1912 when a pipe organ was installed. The old pulpit was moved to the former school hall and is now in the front right corner. In the photograph it was still in the 'school hall.'

the expression of his heart: 'The love of Christ constraineth us!' He never became tired of proclaiming the precious name of his Redeemer: 'The love of Christ. Such is our precious theme! If it be so, can we ever weary? Its greatness, can we ever know? Its plenitude, can we fully contain? Never. Its depths cannot be fathomed, its dimensions cannot be measured. It passeth knowledge. All that Jesus did for His church was but unfolding an expression of His love. Travelling to Bethlehem – I see love incarnate. Tracking His steps as He went about doing good – I see love labouring. Visiting the house of Bethany – I see love sympathizing. Standing by the grave of Lazarus – I see love weeping. Entering the gloomy precincts of Gethsemane – I see love sorrowing. Passing on to Calvary – I see love suffering, and bleeding, and expiring. The whole scene of His life is but an unfolding of the deep, and awful, and precious mystery of redeeming love.' Just as John was known as the apostle of love, so M'Cheyne rightly can be called the preacher of love!

**God's incomprehensible love for sinners**

How did he happen to come to be amongst the people of Dundee? His purpose was to proclaim the unspeakable and incomprehensible love of Christ for sinners. In his ministry, both His 'love of esteem' towards His elect, and His 'love of pity' towards sinners of lost mankind were present. His love towards 'Christless men' is the love of 'infinite pity'. In the same way that Christ once wept over Jerusalem, the teacher of St Peter's heart broke at the sight of the many unconverted. 'Oh that the tears which the Saviour shed over your lost and perishing souls might fall upon your hearts like drops of liquid fire; that you might no more sit unmelted under that wondrous love which burns with so vehement a flame which many waters cannot quench, which all your sins cannot smother – the love that passeth knowledge.' The unquenchable fire of burning love towards sinners remained with M'Cheyne until he was consumed by that same love. 'Oh that God would baptize us this day with the Holy Ghost and with fire, that we might be all changed as into a flame of fire, preaching and building up Christ's church till our latest, our dying hour!' The church needed a spiritual awakening, a revival. It wasn't enough that a few were converted and came to Jesus, while the masses like dry, dead bones remained sitting among the congregation. Should the preacher take pleasure in little fruit and conclude that most of the unconverted would abandon their sinful lives? Was his love for the Saviour, which flowed as myrrh from his lips, satisfied with little fruit, or was he spurred on to beseech the Holy Spirit from on high all the more, to sweep through the city of Dundee?

During the first years of his ministry, his preaching often addressed the question: 'Why is God a stranger in the land?' During the weekly teaching sessions, he discussed periods of church history when the Lord effected a revival, such as in America under Jonathan Edwards's preaching and during the year 1742 in the Scottish parishes of Cambuslang and Kilsyth. At his first Bible class meeting, he spoke on Isaiah 32:15: 'Until the Spirit be poured upon us from on high.' Should the Lord desert Scotland, a country which He had in the past so richly blessed? Should men not fear that 'God be as a stranger and as a wayfaring man that turneth aside to tarry for a night?' M'Cheyne said in a few sermons on Jeremiah 14: 8-9, which he delivered in St Peter's in 1837, that the situation in the country was far from rosy. It was true that more and more young men were equipped to proclaim the gospel with power. The influence of the Evangelicals was increasing at the expense of the lifeless sermons of the Moderates. 'In many parts of Scotland there is good reason to think that God is not a stranger.' But what is the level of spiritual life? Is the gospel bearing plenty of fruit? 'How few conversions are there in the midst of us!' 'How much deadness there is among true Christians.' There is certainly talk of an 'abundance of head knowledge, but ah, where is the simple faith in the Lord Jesus and love to all the saints?' The words of the St Peter's pastor revealed a deep concern about the status quo. Would the bones be given new life again? He urged his congregation to pray for an outpouring of the Holy Spirit.

**Hope of blessing**

Yet he wasn't left hopeless. In a sermon on 'Christ's compassion on the multitudes', which he delivered on 12 November 1837, he remarked in his conclusion: 'I have a sweet persuasion in my own breast, that if we go on in faith and prayer, building up God's altars that are desolate, God will hear the cry of His people, give them teachers according to His own heart, and that we shall yet see days such as have never before shone upon the Church of Scotland – when our teachers shall not be removed into corners anymore; when the great Shepherd shall Himself bless the bread, and give it to the undershepherds, and they shall give to the multitudes and shall eat, and be filled.'

What, according to M'Cheyne, are the means that the Lord uses to effect general awakening? Besides the prayer of God's children, it is necessary that God's servants preach in the power of the Spirit. M'Cheyne observed that 'there is much unfaithful preaching to the unconverted', many who 'deal faithfully, yet do not deal tenderly'. 'We do not yearn over men in the bowels of Jesus Christ.' 'There is little of this weeping among ministers now. "Knowing the terrors of the Lord", Paul persuaded men. There is little of this persuading spirit among ministers now. How can we wonder that the dry bones are very, very dry – that God is a stranger in the land?' Besides a dearth of compassion, he perceived also a failing amongst preachers to preach on the fullness of Christ. 'It is to be feared there is much unfaithfulness in setting forth Christ as refuge for sinners.' How few followed the example of Paul, who 'determined to know nothing among them but Jesus Christ, and Him crucified'. When all attention is bestowed on Christ, then there are often no 'beseeching men to be reconciled'. 'We do not invite sinners tenderly; we do not gently woo them to Christ; we do not authoritatively bid them to the marriage; we do not compel them to come in; we do not travail in birth till Christ be formed in them, the hope of glory. Oh, who can wonder that God is such a stranger in the land?'

The last lament was uttered during his sermon at the induction of P. L. Miller. There is an urgent appeal made to the minds of the congregation to flee to Christ for refuge. This was the secret of M'Cheyne's preaching: Love's urge and compulsion to flee to the Saviour of sinners. This is a distinguishing mark of the loyal heavenly messenger; it is also the clarion call of the gospel trumpet. In this sermon, he addressed the topic of what it means to be a preacher in his right mind. 'Oh brethren,' he exclaimed, 'it is thus only we can ever speak with feeling, or with power, or with truth, of the unsearchable riches of Christ! We must have the taste of the manna in our mouth, "milk and honey under our tongue," else we cannot tell of its sweetness. We must be hiding our guilty souls in the wounds of Jesus, or we cannot with joy speak of the peace and rest to be found there.' Besides that, 'the faithful minister should feel the presence of a living Saviour'; it is his duty to speak on the prospect of the Day of the Lord, 'within sight of judgment'. 'The terror of the Lord' should compel him to stir souls to discover a living faith. 'You must either get these souls into Christ, or you will yet see them lying down in everlasting burnings.' But what should form the content of preaching? What are the principal topics to be covered? Should sinners not be specifically addressed? 'Would you not tell him his undone condition by nature and by wicked works? Would you not tell him of the love and dying of the Lord Jesus? Would you not tell him of the power of the Holy Spirit?' Concerning this, he quoted Rowland Hill, who was known to have said: 'See there is no sermon without three R's in it: Ruin by the fall, Righteousness by Christ and Regeneration by the Spirit. Preach Christ for awakening, Christ for comforting, Christ for sanctifying.' 'Oh for a pastor who unites the deep knowledge of Edwards, the vast statements of Owen, and the vehement appeals of Richard Baxter!'

**Attention given to the order of salvation**

Besides the presentation of Christ in a powerful manner, M'Cheyne found it necessary to take heed of the Spirit's work in guiding the sinner to the Saviour and thence his abiding in Him. In this regard, he held to a certain order without becoming legalistic. First, it is necessary to discover the disease, before the cure can be applied. 'The first work of the Spirit on the natural heart is to reprove the world of sin. Although He is the Spirit of love, although a dove is His emblem, although He is compared to the soft wind and gentle dew, still His first work is to convince of sin. If ministers are filled with the same Spirit, they will begin in the same way.' The preaching of the law is necessary to help souls discover the truth about themselves and thereafter come to Christ. 'Men must be brought down by law work to see their guilt and misery, or all our preaching is beating the air.' The conviction of guilt is indeed no condition to receive salvation, but 'it is God's usual method to awaken them, and bring them to despair of salvation by their own righteousness, before He reveals Christ to them'.

When M'Cheyne spoke to 'awakened sinners', then he meant those who had come to a realization of their misery by means of the law. The second part of the Holy Spirit's work is 'to lead to Christ, to speak good news to the soul'. The latter includes the preaching of 'a full, free, divine Saviour', according to him, 'the most difficult part of the Christian ministry'. There are no conditions attached to the preaching of Christ, and it is not only for those who 'are awakened', but the invitation is extended to all. The message must focus on receiving Christ, just as He is presented in the gospel. This urgency should never be absent, so that the following applies to all heavenly heralds: 'Exhort, beseech men, persuade men; not only point to the open door, but compel them to come in. Oh, to be more merciful to souls, that we would lay hands on men and draw them in to the Lord Jesus!'

The call to conversion and faith should go hand in hand with a clear presentation of the truth concerning salvation in

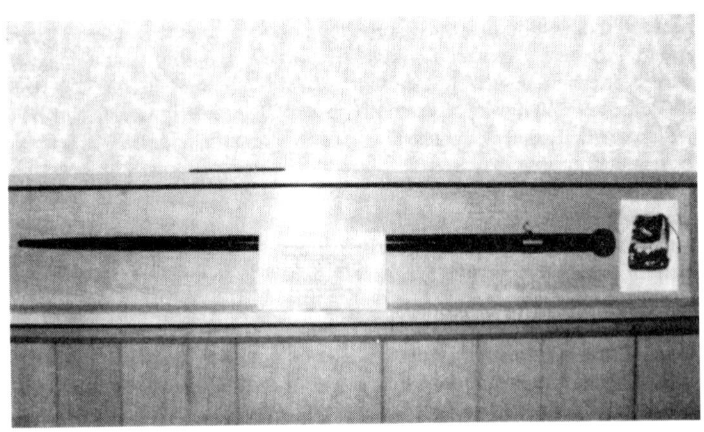

Walking stick of M'Cheyne, kept for years in M'Cheyne's Memorial Church, now in Free St Peter's. On it is a Latin inscription. The stick was a present of his friend Robert MacDonald of Blairgowrie. M'Cheyne lost this stick in Poland on return from his journey to Palestine, but it was found later on.

LATIN INSCRIPTION ON SILVER FERRULE

"HOC BALCULUM, VIRI REVERENDI DILECTIQUE ROBERT McDONALD, BLAIRGOWRIE MINISTRI MILES DIVI, PEREGRINATNS MEAE PER EGYPTAM, PALESTINAM ALAISQUE TERRAS, COME FIDELIS IN POLONIA RELICTUM SED DENIQUE RECUPERATUM ATQUE IN PERPETUAM TAM DATORIS AMICITIAE QUAM ITINERIS ET LABORUM JUCURIDORUM MEMORIUM"

ROBERT MURRAY McCHEYNE OF ST. PETER'S
DUNDEE ECCLESTIC A.D. 1842

TRANSLATION OF LATIN ENGRAVED ON SILVER FERRULE

THIS STICK, PROPERTY OF THE GENTLEMAN THE REVEREND AND BELOVED ROBERT McDONALD OF BLAIRGOWRIE MINISTRY, IS A SOLDIER OF GOD, THE COMPANION OF MY JOURNEY THROUGH EGYPT, PALESTINE AND OTHER COUNTRIES.

THE STICK WAS LEFT BEHIND IN POLAND BUT FINALLY RECOVERED AND WILL BE KEPT CAREFULLY IN EVERLASTING MEMORY OF THE FRIENDSHIP GIVEN AS MUCH AS THAT OF THE JOURNEY AND OUR HAPPY TOILS.

ROBERT MURRAY McCHEYNE OF ST. PETER'S
DUNDEE ECCLESTIC A.D. 1842.

Christ: 'Some good men cry, "Flee, flee," without showing the sinner what he is to flee from; and again, they cry, "Come, come," without showing plainly the way of pardon and peace. These men act as one would run through the streets crying, "Fire, fire," without telling where. In the preaching of the apostles, you will observe the clear and simple statement of the truth preceding the warm and pathetic exhortation.' Besides a clear presentation of the truth, it is necessary above all to be girded with power from above. Thus he added to what Miller said: 'Pray that you may be filled with the fire of the Spirit, that you may pierce into the hard hearts of unconverted sinners.'

Although the servant of God may bring the gospel with much anointing of the Spirit and may lay down the salvation truths with much clarity and power, yet it is the One who sends alone who grants the blessing. According to His promise, the fruit will be forthcoming, because the Word does not return void. 'Success is the rule under a living ministry; want of success is the exception.' There is no reason why one should be discouraged if there is no visible blessing. It is necessary to persevere in prayer in order that souls be saved. 'Do not rest without success in your ministry.'

'Preach the word; be instant in season, out of season; reprove, rebuke, exhort with all long suffering and doctrine.' These words of Paul to Timothy impressed themselves on the heart of the new preacher of Dundee. 'Preach the Word', was also the mandate which he had received from the One who had commissioned him. He expressed it concisely thus: 'The words of the Bible are just the breathings of God's heart.' However, without the Holy Spirit, the Scripture is a letter which kills. 'A sword lying on the ground is a dead thing – it can do nothing. But let the warrior snatch and brandish it – it lives, it glows. So is it with the Word – in itself, or in mouths of wisest of men, it is dead. We speak, it touches not. The Spirit takes it in hand, it lives – the living Word.' M'Cheyne didn't wish to underestimate the Word, but he only wished to make it clear that without the enlightening work of the Spirit it served no useful purpose.

**A lively proclamation of the Word**

M'Cheyne's preaching was a lively ministry of the Word. He was an interpreter of the Scriptures, instructed in the kingdom of heaven. Bonar records: 'It was his wish to arrive nearer to the primitive mode of expounding Scripture in his sermons.' Hence, when one asked him if he were never afraid of running short of sermons some day, he replied: 'No, I am just an interpreter of Scripture in my sermons; and when the Bible runs dry, then I shall.' In his interpretation, he didn't allow himself to be guided by subjectivism or adaptations of the text to suit a distorted allegory, but he strove 'at all times to preach the mind of the Spirit in a passage'. He allowed the Scriptures to speak, and expounded his text within this context. He preferred certain texts, and yet he tried to maintain a balance in his choice, as can be seen in his attempt not to neglect the Old Testament. He was especially fond of the Song of Songs, because it embraced the heart of Christ and His bride, the church. According to Kirkwood Hewat, one of his qualities was 'that he was skilful in the selection of his texts as well as in the exposition of them. He "sought to find out acceptable words" in order that they might be as "goads" and "nails", stimulating and strengthening. And one could not fail to see that he was looking up to the great Master of assemblies to make them effective in applying the truth, as He alone could.'

He proceeded from three or four major points of departure in the construction of his sermons. First of all, he usually demonstrated 'the position it occupied in the context ..., and thereafter he defined the instruction in the text itself which was followed by his chief sermon divisions'. One of his friends observed here that these points 'were not the milestones that tell you how near you are to your journey's end, but they were nails which fixed and fastened all he said. Divisions are often dry; but not so his divisions, they were so textual and so feeling, and they brought out the spirit of a passage so surprisingly.'

What was the essence of his sermons? Bonar summarized it concisely: 'The things of the human heart, and the things of the Divine Mind.' He possessed a deep and personal experience of both issues, which were closely related to the truths he had himself extracted from the Word. Bonar records: 'From personal experience of deep temptation, he could lay open the secrets of the heart, so that he once said, "he supposed the reason why some of the worst sinners in Dundee had come to hear him was because his heart exhibited so much likeness to theirs".'

However, Christ outshone everything else in his ministry of the Word as a whole. He preached Christ 'from whom all doctrine shoots forth as rays from a centre', and not merely doctrine. Christ is the Alpha and the Omega of the message. Dogmatic problems should never be allowed to usurp the place reserved for Him alone. This was exactly the distinguishing mark of the Moderates' preaching: Christ was used as a breech-block of their boring doctrines and digressions on virtue and holiness. All riches and gifts of God are revealed in Christ. A sermon is no summary of general doctrines, but instead it is the proclamation of the living Redeemer. And he often expressed a dislike of the phrase 'giving attention to religion', because it seemed to substitute doctrine, and a devout way of thinking, for Christ Himself.

**Sermon preparation**

We have noted how hard M'Cheyne worked at his sermon preparation. Besides struggling in prayer for the enlightening of the Holy Spirit, he made much preparatory study, although he ran short of time to plan his sermons thoroughly. It was his daily interaction with the Scriptures, above all, that determined the content and form of his sermons. According to Bonar: 'Much of his Sabbath services was a drawing out of what he had carried in during busy days of the week.' He usually made a sermon outline on Friday, which he reread on Saturday. His choice of texts was the most difficult task. One Friday evening he had no idea what the topic for his sermon on Sunday would be. On the Sunday itself he in fact did no more sermon preparation. In every respect, he demonstrated a systematic and orderly method of working, which he had acquired chiefly during his study years.

Since losing his sermon outline in Larbert, this no longer accompanied him to the pulpit. In reading his sermons, we are sometimes made aware of how dependent he was on the ministry from above. Thus he wrote at the beginning of an outline: 'Oh that my tongue were the pen of a ready writer.' We find elsewhere among his notes such remarks as: 'O Life of the world, help me', and 'Out of my weakness make me strong; send showers of the Spirit.' Besides the original text of the Bible, he made use of many theological, exegetical and homiletical books in his preparatory study. He also used the works of other theologians, especially those of Edwards, Rutherford and Bunyan. His manner of sermon preparation changed with the passing of years. In the beginning, he wrote a long introduction, followed by a short definition of the teaching which his text contained. Later, the prologue became shorter and the summary of the teaching disappeared. He didn't write down his sermon applications, but these came straight from the heart, and he borrowed from no one. Bonar witnessed this aspect of his preaching: 'They were poured forth at the moment when his heart was filled with his subject; for his rule was to set before his hearers a body of truth first ... and then urge home the application.'

Besides his Sabbath sermons on a diversity of subjects and Scriptural passages, there were the striking Bible lectures he delivered on Thursday evenings. Thus in 1838, he dealt with the 'Expositions of the Epistles to the Seven Churches of Asia'. He discovered a reflection of the condition of the church in his times, especially in the letter to the Laodicean church: 'The Church had two peculiarities: lukewarmness and self-righteousness.' The situation was certainly serious but not hopeless. God's promises offer sufficient grounds for beseeching Him to send a revival. 'And he has knocked at your hearts, in these seven epistles; the Lord has been in this place, although you knew it not; He has stood until His head is filled with dew, and His locks with the drops of the night. He has pleaded by His blood and by His tears.' At this point we discern an important distinguishing mark of M'Cheyne's preaching: He plainly laid his finger on the wound and described, in vivid imagery, his congregation's spiritual condition, but he sent no one home without having opened wide the door of grace. Even in the story of a disloyal Judas, we find a model of the Saviour's compassion and patience. In Larbert he preached on the betrayer, describing it in his diary thus: 'Afternoon, on Judas betraying Christ; much more tenderness than ever I felt before. Oh, that I might abide in the bosom of Him who washed Judas's feet, and dipped His hand in the same dish with him, and warned him, and grieved over him.' His sermon on John 13:21 with the heading, 'Jesus, melting the betrayer', is a striking example of his deep insight into Christ's compassion for the most godless sinner. Besides Larbert, he delivered this sermon also in Dunipace, Dundee and Errol.

M'Cheyne was no boring preacher. He had the gift of eloquence, although this was dominated by a peculiar anointing of the Holy Spirit. The people hung onto his words, both on Sundays as well as during the week, although his congregation was more involved in his preaching during the Bible classes than on Sundays. The services during the week were a great blessing, particularly to those souls who were eager to receive salvation: 'There is a stillness to the last word – not as on Sabbaths, a rushing down at the end of the prayer.' On Sundays, St Peter's was overcrowded. M'Cheyne had every advantage: His voice was melodious, he possessed much competence, and his attitude demanded respect. A farmer once remarked to Andrew Bonar: 'Before he opened his lips, as he came along the passage, there was something about him that sorely affected me.' 'He was at home in the pulpit,' where he was totally in his element. He was of average height; he was 'of fair complexion and attractive appearance, of erect posture and nimble movement.' Only his eyes were less than good, so that he often wore glasses. However, of greater importance than his outward elegance, was the fragrance of Christ that he demonstrated in every way. His gravity and piety were genuine and sincerely meant. Matters of insignificance were never addressed in the vestry, but an atmosphere of deep earnestness prevailed. He was well aware that he was speaking in God's presence and that the blood of souls would be required from his hand. It was driven home to Bonar when he wrote: 'Surely in going forth to speak for God, a man may well be overawed! Surely in putting forth his hand to sow the seed of the kingdom, a man may even tremble.'

**Influence of Chalmers**

In his presentation of the doctrine, he heartily agreed with the Westminster Confession of Faith, which he had signed at his ordination. He was no theologian, and yet he emphasized certain aspects during his sermons which presupposed the influence of his professor, Thomas Chalmers. However, he didn't agree with him in every respect. Chalmers stressed the gospel offer; he was of the opinion that the teaching on election should never dominate one's proclamation of the message. In this connection, he emphasized points other than those the Westminster Confession had laid down, without deviating from it. M'Cheyne was a great champion of an unrestricted invitation in preaching – and that he shared in common with Chalmers. However, he guarded himself against a denial of God's sovereignty in the deliverance of sinners. Obviously, he thought that it was useless to reason over the tension which existed between election and responsibility. He stood in awe of the counsel of God, but never reduced His sovereignty to a subject of speculation. At one time, he called out: 'Oh, most mysterious electing love!' Bonar observes: 'He saw no inconsistency in preaching an electing God who "calleth whom He will", and a salvation free to "whosoever will"; nor in declaring the absolute sovereignty of God, and yet the unimpaired responsibility of man.'

In imitation of some theologians, he didn't wish to play the dogmas off against each other, but 'he preached Christ as a gift laid down by the Father for every sinner freely to take'. Precisely God's free grace and eternal mercy made room in his eyes for the possible salvation of the worst of sinners. God's absolute power may never be defined as a shackle, which results in people becoming desperate; the liberty of grace means precisely that nothing in a person can make him eligible to cooperate towards his salvation. 'Ah, learn there is enough for you all. I know well that none but God's elect people will be persuaded to come to the blood of Christ – yet there is enough in Christ for you all ....' M'Cheyne preached the full counsel of God. In everything, he strove towards a balanced proclamation of God's Word without partiality.

We find portrayed in all his sermons the balance, as well as diversity, found in the Bible. The fall and redemption; the impotence of unbelief and the obligation to seek salvation; God's offer and His omnipotence; the simplicity of faith, but at the same time its impossibility; the saving and common operations of grace; God's wrath and righteousness, but at the same time His compassion and love; eternal salvation and eternal damnation; the sad state of the church and the promises of revival; the righteousness of Christ in contrast to the self-righteousness of the virtuous; the glory of the Mediator and the depravity of the sinner – these are subjects which he addressed again and again. Besides topical events, such as the conversion of the Jews and the second advent of Christ, his sermons dealt generally with matters concerning the doctrine of God's grace. The practical effect and personal application received more attention than the explanation of the teaching. His departure point for his sermons was an actual situation in his congregation, which for the most part consisted of the unconverted. He addressed his congregation not as believers or 'called saints'. In the days when St Peter's was visited by a revival, he had to say: 'We get on so slowly, because of so many unconverted people among us, and because there are so many who are only "babes" in Christ.'

Clock and chairs in the vestry of St Peter's, a gift of his Tuesday Evening Bible Class. The other photograph is of the silver inscription. Both, clock and chairs were stolen from St Peter's.

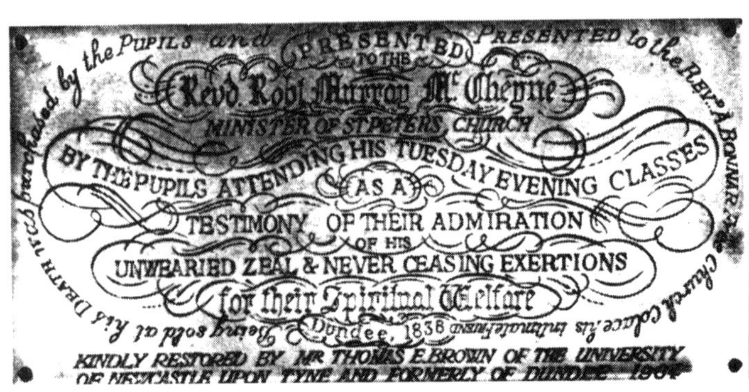

He was aware that the spiritual level of his congregation was below the mark, and thus the revelatory aspect of his sermons set the most important tone, although this was always governed by the lovely sound of the gospel trumpet. In a sermon on God's sword of revenge, he referred in the conclusion to the elderly people, in order to describe their state outside of Christ: 'I have shown you plainly out of the Scriptures what your case is: First, that you are condemned already. Second, that God's sword is ready. Third, that it may come down any moment. Fourth, that God has made you no promise to stay His hand. And fifth, that it will be a sore slaughter.' The young children were included in an earnest warning concerning their eternal destiny if they should die unconverted: 'Think this, little children, you are the pride of your mother's heart, but have gone astray from the womb, speaking lies. Little children who are fond of your plays, but are not fond of coming to Jesus Christ, who is the Saviour of little children, the sword will come on you also.' It was the compassionate shepherd of St Peter's greatest longing that his penetrating words strike all of his congregation. Often impressions would be made in the conscience, but the heart itself remained unmoved. 'Dear friends, ye are my witnesses. I do not know, but I believe I am not wrong in stating that by far the greater number of you have been under remorse at some time or another.' Thus he spoke. He named four causes for these impressions vanishing so quickly: the first is that 'they never are brought to feel truly lost'; furthermore that 'they never saw the beauty of Christ'; then that 'they never had heart hatred of sin'; and in conclusion, 'they have no promises to keep their impressions.' M'Cheyne had no promises for souls outside of Christ, because these would be rejected because of their unbelief. Thus he concluded a sermon on 29 January 1837, on Deuteronomy 33:29, with these words: 'But ah! poor Christless souls, there is no promise of the Spirit to you. All the promises are yea and amen in Christ. Out of Christ there is no promise – nothing but wrath. You have no everlasting arm underneath you. You are sensual, not having the Spirit. There is no sin into which you may not fall. The sins that make men shudder and turn pale, you may commit. God has nowhere promised to keep you from them.... O poor souls! that are growing still on the stock of the old Adam, you cannot but bear evil fruit; and the end will be death. Oh, that you would go away and weep over your miserable estate, and cry to God to bring you among his happy Israel who are chosen, justified, sanctified, saved by the Lord!'

### The deceitful heart

He was acquainted with the deceitful nature of the heart from his own experience and also from his association with his 'sheep'. In a sermon on 'The Heart Deceitful', he depicted the hypocrisy of man. Man deceives not only others, but himself too. He worked on the last point in particular: 'Ever since my coming among you,' he told his congregation, 'I have laboured with all my might to separate between the precious and the vile. I have given you many marks by which you might know whether or not you have undergone a true conversion, or whether it has only been a deceit of Satan.' Thus he attempted to discern between the precious and the wicked.

The work of sanctification in a person's life can possess a semblance of truth, but its root is deceit. 'Often a man is deeply concerned about his soul; he weeps and prays, and joins himself to others who are inquiring. He now changes his way of life, and changes his notions; he talks of his experience, and enlargement in prayer; perhaps he condemns others very bitterly; and yet he has no true change of life – he walks after the flesh still, not after the Spirit.' With all his heart he tried to shake such in order to awaken them: 'Oh, do you not see it is a gone case with you? Oh, if your heart be desperately wicked, and His pure eye ever poring on it, what can you expect but that He should cast you into hell? Oh, flee to the Lord Jesus Christ for shelter – for blood to blot out past sins, and righteousness to cover you.'

Although all that belonged to man's nature was cut off with

the knife of conviction, even including his pious flesh, it never was his intention to pave the way to God with conditions. Despite the fact that he kept a certain order in the application of salvation, and that he emphasized the importance of the effect of the law in the discovery of guilt, in no way did he wish to exclude anyone from the cross of Calvary. The way to the Saviour is open even to the hardened and most indifferent sinner. 'And now, since the glittering blade is bathed in the side of the Redeemer, the guiltiest of sinners – whoever you be, whatever you be – may enter in over His bleeding body, may find access to the paradise of God, to eat of the tree of life and live for ever. Come quickly, doubt not; for He says, "I am the way".' Although most people do never come to the Saviour and few will be saved, it is still a word of truth: 'Ah, no, the most never come to Jesus, and are lost! but this shows that any sinner may come, even the chief of sinners, and take Christ as his own Saviour.' To reject the offer is to insult a God of love. When God's Spirit illumines what is within the heart, the sinner in particular sees that he has despised this love. 'Sin is seen now as done against Jesus Christ and His love.'

Which truth cuts deeper, the conviction by the law or the conviction by means of the gospel? It is precisely the offer of grace that is, according to M'Cheyne, 'the most awakening truth in all the Bible'. 'It is commonly thought that preaching the holy law is the most awakening truth in the Bible ..., and yet to me there is something far more awakening in the sight of a divine Saviour freely offering Himself to every one of the human race.' Hence he eagerly grasped every opportunity to introduce the Saviour to people. We often come across passages in his sermons such as the following: 'To every man and woman and child I do now, in the name of my Master, make full, free offer of a crucified Saviour to be your surety and righteousness, your refuge and strength. I would let down the gospel cord so low, that sinners, who are low of stature, like Zacchaeus, may lay hold of it. Oh, is there none will lay hold on Christ, the only Saviour?'

**The love of Christ**

'The love of Christ constraineth us.' This was the motive for his powerful ministry. It was his pleasure and desire to glorify Him alone. The sinner's attention was continually directed to His blood; what concerned him was a knowledge of the precious Redeemer. 'Keep a continued gaze. Run, looking unto Jesus. Look, till the way of salvation by Jesus fills up the whole horizon, so glorious and peace-speaking.' Preaching is nothing other than the ministry of reconciliation. 'We preach Christ crucified.' 'Here it is plain the preaching of the cross and the preaching of Christ crucified are the same thing.' The cross of Christ is also an expression of God's love. 'That little word implies the whole glorious work of Christ for us. It implies the love of God in giving His Son.' Christ was the rich content of his preaching. He wished to proclaim nothing else. Words proved inadequate when expressing the lovely and beloved nature of His character and Name.

He possessed a deep knowledge of Him who is 'fairer than the children of men'. He himself could repeat from his own experience, that which he witnessed in Paul: 'Paul got such a view of the glory, brightness, and excellency of the way of salvation by Jesus, that it filled his whole heart. All other things sunk into littleness. Every mountain and hill was brought low, the crooked was made straight, the rough places smooth, and the glory of the Lord was revealed. As the rising sun made everything else disappear, so the rising of Christ upon his soul made everything else disappear. Jesus suffering for us filled his eye – filled his heart. From the cross of Christ a ray of heavenly light flamed to his soul, filled him with light and joy unspeakable.' He felt that God was glorified and he was saved; he cleaved to the Lord with full purpose of heart. Like Edwards, 'I was unspeakably pleased.'

How does one find the way to Christ? How do we come to Him? M'Cheyne had but one answer to these questions: 'Believe in Him and receive Him.' According to its character, faith is to be appropriated and focused entirely on Christ. What is required is a simple trust in Him, just as He is introduced in the gospel. 'It gives me no comfort to know that Christ is a precious Saviour to others, unless He is a precious Saviour to me.' Is man capable of believing in his own strength? The soul has no strength of itself, but here he did not stop: 'You say you cannot look, nor come, nor cry, for you are helpless. Hear then, and your soul shall live. Jesus is a Saviour to the helpless. Christ is not only a Saviour to those who are naked and empty and have no goodness to recommend themselves, but He is a Saviour to those who are unable to give themselves to Him. You cannot be in too desperate a condition for Christ.'

The operation of faith in the heart of the sinner in general is preceded by a work of conviction or 'awakening'. In February 1837, M'Cheyne preached two sermons on this subject entitled, 'the order of salvation', in which he referred to John 16:8: 'And when He is come, He will reprove the world of sin, of righteousness, and of judgment.' For the 'awakened souls', who sought the way to Zion out of fear, he had a special word in nearly every one of his sermons. It is necessary that the sinner be observed in accordance with his state outside of Christ. This convicting work is 'a feeling of the loathsomeness of sin' and nothing more. The convinced heart is 'wounded, not broken'. The law is no more than a 'schoolmaster to bring us to Christ'. It injures without offering any healing balm. Many are awakened who never come to Christ. Although such a person has an awareness of 'his own helplessness to make himself better', the heart is not truly contrite, and it is the latter which is the fruit of God's forgiving grace.

He gave a well-defined description of the various aspects of the preparatory work of God's Spirit. Besides the conviction by means of the law, there is also a conviction by means of the gospel. The latter directs itself towards the sin of unbelief, 'Because they believe not in Jesus. This is the strongest of all arguments, and therefore is chosen by Christ here.' This conviction is deep, and concentrates especially on religious man's enmity to the cross of Calvary. Thus the gospel is no longer viewed as an offer without engagement, and man can no longer hide behind his own impotence. His obstinacy finally pierces the heart. 'He sees plainly that Christ is an almighty Ark riding over the deluge of God's wrath. He sees how safe and happy the little company is that is gathered within; but this just makes him gnash his teeth in agony, for he is not within the Ark, and the waves and billows are coming over him. He hears that Christ hath been stretching out the hands all the day to the chief of sinners, not willing that any should perish; but then he never cast himself into these arms.' How could he portray the affliction of such a soul, who realized that he had sinned against a loving Saviour!

**A loving message**

The impression we receive of M'Cheyne's preaching is one of earnestness and compassion. In the opinion of William Lamb, who joined him in his ministry in 1840, he was 'such a zealous and indefatigable servant of Christ'. How beautifully affectionate were M'Cheyne's addresses! He draws you to Christ. Today, he said, 'Christ has brought us into green pastures and by still waters, but would we follow the Shepherd into deep valleys of affliction and trial?' He proclaimed such grassy pastures, but also the valleys of humility. He continually displayed a mirror before his congregation in St Peter's. The gospel is more than a mere presentation of green pastures, because the seed should be sown in well-prepared soil. All that concerned him in the first place was that there should be fruit. When he saw what were often the effects of his preaching, he was most distressed. 'Ah! my friends, is not this just the way with our congregations at this day? Abundance of head-knowledge, but, ah! where is the lowly heart that loves the Saviour? Abundance of orthodoxy and argument, but ah! where is the simple faith in the Lord Jesus, and love to all the saints? Does not the Saviour say, when He looks down on our churches: "There is no breath in them"?'

The concern for his sheep made his preaching more

penetrating. He continually besought God for a revival in St Peter's and Scotland in general. He could not tolerate the lukewarmness of the Laodicean church. His sermons to his congregation between the years 1836 to 1838 were soaked with tears concerning the division of Zion, but were also born out of the struggles in his inner rooms when he besought God to pour out His blessings on the nation. On 1 July 1838, on account of this situation, he preached on the rich promise in Isaiah 44:3: 'For I will pour water upon him that is thirsty, and floods upon the dry ground: I will pour my spirit upon thy seed, and my blessing upon thine offspring.' He expanded the third point of his sermon with the following: 'God pours floods on the dry ground.' He remarked here: 'The dry ground represents those who are dead in trespasses and sins. Just as you have seen the ground, in a dry summer, all parched and dry, cracking and open; yet it speaks not – it asks not the clouds to fall; so is it with most in our parishes. They are all dead and dry, parched and withered – without a prayer for grace, without even a desire for it. Yet what says God? "I will pour floods upon them."' And he then proceeded: 'Learn, Christians, to pray for floods. It is God's Word – He puts it into your mouth. Oh! do not ask for drops, when God offers floods. "Open thy mouth and I will fill it."'

As the year 1836 drew to a close, he preached on 'The vision of dry bones'. How necessary it was for the unconverted to be awakened out of their spiritual death! How he looked forward to a move of God; hence his message: 'O ye dry bones, hear the word of the Lord.' It is precisely preaching that is instrumental in bringing them to life. A year later he spoke about 'The work of the Spirit', from Genesis 1:2, 'And the Spirit of God moved upon the face of the waters.' Thus the Holy Spirit strove with the inhabitants of Dundee. 'O! let those of you that are living in sins, learn what a loving Spirit is now striving with you.' Thus his expectation was in the outpouring of the Spirit of 'grace and supplication' over his sheep.

### His sermons from the first years

His sermon outlines during the first years of his ministry in Dundee reveal a great variety of subjects, which can, however, be summarized under two headings: the law and the gospel. Thus he dealt with Mark 16:15 on 5 March 1837: 'Go ye into all the world'; John 14:9 on 31 December 1837: 'Have I been so long time with you, and yet hast thou not known me, Philip?'; John 7:37 on 22 October 1837: 'If any man thirst, let him come unto me, and drink'; John 5:40 on 30 July 1837: 'And ye will not come to me'; and about 'a crying soul', from Psalm 42:1 on 4 November 1838: 'As the hart panteth after the water brooks.'

His diary regularly records his sermon notes. During the evening of 7 October 1838 he preached at the Gaelic Chapel on: 'I know that my Redeemer liveth', with more seeming power on the people than for a while. 'I never remembered of compelling souls to come in to Christ so much as in that discourse.' On 14 October that same year he preached on 'Forgiving injuries'. Afternoon – on the Second Coming: 'Let your loins be girded about', etc. 'Felt its power myself more than ever before, how the sudden coming of the Saviour constrains to a holy walk separate from sin.' He preached also to seamen. The ship 'Dr. Carey', named after the Baptist missionary to India, lay moored in Dundee harbour on 23 October 1838. 'About 200, very attentive and impressed alike.' On 'I know that my Redeemer liveth': 'May the seed sown on the waters be found after many days.'

Besides an urgent appeal to the unconverted, his sermons contained much comfort and counsel for God's children. He knew from experience about the temptations which disturb the soul, of the doubts that grip the heart. It is not only necessary to come to Christ, but also to grow up in Him. Thus the shepherd of St Peter's led his 'sheep' not only to Jesus, but he also followed them in times of anxiety and strife. Is not the sanctification process the very purpose of glorifying God's work on earth? In a sermon which he delivered in St Peter's on 29

John V. 40.

'Ye will not come to me that ye might have life'.

Doctrine. The reason why men do not come to Jesus for life is that they will not. –

Introd. Nothing more sad – nothing more strange than this – when there is a Saviour that is enough for all the world so few should come to him –
If a life boat were sent out to a wreck sufficient to save all the crew – and yet came back with less than half of them – you would enquire with anxiety why the rest had not come in and been saved
So when Xt has come to seek & save that which was lost, and yet the great majority are unsaved – it behoves us to enquire why are so many lost. –

First page of a sermon sketch on John 5:40, 'Ye will not come to me that ye might have life'.

January 1837, he offered counsel to young believers. He described their condition as one who 'has come to peace in Jesus'. 'No sooner has he found the sweet calm of a forgiven soul, than he begins to know the bitter anxiety of a soul that fears to sin. He fears now that he might go back to the world.' Then the young believer 'begins to make a great many resolutions in his own strength'. Legalistic sanctification is crouching at the door. How should such an insecure soul react? 'When sins arise, when the world sets in like a flood, when temptation comes suddenly upon you, lean back upon the almighty Spirit, and you are safe.' Then he used the illustration of a child learning to walk. While trying to take a few steps forward, he would threaten to fall at any moment. What does such a child do? 'Does it not yield itself up into the mother's arms?' When it cannot go, it consents to be carried; and so do you, feeble child of God. 'God hath given you cleaving faith to cleave to Christ alone for righteousness; has given you the peace of the justified.' Isn't the only way to progress in sanctification to follow and hold fast to the Lamb? What is often the fault in the believer's life? 'It is because your eye is fixed anywhere but on Christ.'

**Christ central**

'Jesus alone' applies both to the unconverted as well as to the converted. This was M'Cheyne's message 'in demonstration of the Spirit and of power': Christ our righteousness and holiness; Christ our perfect Redeemer. He continually directed his congregation towards Him and away from himself.

During the first year of his ministry in Dundee, he paused one Sunday at Hebrews Three: 'Consider the Apostle and High Priest of our profession, Christ Jesus', a word of comfort to the fainthearted and doubting Christian; also a word of admonition and warning for those who continued to live without Him. No one left the church without first having heard a word addressed to him. He spoke to the unconcerned in the following manner: 'Stop, poor sinner, stop and think. Consider your ways. Oh sinner, will you ever doubt any more whether God the Father be seeking thy salvation; whether the heart of Christ and of His Father be the same in this one grand controversy?' To God's children: 'Oh, believer, consider this apostle of God; meditate on these things; look and look again, until your peace be like a river and your righteousness like the waves of the sea, till the breathing of your soul be, Abba, Father! "There is a fountain of salvation in the blood of Christ." Oh, happy believer, rejoice evermore! Live within sight of Calvary, and you will live within sight of glory.... Consider the greatness and glory of Christ who has undertaken all in the stead of sinners, and you would find it quite impossible to walk in darkness, or to walk in sin. Oh, what mean, despicable thoughts you have of the glorious Immanuel! Lift your eyes from your own bosom, downcast believer; look upon Jesus. It is good to consider your ways, but it is far better to consider Christ.'

M'Cheyne's trumpet sounded both curse and blessing, admonition and comfort. The people streamed to hear the anointed shepherd speak. Kirkwood Hewat records, 'What a joy it is to come under the quickening and refreshing influence of a living preacher, a true man of God, whose face, like the face of Moses, shines as if fresh from the holy mount!'

M'Cheyne didn't possess this glory in himself, but together with Moses he would continually cry out: 'Show me Thy glory.' This glory of Christ did not only shine through his heart, but also gave off a rich and brilliant radiance in the pulpit of St Peter's in Dundee. As such he belonged to the inner circle of Jesus' three disciples, who were witnesses of their Master's glorification on the Mount. Unconscious of the fact that it applied to himself, he delivered a sermon concerning the glorification of Christ: 'There have always been men in the church greatly honoured by God. Some are not only of the twelve, but of the three. There are many in the church who have been eminent believers. Ah brethren, covet earnestly the best gifts. It is good to be among the twelve, but it is far better to be among the three.'

St Peter's about 1870.

# Chapter 8

# THE RIGHT HAND OF FELLOWSHIP

## Celebration of the Lord's Supper

'The Lord's Supper is the sweetest of all ordinances.' Thus began M'Cheyne's short treatise, 'This do ye to My remembrance.' The sermon is for everyone, 'but the Lord's Supper is the children's bread; it is intended only for those who know and love the Lord Jesus'. 'When the minister offers the bread and wine to those at the table, this represents Christ freely offered to sinners, even the chiefest.' However, receiving bread and wine means more than merely an 'appropriating act of faith'. It is also more than a fortification of the heart that has been assailed by temptation, or a reflection on the sufferings and death of the Saviour. 'The Lord's table is not a selfish, solitary meal,' he said. It also constitutes a sharing in fellowship with all true believers. Jesus said: 'Drink ye all of it.' This is a sign of one's love for one's brothers, 'a sweet feeling of oneness with all those who love the Lord Jesus in sincerity, a heart-filling desire that all should have the same peace, the same joy, the same spirit, the same holiness, the same heaven with yourself.'

'I believe in the communion of saints'; this was to him no hollow echo of the Apostolic Credo of the church of all ages, but true practice, originating from a real desire within his soul. The communion seasons in St Peter's were feast-days for God's children. Bonar thought back with melancholy to the 'blessed Communion Sabbaths' 'From the very first these communion seasons were remarkably owned of God. The awe of His presence used to be upon His people, and the house filled with the odour of the ointment, when His name was poured forth.' In this connection he mentioned Song of Songs 1:3: 'Because of the savour of thy good ointments thy name is as ointment poured forth, therefore do the virgins love thee.'

The Communion Seasons were not to be thought of apart from the rich tradition of the Church of Scotland. There were usually one or two celebrations in one year. M'Cheyne found it necessary to administer the Lord's Supper four times a year, thus deviating from the rural practice. In reality, he was an advocate of a weekly remembrance, because that agreed with the practice of the first Christian communities in apostolic times. The preparation week began on Sabbath with an Ante-Sacramental sermon. The following Thursday he held two Fast Day services for personal piety and prayer. On Friday and Saturday there were more preparatory services and on the Monday following the holy communion there was a solemn thanksgiving service.

The Sabbath was 'the great Feast Day'. The services were long, because only a few believers could sit simultaneously at the table, due to a shortage of space in the church building. Thus the entire celebration continued sometimes for more than seven continuous hours. Hewat relates that on the day 'immense crowds assembled, with a large muster of ministers'. Before the actual administration of the sacrament, a minister would deliver the Action Sermon, which included the invitation to everyone. A separate address was also delivered, during which time it was emphasized who the true communicants were and who did belong to the table. M'Cheyne held the practice of *fencing of the table* in high esteem, because few were themselves entirely aware of the holiness of the Lord's Table. However, his invitation was rich and loving. Listen to it: 'Ah brethren, herein was infinite love. Infidels scoff at it, fools despise it, but it is the wonder of all heaven. The Lamb that was slain will be the wonder of all eternity. Today Christ is evidently set forth crucified among you. Angels, I doubt not, will look down in amazing wonder at that table. Will you look on with cold, unmoved hearts?' After the elders had distributed the bread and wine to the sitting communicants, a number of ministers gave brief addresses at the table. Four or five of his own circle of friends, such as Andrew and Horatius Bonar, Alexander Somerville, Alexander Moody Stuart, Robert MacDonald and James Grierson, acted as his own assistants. Besides his own congregational members, many were attracted to Dundee from towns and villages nearby to participate in the feast.

The third communion after his induction was truly a feast day. It was 1 April 1838 when M'Cheyne related these experiences in his diary: 'sweet season we have had. Never was more straitened and unfurnished in myself, and yet much helped. Kept in perfect peace, my mind being stayed on Thee. Preached on "My God, my God", etc. (Ps. 22:1). Not fully prepared, yet found some peace in it. Fenced the tables from "Christ's eyes of flame". Little helped in serving the tables. Much peace in communing. Happy to be one with Christ! I, a vile worm; He, the Lord of righteousness.' A few brothers in the faith offered him on this occasion 'the right hand of communion'. Alexander Cumming of Dumbarney served a few tables; his friend Alexander Somerville 'served three, and preached in the evening on "Thou art all fair, my love". Very full and refreshing. All sweet, sweet services. Come thou north wind, and blow, thou south, upon the garden! May this time be greatly blessed!' Moody Stuart and Robert Candlish were there also to give 'a good preparation for this day'. M'Cheyne reflected on this occasion, viewing it as an oasis of refreshment and joyful celebration of God. The text which Cumming chose appealed to him: 'When the poor and needy seek water.' He was concerned that he should receive a blessing merely for his own soul, but his thoughts were concentrated on the welfare of his own congregation: 'Lord, grant some awakening this day, to some bringing peace, comfort to mourners, fullness to believers, and an advance in holiness in me and my children (3 John 4). Lord, wean me from my sins, from my cares, and from this passing world. May Christ be all in all to me.'

In autumn of 1838, M'Cheyne delivered a sermon at holy communion on: 'My soul thirsteth for God, for the living God: when shall I come and appear before God?' (Ps. 42:2). It was an attempt to encourage those who were disheartened in the faith. 'The moon does not always shine in a cloudless sky. The ships do not always sail on a waveless sea. The believer does not always walk in the smile of the Father.' It was precisely for such that the Lord's Supper was a means of encouragement. 'Put away entirely the question as to whether you ever believed before. Believe now. This ordinance is peculiarly fitted for you. You say you cannot realize a Saviour; well, here He is set forth plainly in bread and wine: "This is My body, broken for you." You say: "But how shall I know He is a Saviour to me?" See here the bread is freely offered: "Whosoever will, let him take the water of life freely." You say: "But how do I know He is still offered to me?" I answer, "Yet there is room. Here is bread enough."'

The Communion Seasons were pre-eminently days of fellowship with one another. It was the pastor of St Peter's pleasure to meet his brothers in the faith once again. He was the prominent figure of the group of young ministers who exercised a great influence on the spiritual life of the Church of Scotland at that time. They were instrumental in bringing many into contact with the gospel of Christ, and that not without fruit. A new era was approaching; days of rich harvest were in the offing for the church of Christ. It was precisely the communion seasons which were a demonstration of the Word of God having taken root in many hearts.

Although M'Cheyne was truly attached to his own congregation, yet he never refused an invitation to preach elsewhere. Thus, more than once he assisted his friends, Alexander Somerville in Glasgow and Andrew Bonar in Collace, with the administration of the holy sacrament. The same applied to James Grierson of Errol and Alexander Moody Stuart of St. Luke's in Edinburgh. Bonar witnesses that 'his occasional visits during these years were much blessed. At Blairgowrie and Collace his visits were longed for as times of special refreshment.'

**Church extension**

Besides these, his own bosom friends, he received in 1837 many more contacts, when he became secretary of the committee for Church Extension in Forfarshire. Chalmers's plan for increasing the number of church buildings gradually began to take shape. M'Cheyne received many visits in connection with the planting of new churches. He journeyed on Tully to places miles from Dundee, places he had never visited before. Thus he came in February 1838 to the region of Montrose, in the vicinity of an unusual bay. Snow covered the landscape and it was easy for the faithful animal to make progress. He could, however, not pass by the birth place of John Erskine of Dun. He was one of the first Superintendents from the time of the Reformation, and had himself at the time begun with church extension plans. Chalmers too was present in Montrose. It was a pleasure to meet his old teacher there. He sat opposite him and looked with high esteem into his 'venerable countenance expressing peace and goodwill to men'. How pleased he was that this man of God with his great talents had given himself for the sake of Christ! He felt puny in Chalmers' presence. 'O good grey head which all men knew!' M'Cheyne still felt uncertain in the vineyard of God's church; hence he conducted himself modestly. He also had contact with Nairne from Dunsinane through the Church Extension committee. In a letter to him, he wrote the following significant words: 'I have little courage,

Parish Church Abernyte.

Parish Church Errol, built in 1820

little anything, but I just give my hand to Him as a little child does, and He leads me, and I am happy; what do I desire more?' In church matters too, he never forgot the individual. He never worked for church organizations from behind a mask of reservation but rather radiated a spirit of openness and love.

M'Cheyne offered his talents untiringly in the service of Christ's church. In December 1838 he once more visited Montrose, where he spoke before an audience of eight or nine hundred people on the topic of church extension work. 'Tried to do something in the Saviour's cause, both directly and indirectly.' He was convinced that the number of preaching places, where the gospel could be proclaimed, should be increased. Thus he wrote to Roxburgh: 'Every day I live, I feel more and more persuaded that it is the cause of God and of His kingdom in Scotland in our day. Many a time, when I thought myself a dying man, the souls of the perishing thousands in my own parish, who never enter any house of God, have lain heavy on my heart.' The Lord alone can give the increase, but the labourers in the vineyard should sow the seed. In order to sow, there was a need for more church buildings. 'These new churches were to be like cisterns ready to catch the shower when it should fall, just as his own did in the day of the Lord's power.'

'Oh that Thou wouldest rent the heavens ...!' This was the plea which M'Cheyne and his friends directed heavenward. Two or three of them met together regularly in the environs of Dundee in order to plead for revival. Their souls longed 'for the same waterbrooks'. The entire day was spent in prayer and confession of their sins. In the evening the congregation would gather together with their host. Together with him they would then 'unitedly pray for the Holy Spirit being poured down upon the people'. M'Cheyne expected much from concerted prayer. He imitated the example here of Jonathan Edwards, who had eagerly exerted himself on behalf of this cause. He did not allow himself to be overpowered by despondency. Together they pleaded with God to pour out His Holy Spirit,

Robert MacDonald D.D.

James Hamilton D.D.

St Luke's Church, Queen Street, Edinburgh, built in 1837

according to faith in His promises: 'For I will pour water upon him that is thirsty, and floods upon the dry ground.' When M'Cheyne heard from an elderly woman 'how the river of joy and peace in believing had that Sabbath most singularly flowed through her soul', he included a remark in his Notebook: 'This seems a fruit of our prayer meeting, begun last Wednesday at Collace – one drop of the shower.'

**Relationships in the 'Carse'**

From 20 September 1838, his bosom friend, Andrew Bonar, was minister in Collace. How happy he was that Andrew had taken up pastoral responsibilities a few miles from Dundee. The notes in his diary were written from his heart: 'Present at A.B.'s ordination at Collace with great joy. Blessed be God for the gift of this pastor. Gave testimony to the word of Thy grace.' Collace is situated in the prosperous area of the Carse of Gowrie, which is situated to the west of Dundee. In the years 1838 to 1843 this region was 'an electric spot'. The undulating and hilly landscape adjoining the bay of Tay concealed places such as Errol and Abernyte. M'Cheyne was regularly to be seen in this region on his Tully. He attended the Lord's Supper more than once in Robert MacDonald's church. The latter served in the Blairgowrie region of Perthshire, situated further north. These were days during which 'the desert began to rejoice and to blossom as a rose'. The Rose of Sharon shone especially when the table was prepared and the cup of Christ's love overflowed in many hearts. Then the following was experienced: 'He maketh me to lie down in green pastures; he leadeth me beside the still waters.'

M'Cheyne preached on 2 December 1838 in Errol, where he had spent the night before his ordination in St Peter's. Now he was present to assist in the administration of the Lord's Supper. In his diary he wrote: 'Heard Mr. Grierson preach on Christ's entry into Jerusalem. Served two tables. Evening – preached to a large congregation, on "Unto you, O men, I call," etc. The free invitation of the Saviour. May some find Him this day!'

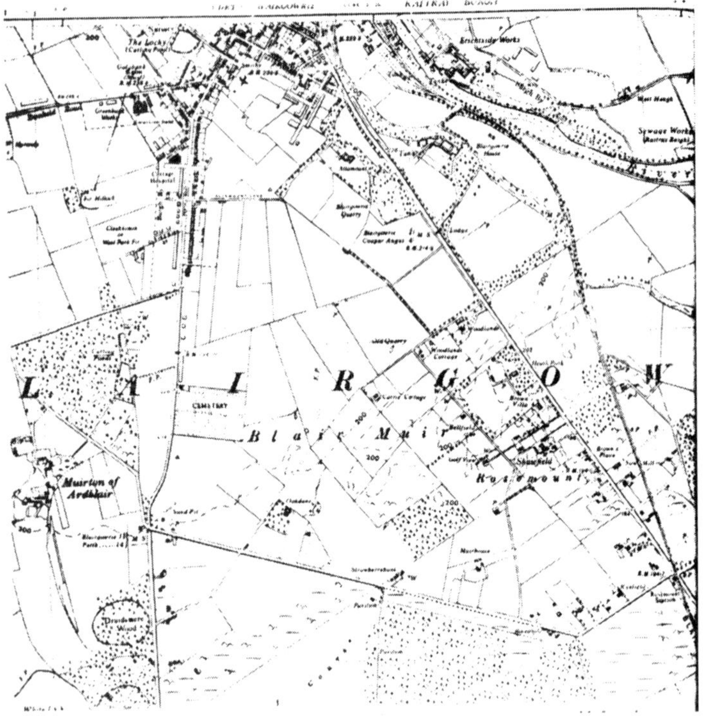


Map of Blairgowrie on which 'Heath Park' can be seen. The summer home of the family of Thain was almost completely changed and is now a guest house.

M'Cheyne knew Grierson already from his visits to Ruthwell, because it was Grierson's birthplace. Since 1819 he had been stationed in Errol, where he had worked with much blessing among the people. Many were converted, especially during the year 1820. He also made a deep impression on the harvesters, who during harvest time came to Errol from the north. The fertile soil of the Carse attracted many labourers from elsewhere. By means of Grierson's ministry, some could enter into the full barns of corn made possible by Jesus who is greater than Joseph.

**James Hamilton**

M'Cheyne often preached in nearby Abernyte. Here his friend, James Hamilton, was assistant pastor. He would shortly leave for the Scottish congregation of Regent Square in London. He took a great liking to Hamilton, who was a year his junior, and he soon invited him to assist him with communion at St Peter's. Hamilton was very fond of M'Cheyne. He heard him preaching for the first time in St Luke's, Edinburgh, while he was still a student. Initially, he could appreciate his melodious voice, but that was due to his own 'cold hearted' attitude at that time. At a later stage, he could recall much of the sermon, except that M'Cheyne had said: 'Lord, stay Thy hand, for Thy servant is but an earthen vessel, and can hold no more.' Hamilton later eagerly preached in St Peter's. He wrote concerning this: 'It was pleasant to preach in St. Peter's Church. The children on the pulpit stairs, the prayers in the vestry, the solemn and often crowded auditory, the sincerity of all the worship, and the often-felt presence of God.'

It was as if Hamilton was cast in the same mould as his friend, and hence they got on so well together. He was theologically better qualified, and the many books that he wrote through the years testify to this. When he was seventeen years old, he wrote biographies about Baxter, Edwards, Boston and others. Candlish wished Hamilton to become his assistant minister in St George's when he heard of his great talents. Mr.

Nairne of Dunsinane, who sought an assistant for Abernyte, was in tears when he heard Hamilton preach. 'This is the minister for Abernyte,' he called out. Abernyte was one of the smallest parishes in the country; it was a village surrounded by a wealth of natural beauty. The Rossie bush covered the scattered homes as a mantel; the view of Tay Bay was brilliant, and on a clear day the contours of Dundee were visible through the trees.

Hamilton felt completely at home during his stay in Abernyte. He gave his impressions as follows: 'We look down on the rich Carse of Gowrie, the Firth of Tay, and the coast of Fife .... There are some pleasant walks, and some lovely retired spots. Today I sat a long while at the foot of a cascade which tumbles from the most romantic hill I ever saw.' He knew this region from the time that his father was the preacher in St Andrew's Chapel, Dundee. At this time the population of Abernyte totalled not more than 280 souls, of which 130 attended church. The moving of God's Spirit was certainly noticeable. From the beginning, God began to work in the Bible Class which Hamilton led. His friends, M'Cheyne and Bonar, who preached there regularly, noticed too that the Lord was present in this place. But when would the waters of revival flow in abundance?

The bond between M'Cheyne's friends was strong and intimate. A regular correspondence kept the contacts alive. Hamilton witnessed: 'It was always quickening to hear from him. It was like climbing a hill, and when weary or lagging, hearing the voice of a friend who has got far up on the sunny heights, calling you to arise and come away.' Andrew Bonar describes M'Cheyne's letters as 'the fresh thoughts and feelings of his soul at the moment he took up his pen'. They depict his tender fellowship with the King, which he also revealed in his relationships. Strictly speaking, his religion possessed no formality, but was simply fellowship with God. Originating from this deep bond with his Saviour, he maintained contact with those who had received a similar precious faith, as for example Robert MacDonald from Blairgowrie, who wrote to him in October 1837 as follows: 'Let me hear from you soon, for a letter of Robert M'Cheyne is peculiarly refreshing.'

Where did the St Peter's pastor make the acquaintance of MacDonald, who wrote to him in January of 1840: 'Oh that I had the simple childlike submission you speak about'? MacDonald, who was the same age as M'Cheyne, had studied in St Andrews and in Edinburgh, where he had met his friend. In June 1837, he began his ministry in the splendidly situated Blairgowrie, in the mountainous region of Perthshire. It was situated with Rattray on the river Ericht, which made its way through an undulating landscape from the spectacular mountain pass and Strathmore. As in M'Cheyne's case, a brother's death had been instrumental in initiating spiritual life. Obviously, he had high expectations of his first preaching post, to which his induction text witnessed: 'I have much people in this city' (Acts 18:10).

It was an extremely extensive parish consisting of two thousand inhabitants in the built-up area, and 1,500 more in the country. Blairgowrie, where he began to sow, was certainly not a dead field; the Lord had 'a seed of righteous', a palm tree in the court of God's house, as it were. Soon the parish became the centre of a spiritual revival in the region. The annual youth meeting, which M'Cheyne considered so worthwhile, yielded much fruit. Some time later, MacDonald asked him in a letter: 'Does the work of God still go on among your people? There is a decided improvement in the ministers here – more prayer and faith and hope.' Then the sluice-gates of heaven were opened over Blairgowrie. By 1837 it was not yet over. MacDonald greatly valued the presence of his friend from Dundee at communion. For the first time, in a letter dated 16 October 1837, MacDonald made an appeal to him. His own life too knew the calling to the mission field. Thus he wrote: 'The neglected field in which I am at present, calls so loudly for a faithful labourer.' He could find no cause for leaving his new congregation. He considered it necessary that the Lord continue His work in him because he yet lacked a total submission to

Andrew A. Bonar D.D.

Alexander Neil Somerville D.D.

Parish Church, Collace.

His will, which he saw so powerfully and abundantly exemplified in his friend. 'I require the smartings of my heavenly Father's rod,' he openly declared. It was precisely the tribulations that were needed to make him plead more fervently for the breath of the Holy Spirit in his ministry of the Word. The trials were but a purification for his friend, whom he highly respected. M'Cheyne could, however, not boast of his trials when he wrote to his friend: 'You will be thinking my affliction is teaching me much, by my saying these things. Oh, I wish it were so! Nobody ever made less use of affliction than I do. I feel the assaults of Satan most when I am removed into a corner.'

**Andrew Bonar in Collace**

How was Andrew Bonar faring in Collace? Together with Alexander Somerville and M'Cheyne, he belonged to the spiritual triumvirate. We have already met Andrew as a student in Edinburgh. In 1810, his cradle stood close to M'Cheyne's parental home. In contrast to Robert, his was a godly upbringing; and yet, for twenty years, he remained estranged from Christ. The sermons of Edward Irving, and books such as *Rise and Progress of Religion* by Philip Doddridge, made a deep impression on his heart. He began writing in his diary when he was eighteen years old. At this time, he was continually reminded of his lost state before God.

Meanwhile he launched into his theological studies as Robert had done. He came to know Christ through a sermon delivered by John Purves from Jedburgh, but his modest faith lacked a solid foundation. By means of his reading *The Christian's Great Interest* by William Guthrie, the Lord had given him light upon his spiritual way. From this time on he steadfastly trusted in, and firmly fixed his faith on, the Lord Jesus and His finished work. He then received personal assurance about the forgiveness of sins and his state before God. From this time on his soul focused more on Christ and his Mediatorial work than on the inner marks of grace. His daughter later observed: 'While others were stumbling at dark doctrines, or searching into the depths of their heart's sinfulness, or looking within for signs of their regeneration, he was pressing on in a life of rejoicing and ever nearer fellowship with Him whose voice at the first had whispered in his ear, "son, be of good cheer, thy sins are forgiven thee".' Since that time he never had reason to doubt his own personal salvation.

Subsequent to the completion of his studies, he became assistant to Purves of Jedburgh, where he began his work in God's vineyard with great enthusiasm. Bonar's life was one of intercession, as was that of his bosom friend. On 9 July 1835, he recorded in his diary: 'I resolved in the strength of the Lord to rise at six o'clock at least ... O may the spirit of prayer be given me every day, and the gifts of the Spirit.' We read that one day in 1842 he spent six hours in the church praying, searching the Scriptures and confessing his sin. With a deep sigh he cried out: 'Prayer! Prayer! prayer must be more a business than it has been.' Andrew Bonar lived close to the Lord. He never became weary in His service of love. Instead he would complain about his daily engagements and his professional shortcomings. A life lived in intimate and dedicated fellowship with God is also a humble life. 'I wished for deeper views of my sinfulness in its length and breadth, that I might feel as Paul, and go to present myself just as an empty vessel which the Lord is to fill.'

Bonar arrived in Collace in the disposition of his heavenly Master. In spiritual terms, it was a dry, sandy desert in contrast to Blairgowrie. The previous preacher had engaged his people's attention with dry explanations of Scripture. Collace was situated in Perthshire, north of the road connecting Dundee to Perth. How often M'Cheyne enjoyed looking up his friend by following the narrow road which took him between the green hills. From the hill of Dunsinane he enjoyed the view of the different counties. Many ruins dating back to antiquity were to be found there.

The heritor of Nairne introduced Bonar here, in the same way he had Hamilton in Abernyte. The first mentioned had also insisted that M'Cheyne should leave Dundee and come to Collace. M'Cheyne's reply was abundantly clear: 'No, but I will tell you of a much better man', whereupon he mentioned his friend Andrew. How pleased Robert was when Bonar arrived, and the latter soon felt quite at home there. On the day of Bonar's ordination, as he was riding through the bush which led to the splendid little medieval church, he reflected on the words: 'Ye shall receive power.' How happy Andrew was too when, besides his parents, sister and brother, he saw his friends, M'Cheyne, Robert MacDonald and others. 'O may I have true grace and apostleship from this hour.'

When M'Cheyne learned that Andrew would go to Collace, he immediately wrote him a letter. He found it necessary to encourage and strengthen his heart: 'Dear Andrew, forgive thy younger brother speaking to thee as if he were an elder – one that must ever sit at thy feet and walk in thy footsteps, following thee in as far as thou followest Christ ... I hear of your preaching, and am refreshed by the very echo of it ... My people have a great attachment to you ... I long to know all your feelings. May the Lord appear to you saying, "Fear not, for I am with thee – for I have much people in this parish".' How he encouraged his friend and brother! This was certainly necessary, because the welcome he received from the congregation in Collace was not a hearty one. His congregation was not impressed with his first sermon. There were barely six practising Christians in Collace! It was precisely this reason that necessitated his arrival. His first manse was 'Dunsinane House', and from there he went to Kirkton, to 'an old-fashioned, ivy-covered house by the roadside, close to the church'. Here his friend from Dundee appeared more than once on his Tully.

M'Cheyne dearly loved the town that lay concealed among the trees and hedges of the fertile landed estates of Strathmore. When he arrived one wintry day at the manse he said: 'I have been riding all the day today through the pure white snow, and that verse has been in my mind all the time: "Wash me, and I shall be whiter than snow".' Snow was certainly the subject of his meditations. He was not far from Collace when he walked through the snow and addressed a passer-by. 'Do you know what is whiter than snow?' he asked him. The man understood what he meant. 'Yes,' replied M'Cheyne, 'there is one thing that is whiter. It is the soul that is washed in the blood of Christ.' Christ was the focus of Andrew Bonar's life and preaching. He once prayed in his own church: 'Lord, never let any one occupy the pulpit who does not preach Christ and Him crucified.' On one occasion he preached in St Peter's from the text: 'Thine eyes shall see the king in his beauty.' As they walked to the manse together, M'Cheyne said to him: 'Brother, I enjoyed your sermon; to me it was sweet. You and I and many, I trust, in our congregations shall see the King in His beauty. But, my brother, you forgot there might be many listening to you tonight, who, unless they are saved by the grace of God, shall never see Him in His beauty.' In a brotherly way, he pointed out that Andrew should never forget the unconverted!

Andrew Bonar was also a bachelor. In 1848 he married Isabella Dickson from Edinburgh, whom M'Cheyne had been instrumental in leading to Christ. Thus both held each other in high esteem and considered each other more advanced in the faith. How supportive was the St Peter's pastor of Collace's pastor! 'O what I wonder at in Robert M'Cheyne more than all else is his simple feeling of desire to show God's grace, and to feed upon it himself.' It was a great honour for Bonar to host such a guest at his manse. The first years in Collace were a time of ploughing the rocky soil, and when the gentle rains of the Spirit began to fall on that region, the village remained in the 'shadow of the showers'. However, even there the Lord would hear the prayers of His servant.

M'Cheyne loved the parish and its inhabitants and enjoyed staying in his friend's manse. The aged house-servant respectfully took note of this preacher's conduct: 'Oh, to hear Mr. M'Cheyne at prayers in the morning!' he cried out. 'Ye would hae thocht the very walls would speak again. He used to rise at six on the Sabbath morning, and go to bed at twelve at night, for he said he likit to have the whole day alone with God.' Thus Andrew Bonar's friend spread the fragrance of Christ! Andrew himself felt attached to him with unbreakable ties of affection.

**Alexander Somerville**

On 30 November 1837, Alexander Neil Somerville preached his first sermon in the *Quoad Sacra Chapel* in Anderston, Glasgow. M'Cheyne had spent his school and student years with him. On one occasion he wrote to Robert: 'Perhaps we may get a lodging near each other in the golden streets of the New Jerusalem.' For nearly his entire life, Alexander remained in Glasgow, although the world was his parish. For fifty-two years he laboured in God's vineyard and, in his old age, he still bore fruit and was 'fat and flourishing' (Ps. 92). He travelled to Spain, India, France, South Africa, Greece and many other lands to testify to his Saviour. Both friends longed to become missionaries, but the Lord guided their lives differently. During M'Cheyne's stay in Larbert and Dunipace, it became his habit on a Sunday morning to stroll past the houses close to his host's lodgings and awaken the late sleepers. He called out to them not to neglect attendance of the services, for which they were always grateful. But the people soon realized that his motivation was to win their souls for Christ.

**Horatius Bonar**

Andrew Bonar's elder brother, Horatius, was also a friend of M'Cheyne's. From 1837 he was the minister at the North Church in Kelso, situated near the River Tweed on the southern border of Scotland. M'Cheyne travelled south more than once to assist him with the Lord's Supper. They held one another in high mutual regard. Horatius developed into a prominent preacher, whose words commanded much respect. He was well-known for his hymns, which affectionately depicted the walk of God's children in His presence. Both Bonar brothers were men who lived in expectation of the return of Christ. Their

Alexander Moody Stuart D.D.

Horatius Bonar D.D.

future hope, however, did not detract from the simple gospel message. In looking back, Horatius declared that 'the burden of our good news' was: 'Righteousness without works to the sinner, simply on his acceptance of the divine message concerning Jesus and His sufficiency.'

M'Cheyne visited Kelso eagerly, about which he wrote at a later date: 'Sweet are the spots where Immanuel has ever shown His glorious power in the conviction and conversion of sinners. The world loves to muse on the scenes where battles were fought and victories won. Should not we love the spots where our great Captain has won His amazing victories?' During this time there was also a move of the Spirit there.

Both friends were in agreement as to the method of proclaiming the gospel, as well as the way of sanctification. Without fear of encountering a brick wall, M'Cheyne could write to him: 'I have great desire for personal growth in faith and holiness. I love the Word of God, and find it the sweetest nourishment to my soul. Can you help me to study it more successfully? The righteousness of God is all my way to the Father, for I am the chief of sinners; and were it not for the promise of the Comforter, my soul would sink in the hour of temptation.'

**Alexander Moody Stuart**

The friendship with Alexander Moody Stuart dates back to M'Cheyne's student years. The former was full of wonder at their first meeting. 'It was to me a golden day when I first became acquainted with a young man so full of Christ.' M'Cheyne introduced Andrew Bonar and later his brother Horatius, as well as Alexander Somerville, to him, whereupon they held their weekly prayer meeting. Moody Stuart's remark concerning him speaks volumes: 'I cannot understand M'Cheyne; grace seems to be natural to him.'

Stuart was born in Paisley in 1809. His father's death, as well as the loss of his two elder brothers, caused him to reflect on eternal things. Initially he possessed the religion of the rich young man, which was revealed to him in a sermon delivered by a preacher from New Town in Edinburgh. At the end of the service, the following resounded in his ears: 'All these things have I kept from my youth up; what lack I yet?' Dr Robert Gordon offered him insight into the meaning of Christ's work as Mediator, and Walter Marshall's book, *The Gospel Sanctification*, made him aware that his religion was built on sand. He came to the realization that a chasm existed between God and his soul: 'I was lost and dead, without any power either to pray or to believe; there was free salvation in Jesus Christ for the chief of sinners in believing on Him, but in Him I never had believed, and could not now believe. Standing stripped and ashamed, with no power to put on the clothing of the Lord Jesus Christ, I could do nothing, and made no attempt.' As a lost and dead sinner he found himself at the feet of Christ. Now he could truly admit that he had embraced His righteousness.

M'Cheyne often travelled to his parents' city to be present at the celebration of the Lord's Supper in St Luke's. Moody Stuart's church in Young Street was taken over by Dr Candlish on 28 May 1837. M'Cheyne also made the acquaintance of the well-known Dr John Duncan, who afterwards became professor of Oriental languages. The 'Communion Seasons' were oases in the desert. There probably existed no other congregation where services were so well attended by God's children as here. Moody Stuart's efficacious preaching, based on personal experience, attracted many. He knew, even as his friend from Dundee, what it meant to live in close communion with the Lord. On the occasions of the Lord's Supper, his manse resembled the Upper Room of Acts 1:14, where 'these all continued with one accord in prayer and supplication', as the first disciples had gathered prior to Pentecost. The friendly conversations were extremely profitable for their souls. When M'Cheyne and other friends came to visit him, it was as if Moody was entertaining angels. The ministry of the sacrament was solemn and impressive. An absolute silence prevailed over the congregation when the preachers, and sometimes the elders, would come forward to administer the symbols of bread and wine to the many who were present.

M'Cheyne also maintained contact with Moody Stuart outside Edinburgh. At the Carse of Gowrie, 'on a lovely knoll not far from Rait, and across the glen ... stands Annat'. Here Moody had a summer cottage built. In these splendid surroundings he enjoyed not only the beauty of nature, but also the company of his friends. James Grierson, Andrew Bonar and Robert M'Cheyne would meet together in the shady garden. Many years later, Moody remembered Robert and Andrew sitting next to each other on the garden bench, not merely to carry on conversation, but also to participate in reflection and prayer. It was as if time stood still here. 'The thought was very pleasing to me,' related Moody Stuart, 'that at that same hour they might also be recalling our hallowed converse in the earthly garden and expecting me, though greatly less worthy, soon to join them in the heavenly paradise.' The garden in Rait resembled an entrance to heavenly bliss. Andrew Bonar and Robert Murray M'Cheyne were already dead when the aged Moody Stuart remembered the times of communion they had enjoyed together.

M'Cheyne regarded these visits, in the first place, not merely as a time of socializing, but as a time to be of use to each other. He always broached the topic of eternal matters in his discussions and if that did not succeed, he remained silent. He did this in a natural way, and he never forced his will upon another. He likened the fellowship they enjoyed to a garden containing fruit trees. With a reference to Song of Songs 4:16, where we read that the wind of God's Spirit is entreated to blow over the people of God 'that the spices thereof may flow out', he observed that believers also possess spices which cause them 'to be attractive'. These spices were not lacking in his own life. It could possibly have been in Alexander Moody Stuart's cottage garden, that he, 'sitting under a shady tree, and casting his eye on the hospitable dwelling in which he found a pleasant retreat ...', wrote a short poem that bore the inscription: 'Peace to this house!' This was certainly the longing of his heart. He concluded the poem with:

May the dove-like Spirit guide them
To the upright land!
May the Saviour-Shepherd feed them
From His gentle hand!

**The Thain family**

At the beginning of their friendship, most ministers of the 'M'Cheyne group' were still unmarried. After he had lived with his sister Eliza in the Strawberry Bank manse of Dundee for two years, M'Cheyne turned twenty-five years old. There was talk of an association between him and Jessie Thain, but no evidence for this has ever appeared. Jessie was a daughter of John Thain, a merchant and shipowner by trade, who during the winter months lived in Park Place, Dundee. However, he spent the summer months in Blairgowrie. Here he had purchased a large country house, that bore the name 'Heath Park'. Thain was an elder in Robert MacDonald's church and for some time was Trustee of St Peter's, where he attended church during his stay in the city. Together with his wife, he formed part of the preacher's inner circle of friends.* The friendship was strong. Mother Thain in particular wrote long letters to M'Cheyne, the spiritual father who was instrumental in the conversion of her daughter, Jessie. M'Cheyne also corresponded with Jessie's brother, Alexander, who would later become pastor of the Free Church in New Machar. It was a family in which the fear of the Lord prevailed.

Subsequent to her conversion, Jessie wished to work in God's kingdom. She was pleased to be permitted to lead a Sabbath School class that was under the supervision of the elder, Edward Caird. M'Cheyne wrote to his mother that this gladdened his heart: 'I shall be quite delighted if Jessie is able to take a small part in the Sabbath School. She knows it is what I always told her, not to be a hearer of the word only, but a doer. It is but a little time, and we shall work no more here for Him.... He hath an unchangeable priesthood ...' Jessie was not yet strong in her faith, which caused M'Cheyne to write: 'Tell Jessie to stay herself upon God. Jesus continueth ever ...' He lovingly followed the fortunes of the family to whom he felt so attached. He had a spiritual bond with Jessie, but whether they meant anything more to each other is not apparent from the letters. Jessie was despondent when she did see Robert, but was this due to their spiritual relationship? Did she perhaps nurture a desire to take care of him and share her life with him? She was certainly friends with his sister Eliza.

**Relapse**

The contact with the Thain family was particularly intensive; M'Cheyne often visited the villa 'Heath Park', where he enjoyed not only the quiet beauty which the Perthshire countryside afforded, but also the conversations about spiritual matters. The Thain family was to M'Cheyne as the family of Bethany was to the Lord Jesus. M'Cheyne gave Bible studies on the latter at this time. He was aware of their needs and anxieties.

The Thain family was concerned about their friend's health, which had deteriorated with the passing of time. It had been reasonably good during the first years of his stay in Dundee. However, at the end of 1838, he had a relapse and the following year he experienced a heart-rhythm disorder. He consulted certain doctors in Edinburgh, especially Dr Alison, who was of the opinion that his troubles had developed from nervousness. He was required to rest up completely, resulting in the abrupt termination of his work. In addition, the doctors were afraid that his lungs would be affected should he not relinquish his extremely busy activities. He would have to avoid every form of exertion to give his heart a rest. There remained no other course of action except to move from Dundee to Hillstreet, Edinburgh, his parental home.

He wrote to his friend James Grierson from there: 'The

beating of the heart is not now so constant as it was before. The pitcher draws more quietly at the cistern; so that by the kind providence of our heavenly Father, I may be spared a little longer before the silver cord be loosed, and the golden bowl be broken.' What a contrast to the first months after his arrival, when he wrote to his mother: 'My cough is turned into a loose kind of grumble, like the falling down of a shower of stones in a quarry, and I am well and lively in all other respect'! When his mother recommended that he take some 'gruel with white wine', he answered her that he knew of no better remedy than to preach frequently, because 'it is the best cure for all slight colds'. He did not take his poor health and weak constitution seriously, and flung the advice of his family doctor, Dr Gibson, to the winds. It had now become serious, and he was well aware that he was now well and truly out of circulation.

On receiving the letter from his friend, Grierson was perhaps reminded of the incident that occurred in August, 1838, when M'Cheyne accompanied Dr Thomas Guthrie on a journey and visited Errol with a view to Church Extension. In a letter addressed to Eliza, Robert described an accident that occurred in Grierson's garden. The concerned sister was happy that it turned out well, and could not neglect including on the back of the letter: 'Robert, from Errol. "He keepeth all his bones; not one of them is broken."' What actually happened? There was a horizontal bar used for gymnastics in the garden erected by M'Cheyne himself for his friend's son. However, when Robert, lean frame and all, gripped the bar and swung through the air, one of the supports broke and with a loud thud he fell to the ground. He was unconscious when his shocked friends lifted him up and carried him inside. Happily, he soon came around, and although he complained of a pain in his chest, he seemed to have done himself no serious injury. After two days rest, he once again saddled his pony and the next Sabbath preached in his own church. However, Guthrie relates in his own autobiography that this accident was the beginning of all

Janet M'Culloch, Mrs Coutts (1776-1849).

the physical ailments that would affect him in the future.

The Dundee congregation was certainly distressed when it became obvious that they would provisionally be losing their minister. The worst of it all was that he would be out of the neighbourhood. Letter after letter arrived at Hill Street. A poor woman mourned the loss of 'our golden candlestick and bright star'. Three members of St Peter's placed their names on a petition to receive more information about his health. They wrote, 'When the heart is full, the lips must speak.' An elder suggested that he write a weekly pastoral letter, which would be read before the gathering once a week on Thursdays. A few members of the congregation came together on a Monday evening to pray for the recovery of their pastor and teacher.

On 5 January 1839, M'Cheyne wrote to Grierson: 'I hope this affliction will be blessed to me. I always feel much need of God's afflicting hand. In the whirl of active labour there is so little time for watching, and for bewailing, and seeking grace to oppose the sins of our ministry, that I always feel it a blessed thing when the Saviour takes me aside from the crowd, as He took the blind out of the town; removes the veil and clears away obscuring mists, and by His Word and Spirit leads to deeper peace and a holier walk.'

M'Cheyne was in need of patience. He was aware of his own carnality and pride. His indwelling sin continually beset him. He still clung to material things, was busy with himself, and lacked the unselfish surrender of his will to his Master. Certainly, he desired nothing other than to live for God and to follow Him daily, both via well-known and difficult paths, but his sinful nature would not allow it. 'Ah, there is nothing like a calm look into the eternal world to teach us the emptiness of human praise, the sinfulness of self-seeking and vain-glory, to teach us the preciousness of Christ, Who is called "The Tried Stone".'

M'Cheyne continuously lived with the realization that he could suddenly be summoned into the next life. He often had a premonition that this day would not be afar off. '...My sickly frame makes me feel every day that my time may be very short.' It was as if he, the dying one, spoke to the dying. But how could he leave his own flock behind? Would the revival, for which he had so longed, pass by St Peter's, or would his successor rejoice in a rich harvest of souls? If he should flourish for a period, would that not flatter his pride? In a letter dated 18 January, he wrote: 'I sometimes think that a great blessing may come to my people in my absence. Often God does not bless us when we are in the midst of our labours, lest we shall say, "My hand and my eloquence have done it." He removes us into silence, and then pours "down a blessing so that there is no room to receive it"; so that all that see it cry out, "It is the Lord!"' Is God's way not to be found in the depths of the sea and are His ways not untraceable? His only desire was to follow after Him, and that was all.

**Pastoral letters**

The sick minister remained with his parents, but his heart was really in Dundee. His first pastoral letter to the St Peter's congregation, on 30 January 1839, bore witness to a longing to be with them: 'God is my record of how greatly I long after you all in the bowels of Jesus Christ; and the walls of my chamber can bear witness how often the silent watches of the night have been filled up with entreaties to the Lord for you all.' It did seem likely that he would be restored to them soon. For him as well as his congregation, this trial was a time of reflection. The mighty One who commissioned His servants led them 'often away into darkness and loneliness and trouble, that He may sharpen and prepare them for harder work in His service'. His congregation needed to abandon their hope in a man. 'Is He not bidding you to look more to the treasure which was in them, and which flows in all its fullness from Christ? It is a sad error into which I see many a Christian falling, that of leaning upon man, mistaking friendship towards a minister for faith on the Son of God.'

In the next pastoral letter he warned them to take hold of the privileges they had enjoyed. 'I have spoken to you from Sabbath to Sabbath in the name of the Lord.... Awaking, inviting, comforting messages you have had.' Where was the fruit? 'Consider how much God has done to save your souls,' he wrote on 27 February. 'Has not the Spirit of God been sometimes present in our sanctuary? Have not some hearts been filled there with gladness more than in the time that their corn and wine increased? What could have been done more for My vineyard that I have not done in it? Now let me ask, what fruit have we borne, grapes or wild grapes? Ah, I fear the most can show nothing but wild grapes! If God looks down upon us as a parish, what does he see? Are there not still a thousand souls utter strangers to the house of God?' He earnestly required everyone to give an account of what they had done with the Word preached. Where was the self-discovery and the knowledge of deep depravity? 'What fruit of self-abasement is there in you?... what fruit of believing is there in you. Have you really and fully uptaken Christ as the gospel lays Him down?' Did St Peter's display more of the picture of the barren fig tree than a conformity to Christ?

Thus he roused his congregation to take a retrospective view.

I Observe - He knoweth the way that I take - What sweet comfort there is in these words - He that redeemed me - He that pities me as a Father - He who is the only wise God - He whose name is Love - He knoweth the way that I take -
The ungodly world do not know it - The world knoweth us not even as it knew Him not. A Stranger doth not intermeddle with the joys or with the sorrows of a child of God. When the world look on your grief with unsympathising eye you feel very desolate - your soul is exceedingly filled with the scorning of those who are at ease - But why should you? He that is greater than all the world is looking with the intensest interest upon all your steps.

Part of a copy of a pastoral letter. The originals of the pastoral letters are kept now in Free Church College, Edinburgh.

Such a disposition is useful for planning how to proceed further. He reminded them of his arrival more than two years ago. 'When I came to you at the first, it was not of my seeking. I never had been in your town, and knew only one family in it. Since that day "Ye know after what manner I have been with you at all seasons", and how, as far as God gave me light and strength, "I have kept nothing back that was profitable unto you, but have showed you, and taught you publicly, and from house to house."' He had certainly had their salvation, in mind and had admonished them with many tears. Surely he had pointed them to the only grounds of their salvation and had forestalled all false teaching. 'Remember it is not your own natural goodness, nor your tears, nor your sanctification, that will justify you before God. It is Christ's sufferings and obedience alone.' Thus he declared himself innocent of their blood. 'If you die, it is because you will die; and if you will die, then you must die.' The children of God also received a word, of comfort and admonition. His mission was to graze the lambs and guard the sheep. 'Now, when He sends me away, I would humbly return his own words to Him, saying, O Shepherd of Israel, feed my sheep, feed my lambs, feed my sheep. Little children, love one another ...' Was this a final farewell? Would he never see them again? Meanwhile, the Lord had so ordained it that another task awaited him. His way led him to 'the promised land', not to the heavenly Canaan alone, but to the land where his Master had once trodden with blessed steps. Circumstances unexpectedly opened a marvellous way for him. It, however, signified a great disappointment for his own flock. The work in Dundee seemed about to come to an end. Yet God's ways are well-beaten ways, because for St Peter's, providence meant another way to His sanctuary. 'My glory will I not give to another', that is the lesson God's children and servants continually must learn. Now the real harvest would be forthcoming; now the trees would be overladen with fruit in abundance!

It was a bitter experience for M'Cheyne to have to leave his congregation. The fellowship with the true 'lambs and sheep' was dear to him. He was aware too that his congregation was a praying people, who brought him before the throne of grace. The letters that he received daily from Dundee, were a few signs of the heartfelt solidarity that existed and, as a threefold, cord seemed to be unbreakable. These were letters which sometimes contained many mistakes, but nevertheless contained golden notes of love. These tokens of love from simple souls were just as dear to him as the gracefully written letters of men such as Robert MacDonald and James Grierson. Thus he received in January 1839 a note from Ann Phin from 'Robertson Lane, Hawkhill'. Ann was concerned about her 'dear pastor', 'For the one day I hear that you are thought dying and the other you are better.' She missed him a great deal and prayed fervently for his recovery. However, the Lord kept His side of the bargain 'for while we were wandering without a shepherd, I and some more went to the Rev. Mr. Baxter of Wallacetown.' By the latter she had meant John Baxter who, a short while before, had become minister of the new Hilltown church.

During the same month he received a few letters from Mrs Likely, who poured out her heart to him. She saw God's punishing hand in the departure of her pastor. Was it not due to the 'carelessness' of the congregation, as well as the 'elders and managers', that His chastising hand had come down upon the congregation? Yet the people were praying for him, and the youth too. She wrote to him about the Sabbath School children; she wrote how 'affecting it is to see our dear little scholars waiting with tears in their eyes to have you prayed for'. Were there not prayer meetings held in the school room on his behalf? 'At our second meeting for prayer in the school room last night again Mr. Caird opened it, our dear schoolmaster, next David Brown, next our dear friend James Wallace, precentor.' These were three elders who were a great support to M'Cheyne. Mrs Likely also related how Andrew Bonar had preached the past Sabbath on three occasions, and had visited the sick on the Monday.

The Lord never abandoned his heritage. He provided other pastors who also had a heart for Jerusalem and comforted His people. Continual prayer was made on behalf of the sick pastor, that he might return to their fellowship once more. Similar intercession had once been made for the apostle, Peter. Now they would have to learn, more than they had done in the past, to follow the great supreme Shepherd. Andrew Bonar wrote after his visit to St Peter's: 'You have left your sheep in the hand of the Good Shepherd. I heard the bleating of some of them, but the Lord will feed them.' It was necessary to wait for God's perfect timing. Bonar was convinced that M'Cheyne's departure was a part of His wise plan. 'I have been thinking that in our day there is such need of the Spirit that it would not be surprising if God were to lead those of His servants who will pray into a desert place apart, taking Elijah from the thousands of Israel, to whom he might have testified, in order to watch solitarily on Carmel and pray seven times for the coming of the rain.' God would surely send the gentle rain of His Holy Spirit upon the flock of Dundee too, 'that my house may be filled'.

* Several women were among M'Cheyne's extensive circle of friends. Indeed, godly women such as Mrs Coutts and Miss

Collier, both of whom were his friends, regularly had contact with him. They appear more than once in his correspondence. Miss Collier was a daughter of a gentleman farmer from Dairsie in Fife, and Mrs Janet Coutts, Dr M'Culloch's daughter, who himself was minister in the same place. Janet was married to Robert Coutts, the minister of Brechin. The Coutts, M'Culloch and Collier families belonged to the pious Evangelicals, who during the age of the Moderates kept the flame of God's fallen Zion burning. Mrs Coutts was also a friend of Chalmers, with whom she had a special spiritual bond.

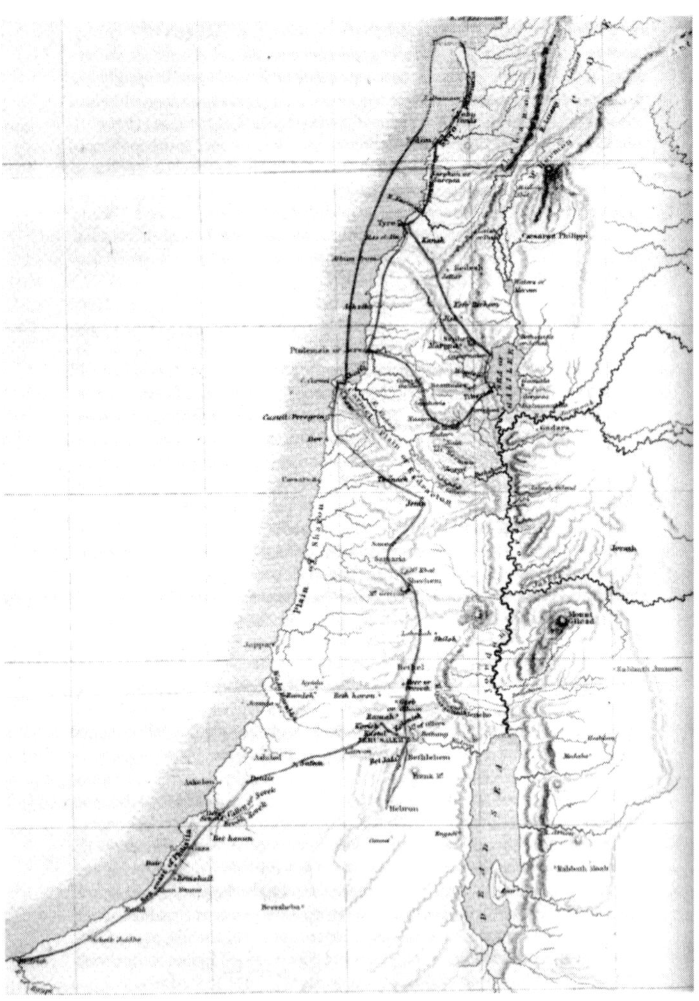


Map of the route of the deputation in Palestine.

# Chapter 9

# TO THE PROMISED LAND

**Much attention for the Jews**

'The time is coming when a voice shall be heard saying to Jerusalem: "Arise, shine; for thy light is come, and the glory of the LORD is risen upon thee." ... Like the rising sun appearing above the hills, tinging all Mount Olivet with living gold, then pouring down upon the prostrate ruins of Jerusalem, till the holy hills smile again in his cheering ray; so shall it be with desolated Judah. Christ shall arise upon their souls, the day shall dawn, and the day-star arise in their hearts. Christ shall appear beautiful and glorious, and they shall submit with joy to put on His imputed righteousness. His glory, his beauty, his comeliness shall be seen upon them.'

This is the beginning of a sermon of M'Cheyne on Isaiah 60:1. It was as if he viewed the day approaching, when the God of Abraham, 'who cannot lie', would fulfil his promise to pour out the Spirit on the fallen house of Israel. The superscription of this sermon bears the concise but powerful title: 'Arise, Shine'. He added that, besides delivering this sermon in

Dundee, he had preached it in five other places, among which were Anderston, Glasgow (Somerville's congregation) and St George's in Edinburgh (Dr Candlish's congregation).

For a few years now M'Cheyne had shown a great interest in the Jewish people. He was absolutely convinced that the Lord had not abandoned His covenant people, but that they would be brought to a knowledge of the true Messiah in His time. His interest in unfulfilled prophecy was instilled by Edward Irving's lectures. From a serious study of God's Word, the conviction grew that the scattered Jews would return to their own land and indirectly 'give life to a dead world'. It was his fervent longing that the Lord would quickly fulfil the promises, which he found so profoundly expressed in the eleventh chapter of the epistle to the Romans. He wrote: 'To seek the lost sheep of the house of Israel is an object very near to my heart, as my people know it has ever been. Such an enterprise may probably draw down unspeakable blessings on the Church of Scotland, according to the promise, "they shall prosper who love thee".' It wasn't strange that he devoted much time daily to meditation as well as prayer for the promised salvation of the errant Israel.

In a sermon delivered in Dundee, he stated that the gospel should be proclaimed in the first place to the sons and daughters of Israel. He then listed four reasons supporting this statement. In the first place, it was God's command, in the Old as well as the New Testament. Then there were the promises made to the friends of the old covenant people and the threats made to her enemies. Next, he mentioned God's love for His people, even during the exile. This same love is still evident until this day. In conclusion, the nation of Israel was important for the life and welfare of the whole world because she 'shall be as the dew of the Lord'.

The interest in Abraham's posterity was nothing new in Scotland. The well-known Samuel Rutherford wrote and spoke many times concerning an expectation that the Lord would have mercy on the remnant of Israel and reunite them with the

Gentile church. In a letter to Marion M'Naught, written on 7 May, 1631, Rutherford made a plea to pray for 'the incoming of the kirk of the Jews'. Thomas Boston delivered a sermon in 1716 in Ettrick as 'encouragement to pray for the conversion of the Jews', wherein he linked the outpouring of God's blessing on the church to the national conversion of the Jewish people: 'Are you longing for a revival to the churches, now lying like dry bones, would you fain have the Spirit of life enter into them? Then pray for the Jews. "For if the casting away of them be the reconciling of the world; what shall the receiving of them be, but life from the dead?" That will be a lively time, a time of a great outpouring of the Spirit, that will carry reformation to a greater height than yet has been.' M'Cheyne agreed with the same opinion, 'that we might anticipate an outpouring of the Spirit when our church should stretch out its hands to the Jews as well as to the Gentiles'.

It is not coincidental that the interest in foreign mission, a love for the Jewish nation and prayer for revival in his own land went hand in hand. It was precisely the hope of the English Puritans and the Scottish Covenanters of the seventeenth century, before the heyday of God's church on earth, that paved the way for the revival of the next century. The names of Edwards and Whitefield were inextricably linked with this latter revival. An open door to worldwide mission emerged from this future expectation and was compounded by a revival spirit. Men such as William Carey and Henry Martyn were soon followed by hundreds of other missionaries, who brought the gospel to lands as far removed as the islands of the South Pacific. M'Cheyne too was gripped by a zeal to proclaim Christ to the pagans, but he emphasized that the Jews should never be overlooked in the task of worldwide missions.

Since 1809 there had existed in England an interdenominational organization which was engaged in the salvation of the Jewish nation. It lasted until 1837. The General Assembly of the Scottish Church had appointed a commission to look into the welfare of the old covenant nation. Robert Wodrow, an elder from Glasgow, had presented a petition to the highest church assembly requesting a mission thrust to this nation. For years now, Wodrow was accustomed to praying and fasting in seclusion in order to seek God's face on behalf of the nation of Israel. At this time, days of prayer and humiliation were held, when God was beseeched above other things 'if the promised conversion of the old people of the Jews might be hastened'. Prayer meetings were held everywhere. Even a few Moderates gathered round, pleading with much enthusiasm for organized mission work to begin among the Jews in Palestine and elsewhere.

Many took up the task of writing on this subject. Chalmers, in his *Lectures on Romans,* defended the literal explanation of Romans Eleven. In 1839 a series of lectures concerning this topical subject was held in Edinburgh. A number of ministers dealt with aspects of the Jews' interests in the light of God's Word. Men such as Andrew Bonar, Charles J. Brown and Alexander Moody Stuart cooperated on this. The seventh lecture was delivered by Robert Candlish, who spoke on 'The intimate connection between the glory of the church in the latter days and the restoration and conversion of the Jews'. 'And,' he continued, 'then at last, the ancient people of God will appear as the centre of a happy world as bringing in, after many judgments, the glorious harvest of the Gospel. At last, after many fears and many disappointments, that harvest is secured.' What a glorious moment when 'the set time is come', that the Lord shows mercy on His Zion. The conclusion to his speech was inspiring: 'Let us reverently adore the unchangeable majesty of the eternal God and trust in His faithfulness. Our strength may be weakened in the way, our days may be shortened; but He is the same and His years shall have no end. The children of His servants shall continue and their seed shall be established before Him (Ps. 102). Amen.'

### The commissioning of four ministers

In October 1838, Frey, a converted Jew, preached in St Peter's.

M'Cheyne recorded in his diary: 'A Jew, Mr. Frey, preached in my church to a crowded house. Felt much moved in hearing an Israelite after the flesh.' The General Assembly appointed a committee of inquiry with this goal: the acquisition of information concerning the condition of the Jews in Palestine and Europe, and the enquiry into the possibility of establishing mission stations. M'Cheyne, was a member of the committee which had a hundred members. Initially, contact by correspondence was sought with the existing mission stations and consulates abroad. However, the need to review the condition of the Jews on the spot became apparent. Without this it would be impossible to obtain a true picture of the situation. Now that the pastor of St Peter's had to stay in Edinburgh for health reasons, he had time in which to become acquainted with the Jewish question. He held many discussions on this topic with Robert Candlish, who was appointed secretary of the sub-committee of the city. During a conversation between Candlish and Moody Stuart, it was proposed that M'Cheyne should also be permitted to travel to Israel. Perhaps it would improve his health if he experienced a change in climate, and at the same time there was the hope of his 'being useful to the Jewish cause'. This proposition appealed to him immensely, and when his doctor-friends were enthusiastic too, the decision was soon taken. Besides M'Cheyne, the deputation consisted of Dr Alexander Black, a professor of Theology at the Marischal College of Aberdeen, Dr Alexander Keith, minister from Cyrus and author of various books on prophecy, Andrew Bonar from Collace and Robert Wodrow from Glasgow. The last mentioned had to drop out because of health reasons, thus leaving four clergymen. The official charter of the General Assembly's appointment was dated 8 April 1839. The mission was 'to collect information respecting the Jews, their number, condition and character'. The church charged them 'to the favour of Him who is the God of the Jew, as of the Greek, the God and Father of all'. Before this parchment could be signed by the Moderator of the

Robert Smith Candlish D.D. (1806-1873). Alexander Keith D.D. (1791-1880)

The declaration as ratification of the deputation of the four ministers to Palestine, signed on 8th April 1839.

Assembly and the different sub-committees, the company of men had already departed and the Mission of Enquiry could commence.

**St Peter's disappointed**

St Peter's congregation was dismayed and disappointed when they heard of the proposed journey. The hope that he might speedily return was shattered. Who would take care of the flock during his absence? Where was the concern for his congregation, which he had so often evidenced in his pastoral letters? Was the decision not a premature one and made in haste? Bonar hesitated at first in accompanying the group on the mission to Israel, and wrote to his friend that he had great difficulty in leaving his congregation in Collace without a pastor. 'Now, to leave my people in this state seems to me like a shepherd, whose voice his own sheep know ... and then all at once leaving them to the danger of grievous wolves,' according to him, an impossible task.

M'Cheyne was resolute in his decision because he observed God's hand very plainly in the recent events. Could the Great Shepherd not ensure that his congregation be cared for in his absence? Many letters arrived at the postbox of his parental house. With great patience he picked up his goose quill to reply to them. Thus he wrote: 'Unless God had Himself shut up the door of return to my people, and opened this new door to me, I never could have consented to go.' He felt bound with strong bonds to his congregation, but His Father's will was still more important to him. '... God has very plainly shown me that I may perform a deeply important work for His ancient people, and at the same time be in the best way of seeking a return of health.' God's work is not dependent upon any human being. He spoke plainly to Bonar: 'I fear I will need to be a swift witness against many of my people in the day of the Lord, that they looked to me, and not to Christ, when I preached to them.'

His kirk session acted with considerable respect to the decision taken. In a long farewell letter from his elders dated

And now, what remains for us but for the present to say, Farewell. May the God of all grace & all consolation be the companion of your journey. May He refresh your soul by rich communications of His love. May He direct you in safety to the place of your destination: and when you first stand amidst the ruins of that once glorious temple, on that Mount Zion which was "beautiful for situation, the joy of the whole earth," may the Spirit himself come down upon you "as the dew of Hermon, and as the dew that descended upon the mountains of Zion: There may the Lord command the blessing, even life for evermore." Again, we commend you to the keeping of the God of Abraham, and of Isaac, and of Jacob; and with every expression of affection and esteem, we remain

Yours most sincerely

Peter Thomson, David Brown Elder, Alex Martin Elder, Alex Ogilvy, Thomas Mackay Elder, Geo Alexander, W Gibson Elder, James Hill Elder, David Baxter Elder, David Kay Elder, Joseph Thomson, James Thomson Elder, Wm Gibson, James Graham

Part of the letter of the Kirk Session of St Peter's before McCheyne's departure to Palestine.

Interior of the National Scottish Church in Regent Square London.

11 March, he was informed of their consent to his proposed journey. The cause of Christ was at stake and that wasn't limited to the city of Dundee alone. Before they placed their signatures at the foot of this sincere letter, they wished him God's blessing: 'May the God of all grace and of all consolation be the companion of your journey. May He refresh your soul by rich communications of His love. May He induct you in safety to the place of your destination, and when your feet stand amidst the ruins of the once glorious temple, on that mount Zion, which was "beautiful for situation, the joy of the whole earth", may the Spirit Himself come upon you "as the dew of Hermon, even the dew that descended upon the mountains of Zion: There may the Lord command the blessing, even life for evermore!" Again, we commend you to the keeping of the God of Abraham, and of Isaac, and of Jacob.'

A few elders came personally to bid their pastor farewell. Edward Caird's letter was particularly comforting, especially the beginning: 'The everlasting love of our Father be with you now and for ever, constraining you always to count all things but loss for the excellency of the knowledge of Jesus Christ and Him crucified, accounting it always as a faithful saying: "If we be dead with Him, we shall also live with Him, if we suffer with Him, we shall also reign with Him."' In his last pastoral letter (dated 20 March 1839) before embarking on the long journey, M'Cheyne pertinently addressed the condition of the many unconverted in his congregation rather than his preparations. His concern for them was greater; how many shall be saved at last? 'I cannot be blind to the many dangers that accompany foreign travel, the diseases and accidents to which we shall be exposed; but if, through your prayers, I be given to you again, how many blanks shall I find in my flock!'

The moment of departure was at hand. He had to arrange one further matter: He needed a substitute, who would be willing to accept the responsibility for his congregation in his absence. His attention was drawn to the young William Chalmers Burns, 'son of the minister of Kilsyth', who had recently completed his studies and had been given the authority to preach. 'He is one truly taught of God – young, but Christ lives in him.' Burns was actually at the time considering a missionary assignment to India. When M'Cheyne wrote that he was the answer to his prayers, he didn't dare to turn down the request. What must have been his thoughts, when the renowned and well-respected minister wrote to him: 'I hope you may be a thousand times more blessed among them than ever I was. Perhaps there are many souls that would never have been saved under my ministry, who may be touched under yours.' M'Cheyne could now depart with full assurance in his heart. His health improved somewhat. He wrote to Mrs Thain: 'I feel much better than usual today; but I have returns of my beating heart occasionally. When my heart afflicts me, I say to myself: Farewell, blessed work of the gospel ministry! happy days of preaching Christ and Him crucified! winning jewels for an eternal crown! And then again, when it has abated, I feel as if I would stand up once more to tell all the world what the Lord of glory has done for sinners.'

**The journey to Palestine commences**

On 27 March 1839, fully prepared, M'Cheyne made his way up the gangplank of the ship that was to transport him to London. A small gift Bible from the Thain family was a 'pocket companion for Immanuel's land'. His concerned father sent him a letter with a packet containing oddments for the journey. He thought it necessary to include a Scottish plaid; and he advised him to procure a travelling bag in which he could pack all his clothes so that he wouldn't become frustrated when he needed something. 'You will find your maps in the other portmanteau,' he added. He was afraid that Robert would be too tired in London, and wrote: 'seeing so many people and speaking so much will bring back your complaints. Can't you take things more coolly?'

On the way to London, he passed a rocky island named Bass-Rock, which reminded him of the Covenanter prisoners two centuries earlier who had suffered there. 'What a different voyage I and my brethren are going; not to be imprisoned for the truth, but to try and bring it within reach of the prisoners of Israel.' He noticed the sea-gulls following the boat: 'So my soul follows Christ, not as I would desire, for then I should never wander from Him.'

The other travel-companions arrived a few days later in London. On 9th April, a solemn farewell service was held in the Scottish Regent Square Church, where 'many converted Jews and friends of Israel were present'. Three days later the company sailed for France. When Robert saw the chalk-cliffs of Dover fading away in the distance behind him, he wrote: 'Who can tell when we shall look upon them again or in what circumstances – or if at all? We may see the shore of a better country – the true home, the heavenly – before then.' Thus the coast of his beloved country vanished beyond the horizon and he landed on the European mainland. His glimpse of the French capital city was both disappointing and saddening: 'There is a look of vice about the streets of Paris.... I do not think it can be lawful to be a Christian and live in Paris.' It was a great trial to his faith to spend the Sabbath in this worldly city, but fortunately for him he received relief when he listened to Frederic Monod preaching a sermon: 'To open the blind eyes' in the Huguenot Church.

The journey continued from there to Dijon, a city where approximately four hundred Jews lived; thereupon they departed for the Rhone River, which they followed until Marseilles. He enjoyed the splendid scenery, with its many vineyards. 'Some of the fields are ploughed in the circular manner, as in the Carse of Gowrie,' but where were the fertile fields, ploughed and sown by God's Spirit? On arrival in Genoa, M'Cheyne began a long letter to his sister Eliza. His thoughts were still back in Dundee: 'I am anxious to know how the sacrament was conducted in St. Peter's...; if there were marks of good done to perishing souls.' The Italian fare was certainly different from what he was accustomed to back home: 'It begins with different kinds of fish, then eggs dressed in various ways, then mutton, beef, chicken, messes without a name, young peas and potatoes of this year, oranges, figs, nuts, and fruits of all kinds; the only beverage was wine. How happy I shall be to get back to plain fare again. Oh, for a cup of tea!' He thought the Palace of Genoa was brilliant: 'O biache palazzo di Genova.'

**Landing in Alexandria**

On April 26, the ship raised anchor in the harbour of Leghorn, where they had met with some countrymen besides many Jews. From there they sailed for Malta. 'I am mercifully preserved in health, as are all my companions,' he wrote to his sister. 'Andrew is sometimes a little sick at sea, but it soon wears off. Dr. Keith hurt his foot in Paris, which troubles him a little. Dr. Black is indefatigable, and stands all his fatigues wonderfully.' The journey over the Mediterranean Sea continued on towards Alexandria, where the Scottish deputation landed on 13 May.

Mooring fast in this centuries-old city harbour was an experience in itself. 'You cannot imagine,' wrote M'Cheyne to his parents, 'it baffles all description: boys with donkeys, men with camels, wild-looking porters, Greeks and Turks, all roaring in sonorous Arabic, all eager to be at ourselves and our luggage!' The Scottish servants of the gospel viewed with amazement the bustling city life of the East. They attended a synagogue service in the city, where only ten Jews were present. At the conclusion of the service, they related how they 'had come from Scotland out of love to their souls. We spoke of Messiah, how He came the first time to die for sin, and is coming soon the second time to reign in glory'.

Islam reigned supreme in Egypt also. The ministers were astonished at the idols of Mahomet, the false prophet from Arabia, which held so many souls in their power. When, on 19 May, they were honouring the Sabbath rest and were passing the afternoon in the shade of some fig trees, they were all at once surrounded by twenty half-naked farmers. 'We felt it painful to be among these ignorant, miserable people, and not be able to tell them in their own tongue one word of the great salvation. It stirred us the more to cry, "Thy kingdom come!"' With great emotion M'Cheyne shouted: 'Oh that I could speak their language, and tell them of salvation.' They passed the fertile Nile delta, Damietta and Rosetta, and travelled in the direction of the Desert of Shur.

Now preparations had to be made for the journey through the desert. Clothes and blankets were purchased and 'nice pillows also which Jacob had not when he slept at Bethel'. Donkeys, riders and tents were hired. Two guides were to lead them: Ibrahim, 'a handsome small-made Egyptian' and Achmed the cook, 'a dark good-natured fellow with a white turban and bare black legs'. Thus 'the pilgrims' journeyed into the barren desert. In his thoughts, Robert saw his concerned mother sitting, while reading this letter: 'You will be anxious, my dear Mamma, but you must just be still, and know that God is.' Just as the cloud and fiery column preceded Moses and his followers, surely the protective angels would form a fiery wall around them. They followed the coastal region of what was formerly the land of the Philistines, in the direction of the promised land. The desert journey became an experience to be remembered. Concerning the solitude of the vast, sandy plains, M'Cheyne wrote: 'It is a remarkable feeling to be quite alone in a desert place; it gives similar feelings to fasting; it brings God near.... It is a strange life we lead in the wilderness. Round and round there is a complete circle of sand and wilderness shrubs; above a blue sky without a cloud, and a scorching sun.' He wrote to John Bonar in Larbert: 'I had no idea that travelling in the wilderness was so dreadful a thing as it is.'

On Saturday, 25 May 1839, they mounted their camels at sunrise. 'The sunbeams glanced along the level plain of the wilderness, scorching our hands and faces, for we were journeying nearly the east.' The heat increased as the hours passed and the slow gait of the camels 'often produced an irresistible drowsiness'. Suddenly the interpreter gave a cry; Dr Black had fallen from his camel into the sand. 'We immediately slipped down from our camels and ran to the spot.'

Map of the journey of the deputation to Palestine.

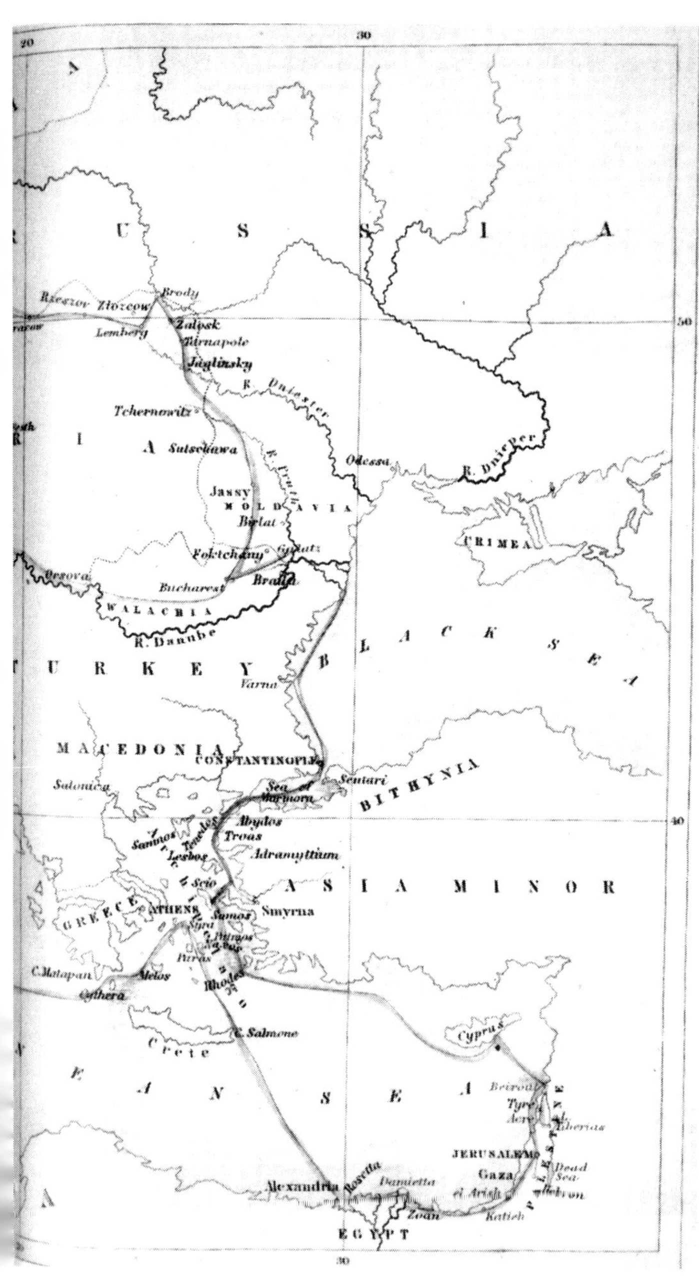
RUSSIA
Brody
Zloczow
Lemberg
Zalosk
Tarnapole
Tchernowitz
Sutschawa
R. Dniester
Odessa
R. Dnieper
R. Pruth
Jassy
MOLDAVIA
Birlat
Foktchany
Galatz
Bucharest
Braila
WALACHIA
R. Danube
CRIMEA
BLACK SEA
TURKEY
Varna
MACEDONIA
CONSTANTINOPLE
Salonica
Scutari
Sea of Marmora
BITHYNIA
Abydos
Troas
Lesbos
Adramyttium
ASIA MINOR
Scio
ATHENS
Samos
Smyrna
GREECE
Syra
Patmos
C. Matapan
Melos
Cythera
Rhodes
C. Salmone
Crete
Cyprus
Beirout
Tyre
Acre
Tiberias
JERUSALEM
Gaza
Dead Sea
el Arish
Hebron
Alexandria
Rosetta
Damietta
Zoan
Katieh
EGYPT

For a time he lay there unconscious, but slowly he came to. What did this accident signify? 'Is it a frown on your undertaking?' God's hand was certainly guiding them; He used this fall to open other doors.

Presently, the four neared the borders of Judah. What a happy Sabbath they celebrated on June 2, when together they sang from Psalm 76: 'In Judah is God known; his Name is great in Israel!' M'Cheyne wrote in his letter home: 'Singing praises in our tent is very sweet; they are so frail like our mortal bodies; they rise easily into the ears of our present Father. Our journey through the land of the Philistines was truly pleasant.' They continued farther through the valley of Aschalon, and they saw the hills of Judah looming up before their eyes. The landscape changed into 'wild rocks and verdant hills'. 'Wild flowers of every colour and fragrance scented our path.... The turtle's voice was heard in the land, and singing birds of sweetest note.' Only the wine grapes were missing; the land of milk and honey was wild and the fertile fields were changed into deserts. The landscape resembled to a greater extent the desolate glens of the Highlands than the fertile fields of the Carse of Gowrie.

**Jerusalem in sight**

It wasn't long before the city of Jerusalem appeared in sight. They beheld 'the city of the great King' for the first time on 7 June 1839. Dismounting from their camels at the Jaffa Gate, they withdrew for a few days to rest after the long journey. For M'Cheyne and his friends, the stay in this centuries-old city meant: 'One of the most privileged days of our life.' But where was the former lustre! 'It is indeed very desolate. Read the two first chapters of Lamentations, and you have a vivid picture of what we saw,' he related to his parents. The view of the city from the Mount of Olives was splendid. 'As you climb up that interesting hill, every step reveals new beauty in the daughter of Zion; or rather, you are forced to say, How beautiful it must have been! The valleys round it are so deep, the mountains so plainly standing round it on every side.'

They spent ten days in the old city of David and they never tired of looking at everything. Here the Saviour walked and here He underwent His vicarious suffering. 'We got a slight view of the Mount of Olives, as we rode toward the Jaffa Gate. The nearer we came to the city, the more we felt it a solemn thing to be where "God manifest in flesh" had walked.' The atmosphere of the city was sombre and poverty prevailed in the streets. From Mount Zion, M'Cheyne wrote to a friend on 12 June: 'We are living in one of the missionaries' houses on Mount Zion. My window looks out upon where the temple was, then beautiful Mount of Olives rising behind. The Lord that made heaven and earth bless thee out of Zion.'

Happily, they met people of the same faith in the idolatrous city. On a number of occasions they visited the house of the English consul, Mr Young, and made the acquaintance of the missionary, Nicolayson, who supplied them with all the information they required. The enmity amongst the Jews was greater in Palestine than in other countries. It was an impossible task for the London Missionary Society to work here. In the city there lived approximately ten thousand Jews, most of whom originated from Mid-Europe and Spain. Generally speaking, they were strictly orthodox and were awaiting the coming of the Messiah. There was great poverty among them, and they were pleased with the British support. The Turkish Governor, who ruled the country, was more liberal than his predecessor had been; he had for the first time in centuries opened the tomb of David to the Jews. The Christians, such as the Roman Catholics, the Greeks and the Armenians, demonstrated greater hatred towards the Jews than did the Moslems.

For five hours Nicolayson helped in answering questions the Scottish Commission had submitted to the delegation. Besides the social condition of the Jews, they wished information on their relationship with Christendom and how mission work was carried out here in the recent past. The London Missionary Society began there in 1820; a Swiss clergyman by the name of Tshudi distributed Bibles. Nicolayson arrived there in December 1825, and his work bore fruit here and there. The first converted Jew was a rabbi, Joseph; he was an educated young man, who subsequent to his conversion had to suffer so much indignity that his baptism had to take place in Constantinople. The Scots were also fully enlightened as to the means which Nicolayson had at his disposal.

It was a pleasure for the tired ministers to take a rest in his house on Mount Zion, where they visited the many sacred spots of the city. They were astonished by the many idols. Fortunately, the memory of their precious Master, who shed his blood here, was uppermost in their minds. A highlight for them was the commemoration of His death in an upper room. Nicolayson preached from 1 John 1:3, 'Truly our fellowship is with the Father, and with his Son Jesus Christ.' Dr Keith shared the symbols of bread and wine and Andrew Bonar preached from John 14:2, 'In my Father's house are many mansions.' 'Feelings of deepest solemnity filled our hearts while we worshipped in an upper room, after such a feast where we had been showing the Lord's death "Till He come" and "His feet stand upon the Mount of Olives". And it was with more than ordinary fervour that we joined in the prayer that Israel might soon have their solemn feasts restored to them.' Having sung the conclusion from Psalm 116 together, they returned by way of Mount Zion and saw the Mount of Olives in the distance, 'on which the last rays of the evening sun were pouring their golden lustre.' When would the Sun of Righteousness rise over Jerusalem?

### At Jacob's well

With regret they bade farewell to the old City of David. Passing through Samaria, they couldn't omit a visit to Jacob's well at Sychar, where Jesus had met the Samaritan woman. It was 20 June when they arrived there. Jacob's well was actually a cave, where indispensable water had bubbled up for centuries. Andrew Bonar wished to descend into the well, but in his endeavour, lost his pocket Bible. 'He could not get it again,

David Roberts (1796-1864), painter who visited Palestine in 1838/1839. He made drawings for reproductions in lithography. He intersected the whole country and left in May 1839 to London, just in the same year that the 'four' made their journey.

Panorama of Jerusalem, after a litho of David Roberts, taken from Mountain of Olives.

"for the well is deep".' This occurrence inspired M'Cheyne to write a poem. Had they now lost their compass for good?

My own loved Bible, must I part from thee,
Companion of my toils by land and sea;
Man of my counsels, soother of distress,
Guide of my steps through this world's wilderness ...

M'Cheyne not only had the Word on paper, but also hid it in his heart. This travel-companion could not get lost, because he kept it as an everlasting treasure. The well-known places of 'the promised land' were but reminders of the precious Word of God. His only comfort was to be found not in buildings of wood and stone, but in the Word of Life, the Word of the crucified and risen Saviour. Thus he could say:

When through the lonely wilderness we strayed,
Sighing in vain for palm-trees' cooling shade,
Thy words of comfort hushed each rising fear,
The shadow of Thy mighty Rock is near.

The Mount of Olives and Sychar focused his thoughts on his Master, but He was no longer to be found here. He is sitting at the right hand of His Father and shall return once more, and hence the conclusion:

Sweet record of the past to faith's glad eyes,
Sweet promiser of glories yet to rise!

They spent one week at the foot of Mount Carmel. 'I plucked a rose of Sharon for you, and concealed it under my saddle,' related M'Cheyne to his sister in the next letter. 'I am of the opinion that the rose of Sharon is the splendid rhododendron, which blooms there in magnificent profusion.' He couldn't help adding: 'It is like Christ, altogether lovely.' While viewing the blue mirror of the Mediterranean Sea, he wrote several letters

Jacob's Well, after a litho of David Roberts.

to his homeland. Of course, he also wrote a lengthy letter to his father and mother, which included a detailed report of his vicissitudes. He had written his last pastoral letter to St Peter's from Leghorn on 2 May 1839, so that he now omitted to write to his congregation. He also wrote to his colleague, John Roxburgh, and to his friend, Robert Macdonald. To the latter he offered an impression of life in the desert: 'Our life in the wilderness was a singular one. Since the day I wrote you, we have never known the luxury of a bed. We spread our mats upon the sand, and God watches over us when we are under the cover of our frail tent as much as if we were within brazen gates and bars. We often hear the cry of the wolves at night; and there are many lynxes and hyenas in this mountain; but God keeps us safely. The burning heat of the desert, the long fatiguing journeys – sometimes twelve hours or fourteen in the day upon a camel – the insatiable thirst, and our weakness, were very trying to our faith and to our temper; it proved us and made us know what was in our heart. Ah, dear friend, wherever we journey, union to Jesus and holiness from His Spirit flowing into us, is our chief and only happiness.'

On Mount Carmel, where once Elijah had prayed, M'Cheyne found a welcome rest. His reflections were focused on the work of his Saviour, whose desire and will it is to sanctify His children. He wished to draw from the source of His merit alone. Here he was inspired to write a poem on the waters of Siloam, in which he remembered to make a personal application:

O grant that I, like this sweet well,
May Jesus' image bear,
And spend my life, my all, to tell
How full His mercies are.

**In Beirut**

The journey continued. From Haifa they travelled by boat to Beirut. Dr Black's health wasn't satisfactory. During the journey through the desert he had been in a state of torment; thrice he had fallen off his camel, and he had suffered heat exhaustion. It was thus decided that he and Dr Keith would make a premature return journey via the Danube, possibly visiting a number of synagogues along the Rhine. Black preached on Romans 5:1, after which he and Dr Keith boarded a steamship bound for Smyrna.

The remaining touring party of two persons walked from the harbour to the mission house. 'Mr. Thomson preached in deeply toned Arabic to an attentive audience of about 130, gathered out of many different countries. There were two Armenian bishops, with clean, venerable beards ..., Greeks and Greek-Catholics, an Abyssinian Christian, and a Druse, converted Jews, American Presbyterians and Congregationalists, and ministers of the Church of Scotland – all different in name, and yet, we trust one in Christ.' The sermon having been concluded, the company celebrated the Lord's Supper in an upper room. 'This was a well of living water at which we were strengthened for our coming journey, and refreshed after the departure of our elder brethren.'

In Beirut, they met up with a converted Jew, Erasmus Calman, who had Palestine at his fingertips and moreover could speak Arabic, Polish, German and English. He offered to accompany them further on their journey. 'With tears on both sides', they took leave of their guides, Ibrahim and Achmed. They had met very few converted Jews. The Jews mistrusted the Christians, especially the Roman Catholics, because of the indignity and persecution they had suffered at their hands for centuries. The friendliness with which the Scottish clergymen treated them fell mostly on good soil and removed all their mistrust.

The Palestinian Jews were certainly better off than their Eastern European counterparts. The British were on the whole highly esteemed by them. Moses Montefiore, both Jew and president of the English Board of Deputies, supported the colonization of Palestine and organized aid for the oppressed

Sir Moses Montefiore (1784-1885).

Lake of Galilee, after a litho of David Roberts.

Jewish people in Damascus and Eastern Europe. The Scottish delegation visited this well-to-do personality on the Mount of Olives in Jerusalem, and met him also during the quarantine on Mount Carmel. Dr Keith tried to steer the conversation around to the already fulfilled prophecies of the Old Testament, but when he proceeded to implicate the gospels and the apostles, it seemed as if Moses wanted to hear no more. This all goes to show that the Lord alone could remove the veil from the heart.

From Beirut they traversed the land in a southerly direction. The deputation visited every city and town in Palestine inhabited by Jews, excluding Jaffa and two small cities. Before they set course for Galilee, they travelled through the mountainous region of Lebanon. These mountains impressed M'Cheyne and reminded him of an essay on 'its scenery and allusions', a description which he had once written as a student for the Exegetical Society. Here he also made mention of Song of Songs 4:15: 'A fountain of gardens, a well of living waters, and streams from Lebanon.' Surely 'the subterranean streams' were a type of 'the unseen supplies of grace, and the well of living water which is in the believer springing up to everlasting life'.

**At Lake Galilee**

To view Lake Galilee was a wonderful experience for the remaining two travellers. His friend, Alexander Somerville, had to sense the atmosphere of this unforgettable event: 'Oh, what a view of the Sea of Galilee is before you, at your feet!... The lake is much larger than I had imagined. It is hemmed in by mountains on every side, sleeping as calmly and softly as if it had been the sea of glass which John saw in.' Many images from the Bible entered his mind here! How could he omit taking up his pen at the very place where his beloved Master had so often tarried? He wrote his poetic lines concerning the Sea of Galilee on 16 July.

How pleasant to me thy deep blue wave,
O sea of Galilee!
For the glorious One who came to save.

One day previously, he had described His Saviour's watch over His disciples' unstable boat in the midst of a storm which had descended upon the lake, as follows:

So have I seen a fearful storm
O'er wakened sinner roll,
Till Jesus' voice and Jesus' form
Said, 'Peace, thou weary soul.'

It was most refreshing to bathe in the clear water of the lake. However, they had to continue on their way. They traversed through the land of Galilee and visited Nazareth, Nain, Cana, Capernaum and other places of interest. A curious Bedouin neared their tent and M'Cheyne could not resist sketching his portrait. By way of Mount Tabor, they set off in the direction of the coast. At the foot of the mount lay six or eight men, who all of a sudden stood up. They stormed down on the Scots, brandishing heavy sticks, but when they saw that the Europeans were not bent on robbing them, they let them pass. At the seaport of Acre they were afforded a magnificent view of Mount Carmel. The sound of the crashing waves elicited the following lines from M'Cheyne's poetic spirit:

O Lord, this swelling, tideless sea
Is like Thy love in Christ to me;
The ceaseless waves that fill the bay
Through flinty rocks have worn their way,
And Thy unceasing love alone
Hath broken through this heart of stone.

This love would in God's time reach the hearts of many thousands of hostile Jews. Trusting in the promise that the

Lord would show mercy on the remnant of Abraham's posterity, he wrote:

> Though scattered now at Thy command,
> They pine away in every land,
> With trembling heart and failing eyes,
> And deep the veil on Israel lies,
> Yet still Thy word Thou canst not break,
> 'Beloved for their father's sake'.

In the belief that the God of Abraham, Isaac and Jacob would return to 'Immanuel's land', the two friends set out once more 'into the coasts of Tyre and Sidon'. It wasn't easy to bid farewell to this country, where 'every hill and valley of which tells of the wonders God hath done'. Beirut once more appeared within view. Here they waited for the Austrian steamer which would set sail on 28 July. In the meantime, the two companions enjoyed the beautiful city. Robert wrote to Eliza, 'I have seldom seen a more lovely place than this.' Now he had time to rest up and catch up on his correspondence. He longed to know how things were faring in Dundee. He also wrote a letter to his friend, Mrs Coutts of Edinburgh. This energetic lady had so longed to accompany them to Palestine. Of course, he greeted her friend, Miss Collier, at the same time: 'Remember that this letter is half to her and half to you. I can never forget her; and hope she still holds up the hands of my successor as she did mine, by the prayer of faith.' He sent a long letter to his friend, 'Alex' Somerville. His mood was sombre with respect to the condition of the Jewish nation, but regarding the country he was enthusiastic: 'I can only say, like the Queen of Sheba, that "the half was not told me".'

The time had arrived to bid farewell to the coasts of Palestine for good. The steamer lay at anchor and ready to set sail for Smyrna. M'Cheyne was in poorer health than on his arrival. During the journey through Palestine he was often exhausted from the heat of the sun and the long expeditions they had to make. In a wonderful way, he was sustained and received renewed strength every day. Even his spiritual condition didn't suffer as a result of the circumstances of the journey. Despite the fact that he felt so tired at evening time, he always looked for an opportunity to pray. His communion with God remained undisturbed. He searched for a cool place under the trees to find solitude with his Saviour. He could 'lie almost speechless for half an hour; and then, when the palpitation of his heart had a little abated, would propose that we two should pray together'. Bonar observed that: 'The fountain springing up unto everlasting life (John 14:14) in his soul, welled forth its living waters alike in the familiar scenes of his native Scotland, and under the olive-trees of Palestine.' He never neglected to pray during his hours of seclusion. Even in a foreign country his life was hidden with Christ in God.

**M'Cheyne becomes ill**

When M'Cheyne embarked for the return journey, he was feverish. In Beirut he had visited a young man from Glasgow who had a fever, and soon he contracted the same fever. The doctor advised him to undertake the journey despite his illness, because he supposed that the fresh sea-wind was better than the heat of the city. But when the ship moored in Cyprus, the fever took a turn for the worse and he became unconscious for several hours. His friends were concerned about his condition and saw how he was tormented by severe headaches. In the end, he hardly spoke. For three days they sailed across the sea, without a physician's help. Only once did the sick man lift up his eyes: when he lay on deck and beheld the Island of Patmos in the distance. It was here that the apostle John received a wonderful revelation of Christ, who appeared to him in glory. The fever took a turn for the worse and it seemed as if he would not again be aroused from his sleep. Would he make it to Smyrna harbour? 'They helped me,' thus he wrote later, 'on deck under the awning; but I felt as I never felt before. I knew I had a Father in heaven who had forgiven and redeemed me, and therefore I resolved to fear no evil.'

On their arrival in Smyrna, he was carried from the ship and taken to an inn. The innkeeper, Salvo, was a man with a kind heart. The walls of the room were extremely thin, the atmosphere was stuffy and the noise of the seamen and other guests caused him continual irritation. He was very happy when he found a quiet shelter in the house of an English chaplain by the name of Lewis, in nearby Bouja. Here he was surrounded by loving care. The Lord raised him up from his sickbed. He later spoke with gratitude about his stay in Bouja; he used to say 'it was his second birthplace'.

Above all else, God's Word was as a medicine for his spirit. He received much comfort from the words of the psalmist: 'Blessed is he that considereth the poor: the LORD will deliver him in time of trouble.' Didn't this text apply to his compassion for suffering humanity? A word from the Psalms, whispered in his ear by his friend Andrew: 'And call upon me in the day of trouble: I will deliver thee, and thou shalt glorify me,' was to him 'as the drop of honey to Jonathan'. The Lord remained by his side, even when he was fearful. He wrote to Somerville: 'My mind was very weak when I was at the worst, and therefore the things of eternity were often dim. I had no fear to die, for Christ had died. Still I prayed for recovery, if it was God's will.'

During his time of sickness, he was not only caught up with his own needs, but he also wrestled 'to pray for a blessing' on behalf of his congregation in Dundee. He wrote to his house doctor, Dr Gibson: 'I really believed that my Master had called me home, and that I would sleep beneath the dark green cypresses of Bouja till the Lord shall come, and that they that sleep in Jesus come with Him; and my most earnest prayer was for my dear flock, that God give them a pastor after His own heart.' However, his work in St Peter's was not yet finished, hence the day of his death had not arrived. The Lord revealed in the midst of all these dangers the truth of Psalm 91: 'For he shall give his angels charge over thee, to keep thee in all thy ways.'

**Smyrna**

The city of Smyrna reminded him of one of 'the seven churches of Asia'. He recalled the Bible classes on 'the happy Thursday evenings', when he had lectured on the subject of these churches. The two companions had no opportunity to visit all of them, but they enquired after their condition which, for the most part, showed no signs of true Christianity any longer. His outlines on the seven churches, which appeared for the first time in 1843, contained a serious warning to all of lukewarm Christendom, which had lost all the splendour of godliness. The weed of Islam had overgrown all but the leftovers of the true faith in this region. Was one of the possible causes not a lack of vigilance and perseverance?

While passing the coast of Troas they recalled the Macedonian man, who from Europe called out to Paul in the spirit: 'Come over and help us!' The ship sailed through the Bosphorus and across the Black Sea towards the Danube. They intended to visit the most important Jewish centres of Eastern Europe on their return journey. It was as if the appeal, 'Come over and help us!', sounded this time from the mouths of the descendants of Abraham. These people were certainly in great need! The massacres had broken and persecuted them, but they weren't destroyed. Despite all the setbacks, the God of Abraham watched over them. This was beyond M'Cheyne's and Bonar's comprehension. Their journey through 'the countries of darkness and of shadow of death' in the vicinity of the Danube confirmed that God would not violate His faithfulness to Israel. They visited Moldavia, Walachia and Austria. The spiritual poverty amongst both Jews and Gentiles appalled them. M'Cheyne tried here too to establish contacts and enter into conversations with the Jews. With Hebrew Bible in hand, he walked up to them and mentioned a text such as: 'In that day there shall be a fountain opened to the house of David and to the inhabitants of Jerusalem' (Zech. 13:1). When would the promised day dawn when they would bow down before the Messiah?

For more than two months they would still be separated from their beloved homeland. The weather was totally different from that of the Middle East. In Bucharest M'Cheyne bought a 'cloak of fox-skin', which kept him 'quite warm night and day'. In Jassy they attended a wedding, which event he related in a letter to Eliza. A description of the bride's finery was accompanied by a sketch. He added mischievously, 'You see what a lesson of modesty the covered faces teach our Scottish brides.' In Austria he was astounded at the idolatry of the Roman Catholic faith. He was shocked, too, by the many crosses and images of Mary, which were plainly visible along the roadside. Indeed the treatment they received in this land was disappointing.

In Poland, M'Cheyne made the acquaintance of two shepherds who apparently wanted to rob him. They assaulted him, and after a struggle enduring fifteen minutes, he lay somewhat stunned on the ground. The ruffians suddenly stood up and within minutes had vanished into the bush. What they were up to, he couldn't say; but he felt that it was God's hand that had protected him.

Poland harboured at this time the most Jews, but the Christians made no attempt to win them to the faith. The darkness of Rome held the Polish people captive in complete ignorance. While attending a church service, where the farmers kissed the image of the Saviour, they were compelled to recall Martin Boos, a pastor from Bayer, who lived at about the turn of the century. While remaining faithful to the Roman Catholic Church, with blessing he proclaimed the Reformed teaching in a remote village! Many times M'Cheyne referred to him in his sermons, as well as in a pastoral letter which he wrote from Leghorn. 'Oh that God would raise up another Martin Boos in this region of gross darkness, to proclaim the glad tidings of righteousness by the obedience of One!' When they celebrated the Lord's Supper with five others in Cracow, the former capital of that country, it was as if they were in a peaceful oasis.

The tired Scots were relieved to be able to rest up in the

Prussian Upper Sylesia. M'Cheyne wrote his congregation a letter from Breslau, which he had begun in Cracow and later completed on 16 October. For five months now he had received no news from Scotland. On a number of occasions subsequent to his last letter from Leghorn, he had taken up his pen to inform his congregation of his vicissitudes. 'At the foot of Mount Carmel I began one letter to you, and again in sight of the Sea of Galilee I began another, but neither did I get finished.' Yet his congregation was never out of his thoughts for one moment. 'In the wilderness, in Jerusalem, beside the Sea of Galilee, at Smyrna, on the Black Sea, on the Danube – you all have been with me. I have, day and night, unceasingly laid your case before God.' He related how he had been rescued from the robbers and his wonderful recovery from a fever. 'I am persuaded we have been watched over by our all-loving Father, who is the hearer of prayer!' It was of great encouragement to him to know that his congregation kept him in their prayers. He certainly longed to be in their presence once again and to proclaim the gospel in St Peter's.

**Good news!**

Finally, the long journey drew to an end. In Hamburg, where they were to embark for London, a surprise awaited them. They could scarcely believe their eyes when they read in the newspapers that a revival was taking place in their country. Their eyes grew bigger at the news that Dundee was included. No better news could have reached their ears. Without them even having suspected anything, the Lord had visited His vineyard. He had heard the prayers of the young St Peter's pastor in a wonderful way. It was no wonder that his longing to see his congregation grew stronger still. The Lord had visited his church in Scotland. He hoped fervently that 'good has been doing in our Church, and the dew from on high watering our parishes, and that the flocks whose pastors have been wandering may also have shared in the blessing'. It was certainly striking and 'it appeared also worthy of special notice and thanksgiving, that God had done this in the very year when the Church of Scotland had stretched out her hand to seek the welfare of Israel, and to speak peace to all their seed.'

On 6 November 1839, the ship sailed up the Thames River, and from London the two companions travelled to Edinburgh. The subcommittee for the Jewish Mission awaited them in the Tolbooth Church, where at that time the General Assembly met together; here they rendered a detailed report of their journey. Dr Candlish's St George's Church was overcrowded when M'Cheyne climbed the pulpit. With much emotion and libertys he spoke on 'our debt to Israel', according to Romans 1:16: 'To the Jew first.' Emphatically, he fixed the congregation's thoughts on the duty of bringing the Jews into contact with the Christ of the Scriptures. 'They are ready to perish – to perish more dreadfully than other men. And have you none of the bowels of Christ in you, that will not run first to them that are in so sad a case?' Was Scotland aware of the many privileges she enjoyed? 'In many respects, Scotland may be called God's second Israel.... No other land has the gospel preached, free as the air we breathe.'

The following still applied, 'Beginning at Jerusalem.' The conversion of the old covenant people was not far off. It was necessary to pray fervently for an outpouring of God's Spirit, not only over Scotland, but also over the remnant of the house of David. The Lord has opened 'a peculiar access to the Jews'. It was a marvel that M'Cheyne and his companions could speak to so many of them. 'In Jerusalem and in Hebron we spoke to them all the words of this life. In Sychar we reasoned with them in the synagogue and in the open bazaar. In Haifa, at the foot of the Carmel, we met with them in the synagogue. In Sidon also we discoursed freely to them of Jesus. In Tyre we first visited them in the synagogue and at the house of the rabbi, and they then returned our visit; for when we had lain down in the khan for the heat of midday, they came to us in crowds. The Hebrew Bible was produced, and passage after passage explained, none making us afraid. In Saphet, and Tiberias, and

Acre we had the like freedom. There is indeed perfect liberty in the Holy Land to carry the gospel to the Jew.'

**Arrival in Dundee**

The congregation of St Peter's longed for their pastor's return. In a letter dated 15 November, M'Cheyne had informed Burns of his arrival. Now that he had heard reports of the great blessing the Lord had poured out on His congregation, it was his fervent desire to know more. 'I cannot rest till I hear from you what has been done among my dear flock. You remember it was the prayer of my heart when we parted, that you might be a thousandfold more blessed to the people than ever my ministry had been.' It was no wonder he wanted to know if this wish had been fulfilled.

At last the time had arrived. 'The first sight of Dundee was animating and refreshing to me; and I felt wonder and thankfulness at the way by which God had led me since I last bade it farewell.' Many stood waiting for him at the harbour. His beadle, James, was the first to jump on board to greet him. In addition, his elders, Mr Neilson and Mr Thoms, and Alexander Thain, and his friend and colleague, Robert MacDonald from Blairgowrie, stood on the quay. A procession proceeded from Perth Road to the manse. It was a Thursday afternoon, and that same evening the prayer meeting was to take place. It seemed as if the tired pastor was to be afforded no chance to recover. He certainly had much to assimilate on his arrival, now that he had heard of all the miracles the Almighty had accomplished in their midst. To see his congregation once more was an unforgettable experience. The church building was overcrowded, and even the steps leading to the pulpit were occupied. The introductory song moved him: he read from Psalm 66 and the sound of many voices was 'so tender and affecting, as if the people felt that they were praising a present God'. The congregation sang in a different way than he was previously accustomed to and it couldn't have been any different! Had the Spirit entered into the dead bones? When he left the church to go home, he had to make a way through the crowd. Much jostling took place as everyone sought to shake his hand. It was as if they wished that he would say one more word to them, and he acquiesced. On arrival home he could do no more than speak from his heart, 'To Thy Name, O Lord, be all the glory'.

M'Cheyne and his friends had accomplished their mission. Black and Keith would arrive some time later in Scotland, because they had to stay over in Budapest for a time due to sickness. Later, Bonar and M'Cheyne would put together a detailed report of their travels that would be printed and read by many thousands. Their journey had stimulated the interest among 'the beloved for the fathers' sakes'. The Irish Presbyterian Church joined with her sister church to emphasize the importance of the mission to the Jews. Thus Bonar and M'Cheyne wrote in the conclusion to their travel report: 'And all who take pleasure in tracing the steps of the Son of man, as he walks amidst His golden candlesticks, cannot but thank God that these two churches have now come forth in their full evangelistic character – preaching Christ and Him crucified to their people at home, and stretching out their hands abroad, with the offer of the water of life to the distant Gentiles and the dispersed of Judah.' The four companions had collected a great deal of information concerning the Jewish condition in Palestine and the Diaspora. They advised beginning with a mission in their own country, because the circumstances here were the most favourable. The Scottish Church focused its attention, however, first on Eastern Europe. Daniel Edward was the first missionary to the Jews. Commissioned in 1841, he worked with much blessing in Jassy, Lemberg and Breslau. He maintained a regular correspondence with M'Cheyne. In the same year, John Duncan was commissioned to work in Budapest. To the latter's first converts belonged the well-known Adolph Saphir and Alfred Edersheim. Thus the work of M'Cheyne and his three colleagues was not in vain.

With emotion, the Scottish Church General Assembly took

note of the report of the four ministers. M'Cheyne's countenance glowed because of the love he felt, and his soft voice trembled when he related to 'the fathers and brethren how his heart burned within him to communicate the vivid feeling of compassion given to himself by seeing the dry bones in the open valley, very many and very dry'. Then while absolute silence reigned, the last words of his glowing speech sounded: 'Shall we be ashamed to drink deeply of the same spirit of which the mighty Paul drank, and to have the same heart? Shall we not wish that every Christian in Scotland might love as Paul loved and pray as Paul prayed?'

Was it not the selfsame spirit that spoke through the words of the Saviour, who wept over Jerusalem from the Mount of Olives? 'If thou hadst known, even thou, at least in this thy day, the things which belong unto thy peace! but now they are hid from thine eyes.' Imbued by the same spirit of compassion, M'Cheyne wrote a poem from a Hebrew song, of which the first and last couplets rang:

Rock and Refuge of my soul,
Swiftly let the season roll,
When Thine Israel shall arise,
Lovely in the nations' eyes!

Rock and Refuge of my soul,
Swiftly let the season roll,
When Thine Israel shall be,
Once again, beloved and free.

# Chapter 10

# STREAMS OF BLESSING

### The necessity of revival

'Every means will be in vain until He pours the Spirit down (Isa. 32:13, 15): "Upon the land of My people shall come up thorns and briers", until the Spirit be poured upon us from on high.' We may preach publicly, and from house to house; we may teach the young and warn the old, but all will be in vain. Until the Spirit be poured upon us from on high, briers and thorns shall grow. Our vineyard shall be like the garden of the sluggard. We need that Christ should awake; that He should make bare His arm as in the days of old; that He should shed down the Spirit abundantly.' These are M'Cheyne's words as he makes an urgent appeal for revival. The prayer of the psalmist who penned Psalm 85 is on his lips: 'Wilt thou not revive us again: that thy people may rejoice in thee?' A revival is necessary, for ministers as well as for the Lord's people, for 'those that were awakened, and have gone back', and for 'barren fig-trees'.

He looked forward to a time of revival and his desire was:

'Oh, lift up your hearts to the Lord for such a time. Plead earnestly the fulfilment of the promise, "I will pour my Spirit upon all flesh." Then this wilderness will become a fruitful field, and its name be Jehovah-Shammah – the Lord is there.' The provision of God's promises is an encouragement to look for revival: 'For I will pour water upon him that is thirsty, and floods upon the dry ground: I will pour My spirit upon thy seed, and My blessing upon thine offspring.'

M'Cheyne lived in the days of fulfilment. The Lord had visited his heritage with his abundant blessings. In a Bible teaching on Matthew 11:20-24, he observed that 'Dundee has been exalted to heaven'. He pointed to the great privilege that would be apportioned to Scotland in comparison with other parts of the world. He had himself seen how 'almost all Asia is sunk under the wicked delusions of Mohammed, or under the idolatries of Paganism. Oh, what grace is it to pass over the fairest provinces of the world, and come to the bleak island, with an open Bible, a quiet Sabbath, and a preached gospel!' The history of his country, in no uncertain manner, demonstrated God's continual care and immense mercy. 'We have had more of the Holy Spirit poured out than ever Capernaum had. I do not know that any country in the world has been visited in this way, as Scotland has been.'

Then he related a few revivals from the past. 'The first remarkable time in Scotland was from 1625 to 1630, when for five years there was an open window of heaven over Scotland.' Men such as David Dickson and John Livingstone were instrumental for an eternal blessing to many hundreds of souls. The next great revival took place in the year 1742, 'when the windows of heaven were opened over Kilsyth and Cambuslang', as well as other areas. 'The third time of love in Scotland was from 1798 to 1800, when the parish of Moulin and some neighbouring parishes were visited in a remarkable manner.' Then came the last outpouring of God's grace: 'The last is in our own day, beginning in 1839, when God opened the windows of heaven.' Thus Dundee too was raised to the skies.

## Dundee richly blessed

On his arrival back from Palestine in November 1839, M'Cheyne became immediately aware that an unusual movement of God's Spirit was at work in the city. Bonar observes that 'the cry of His servant in Asia was not forgotten'. It was while he was seriously ill during his stay in Smyrna that the revival proper began. As he lay before the portals of death, the blessings were being poured out on his congregation. God's work was not dependent on M'Cheyne, or on anyone, for that matter; He wished to make it known that He needed no man. 'He could send forth new labourers and work by new instruments, when it pleased Him.' It was his replacement, William Burns, that He used to 'open the floodgate at Dundee as well as at Kilsyth'.

It was the striking text from 2 Chronicles 5:13 and 14 that M'Cheyne chose for his sermon on the Sunday after his arrival back at St Peter's. It dealt with the dedication of Solomon's temple, to which the ark of God was conveyed. Then this 'wonderful text, "So that the priests could not stand to minister by reason of the cloud: for the glory of the Lord had filled the house of God." ' Apparently a new era had dawned for St Peter's. Many who then heard M'Cheyne remembered years later the impressive conclusion to this sermon, which in summary ran as follows: 'Dearly beloved and longed for, I now begin another year of my ministry among you; and I am resolved, if God give me health and strength, that I will not let a man, woman, or child among you alone, until you have at least heard the testimony of God concerning His Son, either to your condemnation or salvation. And I will pray, as I have done before, that if the Lord will indeed give us a great outpouring of His Spirit, He will do it in such a way that it will be evident to the weakest child among you that it is the Lord's work and not man's.'

Was M'Cheyne not jealous when he understood that in a few months the inexperienced William Burns had received so much blessing on his work? People were afraid that a spirit of envy would prevail amongst members of the congregation. Some said: 'I am of Paul; and I of Apollos; and I of Cephas.' Bonar was convinced that his friend 'had received from the Lord a holy disinterestedness that suppressed every feeling of envy'. It was only God's grace that gave him such an attitude, because M'Cheyne too was a human being, full of sin and shortcomings. He told his friend, James Hamilton, that many were disappointed on his return because they preferred to listen to Burns. This was a lesson to him because he had to acknowledge that 'his sin had been to idolize his congregation, and he felt their estrangement a rebuke from God'. 'My congregation was my idol, I used to think that there were no people like them in the world.' He was too attached to his congregation. He could certainly witness to an amazing, tender presence of God's Spirit when he spoke in St Peter's. While he was leaving Abernyte on one occasion, he said to Hamilton, 'I would beg my bread to get preaching in Dundee.' Now he had to learn that there were other sheep: 'And other sheep I have, which are not of this fold; them also I must bring.' The work of revival wasn't limited to his own congregation alone, but later spread to other places.

God's work wasn't disturbed by bitter rivalry amongst His servants. Burns himself preserved the spirit of gentleness, and evinced a great respect for the St Peter's pastor. M'Cheyne's evaluation of him, when he heard him preaching for the first time, spoke volumes: 'His manner is very powerful – so much so, that he sometimes made me tremble.' Burns had kept him informed of the work of God in his congregation on his arrival back in Edinburgh after the journey to Palestine. His letter, dated 18 November 1839, witnessed to an attitude of humility and worship. The Lord had poured out his blessing beyond all expectations and prayer. His task in Dundee was terminated. 'It will be painful for me to part with your people; but it will be as pleasant as it could be made when I leave them in your hands as their pastor under the chief Shepherd. I pray, as many of them are doing, that your expected meeting with them on

Thursday night may be blessed for the awakening and conversion of many souls. Your letters when absent were much blessed, and not least the two last, which, though they contained less perhaps that was directly hortatory, yet, coming at a time when little goes far, they were the means of awakening some that I have met with. But most of all do I believe that your prayers for your people have been answered in this work of the Lord. Indeed, I do not know how far dependent it may be all found to be on your wrestlings in the Holy Spirit in behalf of your flock, both while among them, and while absent on the Lord's chosen errand.' William Burns was enabled to deny himself, because the honours did not fall to him. The conclusion to his letter in this regard is clear: 'Glory, glory, glory to the Lord Jehovah! "Ye angels that excel in strength, praise Him!" "Come, Lord Jesus, come quickly!" '

**William Burns**

William Chalmers Burns was two years younger than M'Cheyne. He was born in Dun, in Angus-shire, where his father was minister. When he was six years old, the family moved to Kilsyth, a town north of Glasgow. Subsequent to his conversion, he felt called to the ministry. His heart went out to mission work among the heathen. Later, he would go as a missionary to China where he would also, with tireless zeal, win souls to Christ. He, like the pastor of St Peter's, had a heart full of love for fellow sinners. Not long after his conversion, he met his mother in Glasgow, on an extremely busy street. William was deep in thought and therefore failed to notice her. When she began to walk alongside him and to talk to him, he awoke from his meditation and called out, 'O mother, I did not see you!' He was occupied with the immortal souls of people in his midst and their eternal state burdened him.

After M'Cheyne left for Palestine, Burns began his work at St Peter's. The letter which he received from M'Cheyne in Edinburgh on 22 March 1839, was meant to put new heart into him. 'The prayerful are praying for you. Be of good courage; there remaineth much of the land to be possessed. Be not dismayed, for Christ shall be with thee to deliver thee.' The first sermon which he delivered on the first or second Sabbath in April, dealt with Romans 12:1: 'I beseech you therefore, brethren, by the mercies of God, that ye present your bodies a living sacrifice, holy, acceptable unto God, which is your reasonable service.' This truth was prophetical for his ministry and future life. It was an attentive congregation which filled the church building. His words were 'as pins and needles' to stimulate his congregation. There were elderly Christians in St Peter's who later related how their hearts trembled when he stepped into the pulpit of their beloved teacher. The people listened with rapt attention to this young candidate's words.

William Chalmers Burns in Chinese dress. He left in 1847 for the Far East for a missionary task, which had been on his mind for years before.

An elder in the congregation described his ministry thus: 'Scarcely had Mr. Burns entered on his work in St. Peter's here, when his power as a preacher began to be felt. Gifted with a solid and vigorous understanding, possessed of a voice of vast compass and power unsurpassed ... and withal fired with an ardour so intense and an energy so exhaustless that nothing could dampen or resist it, Mr. Burns wielded an influence over the masses whom he addressed which was almost without parallel since the days of Wesley and Whitefield.' From every part of the entire region, people came to the church in Perth Road to hear him preach. In this manner, the young preacher quickly gained their affection.

Burns wrote to his sister on 10 April from his temporary address at 'Seafield Cottage' concerning his first impressions. 'I am not left without many circumstances to encourage me in my arduous labours; not a few hearts seem in a good measure prepared to hear the gospel as the Word of God, and some I have met with whose experience in the spiritual life afford the strongest stimulus to my own growth in grace.' With zeal he visited the sick, taught the youth and prepared his sermons. He spoke to two young people concerning the work of God in their hearts and prayed for them. They wished to attend holy communion. One of them had much difficulty with doubt concerning the genuineness of faith and the other related what a blessing M'Cheyne's preaching had been to her. He wondered at the clear sign of grace that he noticed in some of them.

Thus he looked up James Wallace, a sick youth of twelve years, from Paton's Lane, in whom he observed the true work of God in an amazing way. He asked him a few questions: 'What he needed from Christ.' He said, 'Redemption.' 'Tell me some of the particular things you need.' 'A new heart and right spirit, deliverance from temptations, the world, and the devil.' 'Can Christ give you these great things?' 'Yes.' 'Why can he do so?' 'He is the Saviour of sinners.' 'Do you love Christ?' 'Yes.' 'Why?' 'Because He loved me.' 'Who has taught you?' 'The Holy Spirit.' 'Did you seek Him first, or did He seek you?' 'He sought me; "I am found of them that sought Me not." ' 'Can you ever praise Christ enough?' 'No.' 'Would you like to sing His praise in heaven?' 'Yes, forever.' There followed many more questions, which the youth humbly and respectfully answered.

Burns had much contact with the elders of St Peter's. We read in his diary, 18 April, that he breakfasted with P. H. Thoms, where he also met Mr and Mrs Parker from Aberdeen. Apparently, it was Gavin Parker who was minister of the Union Terrace Chapel. We also read on this day that he accompanied another elder, by the name of Andrew Neilson, to his house. On the same day he met Robert Macdonald from Blairgowrie and 'walked with him to Mr. Thains's'. Later he met the Thain family also in Blairgowrie, and spent one Sunday in 'Heath Park'. He felt quite at home: 'Mrs. Thain is, I think, a truly pious woman, and both she and Mr. Thain with all the family are most kind and interesting.' Their son, Alexander, who would later become a clergyman, lay in bed with scarlet fever; 'on Sabbath night he was very anxious to see me regarding the state of his soul; however, we were afraid to increase the fever, and I only stood at his bedside and repeated a few of the invitations to Christ for all.'

The communion services in St Peter's were welcome times. Cumming and Grierson were present to examine the young candidates who wished to be admitted to the sacrament. Burns spoke to them earnestly; some received a token and some were refused admittance. He realized how necessary the work of God's Spirit was in renewing the people's hearts. 'Oh, what need of the powerful presence of the Holy Ghost, without whom a free Saviour will, and must be, a Saviour despised and rejected of men! How hard it is to unite in just proportions the humbling doctrine of man's inability to come to Christ without regeneration, and the free gospel offer which is the moral means employed by God in conversion! Oh, Spirit of Jesus, my Saviour, lead me, a poor, ignorant, and self-conceited sinner, to the experience of this great mystery of grace, that I may know how I ought to declare Thy glorious gospel to perishing fellow sinners! Amen.'

It dawned on Burns more and more that a revival was necessary. He not only addressed this theme, but it also burned within his soul. This fire stirred him all the more when he read the well-known book, *Fulfilling of the Scripture,* by Robert Fleming. 'But O for a revival of that experimental deep-laid religion which Fleming valued and exemplifies so fully in his pages! "Awake, awake, O arm of the Lord! awake as in the ancient days, in the generation of old."' His longing for the outpouring of God's Spirit in the church became stronger by the day: 'Come from the four winds, O breath, and breathe on these slain that they may live.' Would the Lord use him for this work? He didn't view himself as possessing the capability. When he heard that someone was awakened by his sermon on Psalm 71:16, he wrote: 'O marvellous grace, that the Lord should regard at all my carnal, self-seeking ministry; to Him be the glory eternally.... Lord Jesus, the good Shepherd, lead this wandering sheep to Thy fold; even now do Thou fan into a flame by the quickening breath of Thy Spirit that smoking flax which Thou hast touched with the heavenly fire of Thy matchless grace, and give me grace – the grace of the indwelling Spirit to fit me for feeding the lambs and tending the sheep. Thy blood and obedience freely offered to sinners of the deepest dye, are all my pleas with the Father. Come, Lord Jesus, come quickly, and cause many to say with hearts smitten with the rod of Thy strength, "We would see Jesus". Amen.'

Burns noticed with pleasure that the Holy Spirit blessed his work in Dundee during the first few months. The people were gripped by his sermons, but he observed many shortcomings and imperfections in his work, which made him feel dissatisfied. On the other hand, he had something to thank the Lord for, because he wrote thus: 'During the first four months of my ministry which were spent at Dundee, I enjoyed much of the Lord's presence in my own soul, and laid in large stores of divine knowledge in preparing from week to week for my pulpit services in St Peter's Church. But though I endeavoured to speak the truth fully, and to press it earnestly on the souls of the people, there was still a defect in my preaching at that time which I have since learned to correct, namely, that partly from unbelieving doubts regarding the truth in all its infinite magnitude, and partly from a tendency to shrink back from speaking in such a way as visibly and generally to alarm the people, I never came, as it were, to throw down the gauntlet to the enemy by the unreserved declaration and urgent application of the divine testimony regarding the state of fallen men and the necessity of an unreserved surrender to the Lord Jesus in all His offices in order that he may be saved.'

In his pastoral conversations, Burns discovered 'that there were not a few to whose conversation, as well as to whose minds and hearts, their own state as sinners under the glorious dispensation of divine grace was become familiar'. Pricked by an arrow of conviction of sins as a result of either his or M'Cheyne's sermons, they felt the burden of sin pressing down on their souls. 'I almost immediately invited from the pulpit all those who were under any anxiety about their souls, and who might wish private direction, to call on me at particular hours for this purpose. And I soon learned from the intercourse to which this led in many instances, that the necessity of union to Jesus, and entire dedication to His service and His glory, was a truth to which the mind of the congregation in general had been brought under your ministry.' The plough of the law had struck many souls, but there was still no power to bring forth a new birth. The workings of God's Spirit down the church aisles were hidden for a long time. Burns focused especially on those convicted souls. With encouragement from God's children he held many conversations with them during the first four months of his stay. This work was also instructive for him: 'I prosecuted my labours among them ... here with great benefit and pleasure to myself, and not without a pleasing testimony in the consciences and hearts of many of the people of the Lord, that I was really teaching some part of the truth "as it is in Jesus".'

Thus Burns grew in his knowledge of his St Peter's 'sheep'. He noticed with gladness that 'many seemed interested, and some of the people of God appeared to be refreshed'. Yet initially there were only a few who were touched in their hearts by his preaching. He faithfully preached his Sabbath sermons and attended the prayer meetings on Thursdays. He was pleased that the men's and women's groups continued to meet together as had formerly been the case. He was shocked by the thought that 'there were hundreds in the congregation and parish, who, with a name to live, were in reality "dead in trespasses and sins".' He knew, without a doubt, of only two or three persons who were touched by his sermons. 'They came to me in anxiety for direction in the way to Zion. I sought to declare the truth of God, both in the law and the gospel, with all faithfulness on every occasion, and to "labour fervently in prayer to God" in behalf of the people at all times; but still there was no appearance of a general awakening among them to the sense of their natural state of sin and misery, and of their absolute need of the glorious Saviour who is offered freely to sinners in the gospel. I always felt as if the ground which was won from the enemy on the Sabbath was lost during the following week.'

Although there was movement in the bones, the breakthrough was yet to come. A few praying societies did meet together to beseech God for revival. 'There appeared to be an increasing earnestness in desire and prayer among the people of God, and especially, I think, among the younger Christians.... They beseeched for a larger outpouring of the Spirit of God, and a more general awakening and converting of souls to Jesus.' He spoke with a woman who told him that she noticed several persons weeping tears on the Sabbath. Burns also noticed a more than unusual earnestness amongst the youth. 'One young man in particular, who has since, I trust, been savingly converted, wept profusely while I was pressing the necessity of a full and immediate acceptance of the Lord Jesus.'

**Revival in Kilsyth**

Burns departed for Kilsyth on 16 July to assist his father during the communion service. There too the stirrings of God's Spirit were noticeable. Approximately one hundred years previously, a general revival had taken place here under the preaching of James Robe. On the commemoration day of Robe's death, his father, William Hamilton Burns, roused his congregation to entreat the Lord to repeat the occurrences in Kilsyth once more. The interest in eternal matters increased. God's people were revived, and prayed continually for streams of blessings to be poured out.

The young Burns preached on Psalm 110:3 the Monday following the celebration of the Lord's Supper: 'Thy people shall be willing in the day of thy power.' He didn't realize that the day had dawned for Kilsyth. When he related, during the application of his message, what great things the Lord had done in the past, there arose an unusual agitation among the people. Burns emphasized with great earnestness that they should be reconciled to God. It was as 'the rushing mighty wind of Pentecost'. Many could no longer control their feelings, and 'broke forth simultaneously in weeping and wailing, tears and groans, intermingled with shouts of joy and praise from some of the people of God'. Many appeared to be struck by convicting power in their hearts. 'Some were screaming out in agony; others, and, among these strong men, fell on the ground as if they had been dead.' Burns had to end his sermon prematurely. 'Such was the general commotion, that after repeating for some time the most free and urgent invitations of the Lord to sinners, I was obliged to give out a psalm, which was soon joined in by a considerable number, our voices being mingled with the mourning groans of many prisoners sighing for deliverance.' More souls were touched through one sermon than was the case for many years previously. The entire city was under the sense of this movement. Did this mean the dawning of a new day for Scotland? Would the sun now shine through all the haziness?

Parish Church, Kilsyth.

The Spirit moved through Kilsyth. Burns was compelled to remain here for three weeks. 'I returned to Dundee on Wednesday, 8 August. In my absence Mr. Lyon, missionary at Banton, in the parish of Kilsyth, came over to Dundee and officiated for me.' In his thoughts, he was still in Kilsyth and, strictly speaking, he didn't expect the revival to spread to St Peter's. 'I was in some degree kept from entertaining by a full conviction that the work at Kilsyth was almost entirely dependent for its origin on the prayers of God's people there, which had been for some time incessant and most fervent; and that it was in a very inferior degree, indeed, connected with any particular instrument employed in preaching the gospel. I entertained perhaps less hope of an outpouring of the Spirit on the people at my return; also, because I was inclined to think, as other people thought, that I must be exhausted by the incessant labours of the preceding fortnight, and that I had rather the idea of taking rest on my return, than of then beginning, and from that time continuing to labour day by day as constantly, and in the same glorious and blessed work, as I had been engaged in at Kilsyth.'

**Revival at St Peter's**

How God's thoughts differ from a man's! Rightly, the news of the occurrences in Kilsyth caused feelings to run high. Bonar wrote: 'All Scotland heard the glad news that the sky was no longer as brass, that the rain had begun to fall. The Spirit in mighty power began to work from that day forward in many places of the land.' At the end of the service, Burns related what had happened to him in Kilsyth and what miracles the Lord had done. Those who saw the need of an outpouring of God's Spirit were invited to remain behind. Approximately one hundred people availed themselves of the opportunity and when Burns addressed them with an earnest word, 'Suddenly the power of God seemed to descend, and all were bathed in tears'.

The following evening there was a prayer meeting in the church. 'There was much melting of heart and intense desire after the beloved of the Father; and on adjourning to the vestry the arm of the Lord was revealed. No sooner was the vestry door opened to admit those who might feel anxious to converse, than a vast number pressed in with awful eagerness. It was like a pent-up flood breaking forth; tears were streaming from the eyes of many, and some fell on the ground, groaning and weeping, and crying for mercy.' From this night on, for several weeks, prayer meetings were held on a daily basis. The fire of the movement struck other churches in the city, such as St David's and the Hilltown church. The entire city of Dundee was moved; it seemed as if it was being transformed.

Margaret Sime was very young when Burns came to Dundee, but she remembered well, at a later date, 'the first night it took place, on a Thursday night in August 1839. The good news spread over the city like fire, and every night, and sometimes in the morning, for many weeks, the church was crowded with seeking souls, and the young people came in great numbers. I was among them, sitting at the foot of the pulpit stairs. It was then that the Spirit of God began His work of convincing me of sin. I can remember weeping bitterly about my soul being lost, and I was often in the enquiry room, sometimes till one o'clock in the morning. Although I could not lay claim to any special text at that time as the means of my conversion, the Holy Spirit of God so drew me and showed me Jesus as the Saviour of sinners, and blessed be His name, He has never left me from that day to this, although I have often grieved Him. It is all due to free sovereign grace. Amen.'

Not everyone was happy that the revival had come to the city. Many believers themselves doubted whether it was genuine; the godless obstinately continued in their sinful ways, 'breathing out threatenings'. However, the work of God continued – in churches, gardens, houses and in open fields. In fact people were praying everywhere; sometimes some would spend the entire night in supplication to the Almighty. Complaints were heard, but also the singing of psalms of praise. There was both sadness and joy. Souls were set free from their bonds of sin and unbelief and rejoiced in God's redeeming grace. Entire households came to believe in the Saviour. It happened in Dundee as we read in Zechariah 12:11: 'In that day shall there be a great mourning in Jerusalem.' It was an unforgettable spectacle: especially the awakened souls who stood night after night before the church doors, to ensure that they would find a seat. Once the services were over, they still would not go away, but instead encompassed the leaders and elders to ask for counsel. Hundreds of souls were starving for the Bread of Life; they came also from the outskirts and surrounding towns to find food for their hungry hearts.

Burns was unable to meet all their needs and thus sought help from elsewhere. At the end of August, William Reid from Chapelshade Chapel and Horatius Bonar from Kelso preached in St Peter's. The church was filled to capacity. Reid preached on a Wednesday evening 'in a very searching manner on regeneration', and Bonar followed him with a message from Job 22:21, 'Acquaint now thyself with him, and be at peace'. It was eleven o'clock when Burns prayed and concluded the meeting. The following evening James Hamilton from Abernyte

St Peter's about 1900.

took over, and this time spoke on the rich young man. Thereafter Burns read about the revival in Kilsyth in 1742. The following evening, John Baxter from Hilltown preached 'with much more solemnity and more of the freeness of the gospel than usual, from Jeremiah 35:15'. Again Burns read to them concerning Kilsyth, and in conclusion addressed Roman Catholics and 'our duty towards them'. The following Thursday he was called to a certain mother of a Roman Catholic family, who was seriously ill. She had summoned the priest, but he could offer her no peace.

Burns spoke a timely word. Not only did the usual churchgoers attend the services, but brazen sinners too. Some drunkards took leave of 'their cup of poison' and their hearts were touched. Indifferent sinners were found on their knees, crying out for mercy; the most hardened were converted.

Thus the work of God's Spirit continued. On 28 August Burns recorded the following: 'On Saturday evening the congregation was large. I preached with considerable assistance from God on Psalm 32, particularly with a reference to the day of fasting, humiliation, and prayer, which by the recommendation of the session I was to intimate for Tuesday, the fair-day. On Sabbath forenoon I preached with much of God's presence and power from John 4:10, and in the afternoon with still greater liberty from Romans 8:34. In the forenoon the church was densely crowded, and in the afternoon every corner was filled, so that I could not, without much difficulty, force my way to the pulpit; hundreds were forced to be excluded. I never felt so powerfully as in the afternoon, the absolute certainty of the believer's acceptance as righteous through Jesus; and the people appeared to be much impressed, although I have not yet heard of any cases of awakening or conversion. In the evening I thought it better not to preach, in order to save my bodily strength for preaching in the Meadows, as I had intimated I would; but being told that a great crowd was assembled, I ran up to renew the charge on Satan's host.... When I went up however, the multitude was dispersed, and we would have given up thoughts of preaching had not a few pressed us to go on.' Thus Burns preached together with P. L. Miller, who would one year later be inducted by M'Cheyne in Dundee. The people continued to come in droves when both teachers spoke, and when they departed the influx didn't cease.

**Expansion of the work**

The church buildings in Dundee seemed too small to contain the great number of interested persons. The large city pastures had to offer relief, and the news that a gathering would take place there on Tuesday spread through the city like wildfire. The city authorities, however, put a hold on the works. Burns discovered a letter at home which prohibited him from preaching in the Meadows. He wrote: 'Which did not surprise me, but led me to meditate solemnly on that approaching conflict with the world and Satan in which many will probably be called to die for the name of Jesus. O Lord! may Jesus Christ be magnified in me whether by life or by death!'

The crowd that had flooded into the meadow were told that the gathering wouldn't take place there after all; but, the churchyard of St Peter's offered relief! Here the day of fasting was held; it became a richly blessed gathering. A long procession made its way to the churchyard in Perth Road, where many had already gathered together. Baxter opened the service with singing and prayer, after which Burns addressed the large crowd. 'I think the Spirit of God was much among the people of God on this occasion, filling them with joy and wonder at the free and infinite love of Jehovah.' 'I was led to speak in very plain terms of many prevailing sins, and especially of the peculiar sins of the fair-day. I had great liberty from the Spirit of God, I believe, to tell all I knew of the truth on these points, and O, may the Lord greatly bless for His own glory all His own truth which any of His servants have spoken, and pardon through the blood of Jesus all that we have said of our own invention, according to the darkness and folly of carnal reason.' Miller and Walker from Edinburgh also spoke on this unforgettable day.

The revival continued into September. The fire seemed inextinguishable. Many ministers came to Dundee to observe with their own eyes the heavenly miracles. Thus, Alexander Somerville and John MacDonald, the well-known 'Apostle of the North', arrived at the city on the Firth of Tay. Cesar Malan from Geneva, in Switzerland, visited Burns unexpectedly. He was accompanied by Robert Haldane, the Scottish lay preacher, who at the time gave the initial impetus towards a revival in Calvin's city. Malan preached on the words of the Saviour: 'Peace I leave with you.' He strongly emphasized the duty of believing in Christ, as revealed by God's plain testimony. In this way, the weeks went by in Dundee St. Peter's was filled with many souls eagerly desirous of salvation, as well as guilty consciences in the light of God's holy law. The influx of hearers was so great that Burns had to look for a larger church building, which he found in St David's. Since June of that year, George Lewis had been minister there. He spontaneously placed the largest church building in the city at their disposal.

In contrast to M'Cheyne, William Burns experienced his days of spiritual darkness. He would be off his stroke that he dared not ascend the pulpit. The adversary tried to persuade him that he would dishonour God in his speech. Fortunately, the bonds broke once he began to speak. Thus, more and more he learned dependence on his Master. During the months that the revival progressed so powerfully, relief came to his soul. With great joy he saw God's blessing descend on him. He received extraordinary strength to work day after day in God's vineyard. He was often physically exhausted, but again and again he received renewed strength. At the end of one week of continuous work he wrote: '20 minutes to 12 – when this week is expiring, I would again, with praises which must echo through all the arches of heaven, set up my Ebenezer and say, Hitherto the Lord hath helped me! O, what a week of mercy and grace and love! Last week was wonderful, this is much more so; what will the next be? Perhaps it may be with Jesus in glory! O, that it may at least be with Jesus, and that it may redound to the eternal glory of His grace in me and many thousands of redeemed souls! Come, Lord Jesus, come quickly! O scatter the clouds and mists of unbelief, which exhale afresh from the stagnant marshes in my natural heart, the habitation of dragons, and pour afresh upon my ransomed soul a full flood of Thy divine light and love and joy, in the effulgence of which all sin dies, and all the graces of the Spirit bloom and breathe their fragrance!'

Love's fragrance filled many hearts in Dundee. During October, the revival reached a climax when arrangements were made to have Holy Communion. John MacDonald, the minister from the Highlands, who was a blessing to many thousands, including the remote islands of the Hebrides and St Kilda, knew what leading a revival entailed. On 10 October, Burns and MacDonald met at 'Mr. Thains's gate' and thence went to the place of meeting, 'praying each by himself for the solemn work of the evening'. There was such a sense of unity and love. The tables were arranged in St David's. The ministers, Horatius Bonar from Kelso, John Bonar from Larbert, Robert Macdonald from Blairgowrie and Alexander Flyter from Alness, spoke at the Lord's table where the hungry souls were seated, 'many of whom seemed burning with desire after nearness to Jesus'. On this particular evening, three congregations were present, one gathered in the church building and two in the adjoining school classrooms. It was a blessing to experience the nearness of God's love during the ministry of the sacrament.

**M'Cheyne's return**

The day of M'Cheyne's return from Palestine drew near. We have seen how Burns kept him posted concerning the events of this wonderful revival. How happy he was when he received a letter from his colleague! His diary spoke volumes: 'Had a letter from dear Mr. M'Cheyne, written in a spirit of joy for the work of the Lord, which shows a great triumph, I think, of divine grace over the natural jealousy of the human heart. O Lord, I would praise Thee with all my heart for this, and would entreat that when Thy dear servant the pastor of this people is restored to them, he may be honoured a hundredfold more in winning souls to Christ than I have been in Thine infinite and sovereign mercy. Amen.'

When the ship which had conveyed M'Cheyne moored in Dundee harbour, Burns wasn't present to welcome him. However, the following day, at half-past six on 23 November 1839, he met him in the manse. 'I had a sweet season of prayer with him before the hour of the evening meeting. We went both into the pulpit, and after he had sung and prayed shortly, I conducted the remaining services, speaking from 2 Samuel 23:1-5, and concluding at ten. We went to his house together and conversed a considerable time about many things connected with the work of God, and his and my own future plans and prospects. I found he preached to a densely crowded audience on Thursday night, and with a very deep impression, from, "I am determined to know nothing among you," etc.' What a meeting in the congregation of St Peter's after an absence of so many months! M'Cheyne was tired by reason of the journey, but not exhausted spiritually. Bonar wrote about him: 'He seems in but weak health, and not very sanguine about ever resuming the full duties of a parish minister. O Lord, spare Thy servant, if it be for the glory of Thy Name, and restore his full strength that he may yet be the means of winning many souls for Jesus. Amen.'

M'Cheyne resumed once more his pastoral duties. He was grateful for what Burns had meant to his congregation during his absence, but above all for God's wonderful deeds. One month later he thanked his friend once again for the work he had accomplished in St Peter's. 'My dear brother, I shall never be able to thank you for all your labours among the precious souls committed to me; and what is worse, I can never thank God fully for His kindness and grace, which every day appear to me more remarkable. He has answered prayer to me in all that has happened, in a way which I have never told any one.' On the final day of that memorable year, he wrote to him:

'stay where you are, dear brother, as long as the Lord has any work for you to do.' At this time, Burns was in Perth, where a revival was also going on, whereby the hearts of hundreds of souls were touched. He had become a tireless evangelist, sowing the seed of the gospel whenever he had the opportunity.

Before his departure for Palestine, M'Cheyne had thought he was well acquainted with his congregation. He often fancied that his preaching bore little fruit. Now he realized that far more souls had come to the faith through his ministry than he had ever previously dared to imagine. 'I find many souls saved under my own ministry, of whom I never knew before.' Had the Lord in His wisdom purposely hidden this from his eyes, so that he would not pride himself in what God had accomplished through him? Now he discovered 'the bread that he had cast on the waters' a few years previously. Thus he fell upon the one surprise after the next. 'I have seen many of the awakened, and many of the saved; indeed, this is a pleasant place compared with what it once was. Some of the awakened are still in the deepest anxiety and distress.' Guiding these sinners who sought purpose in their lives demanded much wisdom and caution. M'Cheyne was not accustomed to laying hands on anyone hastily. If his counselling led to no more than a conviction of sin, then he tried to discover what was the cause of the hindrance. Horatius Bonar told him that many didn't come to faith: 'They think that coming to Christ is some strange act of their mind, different from believing what God has said of His Son.' He noticed that some of the awakened returned to their old ways. The seed was sown in their hearts, which had caused some concern and movement, but there was no power to be regenerated. Soon it seemed the revival had reached its climax and that its power was beginning to wane.

M'Cheyne followed up the permanent fruit with great interest. The plentiful rains were necessary to water the plants, so that they would find more assurance. The means of grace was present in great proportions and the Holy Spirit's dew was certainly not lacking. Yet, there was a great need for aftercare. The faithful shepherd visited many homes in the West End to offer counsel, especially to the fainthearted, so that they might grow up in the knowledge and grace of Christ. What happened in St Peter's resembled the time subsequent to the outpouring of the Holy Spirit at Pentecost, when much love was evident among God's children. The prayer meetings, in particular, awakened the fires of love. Prior to the revival taking place, a few of these meetings had been held in the congregation. Now he observed that there were 'thirty-nine such meetings held weekly in connection with the congregation, and five of these were conducted and attended entirely by little children'. Many young hearts were drawn to Jesus through the preaching of Burns and others. 'God has so greatly honoured their labours, that many children, from ten years old and upwards, have given full evidence of their being born again,' related M'Cheyne.

He was indeed pleased to meet so many children, in whom the work of God was so wonderfully displayed. Besides the many whom he admitted to communion, he met many on the street, in their houses or at Sabbath School. He was often amazed at the answers they gave to his questions. 'One eleven-year-old, is a singular instance of divine grace. When I asked if she desired to be made holy, she said, "Indeed, I often wish I awa, that I might sin nae mair." A. L. of fifteen is a fine tenderhearted believer. W. S., ten, is a happy boy.'

**Prayer meetings**

Was A.L, whom he mentioned, perhaps Alexander Laing, a young boy of fifteen years old who lived on the east side of 'Miller's Wynd, Hawkhill'? His house was no more than a *auld clay biggin*, the mud-hut of a stonemason. His mother had died nine years before, and his sister Margaret had been left with the task of caring for her brothers, Alexander and Jamie. She feared the Lord; the hearts of both brothers were touched during the revival. Alexander was sad that his younger brother backslid with the passing of time, until the Lord overcame his obstinacy. We shall hear more of him later, but it is important to know that Alexander, the simple sailor, held meetings in the attic of his parental house. As with the other prayer meetings, the pastor of St Peter's wished to learn more about the children's evening meetings which took place in this poor house.

Alexander wrote the teacher a short letter, in which he explained in broken English the reason for their gathering. It was the beginning of December when this scrap of paper was delivered to the manse on Strawberry Bank. He first informed M'Cheyne that the Lord had delivered him from hell and that he needed to read, speak and pray with a few young people 'I hope that by the power of Jesus and the words that we read I hope that He will put it to the hearts, for He hath said where there is two or three meet in His Name there will He be in midst of them.' Alexander had brought together no group in his own name, but he had called them on the strength of God's promises alone. He pointed out still more Bible texts to show that meeting together to pray was no mere human matter, but a command of Christ Himself, who has promised not to

Beloved if God first Loved us
we ought also to Love one another
grace be with you mersy and
peace from the father and from
the Lord Jesus the son of the
father in thruth and Love
and we have our Meetings
on monday and on Saturday
nights no more at present but
remains your servent
Alexander
Laing

End of the letter from Alexander Laing.

Pray for us & we will pray for you
I am by the Grace of God [illegible] what I am
My fellow Brother that helps me
John Smith. Thomas Brown
We hope that you will visit us any week night, send answer
with the Bearer when you will come. Isles Lane, Hawkhill, Dundee
183[illegible]

End of a letter, written by John Smith and Thomas Brown in December 1839, referring to their Prayer Meeting.

withhold His merciful blessings from such. Thus he led the prayer and singing 'with no little fervour and unction', as reported in the Dundee newspaper by a visitor to this prayer group more than sixty years later. Every young person was invited to pray out loud and if the person didn't dare, then he asked him 'to say aloud the Lord's prayer from the heart'. He led the prayer gatherings out of love for those who followed the same Saviour. In conclusion, he wrote that the meetings were held on Monday and Saturday evenings.

At the same time, two boys, Tom Brown and John Smith, knocked on the door of the manse. The manservant opened for them and escorted them to the kitchen, whereupon he walked down the passage and knocked on the door of the minister's study. Tom and John had brought a letter, which they handed over to their beloved teacher. The latter wished to learn more about the prayer meetings which they had organized. 'He came to us wearing a dark dressing gown, and received our paper; but I cannot recollect any more – perhaps the excitement had driven the remainder of the interview out of my mind,' thus wrote Smith years later. Tom Brown lived in the Small's Wynd orphanage and he led the gatherings for a small number of boys and girls in Isles Lane. At first they met in a remote place, but later they managed to obtain a room, and they were permitted to use a classroom of a school building as well. Margaret Sime relates later that these youths 'often led the meeting with great power in prayer'. A group met together nearby the manse as well, concerning which someone commented: 'A young girl, one of the party, led in a prayer most beautifully, and so the blessed work commenced amongst us, when our young hearts were thrilled.' However, Tom's group was larger. This appears to be the case from the names that were written in the letter to M'Cheyne in decorative style. John's father had probably written it as he had mastered the art of calligraphy.

The names of eighteen boys and twelve girls were written in two columns. John Smith had written the letter and Thomas Brown was 'my fellow brother who helps me'. Or was it the

List of Boys and List of Girls.

| List of Boys | List of Girls |
|---|---|
| James Dow | Isabella Oliver |
| David Robertson | Mary Dow |
| George Guthrie | Isabella Smith |
| Alexr Gilchrist | Agness Smith |
| William Gilchrist | Isabella Guthrie |
| David Edwards | Mary Yule |
| John Stewart | Mary Bell |
| William Mude | Kity Stewart |
| James Reid | Ellison George |
| James Smith | Mary Bruce |
| John Reid | Elizabeth Reach |
| Thomas Stewart | Agness Robertson |
| David Sim | |
| William Wright | |
| John Bell | |
| Alexr Boulfoure | |
| Peter Smart | |
| James Nicoll | |

Peter Stewart
Margret Tosh
Alison Scott
Jane Croll
Jean Balfour
Margret Sime
Maryann Langlands
Helen Kidd
Margret Scott
William Smith

Those attending the Childrens Prayer Meeting, in a letter of 9 December 1839.

other way round? In any case: the teacher was also welcome to attend their gatherings. 'None of the members are above fourteen years of age.' They gathered together every evening at six o'clock. 'In our meeting we pray for you and for him,' the latter referring to William Burns. It must have been moving for M'Cheyne to read that it was children who pleaded with the Lord to open the door of His Word, that he might 'speak the mystery of Christ'. 'The Lord says that He loves prayer meetings, I love them that love me and they that seek Me early shall find me'; that was, according to both youths, the reason for their gathering. The psalmist confirms this does he not, 'The Lord commanded the blessing'?

There was another meeting of young children of approximately twelve years of age. Margaret Sime's father took over the lead of this children's group, which met in his own house, 'on the Sabbath night after the Sabbath School'. 'I remember Mr. M'Cheyne visiting us one night, and he spoke from Proverbs 9:13 to the end – a very solemn warning: "A foolish woman is clamorous: she is simple, and knoweth nothing'", thus wrote Margaret later. How would he explain this text to the children? She asked a year later to be permitted to participate in communion when she herself was barely twelve years old, as did other children from this group. On 9 December 1839, the children wrote a long letter to their pastor. 'We will tell you first its rising and second of the manner it is conducted.' At Sabbath School they heard about 'the chains in which Satan held his slaves and then of the love of Christ in breaking the chains. Then we felt we had been bound with chains and many of us burst in tears and we met in our house to pray that God breaks these chains.' They were told that they were too young to pray together, so they looked for a place in the open air, 'until Thomas Sime, one of our teachers, gave us his house.' This was in Wattstreet, Hawkhill, not far from Tom Brown's group. They prayed to the Lord to bless the preaching and the Sabbath School lessons, read portions from the Bible and sang psalms. The letter concluded by listing twelve children's names.

Then there was another letter from Agnes Crow, who reminded M'Cheyne of his words, that his church 'may become a Bochim or place of weepers; and since the Spirit of God came among us with power and brake the rocky hearts in pieces on many the tears be felt down the cheek that never was seen to weep for sin before'. She also gave expression to 'the boundless love of God in Christ' to deliver sinners from their sin. Mrs Likely told him of a small gathering of women around her sickbed, and rejoiced in the 'many brought to Christ of whom Mr. Burns never knew, and a great number more under your own ministry'.

Andrew Cant, together with James Paton, led 'a meeting held for praise, prayer, and mutual edification in the house of Louisa Lindsay, Tait's Lane, Hawkhill' on Sundays at seven o'clock in the morning, as well as in the evening. He listed all the names of this group of elderly people, and in conclusion it was his wish 'that the Holy Spirit may descend in rich abundance in our souls'. Jane Petrie met with a group on a Sunday morning in James Wallace's house in Paton's Lane near Perth Road, not far from the church. From the list of names it appears that this was a large group. The neighbours named the gathering place 'the house of prayer'. 'Numbers of the friends of Jesus would meet and sing and pray there, especially on Sabbath morning.'

M'Cheyne read the letters concerning the prayer meetings in his congregation with great pleasure. He remained careful and alert, because he knew his own proud heart only too well. Excesses were not unthinkable, making professional supervision necessary. On 11 December, he wrote in his diary: 'Surely Immanuel is in this place, and even old sinners are flocking to Him. I have got an account of about twenty prayer meetings connected with my flock. Many open ones; many fellowship meetings; only one or two have anything like exhortation superadded to the Word. These, I think, it must be our care to change, if possible, lest error and pride creep in. The only other difficulty is this. In two of the female meetings, originally fellowship meetings, anxious female inquirers have been admitted. They do not pray, but only hear. In one, M. and J. had felt the rising of pride to a great degree; in the other, M. could not be persuaded that there was any danger of pride. This case will require prayerful deliberation. My mind at present is, that there is a great danger from it, the praying members feeling themselves on a different level from the others, and anything like female teaching, as a public teacher, seems clearly condemned in the Word of God.'

Despite the critical marginal notes which M'Cheyne recorded here and there, his opinion of the revival on the whole could be called favourable. In one detailed letter to Andrew Bonar, he gave a report on 2 December 1839 of the work of God in his congregation. 'Many of my own dear children in the Lord are much advanced; much more full of joy, their hearts lifted up in the ways of the Lord.' However, he is afraid 'that the great Spirit has in some measure passed by, I hope soon to return in greater power than ever'.

The fire had somewhat diminished. 'The week meetings are thinner now. I will turn two of them into my classes soon, and so give solid, regular instruction, of which they stand greatly in need.' It was no longer necessary to gather every evening in the church. The time for aftercare had arrived. The subsidence of emotions made way for solid teaching in the Holy Scriptures and the Catechism. M'Cheyne could announce that he had not met 'with one case of extravagance or false fire, although doubtless there may be many'. The waves of the climax had now levelled off to a constant, steady stream.

M'Cheyne thought it a great pity that Burns had taken leave. Out of gratitude, the congregation offered him more than one hundred theological books, as a token of their affection and appreciation. The *Dundee Courier* published an article concerning this on 31 December 1839. In his letter of thanks to Burns, he stressed how highly he honoured his presence: 'You know I told you my mind plainly, that I thought the Lord had so blessed you in Dundee, that you were called to a fuller and deeper work there; but if the Lord accompanies you to other places, I have nothing to object.' M'Cheyne admonished him to continue in humility with his work, 'or you will yet be a wandering star, for which is reserved the blackness of darkness for ever. Let Christ increase; let man decrease.' Reluctantly he allowed his friend to depart, in the knowledge that the work of God doesn't depend on man.

**The Revival proceeds**

With much assistance from his congregation, M'Cheyne took over Burns' work. He preached as follows on Jeremiah 6:14: 'They have healed also the hurt of the daughter of my people slightly, saying Peace, peace; when there is no peace.' 'Much comfort in speaking. There was often an awful stillness.' The fruit continued to be perceptible. A few days later, he visited a sick woman, concerning whom he reported: 'She seems really in Christ now; tells me how deeply my words sank into her soul when I was away.' And 'J. B. walked home with me, telling me what God had done for his soul, when one day I had stopped at the quarry on account of a shower of rain, and took shelter with my pony in the engine-house.' M'Cheyne pointed to the burning oven with the words: 'What does that remind you of?' These words struck home in the man's soul.

With joy he took in a number of young members on the last day of the year 1839. 'Two under eleven years of age have made application to be admitted; four that are only fourteen; three who are fifteen or sixteen.' No wonder that he could enter the New Year with a heart rejoicing in God. He wrote as follows: 'Awoke early by the kind providence of God, and had uncommon freedom and fervency in keeping the concert for prayer this morning before light.'

The progress of the work of God had a healthy effect on M'Cheyne's spiritual life. He didn't mention his poor health at this time. The journey to Palestine had done him good, despite the high fever he had contracted for some weeks. The Lord had done great things for him. His joy was in the God of his salvation. He had visited his remnant and had poured out his mercy on the dry bones. M'Cheyne's years of wrestling in prayer had been heard. The fruit of a 'handful of corn' grains which he had sown over a few years, had begun 'to shake like Lebanon; and they of the city shall flourish like grass of the earth' (Ps. 72:16). The St Peter's minister opened the way through the greater Joseph to the full stores of God's grace, causing the city of Dundee to become a centre of spiritual awakening. 'Dundee has been exalted to heaven,' observed M'Cheyne in one sermon. The surrounding regions also shared in the fruit of the rich harvest. Thus, he wrote on 2 January 1840, when the city of Perth also began to partake in the revival: 'This awakening was the commencement of a solid work of grace, both in that town and its neighbourhood, much fruit of which is to be found there to this day in souls that are walking in the fear of the Lord and the comfort of the Holy Spirit.' Streams of blessings were poured out!

# Chapter 11

# AN ABUNDANT HARVEST

**A rich communion**

'We had an additional communion season at my return from the Continent, which was the happiest and holiest that I was ever present at.' It was for M'Cheyne, who wrote these words in 1840, and many others, a memorable event. The Lord set His seal on the wonderful work of revival. M'Cheyne invited some of his friends to be present at this celebration.

James Hamilton from Abernyte was among those to receive a letter with the request to declare the 'unsearchable riches of Christ'. 'We have the communion on Sabbath. We have no fast day (it being quarterly communion), but only a meeting in the evening at a quarter past seven.' Instead of annually, in 1840, four celebrations were held. 'Come, my dear sir, if you can, and refresh us with your company. Bring the fragrance of the "bundle of myrrh" (S.S. 1:13) along with you, and may grace be poured into your lips.' Unfortunately, Hamilton could not be present with them this time.

Thus holy communion was arranged in the congregation's

midst on 19 January 1840. The church doors opened every morning at ten o'clock and the services lasted until five o'clock in the afternoon. It happened to be a stormy Sabbath morning. A deluge poured down on the roof of the church building. Fortunately, the weather cleared, which M'Cheyne viewed as an answer to his prayer. Before the services could begin, the ministerial brethren gathered together. 'Sweet union in prayer with Mr. Cumming, and afterwards with A. Bonar. Found God in secret. Asked especially that the very sight of the broken bread and poured-out wine might be blessed to some souls, that pride will be hidden from man.'

The church was overcrowded, and many had to be satisfied with standing space. Before the administration of the sacrament, M'Cheyne preached from John 17:24: 'Father, I will that they also, whom Thou hast given me, be with me where I am; that they may behold my glory.' The glory of God radiated forth during the preaching. The love of Christ flowed forth as a stream from his soul. The splendour of God's glory in Christ shone for all to see. He mentioned that 'there were many openings of the veil when the bright glory shone through'; for example, when He changed the water into wine, when He wept over Jerusalem, when He hung on the cross and as He was taken up into heaven. Surely, He radiated the love of God whilst on the cross. 'Every drop of blood that fell came as a messenger of love from His heart to tell the love of the fountain. This was the love of God. He that hath seen a crucified Christ hath seen the Father. Oh, look on the broken bread, and you will see this glory still streaming through! Here is the heart of God laid bare; God is manifest in flesh. Some of you are poring over your own heart, examining your feelings, watching your disease. Avert the eye from all within. "Behold Me, behold Me!" Christ cries. "Look to Me, and be ye saved." Behold the glory of Christ! There is much difficulty about your own heart, but no darkness about the heart of Christ. Look in through His wounds; believe what you see in Him.'

Thus M'Cheyne aroused in his congregation a hunger for

the true Bread of Life. 'The people were in a very desirable frame of attention – hanging on the Word.' With great urgency, he preached the Word, and the Almighty's support gave him strength. 'Had considerable nearness to God in prayer – more than usual – and also freedom in preaching, although I was ashamed of such poor views of Christ's glory.' The Lord was with him also when he delivered his speeches at the tables. He earnestly urged them to examine themselves. At the first table he spoke about Ananias and Sapphira, and at the next: 'My beloved is mine, and I am his.' The hypocrites received an earnest warning not to partake unworthily: 'Oh hypocrite, take heed lest you drop down dead! Draw back that hand lest it wither!' God's children were comforted. He himself looked back on the wonderful way that the Lord had led him: 'I was once of the world – cold and careless about my soul. God awakened me, and made me feel I was lost. I tried to make myself good – to mend my life; but I found it in vain: I sat down more lost than before. I was then told to believe on the Lord Jesus. So I tried to make myself believe. I read books on faith and tried to bend my soul to believe, that so I might get to heaven; but still in vain. I found it written, "Faith is the gift of God". "No man can call Jesus Lord, but by the Holy Ghost." So I sat down more lost than ever. Whilst I was thus helpless, Jesus drew near – His garments dipped in blood. He had waited long at my door, though I knew it not. "His head was filled with dew, and His locks with the drops of the night." He had five deep wounds, and He said, "I died in the stead of sinners; and any sinner may have Me for a Saviour. You are a helpless sinner, will you have Me?"'

He served the first table himself 'with much more calmness and collectedness ...' than he had ever experienced before. Andrew Bonar ministered to the next tables; there were six in total. 'The people more and more moved to the end. At the last table every head seemed bent like a bulrush while Andrew Bonar spoke of the ascension of Christ.' It was as if the glory of the Lord shone around about the church building. A small, young boy mentioned to him as they were departing from the church, 'This has been another bonnie day.' The children too were moved. Alexander Cumming and William Burns spoke in the adjacent school building. Burns had come over from Perth, but returned immediately that Monday. In conclusion, M'Cheyne preached from Jude 24: 'Now unto him that is able to keep you from falling.' The Lord alone received the glory. 'Oh, if anything has been done for your soul, give Him the glory.' Refreshed and strengthened, some of the believers departed from the church building. It was, however, difficult to part from the Lord's presence in this place. Thus a few of them walked into the school and began to sing there. Their pastor joined them and sang along. He addressed them furthermore, 'Behold I stand at the door, and knock.' The Lord was in this place, it was a Beth-El, a house of God. The ladder was lowered down from heaven and the blessings flowed into many hearts. When M'Cheyne eventually walked home, he came across A. L, who said to him: 'Pray for me; I am quite happy, and so is H.' Was it perhaps Alexander Laing whom he accompanied? How thankful everyone was for the abundant evidence of God's favour.

It was probably at this opportunity, or else at the following celebration, that many spent the Sunday night in prayer as did M'Cheyne, in intimate fellowship with his Master, in order to offer thanksgiving to Him alone. A new awakening had begun in the congregation. 'Altogether a day of the revelation of Christ, a sweet day to myself, and, I am persuaded, to many souls. Lord, make us meet for the table above.'

The next celebration of the Lord's Supper took place on 19 April, exactly three months later. Horatius Bonar from Kelso, James Grierson from Errol and the elderly Burns from Kilsyth, father of William, assisted M'Cheyne. Once again it was a 'sweet and precious day'. 'The prayer meeting on the Monday evening following the communion was generally enjoyed by all the Lord's people, and by the ministers who assisted, in a peculiar manner. Often all felt the last day of the feast to be the great day. Souls that had been enjoying the feast were then, at its conclusion, taking hold on the arm of the Beloved in the prospect of going up through the wilderness.' It was not easy to part company with these Elims in the desert of trials. However, the congregation certainly received new strength and comfort enabling them to continue the journey through this wilderness.

**Examination of candidates**

The number of requests for admittance to the Lord's Table increased steadily. Certainly there were refusals, but the majority of the candidates were admitted. Many names were recorded in M'Cheyne's notebook during the period 1840-1842. On 13 April 1840, he spoke to thirty young candidates in private. We read: 'Spoke in private to nearly thirty young communicants, all in one room, going round each, and advising for the benefit of all.' In October there were no fewer than previously. Amongst other entries we read: 'Anxious to come under William Burns. Seems really a child of God, though it is hard to know'; 'I trust has really come to Christ'; 'has come previously unconverted, now evidently under deep concern'; 'Fine, quiet, staid young woman, well-instructed, seems also under the teaching of the Spirit, very silent'; 'seems truly to have got salvation under William Burns.' During March 1841, he wrote: 'Sweet Irish girl. Have you found Christ?' 'I hope and trust I have.' 'Still cares for her soul – this is a young disciple of fourteen and loves Jesus'; 'The blood of Christ gives me peace; Christ is precious to me'; 'Awakened under William Burns, and went back to the world; awakened again at last communion; I trust there is something of God here; very silent. Truly saved, so far as I can see.' During April 1842, we come across the name of Burns a few times. Some of the testimonies are concise but clear: 'I'm a great sinner, but I believe on Christ.' Neither tears nor spiritual experiences formed the foundation of their faith, but the completed work on the cross of Calvary alone. Whenever M'Cheyne perceived some knowledge of this beloved Person in his students, he would immediately accept them into the fellowship of the church.

Mary Wanless was admitted along with thirty other candidates to the Lord's Supper. He questioned her as follows: 'What is your reason for thinking of coming to the Lord's table, Mary?' She answered: 'Jesus says, If you love Me, keep My commandments, and I love Jesus.' 'A very good reason, Mary.' She and her friend, Jessie Chephen, were orphans and reserved a special place in his heart. Following a Thursday morning service, he invited them to his home, took out the Bible and read a few verses explaining these to them. Later Mary remembered the last verse in her old age: 'Be ye therefore followers of God, as dear children; and walk in love, as Christ also hath loved us, and hath given himself for us an offering and a sacrifice to God for a sweet smelling savour' (Eph. 5:1-2). Whereupon he knelt down to pray with the girls. He allowed Mary to pray first, followed by his own supplication, committing the needs of the girls to the throne of grace. They would often be shown hospitality in the manse and prior to M'Cheyne's death, Mary would be permitted to help in the house.

At her first communion, he preached on: 'What have I to do any more with idols?' He related the story of a woman who was offered a garland of flowers, but refused this, saying, 'How could I wear flowers on my brow when Christ wore thorns?' As M'Cheyne said this, the young women at the table pulled the flowers from their hats and trampled them under foot. Since that time, Mary never wore flowers in her hat again. It was in October 1840 that she participated for the first time, and by the time of the next service two young communicants, James Wallace and James Laing, had died. M'Cheyne's words were emotionally charged: 'There were two with us at last communion, and now they are sitting at the table above.'

It was worth noting how many were admitted between the ages of twelve and fifteen years. The daughter of an elder by the name of John Mathewson, who later became Mrs W. Nairn, was admitted whilst merely twelve years of age. Mr Reid thought her too young, but M'Cheyne said, 'If I was not too young to be in Christ, I was not too young to be at His table.' She later became seriously ill and they feared for her life. Her father requested that intercession be made on her behalf. When he arrived home after the service, he noticed that the situation was no longer life-threatening, and from then on she showed signs of improvement. M'Cheyne believed in the power of prayer. An anonymous letter to his address informed him of a family in great need. A daughter 'suffers under the deep affliction of budwing', by which her husband had fallen into grave errors, and 'of which the apostle speaks in such strong terms'. The spiritual powers of the evil one were let loose on this family, but the unknown writer believed that God exists and is willing to listen to prayer. Could M'Cheyne have ignored this cry for help?

His people's needs were also his. His concern for the awakened sinners' souls in particular resulted in intercession and care on their behalf. He always directed their attention to Christ alone, who is powerful to sever the shackles of sin and unbelief. He rejoiced in hearing that the arrows of conviction had touched hearts, but his mind was only set at rest once he knew that their souls were hidden in Christ. There remains preserved a short letter which he wrote to Miss Katherine Duncan of Small's Wynd on 14 January 1840. He requested this lady to visit Elspeth Robertson, 'the old woman you spoke of above the Lows in Tait's Lane. ...Tell me whether you think the Lord has opened her heart to believe in Jesus. You can understand a woman's heart better than I can do.' Thus he tried to get to know his congregational members; he bore them all in his heart. He was happy with the rejoicing and sad with the downcast.

In 1841, during a time when unemployment was rife, on returning from a meeting at Invergowrie, he encountered the orphan girl, Mary, who happened to be unemployed and was consequently without food. 'I hear you are out of employment, Mary; take this.' He offered her five shillings, but Mary refused them. 'You are a very bad-mannered girl, Mary; if you will not take it from me, take it from Christ, as we are Christ's stewards.'

**Prayer with fellow ministers**

M'Cheyne enjoyed good contact with his fellow labourers in the city, especially during the time of the revival. He was pleased that Patrick Miller, the friend from his youth, joined the ranks of the ministers. He also related well to John Roxburgh of St John's, John Baxter of Hilltown church and George Lewis of St David's. They met together every Monday morning to pray for the needs of the city. He never neglected to show up at these gatherings, the first of which took place in the vestry of St David's on 8th December 1839. 'The Lord answers prayer; may it be a great blessing to our souls and our flocks.'

The needs of the entire city weighed upon him. It gladdened him that new churches were built. It was also decided to erect a church for seamen. According to M'Cheyne's opinion there were no such things as church walls or district boundaries. His sphere of labour was the world of sinners. Thus he wrote on 7 April 1840: 'Impressed tonight with the complete necessity of preaching to my people in their own lanes and closes; in no other way will God's Word ever reach them. Tonight spoke in St Andrew's Church to a very crowded assembly in behalf of Israel. Was helped to speak plainly to their consciences. Lord, bless it! Shake this town!' He was interested too in the work among the seamen. He was deeply involved in the work of the Seaman's Society, an institute for seamen, which appointed a permanent minister, James Law, in May 1840. Furthermore, he kept contact with the Deaf and Dumb Institute. On 21 August of the same year, he became a member of the commission which decided upon the admission of pupils. In this way he contributed to the social work of the city.

There was not only hope for Dundee, but for many other places in Scotland. M'Cheyne was of the opinion that there was never before a time 'when the Spirit of God was more present in Scotland'. He mentioned Kilsyth, Dundee, Perth,

Collace, Blairgowrie, Strathbogie, Ross-shire, Breadalbane, Kelso, Jedburgh and Ancrum, where the work of revival had begun to take root. William Burns was to be found in many of these places. After his time in Dundee, Burns found work in the nearby city of Perth. He received much support there from John Milne of St Leonard's Church, with whom M'Cheyne shortly afterwards established ties of friendship. The letters they sent each other showed something of Christ's love. 'My dear brother, I long after you in the bowels of Jesus Christ.' Because thousands turned up in front of the church building to hear the young evangelist, Burns made his way to a place in the open air. A bar-keeper was powerfully converted and shut up his shop. The Spirit of the Lord worked powerfully in many souls. Milne was made of the same stuff as Burns and M'Cheyne, and assumed the lead after the first had left. Perth was richly blessed during the revival.

On leaving Perth, Burns journeyed farther to Aberdeen. The opposition there was great, but the grace of God also persisted in this 'granite city'. Thereafter he departed for the mountains of Breadalbane adjoining Loch Tay, whence he went to Moulin; these were places and districts where earlier revivals had taken place. A restless traveller, he departed yet again, this time for the city of Newcastle in England. He never forgot his brother in Dundee, and the reverse was also true. Both kept up a regular correspondence. At the end of December, Burns informed his friend about the progress of God's work in Perth: 'Last night, the work was so glorious that hardly one out of about a hundred and fifty seemed free from deep impressions of the Word and Spirit of Jesus, and many were evidently pricked in their hearts, while some heavy-laden souls emerged into the liberty of the children of God.' In June he wrote concerning the county of Fife, describing it as 'poor parched Fife, the Valley of the Shadow of Death', but a month later he announced that he had spoken in Anstruther, Chalmers's birthplace, to a large crowd in a tent in the churchyard.

M'Cheyne wrote to him on 10 June concerning his visits to

the surrounding district. He found himself in places where people had expected Burns to be: 'It would be very gratifying, if you are not better engaged, if the Lord would direct your steps towards us. You may be sure I ever follow you with my prayers and earnest longings of heart that God may humble, purify, and make use of you to carry glad tidings of great joy to the inmost hearts of poor, guilty, perishing sinners, whenever you go.' He considered his brother in the faith more highly than himself. With joy he heard about the fruit the young evangelist had reaped by God's grace. What was his deepest wish? Thus they encouraged one another in the most holy faith. Burns still needed M'Cheyne to pray for him, and urged him to unite with him 'in wrestling with the Lord that He may pour out His fullness'. In himself he was incapable of anything because he was mere clay in the hands of the potter. Therefore he needed the prayers of 'the children of God in Dundee'. 'O, how glorifying to Him that the walls of Jericho should fall at the blast of a ram's horn! that the mountains should be thrashed to dust.' Nothing is a match for God's almighty power.

**Revival in the 'Carse'**

After Burns' departure from Dundee, he regularly visited the Carse of Gowrie, the fertile region to the west of this city. In November of 1839, he arrived at Abernyte, where James Hamilton worked, and here he preached before an attentive audience on the words, 'For God so loved the world....' Here the Lord touched souls and tears were shed. The effect was less noticeable in Longforgan, but Burns knew also of awakened souls in this town. In March 1840, he visited Kinfauns, where he spoke with much freedom on Matthew 11:28. The service lasted three and one-half hours. In 1842 he made three journeys through the Carse and visited Collace, Abernyte and Kilspindie. Naturally he didn't omit to visit Errol, where James Grierson had laboured so long with much blessing. Only once he failed to turn up, because he felt bereft of God's help. Then Grierson took over and 'preached with wonderful comfort and help to many'.

With regard to the revival in Dundee and other places in the Carse, Collace lagged rather behind. Most of the members of Andrew Bonar's church were content with their form of religion. It wasn't easy to awaken them from their false comfort. A young woman, Elizabeth Morrison, was awakened in Dundee, but not yet delivered. Bonar and Cumming prayed together in Perth after the presbytery meeting and became aware of God's presence. 'I feel that for the relief of anxious souls I must betake myself to prayer; the Holy Ghost can show them the object Christ.' When he returned once again to Collace, Elizabeth came to tell him that her soul had found peace and that was at the same hour the two ministers were in prayer together! Thus he beseeched the Lord all the more on his congregation's behalf.

After a few months, there came a movement in the silent valleys of the parish. 'And it was in the spring of this same year, that in Collace, at our weekly prayer meeting, when two brethren were ministering, we received a blessed shower from the Lord.' During a prayer meeting in April, Bonar as well as Alexander Cumming and his brother, Horatius, preached. The last mentioned spoke on the Samaritan woman. 'While he was pressing on all present the immediate reception of the offer of the living waters, many burst into tears, old and young, and among the rest, several boys of twelve and fourteen years of age.' The entire congregation was impressed, and disheartened souls surrounded the teachers after the service to ask for counsel. Thus the revival began unexpectedly in Collace. It was no early dew which soon vanished, because for months there was talk of a work of conviction and deliverance of lost souls. Full of hope, Bonar wrote at the end of his report: 'We have seen the steps of our God and King in His sanctuary, and we expect Him again.'

M'Cheyne also went regularly to other places where the Lord had poured out His Spirit. More than once he visited the southern cities of Jedburgh and Kelso, where Horatius Bonar lived, such as in February 1841. He spoke to a girl in Kelso as follows: 'Christ gives last knocks. When your heart becomes hard and careless, then fear lest Christ may have given a last knock.' His visits and the work of Horatius Bonar were richly blessed to the many souls in that picturesque town on the river Tweed. M'Cheyne ended his letter to his friend: 'I am humbled and cheered by what you say of good done in Kelso.' M'Cheyne too needed to be appreciated, although he was apprehensive of the praise of men. Hence he always urged his brothers towards sanctification. We come across it in his letters continually, such as for example those of 18 August 1842, to Horatius: 'I have great desire for personal growth in faith and holiness.' This was one of the most important fruits of the revival, in which the ministers also shared. He ended with the wish which spoke volumes, 'May we be kept in the shadow of the rock. Farewell! May Jesus shine on you.'

The year 1840 meant an abundant harvest for many places in Scotland. Dundee could also share in 'the rain upon the mown grass'. The streams of blessing, which the previous year had suddenly poured down, changed to a gentle rain which fell steadily. The fire of the first love became dampened. At the beginning of the year, M'Cheyne already perceived 'tokens of backsliding', in both the believers as well as those who were being awakened. It was a case of all that glitters is not gold. The counterfeit work was not visible to the naked eye at first; Satan tried to imitate and upset God's work. The wise teacher called out honestly: 'What blind creatures ministers are! Man looketh at the outward appearance.' There were those who were awakened out of their spiritual sleep who still didn't come to Christ and who often returned to their former life. 'That many, who promised fair, drew back and walked no more with Jesus, is true. Out of about eight hundred souls who, during the months of the revival, conversed with different ministers in apparent anxiety, no wonder surely if many proved to have been impressed only for a time.' M'Cheyne knew the books of

Jonathan Edwards, who during the great revival in Northampton had experienced the same, and M'Cheyne learned from this how closely the genuine work of God's Spirit resembled the spurious work of Satan. Edwards' contemporary, David Brainerd, whom he deeply respected, witnessed also an apostasy among the Indians. It was the rain shadow of the revival in Dundee, which put M'Cheyne in a sad mood.

Was this a demonstration that the movement consisted only of passion? Were those who had condemned the occurrences in Dundee merely as enthusiastic, correct in their estimation? A careful examination led M'Cheyne and his colleagues to the conclusion that the work as a whole revealed a Biblical course of events. God's Word teaches that there is chaff among the corn. Andrew Bonar addressed this point: 'We have the authority of the Word of God, declaring that such backslidings are the very tests of the true church.'

Then there was the criticism of some who maintained that the Lord had used only young ministers to lead the revival. Bonar answered this form of criticism: 'But herein it was that sovereign grace shone forth the more conspicuously. Do such objectors suppose that God ever intends the honour of man in a work of revival? Is it not the honour of His own Name that He seeks?' In contrast, the many fruits of their defective labour were constant. There was a close relationship between the believers and those who were newly converted. Love, as the sign of perfection, radiated forth from the leaders as well as from the congregational members to 'them that are without'. There was a unity in genuine faith, which worked together for the edification of the body of Christ. Great watchfulness was certainly required, because Satan wasn't inactive. M'Cheyne became more careful, and 'became more than ever vigilant and discriminating in dealing with souls'. He saw that many allowed themselves to be led more by their feelings, and that tended to make him more critical and detached in his judgment of souls who considered themselves among the converted.

The revival movement had set many tongues wagging. The

New Machar
25 January 1841.

Revd. Sir,

A Committee of the Presbytery of Aberdeen, being engaged in collecting information on the subject of Revivals, and having been informed that Revivals have lately taken place in your Parish or District – have directed me to address to you the subjoined list of queries, with an earnest request that you favor them with an early answer –

By the term Revivals the Committee understand real or supposed conversions from sin to holiness; or awakening resulting from certain known means assumed to be originated and applied by the Spirit of God.

The beginning of a letter from the Presbytery of Aberdeen, dated 25th January 1841

press too paid much attention to the occurrences connected with this movement. The Moderates were most severe in their criticism. A commission from the Presbytery of Aberdeen was instructed to make an examination of the motive for and the result of the spiritual revival. In December 1840, the Presbytery formulated fifteen questions, which were sent to places where there was talk of such a movement having taken place. M'Cheyne too was sent these questions, which he attempted to answer with as much lucidity as possible. The letter from the Presbytery dated 25 January 1841 was answered in March by M'Cheyne. He supplied a detailed report of the facts, as well as the developments of the revival in his congregation. In positive comments, he described the extent of the work of God: 'The parish is situated in the suburb of a city containing 60,000 inhabitants. The work extended to individuals residing in all quarters of the town and belonging to all ranks and denominations of the people. Many hundreds, under deep concern for their souls, have come, from first to last to converse with the ministers: so that I am deeply persuaded, the number of those who have received saving benefit is greater than any one will know till the Judgment Day.'

M'Cheyne didn't perceive excesses. There was no such thing as spiritual revelation beyond the bounds of God's Word; the preaching of the Word was the most important medium to awaken sinners and to lead them to Christ. The plain message of the gospel accomplished great miracles by the working of God's Spirit. The ministers preached nothing special, but merely the gospel, in manner 'fully, clearly, solemnly; with discrimination, urgency, and affection'. 'Some of them have been particularly aided in declaring the terrors of the Lord, and others in setting forth the fullness and freeness of Christ as the Saviour of sinners.' The Lord blessed this simple word, enabling hundreds of souls to be converted.

**The height of the revival ends**

After the ebb of the highlight of the revival, the congregational life of St Peter's revealed a stream 'flowing gently; for the heavy showers had fallen, and the overflowing of the waters had passed by'. God's work continued now in silence. Exclamations of souls in distress during the services were less and less frequent. In July 1840, M'Cheyne noted down that a few of the congregation were 'crying out in extreme agony', but such incidents became more the exception rather than the rule. When William Lamb established himself as a graintrader and shipper in Dundee, the afterglow of the movement was still noticeable. This young man reproduced his impressions of the congregational life in a diary from 3 April. He, together with his brother John, 'arrived at Dundee from London after a good and safe passage'. On the first Sabbath, he attended Roxburgh's church in the morning and St Peter's in the evening. He had already heard about M'Cheyne while still in London, but it was another thing to sit among the audience of this man of God. 'I greatly enjoyed the preaching.' He decided immediately to request a seat and to join this congregation. His wish was that he might 'derive much strength from the ministrations of His servant'. He was not disappointed in his choice, because

Cottage in which James Laing lived. It was in Miller's Wynd, east side, one of the many streets between Hawkhill and Perth Road. After a drawing in a Dundee newspaper of the beginning of 20th century.

the preaching was a great blessing to him. 'How beautifully affectionate were M'Cheyne's addresses! He draws you to Christ. Today he said, "Christ has brought us into green pastures and by still waters, but would we follow the Shepherd into deep valleys of affliction and trial?"' This brought Lamb to self-examination: 'I felt composed and comforted, though downcast, because of my walking too much away from Christ.'

The Sabbath services, as well as the weekly prayer meetings in St Peter's, were impressive. The young people didn't forget M'Cheyne, because they had a special place in his heart. What struck Lamb was that so much work was done among the younger generation. 'There were large Sabbath Schools, and in addition something like what we would now call a children's church.' How the children loved their pastor! Even more than his words, his appearance to many of them left an indelible impression behind. In 1903 a certain J. S. M. gave his impressions of days long ago in one particular issue of a city newspaper, after he had heard and met M'Cheyne. 'Dear memory of Robert M'Cheyne, how his figure starts up to the mind's eye once more! The tall and somewhat slim, but graceful and willowy form, the longish neck, the head slightly bent or stooping, the measured, gentle step as he walked along, with looks absorbed, "unhasting, unresting", could never be forgot.' The writer was ten or eleven years old when M'Cheyne walked behind him on the south side of Perth Road 'from about the top of Westfield Place'. Before he became aware of it, M'Cheyne had grabbed him around the waist and gripped him tightly with his arm. He questioned him about his family and whispered in conclusion some friendly words in his ear. 'M'Cheyne's arm, his hand, his voice, remain an ineffaceable consecration.'

**Jamie Laing**

The walls of the poverty-stricken house of father Laing in Miller's Wynd also witnessed to a similar memory. In the previous chapter we made the acquaintance of the prayer group of a young seaman, Alexander Laing. His younger brother, Jamie, lay sick in bed when the beloved minister crossed the threshold of the humble home many times to visit the youth. 'James Laing was born on 28 July 1828 and lost his mother before he was eight years old.' As a child he was as naughty as other children, although he was more retiring by nature. During the revival in the autumn of 1839, he was discovered by his sister, Margaret, together with his brother, Alexander, on his knees in fervent prayer to God. These strong impressions vanished as snow melts in the midday sun, until one day, in great unrest, he confessed to his sister, 'There's me come awa' without Christ tonight again.' During a prayer service one Thursday night, he was deeply touched along with others and joined those who remained behind. This solicitude too, however, passed over.

When he arrived home from Sabbath School, which was

held in the same avenue as his home, he was moved more than once. The teacher tried always to speak to the hearts of the children and to point them to the necessity for conversion. His eyes became filled with tears too at the home devotions, but when he went to join his friends there wasn't much to be seen of his tears. His health was suffering; it seemed as if he were experiencing the same attacks of fever that had caused his mother's death. In order to recuperate, he went in June 1841, to another region, but this didn't benefit him much. The youth evidenced a knowledge of discrimination – that he sensed that anxiety of the soul and solicitude were not the same as 'to be in Christ'. He realized full well what he missed, but didn't know how he could obtain it. While sitting before a hearth-fire, a woman read from a book by an author of yore. The section she was reading concerned unforgettable impressions, and she inquired of Jamie if he ever had impressions. He replied, 'I can never forget it; but we cannot seek Christ twice.' Christ knocked on the door of his heart, but he didn't wish to hear.

'The day of Immanuel's power, and the time of love, was, however, near at hand.' It was October when a biting wind blew through the lane and over the clay hut. The weather didn't assist in his recuperation and his health deteriorated noticeably. He was actually more concerned about his soul than about his physical well-being. One evening his sister heard him calling out, 'Oh Jesus, save me, save me!' A few days later M'Cheyne visited the sick youth, who sat on the hearth. When the teacher told him that Jesus came into the world to save sinners, he began to cry. What actually held him back from fleeing to take refuge in Jesus? In a simple manner, the minister tried to refute the arguments against an unconditional surrender. He departed from the youth, leaving him behind in deep dismay. Margaret wished to know more about this and asked him if he was seeking Jesus, upon which he replied in the affirmative. Hereupon she asked him if he wanted to eat something, which he answered by saying: 'No; but I would take a bit of the Bread of Life if you would give me.' 'I cannot give you that; but if you seek it, you will get it,' was her reply.

The Lord impressed upon his heart a genuine need for the Saviour. He remained in constant prayer and reflection until the evening. When he went to another room, he asked, 'Have I only to believe that Jesus died for sinners? Is that all?' The simplicity of faith, but also the impossibility of believing in Christ, were the matters that the Holy Spirit drew to his attention. Not only that, because thereupon he spoke: 'Well, I believe that Jesus died for me, for I am a poor, hell-deserving sinner. I have been praying all this afternoon that when Jesus shed His blood for sinners, He would sprinkle some of it upon me, and He did it.' Then he picked up his Bible and read from the letter to the Romans chapter 5: 'While we were yet sinners, Christ died for us.' With great joy, Margaret heard this simple and yet clear testimony from her younger brother. She cried with joy when he said, 'I am not afraid to die now, for Jesus has died for me.' Thus there was joy not only in this poor home, but also in heaven.

How happy M'Cheyne was that the light had risen in Jamie's heart. His many visits to his sickbed were a refreshment and encouragement to him. The Word of God became Jamie's best food. His face beamed with pleasure when his beloved teacher explained Bible texts to him. His body became weaker and weaker, but his soul increased in knowledge and holiness. A few of M'Cheyne's colleagues visited him to rejoice in God's wonderful way. Cumming of Dumbarney asked him if he experienced much pain, to which he replied, 'Sometimes.' 'When you are in much pain, can you think on the sufferings of the Lord Jesus?' The youth's reply amazed the teacher, 'When I see what Jesus suffered for me, it takes away my pain.' Miller, the minister from Wallacetown church, visited Jamie too on one occasion. He asked him if he longed to be restored to full health. Succinct and powerful was his reply, 'I would like the will of God.' 'But if you were getting better, would you just live as you did before?' His answer proved his deep self-knowledge, '... If God did not give me grace, I would.'

M'Cheyne was often astonished at the knowledge Jamie displayed of 'the way of pardon and acceptance through the doing and dying of the Lord Jesus, laid to our account'. Never before had he observed it thus in a child of his age. When he wished to know from Margaret when James for the first time became convicted of his sins, the youth interrupted his sister by saying, 'Ah! but we must not lean upon that.' He meant to say that 'past experiences are not the foundation of a sinner's peace'. The reconciliatory merits of Christ were the only resting-point of his soul. Andrew Bonar, too, who visited him more than once, was surprised at his great faith and insight into the teaching of God's grace.

Jamie was moved by the lot of his fellow man just as M'Cheyne was. He could not keep quiet before others, such as when his Sabbath School classmates visited him. Quietly they stood gathered around his bed. He spoke to them as follows: 'You all know what I was; I was no better than you; but the Holy Spirit opened my eyes, and I saw that I was on the very brink of hell. Then I cried to Jesus to save me and give me a new heart; I put my finger on the promise, and would not come away without it. And He gave me a new heart; and He is as willing to give you all a new heart. I have sinned with you; now I would like you to come to Christ with me. You would be far happier in Christ than at your play.' He warned them earnestly concerning the coming judgment. 'Go and tell Jesus,' he admonished them in conclusion, 'that you are poor, lost, hell-deserving sinners, and tell Him to give you a new heart. Mind, He's willing, and oh, be earnest! – ye'll not get it unless ye be earnest.'

The wonder of grace became more and more amazing to Jamie. Often he would say to his sister: 'Ah, Margaret, I wonder that Christ would look in here and take us.' Then again, 'Why me, Lord, why me?' He was not better than the others; it was the mercy of God alone that had saved him. Often he would complain about his cunning and sinful heart; he was attached to holiness and longed to be delivered from his body of sin and death. Then he prayed, 'Come, Holy Spirit, and make me holy – make me like Jesus.' This holiness he found in Christ alone, his Substitute; he himself remained fleshly and condemnable. 'Oh Margaret, I see it must be all Jesus from beginning to end!'

Satan often tormented him with temptations. These were not only directed at sinful desires, but also at seemingly commendable deeds. Jamie related to M'Cheyne how he was spurred on by the devil to seek help from pious people. He had already prepared what he would say to the evil one. 'It is Christ I want.' Then the evil one accused him that he couldn't receive salvation because he had been converted while in bed. Then he called out, 'If I perish, I'll perish at Christ's feet.' Sometimes he would complain of a spiritual darkness which came over his soul. Then he doubted if he actually knew Jesus. M'Cheyne then instructed him how he should manage his soul. This teaching was the means of strengthening his faith in days of darkness. A believing woman once asked him, 'When you are in darkness, Jamie, how do you do? Can you go to Jesus?' In his own pithy manner, he answered her, 'Annie, woman, I have no ither gate to gang.'

Prayer in solitude was the breath of his soul. As long as his body allowed, he would spend hours on his knees. It was his food and drink to be in fellowship with his God. Thus he lived until his death, or to put it in a better way, until the beginning of his glorification above. 'I long to be with Jesus. I long to see Jesus who died for me.' On the last day of the year 1841, he told his sister what his most beautiful New Year's gift would be: 'I would like a praying heart, and a heart to love Christ more.' He received much comfort from Psalm 23: 'Yea, though I walk through the valley of the shadow of death, I will fear no evil.' Despite the darkness which often overcame him, the Lord was beside him.

In the same area there lived a young woman, who during the same winter was brought to Christ. She died in complete happiness and went ahead of Jamie in the joy of her Lord and God. When he heard of her deathbed, he said, 'I wish I had been away with her; but I must wait the Lord's time. Betsy is singing now, and I will soon be there too.'

His time drew near in haste. In the summer he heard of James Wallace's death. He had been a youth who possessed the gift of edifying others by means of prayer. Jamie Laing was well acquainted with him and was jealous that he was in glory. During the last weeks of his life, the Lord still had work for him to do. David, an anxious youth who often saw him, asked him, 'Will you get to heaven?' 'Oh yes! all that believe in Christ get to heaven, and I believe that Jesus died for me. Now, David, if I see you on the left hand, you will mind that I often bade you come to Christ.' The last time that M'Cheyne visited the dying youth, he was accompanied by P. L. Miller and R. Smith, the last mentioned being a missionary to the Jews. M'Cheyne asked him for his prayer requests. Jamie answered, 'Dying grace.' Jamie gripped the missionary's hand tightly and added, 'God's people have much need to pray for you, and for them there.' In the same week he passed away in the joy of his Lord and God. He felt strongly that he needed grace to die, when he spoke to his sister, 'Ah Margaret, I wonder that Christ would look in here and take us.' Now the time had arrived to say farewell. He gave away his possessions; his new boots and Sunday clothes were intended for a poor youth, 'that he might go to the church'; he gave his father the book *The Dying Thief*; *Dewdrops,* from which he had received so much blessing, to his brother, Alick. Under his pillow he found a coin; it was intended for the purchasing of Bibles 'to them that had never heard of Christ'.

On the day he died he didn't say much. Margaret wished to watch over him at night but Jamie thought that unnecessary. It was during the middle of the night that she stood by his bedside and saw that the end was drawing near. She called her father and tried to hide her tears. Jamie saw that she was crying and spoke in a calm tone: 'Oh, woman, I wonder to see you do the like of that!' Thereafter he passed away in the arms of his Saviour, who had purchased him with His blood and also had prepared a home for him in the celestial city. It was Sunday morning at about one o'clock that he passed away. M'Cheyne wrote a report of his conversion and holy death on 11 June 1842, under the title 'Another Lily Gathered'. This beautiful lily continued in the prime of life on to higher glory. The following poem, written by his minister one year before his death, entitled 'The child coming to Jesus', became fulfilled in Jamie's experience:

Gentle Shepherd, on Thy shoulder
Carry me, a sinful lamb,
Give me faith, and make me bolder,
Till with Thee in heaven I am.

**Johnnie Thain**

Johnnie Thain was 'Another Lily'. He wasn't among the poor of the city, as Jamie Laing had been. His parents owned both a summer and a winter house. His mother wrote letters to her spiritual father, the minister of St Peter's, from 'Heath Park', the family's summer villa in Blairgowrie. Alexander Thain, his elder brother who studied in Edinburgh, also knew how to reach him by post. The little Johnnie Thain wrote a letter to M'Cheyne from the large house in Park Place, Dundee. He knew how to contact M'Cheyne because the latter was then staying with his friend, Andrew Bonar, in Collace, in order to round off their travel report on their journey to Palestine. His letter was drafted in neat school handwriting and dated 21 January 1842. What induced the youth to write to M'Cheyne? He was struggling with his health and it was not well with his soul. He thought it a great pity that he no longer often heard his teacher preaching. 'The Lord has thought it necessary to afflict me to try and bring me to himself. He hath said, "He doth not afflict willingly, nor grieve the children of men." I feel I am a lost sinner, but Christ has said, "him that cometh unto me I will in no wise cast out". I would like to be his, to be saved in the Lord. O may the Lord bless this affliction to my soul and make me one of his lambs.' Besides his spiritual

Park Place 21st Jany

My dear Mr McCheyne

I have been thinking that I would like much to write you a note, hoping you will take the trouble to write me, as I am not well and very seldom get to hear you preach. The Lord has thought it necessary to afflict me to try and bring me to himself. He hath said; "he doth not afflict willingly nor grieve the children of men" I feel I am a lost sinner, but Christ

Letter of Johnnie Thain, 21st January 1841.

affliction, Johnnie couldn't omit to inform M'Cheyne that his brother had met a Jew while visiting Mrs Coutts.

The youth quickly received a reply. 'My dear boy!' wrote M'Cheyne, 'I was very glad to receive your kind note.... You are very dear to me, because your soul is precious; and if you are ever brought to Jesus, washed and justified, you will praise Him more sweetly than an angel of light. I was riding among the snow today, where no foot had trodden, and it was pure, pure white; and I thought again and again of that verse: "Wash me, and I shall be whiter than snow." That is a sweet prayer; make it your own. Often go alone and look up to Jesus who died to wash us from our sins, and say, "Wash me."' How he inspired the boy to be safe in the arms of Christ: 'Remember, Johnnie, you once wept for your soul too, and prayed and sought Jesus. Have you found Him? or have you looked back, like Lot's wife, and become a hard, cold pillar of salt? Awake again, and call upon the name of the Lord. Your time may be short, God only knows.'

Johnnie's time was short. Within one month he was no more. Death snatched him away, but the devil didn't get him as his prey. His wish that the Lord would receive him as one of His lambs was fulfilled. As a lamb, he was taken up into His arms; 'as another lily gathered'. The family of father and mother Thain were plunged into deep mourning. In a letter to his brother, Alexander, M'Cheyne wrote concerning his blessed end. 'I saw your dear little brother twice on his dying bed, and indeed I could not believe he was dying, except that his calm eye was directed to the hills of immortality.... I do trust and believe that he was a saved boy. You know I am rather slow of coming to this conviction, and not fond of speaking when I have not good evidence; but here, I think, God has not left us in doubt.'

M'Cheyne had addressed the young on spiritual matters on more than one occasion at 'Heath Park', the summer home of the Thain family. Then Johnnie had feared that he never would be brought to Jesus. Without Christ he couldn't and dared not face God. Through grace, the Lord had removed this fear from him. He was enabled to believe that Jesus had died for him too. 'He seemed tranquil and happy, even when the pain came on in his head and made him knit his brows.' Thus the youth left this earthly existence, and his end was in peace. His father, mother and sister Jessie were sorrowful and yet glad. 'Your dear little brother lies like a marble statue in the peaceful sleep of death, till Jesus's voice shall waken him. Happy boy! He shall hunger no more, neither thirst any more, neither shall the sun light on him, nor any heat.'

Johnnie Thain's death was unexpected. His life's flame petered out. For M'Cheyne his final hours were unforgettable:

I little thought, when last we met,
Thy sun on earth was nearly set:
I said what I can ne'er forget,
'Dear boy, we'll meet again'.

At the end of every stanza he repeated Johnnie's farewell greeting, which made such an impression on him:

'We'll meet again!'
Everyone stood sorrowfully around his bed.
No hope thy weeping mother had,
Thy sister's face was pale and sad

However, the word of comfort issued by the dying lad was as a balm on the smarting wound: We'll meet again!

I love you well, my mother dear-
I love you all, yet shed no tear-
I'd rather be with Christ than here-
Farewell, we'll meet again.

A few days later M'Cheyne, moved with emotion, stood beside the pit into which Johnnie's coffin was lowered. He mourned with the family, but not without hope!

I saw thee in thy narrow rest,
The clods upon thy coffin pressed;
The clouds dropped tears, yet in my breast
God said, 'We'll meet again.'

**Sermons on death and judgment**

St Peter's congregation was during this time regularly startled by sudden and grievous deaths besides those of Jamie Laing and Johnnie Thain, who died at a tender age. William Lamb wrote in his diary: 'Both young and old – the child and the old man of hoar hairs – had all been laid in the grave.' On Sabbath, 20 February 1842, M'Cheyne preached in the afternoon in an impressive way on Job 14:1 and 2: 'Man that is born of a woman is of few days, and full of trouble. He cometh forth like a flower, and is cut down; he fleeth also as a shadow, and continueth not.' The scope of his preaching was focused on eternity. Perhaps this subject was uppermost in his thoughts because he himself felt he was nearing his own end. He spoke as a dying man to those who were dying. After the death of Johnnie he spoke more than once 'about the future of the unconverted and the reality of eternal judgment. In the last nine months of his ministry he preached in his own congregation at least four times about hell.'

On 15 July 1842, he preached from Mark 9:44: 'Where their worm dieth not, and the fire is not quenched.' He spoke to his congregation in the knowledge of the 'terror of the Lord', in order to persuade them towards faith. How could they hope to flee from the coming wrath? To the unconverted, he spoke: 'Ah, you are fools and you think you are wise; but O I beseech you, search the Scriptures! Do not take my word about an eternal hell; it is the testimony of God, when He spoke about it. O if it be true, if there be a furnace of fire, if there be a second death, if it is not annihilation, but an eternal hell – O is it reasonable to go on living in sin? You think you are wise – that you are no fanatic, that you are no hypocrite, but you will soon gnash your teeth in pain. It will come; and the bitterest thought will be that you heard about hell, and yet rejected Christ. O then, turn, turn ye, why will ye die?'

The thought that he would one day see members of his congregation standing at the left-hand side of the Judgment throne was unbearable. In his memoirs we find the following striking passage: 'As I was walking in the fields, the thought came over me with almost overwhelming power, that every one of my flock must soon be in heaven or hell. Oh, how I wished that I had a tongue like thunder, that I might make all hear; or that I had a frame like iron, that I might visit every one, and say, "Escape for thy life!" Ah sinners! you little know how I fear that you will lay the blame of your damnation at my door.'

M'Cheyne preached with earnestness the importance of death and eternity, but he never sent church members home without pointing out the open door of grace and the only refuge from the flood of God's wrath. On 18 December 1842, he preached from Hebrews 2:3: 'How shall we escape, if we neglect so great salvation?' The offer of God's grace became as a fire from heaven. Lamb added on this day: 'It was a solemn and searching sermon. What a terrible guilt lies at the door of those who hear the gospel, and yet fail to accept its gracious invitations! We need only to neglect what is offered, to perish, and go down to a lost eternity. Who can answer the question of the text?' The well-meaning message of God is no joking matter. M'Cheyne called all to witness the abundant harvest which was gathered in due to the revival. However, where was the fruit? In spite of it, didn't many live on in their stubborn unbelief?

On the last day of the year 1841, he presented the congregation of St Peter's with 'The Saviour's tears over the lost'. Christ weeping over Jerusalem: 'If thou hast known, even thou, at least in this day, the things which belong unto thy peace!' He placed them before the mirror of the gospel: 'For many a year now, I have been preaching peace to you. I have been a peacemaker. And O brethren! why is it that you will not receive it? Why is it that ye do always resist the truth? Why will ye yet despise Christ and His gospel?' Was the Holy Spirit not poured upon Dundee? 'Brethren, you have had such a time, and it was an easy matter for you to be saved – that year when I was away from you; but ah! many of you let it pass by. It may indeed be said of many here, "The harvest is past, the summer is ended, and we are not saved." O brethren! you have been a highly favoured people; but remember these days of gospel mercies will soon be gone, nevermore to return, and if they leave you unsaved, O what miserable wretches must you be throughout eternity!' Then M'Cheyne reminded them of the time of rich harvest that had passed: 'You may never see such a time again, as you saw here in the autumn of 1839. O, if you would be but wise, and know the day of your merciful visitation!'

According to Bonar, M'Cheyne's preaching 'became more and more to him a work of faith', subsequent to the revival. What concerned him was not a beautiful delivery or a large audience. If he found an opportunity to bring the Word to a small town congregation, then he would saddle his Tully with joy. Thus he once had to make a journey to a distant place, 'to give a cup of cold water to a disciple'. He knew that he was called by the Great Commissioner and his salvation rested in Him alone. We often come across words such as the following at the end of his sermon outlines: 'Master help!' 'Help, Lord, help!' 'Send showers' and 'May the opening of my lips be right things'. His manner of preaching was penetrating and focused on eternal salvation. The wrath and judgment of a righteous God on sin frightened him so that he didn't cease to point the way to the ark of salvation with great seriousness and urgency.

**'Daily Bread'**

From which source did M'Cheyne draw the material for his sermons? Was it not from the eternal Word of God? The Bible was his 'Daily Bread', whence he drew treasures. He preferred nothing more than presenting the wealth of the gospel through preaching. In this way, he continually focused the attention away from himself to the Source of the Word of Life. He admonished the congregation to earnestly examine the Scriptures, which alone could explain the way of salvation. On 30 December 1842, he offered them a Bible timetable, 'a Calendar for reading through the Word of God in a year'. 'It has long been in my mind to prepare a scheme of Scripture reading, in which as many as were made willing by God might agree, so that the whole Bible might be read once by you in the year, and all might be feeding in the same portion of the green pastures at the same time.' It was so necessary that the feet of his congregational members were fastened to the Word of God, so that they would be guarded from following wrong tracks and being led astray.

M'Cheyne was concerned for his congregation, and asked them what would happen when the judgment came over the land due to the contempt for God and his commands. 'There is need now to ask that solemn question: "If in the land of peace, wherein thou trustest, they wearied thee, then how wilt thou do in the swelling of Jordan?" How necessary it is to be ever deeper and deeper confirmed in God's Word by the Holy Spirit. We must be driven more to our Bibles, and to the mercy seat, if we are to stand in the evil day.' Now that yet another year had passed, he asked them where the fruits were. 'The approach of another year stirs up within me new desires for your salvation, and for the growth of those of you who are saved. God is my record how greatly I long after you in the bowels of Jesus Christ.'

The abundant harvest gladdened his heart, but he was concerned about the Word of God being preserved by his congregation. Would they be able to withstand the temptations? Was the seed of the Word sown in well-prepared earth? Surely, what was of concern wasn't quick-germinating plants on 'stony ground', which when the oppression came would shrivel up. Fruit is borne above all in plants which are deeply rooted in the Word. Hence M'Cheyne decided with good counsel: 'Above all, use the Word as a lamp to your feet and a light to your path – your guide in perplexity, your armour in temptation, your food in times of faintness. Hear the constant cry of the great Intercessor: "Sanctify them through Thy truth: Thy Word is truth."'

Ordination of elders, after a painting of John Lorimer (1856-1936).

# Chapter 12

# PRAY FOR THE PEACE OF JERUSALEM

## Ordination of Elders

'My dear brethren, the office of the eldership is a hard work. It is an uphill work; and, therefore, if there is a man in all the world who needs prayer, it is an elder.' M'Cheyne spoke these words on 25 December 1842, at the ordination of four elders in St Peter's. They were David Edwards, Peter Duncan, David Moncur and William Lamb who, for this occasion, walked to the elders' pews in front of the pulpit. The pastor's choice of a text was 1 Timothy 5:17: 'Let the elders that rule well be counted worthy of double honour.' He gave a short summary of the distinction between the teaching and the ruling elders, such as prescribed by the presbyterian system of the Scottish Church. Here he emphasized the 'difficult and delicate duties of elders', such as 'judging of communicants' fitness, admitting to and shutting out from sealing ordinances'. He also mentioned the task of leading prayer meetings: 'Every district should have its prayer meeting.' The ordination followed the sermon. William

Lamb wrote in his diary: 'The minister prayed, and gave us the right hand of fellowship, as did also the elders.'

Prior to this memorable day there were some problems. Lamb, and others too, felt themselves unfit for this ministry. He wrote to M'Cheyne that he felt that he was too young, and besides the experience, he also lacked 'that "fullness of wisdom" mentioned in Acts 6 as forming an essential qualification for the eldership'. Those who were chosen came together in order to deliberate what they should do and to 'lay the matter before the throne of grace'. During this gathering, the old elder, David Kay, entered the room, and thereupon tried to get them to think differently about the matter. M'Cheyne asked Lamb in a letter to weigh up this decision in his mind for a week. The four men again met together. Lamb wrote concerning this: 'Our meeting this evening was pleasant and profitable to us all. I think none of us have entered rashly upon the decision, which is a matter of thankfulness to God; and I take it is as a token of His guiding and eventually bringing us – after weighing well the matter, and I trust, "counting the cost", to the determination to become officebearers and fellow helpers with our pastor in the church of Christ.'

M'Cheyne had confidence in his kirk session. He knew that his elders watched over the congregation, so that he could calmly hand many matters over to them. His poor health still played tricks on him; hence he was pleased with the ordination of four new officebearers. He wrote in his diary: 'This day ordained four elders, and admitted a fifth, who will all, I trust, be a blessing in this place when I am gone. Was graciously awakened a great while before day, and had two hours alone with God. Preached with much comfort on 1 Timothy 5:17.' Did he realize on this Sabbath that the Lord would take him home after a few months? He was still busy with his own congregation and with the welfare of the church in general.

**John Matthewson**

Some of the elders of St Peter's impress one because of their godly walk. John Smith, who together with Tom Brown, led prayer meetings, spoke with much respect about the elder, John Matthewson. 'Since my early days I had known his figure as he walked along the street in Dundee.' Just as other colleagues, Matthewson was a businessman who was not without wealth. Service in the kingdom of God was actually of more worth to him than earthly possessions. He was accustomed to rising at four o'clock to pray and examine the Word of God. For this purpose, he used a list of approximately thirty names of persons which he held up to the throne of grace. When he retired from business, he had more time for a personal examination of the Bible and for the work in God's vineyard. 'He believed greatly in the power and willingness of the Spirit to reveal Christ to us, and he very often spoke of his belief in the power of the Holy Ghost being needed in the sinner's conversion, daily walk, and complete sanctification.' One day he told Smith that the previous night he had experienced 'the most glorious view of Christ he had ever experienced'. 'Oh, we are great sinners,' he said, 'but look at His merits' – so he called out with joy.

It could rightly be said of Matthewson and the other elders that they watched over the souls in the congregation. They

Signing of a declaration of the elders of St Peter's, December 1842.

principles of the Reformation Church of Scotland the great majority of his people as well as of the Elders of this Congregation will feel themselves called upon to leave the Established Church along with him.

Dundee December 1842.

David Moncur
[illegible]
[illegible]
David Edwards
Peter Duncan

David Brown Elder
Peter Thomson Elder
James [illegible] Elder
P. [illegible] Elder
Wm Gibson Elder
James Wallace Elder
[illegible] Elder
Edwd Caird Elder
Andrew Morris Elder

years in those exercises in which we shall spend Eternity — the direct service of God and of Christ. —

Now dear sir farewell, Give my kindest remembrances to Mrs Grierson — Lessy, and the little ones. May they put their trust in God from their earliest years — and may the sickly plant twine the closer round the Plant of Renown —

Ever yours

Robt Murray McCheyne

End of a letter of McCheyne to James Grierson of Errol, 23 January 1840.

were faithful in keeping to the teaching and in carrying out church discipline. Their task constituted, in reality, something of broader scope than merely the congregation of St Peter's. With great interest they followed the distressing events and the developments on the church premises. The end of 1842 saw the struggle on the church front in full swing. Her freedom was at stake, a situation which has frequently occurred in the history of the Scottish Church. In a Declaration, a statement, the St Peter's kirk session gave its opinion. It condemned the manner in which the government intervened in church matters. Christ is Head and King of His heritage and there are no other rulers. There should be no meddling with the freedom of church government nor the calling of a new minister. In conclusion to their statement, the reverend brothers emphasized their 'attachment to the ministry of our pastor, the Reverend Robert Murray McCheyne. For his abundant and devoted labours amongst us, we feel deeply grateful.'

His busy pastoral pursuits didn't prevent M'Cheyne from following with much interest the developments in the wider church context. His task didn't limit him to the walls of Dundee, neither to the welfare of the Jewish nation, but along the lines of John Knox and the later Covenanters, the condition of the entire nation went to his heart. The thrilling events on church terrain followed one another in quick succession, so much so, that it required effort to follow them closely. During his time in the Middle East, he had been deprived of up-to-date information. On his return, he became immediately immersed in the work of the revival, so that he had little time to keep track of the latest developments. In a letter to James Grierson dated the end of January 1840, he wrote concerning his extremely busy existence: 'I expect two communion engagements in the month of February; one at Larbert and the other at Kelso. I am also under promise to speak upon the Jewish cause at Inchture, Arbroath and Montrose, all of which I hope to undertake in the month of February. My own people are in a very tender state – many souls as it were looking in through the gate; some lying helpless, crying for a compassionate look from the heavenly bridegroom. This requires all my strength and care.'

Then he observed: 'I am almost a stranger at the non-intrusion question having been engaged in seeking lost Israel when my brethren were gathering up their fruits and girding their loins for warfare.'

## Non-intrusion

What was meant by the non-intrusion question? The controversial issue of the conflict which dragged on between the church and the government was the so-called right of patronage, also called the right of collation. This right, which originated during the Middle Ages, placed the power to call a minister in the hands of the magistrate and, in the country, in the hands of the landlords. The Covenanters of the seventeenth century, in their struggle against the irrationality of the king who subjected the church at will, had abolished the right of patronage. When in 1712, Queen Anne once again introduced the notorious Act of Patronage, it was strongly opposed. Twenty years later, Ebenezer Erskine could not reconcile himself to this law and chose separation. The problems surrounding patronage came to a climax when the Moderates took charge of this matter. In places where the people wished to have pastors from among the Evangelicals, ministers of a Moderate line were intentionally appointed. The landlords, in general, sympathized more with those who propagated a Moderate way of life.

The resistance against the intrusion of ministers increased at the beginning of the nineteenth century. The people could no longer brook the fact that they were not involved in calling a new minister. When, in 1832, the so-called Reform Bill came into force, whereby many citizens gained the right to vote, the time had arrived for the people to be able to elect their own ministers. In 1833, Thomas Chalmers moved a motion at the Assembly whereby the congregation was granted the right to veto in the calling of a new minister. The right to patronage was maintained, but the people could now reject the decision of the collator by submitting a veto. Despite the resistance of the Moderates, the Assembly accepted this proposal. This Act anent Calls was the first important victory achieved by the Evangelicals in many years.

The success that Chalmers and his allies had achieved seemed now unable to be arrested. The other parties didn't allow themselves to be forced into a corner, however, and an intense struggle, the Ten Years' Conflict, ensued. This determined the outlook of the church for this period. It began in August 1834, when the minister of Auchterarder, a town in Perthshire, died and the Presbytery decided to propose, as his successor, the candidate, Robert Young. The congregation was dissatisfied with this decision and issued a veto. The Presbytery was now required to withdraw the nomination, but the patron wanted to hear nothing of the sort. A long, drawn-out procedure ensued. The Court as well as the House of Lords determined that the Veto Act had no legal ground, because the church had no authority to change to her advantage.

A similar incident occurred in Lethendy in 1837, followed by another in Marnoch, a town situated in Strathbogie, a region to the North of Aberdeen. The Presbytery, which consisted mainly of Moderates, determined the vacancy be filled by John Edwards. The innkeeper alone added his signature to the calling, because the other inhabitants could not accept the teaching which Edwards promulgated. The presbytery wished the confirmation to go through, but the Assembly judged that the right to veto should be exercised in this case. Edwards, himself, applied to the Court of Session, the worldly judge, who proved him right. It became a long, drawn-out procedure, which endured for a few years and resulted in a victory for the Moderates.

Despite the adjournment issued by the Assembly to the ministers of the Presbytery who supported Edwards, Edwards' confirmation was passed. It was 21 January 1841. A thick layer of snow coated the ground as two thousand people walked silently to the old church of Marnoch. They handed in their protest against the arrival of the 'intruder' to the members of the Presbytery. It was in the form of a petition: 'We earnestly beg you... to avoid the desecration of the ordinance of ordination under the circumstances... and as in the presence of the great and only Head of the Church, the Lord Jesus Christ, repudiate and disown the pretended ordination of Mr. Edwards.' The reverend brethren, however, remained resolute. Then the elder, Murray, stood up, asking in a reproachful tone: 'I wish to know on which authority you are here present?' When they dared to answer that they had gathered together in the name of Christ, the entire congregation stood up, took their Bibles, and left the church building in absolute silence. They departed from the church of their fathers with tears in their eyes, never again to return, until 'the temple is purified again, and the buyers and sellers ... are driven from the house of God'.

M'Cheyne, too, stood with heart and soul behind Chalmers and his followers, who strove for 'the Church's independence of the civil power in all matter spiritual'. The right of patronage was, in his eyes, nothing more than a barrier to the progress of the gospel. The revival in religious life should extend to all the

The Church of Marnoch. The sorrowful people left the building because of the intruding minister.

parishes of the land. Entire regions were kept under the power of spiritual darkness by means of the suffocating influence of the Moderates. 'No policy, in his view, could be more ruinous, than that of Moderatism,' wrote Bonar. Bonar once wrote to a friend in Ireland: 'It is a plant that our heavenly Father never planted, and I trust it is now to be rooted up.'

**Opposition from the Moderates**

The Chapel Act presented prospects for the increasing influence of the Evangelicals. Now that the Chapel ministers with their church council had received equal rights in the church meetings, the number of Evangelicals increased. The Moderates watched with dismay as their power stronghold was demolished. In some presbyteries they tried to contradict the decisions of the Assembly, to keep the Chapels from taking part in their own meetings. When their Strathbogie rampart threatened to deteriorate, they were forced to take action. The events that took place in Marnoch were proof enough that the common people wished to hear the simple message of the cross, rather than the dry, traditional sermons of the Moderates. The latter secured the compact through the judge that no minister could cross the boundaries of the region to preach there without their prior permission. When M'Cheyne learned of this unrighteous decision, he said: 'I can say with Paul that I have preached the gospel from Jerusalem round about into Illyricum, and no power on earth shall keep me from preaching it in the dead parishes of Scotland.' The hunger for the living Word in the rural regions of Strathbogie was so great that a few ministers from the South ignored the verdict of the law-court. Thomas Guthrie and Henry Duncan from Ruthwell preached the message of grace and forgiveness to large crowds. M'Cheyne accompanied Mr Alexander from Kirkcaldy on a visit to the district of Deer and Ellon. Over a period of three weeks, he preached here at twenty-four different places. 'Under their preaching the gross darkness of the region began to give way to the light of truth.'

It was a heavy burden for M'Cheyne to behold so many congregations in spiritual darkness through the preaching of the Moderates. He wrote in his diary: 'Have been laying much to heart the absolute necessity laid upon the church of sending the gospel to our dead parishes, during the life of the present incumbents. It is confessed that many of our ministers do not preach the gospel – alas!, because they know it not. Yet they have complete control over their own pulpits, and may never suffer the truth to be heard there during their whole incumbency. And yet our church consigns these parishes to their tender mercies for perhaps fifty years, without a sigh! Should not certain men be ordained as evangelists, with full power to preach in every pulpit of their district – faithful, judicious, lively preachers, who may go from parish to parish, and thus carry life into many a dead corner?' In his mind, he envisaged himself as an itinerant evangelist, and should the church ever have called him to this work, he would surely have considered it!

In the meanwhile, the Church Extension work continued unrelentingly. As we saw earlier, M'Cheyne devoted all his energies to promote the building of new churches as the

Edinburgh Septr 16 – 1840.

My dear Sir

May I beg to remind you that the eleventh day of October, being the second Sunday of that month was appointed by the last General Assembly for a collection throughout the Church in behalf of Church Extension. The Committee earnestly and respectfully entreat that you will have the goodness to interest the people of your Parish, and do all that in you lies to urge forward their liberalities in support of this great cause.

I would further refer your attention to the enclosed Circular, and to the last Annual Report on Church Extension. Thomas Chalmers Convener.

A letter of Thomas Chalmers on Church Extension, 14 September 1840.

opportunity presented itself. In his own presbytery, together with John Roxburgh, he was the driving force behind the establishment of new congregations. Roxburgh had, during his probationary period in Glasgow, made the acquaintance of Chalmers' approach. Since 1837, he had been Convener in Dundee, and M'Cheyne secretary of the Extension commission. Within a short period of time, there arose the congregations of Hilltown and Wallacetown, which were soon occupied by ministers from among the Evangelicals. However, M'Cheyne pointed out that this was insufficient. In a sermon which he delivered in May 1840, he observed: 'In our town I suppose there are at least 15,000 still living in practical heathenism, without having a pastor to look after them. I bless God that there are two new churches nearly ready to be opened.... Still, what are these among so many?'

M'Cheyne was faithful in his attendance at the meetings of the presbytery. His contribution to the meetings was greatly appreciated and 'his candour and uprightness and Christian generosity were felt by all his brethren'. The unity experienced among the brotherhood of ministers of the harbour city was a good foundation on which to rebuild the spiritual welfare of its inhabitants. The necessity of the proclamation of the gospel for everyone meant an increase in the number of church buildings. He portrayed his heart's desire for his city and fatherland in poetic form once again:

A spot so small one pastor can survey:
Give these – and give the Spirit's genial shower,
Scotland shall be a garden all in flower!

**The 'Convocation'**

As already mentioned, M'Cheyne had a great aversion to Erastianism, which gave power over the church to the government. It deprived the church of freedom and meant a denial of 'the Crown Rights of the Redeemer'. When he was asked if a supporter of Erastianism could be ordained, he answered in the negative. A reason he offered was that 'it meddled with the headship of Christ, coming in between Him and His people, saying, "I will place the stars".' With great interest, he followed the events taking place in London, which would decide the destiny of the Scottish Kirk. The House of Lords, which clearly had in mind the example of the English Anglican Church, would not yield to the call for recognition of the Church of Scotland's freedom, which was gained ultimately only at great cost.

The oppressive yoke of the government's efforts began to weigh down even more heavily. The revived church could no longer bear this burden and protested through its representatives. At the end of 1842, the struggle came to a head with far-reaching effects. When the case came before the House of Commons in March the following year, M'Cheyne wrote in his diary: 'Eventful night this, in the British parliament! Once more King Jesus stands at an earthly tribunal, and they know Him not!' The spiritual independence of God's visible church was a matter close to his heart. However, what could he do if the government stood their ground? A threatened split became more of a reality. When he returned to an Assembly in Dundee and his brother in the faith, Stewart, asked what he would do if there should be a schism, he replied, 'I think of going to the many thousands of convicts that are transported beyond seas, for no man careth for their souls.'

The Assembly of 1842 had accepted the Claim of Rights and announced that they refused to obey the unbiblical regulations from London. Her Declaration and Protest was directed at the laws of the British Parliament, which were contradictory to the Union Law of 1707 that united England and Scotland as one nation. The Assembly made an appeal for the freedom of the Church of Scotland, which, in the past, had been ratified by royal decrees. Despite these protests, the Crown had no intention of acting upon the requests of the Assembly. The Evangelicals strove for a nearly hopeless case. It hardly seemed possible to avoid a separation. On 11 August 1840, M'Cheyne attended a gathering of ministers and elders in Edinburgh, to sign the Solemn Engagement. On 17 November 1842 the 'protesters' met in Roxburgh Church in the Old Town of Edinburgh. Four hundred and sixty-five ministers came from all corners of the land to the capital city in order to attend this Convocation. Chalmers preached from Psalm 112:4 before a large crowd in St George's: 'Unto the upright there ariseth light in the darkness ...', and the elderly John McDonald from Ferintosh prayed a fervent prayer.

M'Cheyne attended all the subsequent meetings and diligently made notes of the deliberations in his pocketbook. Many prayers, both silent and spoken, were made to the King of the church for a favourable outcome. M'Cheyne too prayed with emotion, leaving a deep impression on those present. For eight days, a remarkable unity as well as the presence of God's Spirit was among the brothers who championed the salvation of Zion. The St Peter's minister met many colleagues with whom he felt a strong bond. At the first meeting, Henry Duncan said a prayer, which was followed by a supplication from his younger friend. Chalmers ably led the meetings. Many speakers expressed their feelings and encouraged those gathered there. The discussions at meal-times were edifying. M'Cheyne made mention of a few names: Dr McFarlan from Greenock, the elderly father of William Burns, Alexander Keith, his companion on the journey to the Promised Land, not forgetting Robert Candlish of St George's.

The last mentioned was especially clearly audible in his speech. He urged everyone to continual prayer. 'We may be of one mind, and yet there will be much diversity of opinion. We are men who, of ourselves, cannot see one foot in advance, who stagger blindly, and who must feel our way. What has passed among us tonight proves it. It makes us more than ever diffident of our own wisdom. It should throw us more completely and confidingly on the guidance of God's good Spirit.' M'Cheyne felt at home in this company. The following applied during the Convocation: 'Pray for the peace of Jerusalem.' He rejoiced in listening to his old master, Thomas Chalmers, who on Saturday, 'after a amazing speech', moved many to tears, but also knew how to obtain the signatures of four hundred ministers supporting the concluded decisions. When, on the following Wednesday, the final meeting was held, he could heartily agree with the address which he heard, in which was emphasized the importance of 'sealing with one's blood' the decisions of the Convocation.

The unity of the church was a matter close to M'Cheyne's heart. He was pleased when he heard that the Secession Church of Ireland would once again be united with the Presbyterian Church. In the summer of 1840, he visited Belfast as representative of the Scottish Church in order to attend the meeting of the united Synod. His congregation reluctantly allowed him to go yet again. How frequently they missed him when the duties of the country-wide church called him away to places farther afield. Naturally, he tried to find a substitute for himself. This time, however, it wasn't that easy. Even in this situation, however, he saw God's guiding hand, because, as he was about to cancel his journey, he preached from the text, Philippians 3:18 on the subject: 'Enemies of the cross of Christ.' 'When that part was expounded, there was a loud and bitter weeping – probably thirty or forty seemed to share in it; the rest deeply impressed – many secretly praying.' God's work continued in his congregation! Encouraged, he departed for the green island to address the synod of the Irish Church. Joy radiated from the faces of the brothers who, unavoidably, for many years had gone their own ways in separation, but now once more were re-united. The following year, M'Cheyne was invited to visit Ireland for a second time, in order to bring the Word to different places, leaving a lasting impression among many.

**Unity with dissentients**

Despite the strong presbyterian principles to which M'Cheyne adhered, he was tolerant towards dissentients, who possessed a 'like precious faith'. He often allowed ministers from the circle of the 'Dissenters', the seceding churches, to conduct a service in St Peter's. Thus William Borwick of the Bell Street United Secession Church preached one Sunday afternoon in his church, which inspired the elder William Lamb to mention in his diary: 'How pleasing to see these barriers of party Christianity broken down, and the right hand of fellowship held out by one Christian Church to the members and ministers of others.' M'Cheyne wrote an open letter in the magazine *The Witness*, 'The Children of God of every Name in Scotland' and urged that prayer should be made 'for all true Christians', irrespective of their denomination. In December 1839, he spoke at a meeting of the Dundee Wesleyan Missionary Society, the Methodist missionary society, and later on even in their own chapel. The

Moderates protested strongly against his contact with these followers of the Arminian Methodist, John Wesley. They attacked him because he had allowed singing with organ accompaniment in their chapel. M'Cheyne's attitude towards other church affiliations was more tolerant with regard to his sympathizers. He thought that the relationship between a man such as Ralph Erskine and the Anglican, George Whitefield, far from Christian. The impression that he gives of the Erskines, is coloured because of this. Thus, he said at the induction of his friend, P. L. Miller: 'It was said of the Erskines, that men could not see Christ over their heads.' The life of these godly brothers demonstrates exactly the opposite.

In reply to the accusation of the Moderates, he wrote a detailed explanation of his opinion concerning 'Communion with brethren of other denominations' to the *Dundee Warder*. This local newspaper was the mouthpiece of the Moderates, who often criticized the other party in a cynical manner. In a clear way, he stated that the unity of believers is based on the essential points of the Christian faith. Differences of opinion may emerge in ideas about church government and matters of secondary importance, but the bond with Christ determines the unity with each other. Together with John Bunyan, he was of the opinion that these differences provided no obstacle to the participation in holy communion together. He pointed to 'the Lord's Supper in an upper room in Jerusalem', during his visit to Palestine. 'There were fourteen present, the most of whom, I had good reason to believe, knew and loved the Lord Jesus Christ. Several were godly Episcopalians, two were converted Jews, and one a Christian from Nazareth, converted under the American missionaries. The bread and wine were dispensed in the Episcopal manner, and most were kneeling as they received them.' And yet there reigned a sweet communion with Christ and with the brethren. In this connection, he mentioned an incident, when the Methodist, Rowland Hill, was refused admittance to the communion table in a Baptist Church, whereupon his reaction was: 'I thought it was the Lord's table?'

What concerned M'Cheyne was the unity of the Bride of Christ. As such, he knew that he followed in the footsteps of a man like Calvin. The 'temple worship' was sacred to him, and he refused an insipid teacher admittance to his pulpit, though he might be a full-blooded Presbyterian. 'But the living servant of Christ is dear to my heart, and welcome to address my flock, let him come from whatever quarter of the earth he may. I have sat with delight under the burning words of a Lutheran pastor. I have been fed by the ministrations of American Congregationalists and devoted Episcopalians, and all of my flock who know and love Christ would have loved to hear them too.' Even the Roman Catholic priest, Martin Boos, from Germany, whose biography had made such an impression on him, would be welcome in St Peter's. Now Boos was no vigorous follower of the pope, and he studied the teaching of righteousness from a Protestant viewpoint! No wonder that the Jesuits more than once were close on his heels.

M'Cheyne loved this 'evangelical pastor'. 'If dear Martin Boos were alive, pastor of the Church of Rome though he was, he would have been welcome too; and who that knows the value of souls and the value of a living testimony would say it was wrong?' The gentlemen of the city newspaper could keep in mind the conclusion to his account, which he wrote on 6 July 1842: 'If our church is to fall under the iron foot of despotism, God grant that it may fall reformed and purified; pure in its doctrine, government, discipline and worship; scriptural in its spirit; missionary in its aim and holy in its practice; a truly golden candlestick; a pleasant vine. If the daughter of Zion must be made a widow, and sit desolate on the ground, grant her latest cry may be that of her once suffering, now exalted Head: "Father, forgive them, for they know not what they do."'

The love for the Saviour was the goad that urged him on to promote unity among the brothers. He agreed wholeheartedly with the proposal to hold meetings for 'concerted prayer'. In September 1841, he took part in such a meeting, where

Martin Boos (1762-1825), 'evangelical romish pastor' in Gallneukirchen in Bayern.

Christians of all church persuasions were present. 'How sweet are the smallest approximations to unity!' he wrote in his diary. In the midst of the disappointments in the life of the church, he saw these gatherings as hopeful signs of the blessing of the Almighty. The unity, as well as the purity of the visible church, were to him a source of concern and prayer. However, the Holy Spirit alone could unite them and purify the Bride of Christ. All human attempts, without the realization of a deep dependence on His ministry, would ultimately suffer loss. The struggle for the freedom of the church raged with intensity and threatening clouds loomed over God's congregation. In 1841, he preached a sermon on Revelation 3:14-22. He described the situation within the congregation of Laodicea and drew parallels with the situation in his own land. 'Christ's cause is bleeding and torn in Scotland. Men in high places have dashed the crown from His head and trampled it in the dust. Are your hearts bleeding? Are you willing to suffer with Christ's cause?' M'Cheyne's preaching contained no dull message whereby one could lapse into resignation, but it was an urge to lay the hand to the plough. Prayer was the first requisite that was necessary in these circumstances. His congregation was the first in the land that proceeded to hold monthly prayer meetings, after the General Assembly had made a summons to this end. The elders of St Peter's devoted themselves on behalf of the concerns of the non-intrusion party in the city. The Declaration drawn up by the church council witnessed to a great involvement in the welfare of the entire church in Scotland.

**The desecration of the Lord's Day**

Another matter which attracted the attention of the pastor of St Peter's, was the increasing profanation of the Sabbath day. On 18 December 1841 he distributed a booklet, entitled 'I love the Lord's Day'. The motive for this was the decision made by the up-and-coming railway companies to establish train services on a Sunday, the Scottish appellation being Sabbath. Since the time of Stephenson's invention, the production of steam locomotives had boomed and the railway network expanded steadily. It would not be long before Dundee, too, received a railway connection. A storm of protest blew across the land, in the places where the Christian Sabbath was still held in reverence. Prominent church leaders, such as Thomas Chalmers, William Cunningham and Robert Candlish, acted as a mouthpiece for the conservative section of the nation, and were able to exercise much influence. Petitions in writing were delivered to Queen Victoria and letters of protest were sent to the government from all quarters. M'Cheyne's father, too, devoted himself to plead for a Sunday without train travel.

M'Cheyne himself attracted the attention of many by his activities within the Presbytery of Dundee. He was Convener of the recently instituted Sabbath Observance Committee, and in the name of this commission and towards the promotion of the sanctification of Sunday, composed a letter of protest directed at the company which had begun, in 1840, a delivery service between Dundee and Arbroath. Herein he gave vent to his 'deep feelings of righteous indignation'. Without speaking in covert terms, he condemned the procedures of the company: 'Ah sir, speak out your mind! Tell what it is that lies at the bottom of your enmity to the entire preservation of the Lord's

Day.' M'Cheyne called the decision of the management plain blasphemy. 'You proclaim your own shame. You prove, even to the blind world, that you are not journeying to the Sabbath above, where the Sabbath-breaker cannot come.'

Besides his frank petitions, he awakened the believers to pray for the conversion of the Sabbath transgressors. Protestation without prayerfully looking upwards means little to God. In spite of all the attempts, the evil plans were realized. It was not long before the first Sunday train travelled from Edinburgh to Glasgow. His friend, William Burns, stood on the platform of the new station near North Bridge at the moment of departure. He held a short service for a crowd of people, who with tears in their eyes, listened to the compassionate evangelist. He also spent the remainder of the Sunday in the station. The railways stubbornly persisted in permitting trains to run on Sundays. Although Dundee was still deprived of a train connection, it would not be long before steam locomotives cast their stench in front of the St Peter's manse, disturbing the peace in the West End suburb. However, M'Cheyne would not be there any longer when it came into operation.

The pamphlet 'I love the Lord's Day' was directed at all his fellow countrymen. Sunday was no slavish maintenance of a rule in M'Cheyne's eyes, but a feast-day when the resurrection of Christ was celebrated. 'The more entirely I can give my Sabbaths to God, and half forget that I am not before the throne of the Lamb with my harp of gold, the happier am I, and I feel it my duty to be as happy as I can be, and as God intended me to be.' This he wrote to a man from Inverness who asked him whether it was advisable to carry out weather observations on a Sunday. Pharisaical piety was strange to him; his scrupulous conduct of life emerged from a fervent love for God and His commands. Hence the significant title of the composition, an enlarged edition of which was distributed everywhere. His plea for the godly command was strong: 'Oh, Sabbath-breaker, whoever you be, you are a sacrilegious robber!' The Sabbath is a remaining flower of Paradise, it is a 'day of blessing'. It delights the Lord, on this day in particular, to consecrate His Word. 'All God's faithful ministers in every land can bear witness that sinners are converted most frequently on the Lord's day.' 'Unhappy men, who are striving to rob our beloved Scotland of this day of double blessing, "ye know not what you do".' Thus M'Cheyne devoted himself to the ordinances of the house of the Lord. What his Saviour said, applies equally to M'Cheyne, 'The zeal of thine house hath eaten me up.'

**The 'Little Flock'**

M'Cheyne's field of labour was unlimited and extensive, as long as the boundaries of God's kingdom were not exceeded. Nothing was too much for him, if it concerned God's honour. 'Hallowed be Thy name', was the prayer that filled his heart. Whether it was amongst the Jews in Eastern Europe, or in the meetings of the non-intrusion party, or where the call was sent out to maintain the Christian day of rest; wherever the Lord called him to confess His Name and His honour, there M'Cheyne followed without murmuring. Sometimes his congregation was somewhat disappointed because of his absence, but they knew only too well that he didn't neglect them in favour of an honorary post. He was no hireling who was unconcerned with the fate of his own. If he should be gone from the city for a while, he always provided a substitute. It was true that he had less time to devote to his house-to-house evangelization. He served St Peter's faithfully, but he also had to attend to the needs of the worldwide church.

What concerned M'Cheyne was the peace and unity of Jerusalem. It was beside the point to achieve a strong church organization, which would allow no room for the continuation of the Holy Spirit's work. He detested every form of coldness and commercialization on the church premises. In everything, he had his eye on the erection of the church of the beloved of the Lord. He 'spoke comfortably to Jerusalem', and continued to speak words of comfort to God's poor and needy people. They were the genuine, living building-stones of God's house.

God's children should be 'the salt of the earth' and a shining 'city that is set on a hill', a leaven giving the visible church new impulse to the further extension of God's kingdom. This 'charity which is the bond of perfectness', should never be neglected by its teachers. The fragrance of Christ's holiness should clothe the children of God and, 'as the dew of Hermon', in true unity and in 'the bond of perfectness', this fragrance should descend upon the court of the Lord's temple. It was an important task for the St. Peter's pastor to guide this living flock in all circumstances of this hard life. Within and beyond the boundaries of his parish, he gave counsel to many who were struggling with spiritual issues or needed comfort from the Word of promise. The goose-feather was a much used instrument, with which he could write letters to young and old, men and women, in Dundee and its environs. We may suppose that he made use of the night hours for his frequent correspondence.

Bonar observes that 'to many it was a subject of wonder that he found time to write letters that always breathed the name of Jesus, amid his innumerable engagements'. According to him, M'Cheyne's style of writing had much in common with the letters of Samuel Rutherford, 'whose works he delighted to read, excepting only that his joy never seems to have risen to ecstasies'. His heart constantly kept looking up to his Master, and the love which he possessed in such a rich measure streamed between the banks of the canal in his soul, without flooding over into exaggerated emotions. His spiritual life wasn't characterized by many ups and downs, but instead was strongly rooted in God's fatherly love and Christ's compassion. He wrote his letters, which contained so much comfort, from this source. His poetical talent and short and pithy language usage, rendered extra effect to his letters. Thus he wrote to his parents: 'The Tay is before me now like a resplendent mirror, glistening in the morning sun. May the same sun shine sweetly on you, and may He that makes it shine, shine into your hearts to give you the knowledge of the glory of God in the face of Jesus Christ.' Didn't nature frequently afford him images of God's unfathomable love and grace? He often concluded his letters with words such as, 'Oh for drops in the pastures of the wilderness.'

**His correspondence**

His affectionate heart expressed itself especially in the letters to those who were struck down by pressure and trials. He wrote to a member of his congregation about the use of tribulations in building one's personal character. He asked the penetrating questions: 'Does trouble work patience in you? Does it lead you to cling closer to the Lord Jesus – to hide deeper in the rock?' And then a few words in his conclusion: 'Pray for me still, that I may get the good of all God's dealings with me. Lean all on Jesus.' To another, whose brother had died, he wrote: 'There is no true comfort to be found but in Christ. He is a fountain of living waters, and you must go with your thirsty soul to Him and drink.' To a Miss A. S. L. he gave good counsel: 'Keep your eye upon Jesus and the unsearchable riches that are in Him; and may the gentle Comforter fill your soul and give you a sweet foretaste of the glory that is to follow. May He leave his deep eternal impress upon your soul, not healing you and going away, but abiding within you, keeping the image of Christ in your heart, ever fresh and full.' Christ is the great Healer, Who 'in all their affliction He was afflicted'. 'Tell Him all your sorrows, all your doubts and anxieties. He has a willing ear. Oh, what a friend is Jesus, the sinner's friend! What an open ear he has for all the wants, doubts, difficulties of His people! He has an especial care for His sick, weakly, and dying disciples.'

Especially during the time of the revival, many letters arrived for him requesting advice. Thus, a member of the church in Blairgowrie wrote to him about a society that had recently been formed for the edification and deepening of the life of faith. M'Cheyne was pleased that believers were meeting together in this way. It was important that Christ remain central in these discussions. 'Let Jesus come into your meetings and sit at the head of the table. It is a fragrant room when the bundle of myrrh is the chief thing there. Let there be no strife among you, but who to be the lowest at His feet, who to lean their head most fully on His breast. Let all your conversation, meditations, and readings lead you to the Lamb of God.'

He impressed the Parable of the Sower upon a prayer society. This group consisted more of a company of seeking souls than confirmed believers. He pointed out to them the various effects the Word can have. Not everybody will be brought to the Saviour; a thorough self-examination is necessary: 'Many among you, I fear, are like the hard wayside, so that, when the seed falls, it cannot get into your hearts, and the devil plucks it all away. If you find that your liking to the gospel is from the surface, from curiosity or fancy, or love to a minister – if you find that your rocky heart has never been broken by conviction of sin, has never been melted to flow towards Jesus – then you are an empty professor; you have a name to live, while you are spiritually dead.' He believed, however, that among this company there were also genuine plants of God's vineyard to be found, 'like the good ground (Matt. 13:8), who receive the Word into a heart broken up by the Spirit of God – watered by prayer – and who bear fruit unto life eternal.' The Lord looks for fruit from the work of His servants. 'Have you had your hearts broken, dear friends? Has God ploughed up your hard, unbelieving hearts? Have you had real concern for your perishing soul? Have you been driven to your knees? Have you ever wept in secret for your sins? Have you been made to tremble under your load of guilt? Do you come thus to the house of God – your heart like an open furrow waiting for the seed? Inquire earnestly whether the fallow-ground of your heart has ever been broken up (Jer. 4:3). A broken heart alone can receive a crucified Christ.'

A certain J. T. just asked for regulations for the holding of fellowship meetings. Great caution was required when holding such meetings. How often did not pious man stand in the centre

Revd Robert McCheyne
Minister of St Peters
Dundee

Rev Robert M. M'Cheyne
Dundee

Revd Robt M. McCheyne
Strawberry Bank
Perth Road.

Addresses on envelopes of some letters sent to McCheyne.

of the proceedings? M'Cheyne thought it better that believers alone, who agreed with each other and had a need for fellowship, should meet together in this way. 'If four or five of you who know the Lord would meet together regularly, you will find that far more profitable than a meeting open to all.' The danger of spiritual pride should not be underestimated. What is the most profitable form of fellowship? 'The praying meeting I like best is where there is only praise and prayer, and the reading of God's Word.' Other forms are also possible, such as handling a question from the Catechism. The most important thing, however, is that God's Spirit takes the lead, which results in the fruit of genuine humility. 'You require more grace to be kept humble and meek and loving, if you engage in this service.'

**Counselling of souls**

Many letters contained counsel for awakened souls. He spurred them on to surrender themselves to Jesus. When he wrote a letter in September 1842, 'to one awakened', a very little girl had come to his home with the question, 'What must I do to be saved? Poor thing, she has been weeping till I thought her heart would break. She lives several miles off; but a companion was awakened and told her, and ever since she has been seeking Christ with all her heart. I was telling her that sweet verse: "Christ came into the world to save sinners, of whom I am the chief" (1 Tim. 1:15). It will answer you also, dear friend.' 'Perhaps you will say, "But I am too bad a sinner"; but Paul says, "of whom I am the chief". So Christ is willing and able to save you, though you were the chief sinner on the face of the earth.' In the same vein, he wrote to another questioning soul, concluding his letter with a poem by Joseph Hart, 'Come ye sinners, poor and wretched...', which had as its concluding verse:

> If ye tarry till you're better,
> You will never come at all.
> Not the righteous –
> Sinners Jesus came to call.

M'Cheyne never cast anxious souls back on themselves; neither did he comfort them with supposed 'marks of grace', but he always pointed them directly to the cross. Thus, he wrote in November 1841: 'He is not far from any one of us. He is a powerful and precious Saviour, and happy are they who put their trust in Him. He is the Rose of Sharon, lovely to look upon.' 'You are dead; He is the life. You are all wounds and bruises; He is the Balm of Gilead. His righteousness is broader than your sin; and then He is so free.' 'Look at Isaiah 40:1-2: "Comfort ye, comfort ye my people." If you receive Christ as your Surety, you have realized double punishment for all your sins. If you will only open your arms to receive Christ as your Surety, then your iniquity is pardoned, if you will only lay hold on Christ now, you will feel the force of that sweet command, "Comfort ye, comfort ye"; double comfort, double peace, for in Jesus you have suffered double wrath.'

In 1841, he wrote a series of letters to 'a soul seeking Jesus'. He was totally honest with this girl. 'The world will say you are an innocent and harmless girl; do not believe them. The world is a liar.' 'Oh, pray for deep discoveries of your real state by nature and by practice!' 'The discovery of one's guilty state is necessary, although it is not a prerequisite for one's fleeing to Christ. The ground for genuine peace is the righteousness of Christ.' 'Your tears will not blot out sins; they do nothing but weep in hell, but that does not justify you ... Do you thus look to Jesus? Do you believe the record that God has given concerning Him? Do you receive Jesus with open arms? ...' The invitation to come to Him was impressed upon her heart: 'Jesus is ready to wash and clothe you in His own blood and righteousness.' His blood alone cleanses from all sins. 'The pure, full love of God steams through the blood and obedience of Jesus to every soul that is lying under them, however vile and wretched in themselves. This is what Jesus wants. He died to be a shelter for such as you. Do you want love? He is the fountain of love: all the promises of God in Him are yea and in Him amen. I am sure, if you got a glimpse of Him, you would lay your head in His breast and die there.' With heartfelt emotions he ended thus the sixth letter: 'Farewell, dear soul! The Lord feed you sweetly, as he feeds the flowers, by silent drops of dew.'

His letters are full of the riches of Christ. He wrote to Miss Collier on 26 February 1840, from Edinburgh: 'How great is the goodness He hath laid up for them that fear Him! Just as the miser lays up money that he may feast his eyes upon it, so Christ has laid up unsearchable riches that He may supply all our need out of them. Unfathomable oceans of grace are in Christ for you. Dive and dive again, you will never come to the bottom of these depths. How many millions of dazzling pearls and gems are at this moment hid in the deep recesses of the ocean caves! But there are unsearchable riches in Christ. Seek more of them.'

What can be better for one's soul than to look to Him, which name is sweeter than the name of Jesus? He wrote to a fellow minister in Belfast as follows: 'Learn much of the Lord Jesus. For every look at yourself, take ten looks at Christ. He is altogether lovely. Such infinite majesty, and yet such meekness and grace, and all for sinners, even the chief! Live much in the smiles of God. Bask in His beams. Feel His all-seeing eye settled on you in love, and repose in His almighty arms.' What better life can there be than one of following Jesus? Thus, he wrote to the missionary, Edwards, on the blessing of sanctification; painful for one's own existence, but profitable for the heart that longs to pursue Christ, and considers all things loss: 'It is our truest happiness to live entirely for the glory of Christ – to separate between "I" and "the glory of Christ". We are always saying, What have I done? – was it my preaching, my sermon, my influence?, whereas we should be asking, What hath God wrought? Strange mixed beings we are! How sweet it will be to drop our old man, and be pure as Christ is pure!'

This longing for holiness characterized M'Cheyne's life. As the months passed by, so his body became more and more weak, although he also experienced times of recovery. Sickness and bodily ailments took their toll, but the power of the Lord strengthened his spirit. The more his earthly tabernacle became broken, the more he longed for the eternal building the Lord had prepared for him. His heavy task demanded much from his constitution. He was enabled to labour in God's vineyard through the wonderful support that he received, until an end came to his young life.

Since his return from Palestine, his condition had gradually deteriorated. The Thain family from Blairgowrie watched with concern how his physical strength declined. During the Spring of 1840, Mrs Thain invited him to rest up at the splendid villa, 'Heath Park'. M'Cheyne himself longed for a rest, but what was God's will? Thus he wrote to her: 'You know how glad I would be of some such retreat as Elijah had by the brook of Cherith, where I might learn more of my own heart, and of my Bible and of my God; where I might while away the summer hours in quiet meditation, or talking of His righteousness all the day long. But it is only said of the dead in the Lord that they rest from their labours; and I fear I must not think of resting till then. Time is short, my time especially, and souls are precious; and I fear many are slumbering because I watch not with sufficient diligence, nor blow the trumpet with sufficient clearness.' Yet, he still visited 'Heath Park' on more than one occasion to be refreshed there. One day, a friend of John Smith's was visiting him. As she was about to depart, she entered the dining room, which served as a study room for the minister. 'I was delighted to see the beautiful, heavenly expression of his face. We had no serious talk. I only stood beside him for a little, and do not remember anything he said. It was a pleasant incident, and his death so soon after impressed me deeply.'

**Serious illness**

In the same year, he was once again struck down by a serious illness. Concerning this, he wrote to his colleague and friend, Patrick Miller: 'I have had a severe illness of late, and been taught to look more toward the Church above. But I am better, and my heart warms again towards the Lord's work below.' It was 'a dangerous nervous fever', which necessitated his taking a rest for some time. For six days, he was required to remain in bed. Before his fit of fever, he was encouraged by a visit from three people, who told him that they were brought to Christ through his preaching. 'Why,' he noted in his journal, 'why has God brought these cases before me this week? Surely He is preparing me for some trial of faith.' Fortunately, he soon recovered and could write to George Shaw from Belfast: 'I have been only twice in the open air, and cannot yet manage the pen with facility; but I cannot delay writing to you any longer.'

The ordeals increased rather than the contrary. Bonar writes concerning this: 'There were other trials also besides these, which were very heavy to him; but in all we could discern the Husbandman pruning the branch that it might bear more fruit.' In spite of his poor health, friends tried to persuade him to change his post. At the end of 1841, he was once again approached concerning a possible call. It concerned the congregation of Kettle, about which he received a letter from his friend, McFarlane, from Collessie. In a letter, he gave his reply to Mr Heriot from Collessie: 'I feel quite at the disposal of my divine Master. I gave myself away to Him when I began my ministry, and He has guided me as by the Pillar Cloud from the first day till now.' Without definite instructions from the One who had commissioned him, he dared not abandon his St Peter's congregation. 'If my ministry were unsuccessful, if God frowned upon the place and made my message void, then I would willingly go, for I would rather beg my bread than preach without success; but I have never lacked success.' He could not remember a month passing by during which no souls were saved. 'I have four thousand souls here hanging on me. I have as much of this world's goods as I care for. I have full liberty to preach the gospel night and day; and the Spirit of God is often with us. What can I desire more?'

There was still another extensive task that required

completion. Since his arrival back from Palestine, his time was mostly swallowed up by the events surrounding the revivals in Dundee and other places. The same applied to his friend, Andrew Bonar, from Collace. Yet, the notes concerning their journey to the Jewish land had to be compiled, because the church awaited a detailed report including the resultant findings. There was no other alternative but to take time off to do it. In March 1842, M'Cheyne and Bonar held over their own work for a while, in order to produce their *Narrative*. For a month they exchanged congregations, so that Bonar regularly preached in St Peter's. The stay in Collace provided relief for M'Cheyne. He would often go for a walk in the early morning, through the magnificent woods of Dunsinane. He was then taken up with meditation and prayer. His thoughts were directed to the future life. During these four or five months, he also had the opportunity to write a few contributions for a meditative diary, entitled *The Christian's Daily Companion*. Thirty-one Scottish ministers co-operated together on this task. In May, the bulky travel report, supplemented by sketches that he himself had made, was ready to go to the press. Now he could once more devote himself completely to the work among his congregation.

In the summer of 1842, he was attacked by different illnesses. Were these heralds of his imminent death? He continued with his work as long as he was able. In a letter dated 5 November, he wrote: 'I preached twice on Thursday, and once last night, and now I am preparing for tomorrow. I feel, like John the Baptist, the voice of one crying in the wilderness. The mad world presses on like a bird hastening to the snare. They do not know that the dead are there, and her guests are in the depths of hell.' Death held no fear for M'Cheyne. It was not that he didn't dread dying, but the sting of death was removed from him. He was entirely assured of his salvation and could see beyond death and the grave. He was thoroughly convinced that the heart was deceitful and that man could deceive himself concerning eternity. A poem from this time about the wise and the foolish virgins, show that he believed the mere name of Christian was no guarantee that one would enter through the heavenly gates.

How vain the Christian name,
If still you live in sin;
A lamp and wick and flame,
No drop of oil within!

M'Cheyne knew from experience that he was grafted into Christ and that He was the source of his life. The oil of love filled his soul, overflowing in abundance. The fervent love for his Saviour kept the lamps burning . Therefore, he was prepared to meet his heavenly Bridegroom. His wedding day was at hand!

Is your lamp filled, my child,
With oil from Christ above?
Has He your heart, so wild,
Made soft and full of love?

Then you are ready now
With Christ to enter in;
To see His holy brow,
And bid farewell to sin.

# Chapter 13

# 'TREADING THE VALLEY'

## A retrospective view

'It is six years, this day, since I first preached to you, as your pastor, from these blessed words. These years have rolled past us like a mighty river.' M'Cheyne uttered these words on Sunday morning, 27 November 1842. It was a turbulent Sabbath. The morning service was disturbed by a rascal 'rushing into the porch of the church with loud and terrified howlings'. He was able to maintain order with some difficulty. During the evening service, the people were startled by a woman who passed out in the gallery. Just as he was accustomed to doing every year, he commemorated the day of his arrival in St Peter's. He preached from the same text that he had used in his inaugural sermon: 'The Spirit of the Lord God is upon me ... to preach good tidings unto the meek' (Isa. 61:1-3). In addition, he thereby retrospectively mentioned the past, which he likened to climbing a mountain. Halfway up there are resting places, from which vantage point one is able to see how one has progressed. The higher one climbs, the more beautiful is the panorama that unfolds before one's eyes. 'In like manner, in going up the hill of Zion, it is pleasant to come to such a resting place as this day affords, that we may stand and see what progress we have made, and whether we have a wider, brighter prospect of eternal glory.'

Where is the labourer's fruit in his vineyard? He pointed out that many had already gone hence from this life. 'Of some I trust we can say, "Blessed are the dead, for they died in the Lord." ' He believed that many had passed from death to life. His work in Dundee was therefore certainly not in vain. However, he couldn't pat himself on the back. 'In looking back upon my ministry, I am persuaded that this has been the great thing wanting. We have not been like the green olive-tree.' It is the anointing of the Holy Spirit that enables the servant of the gospel to bear fruit in his labours. Subsequent to the resurrection of their Master, the apostles possessed this anointing in rich measure and 'when the Spirit came on them like a mighty rushing wind – then behold what a change!' When compared to the apostles, M'Cheyne thought his work to be deficient. 'We have not been able to say, like the Saviour, "The Spirit of the Lord God is upon me," or you would not be as you are this day. Oh, pray that if God spare us another year, we may be more like the high priest, who first went into the holiest of all, and then came out and lifted up his hands and blessed the people.'

In his natural self he was no trustworthy servant of the Lord. His awareness of his own shortcomings made him from his perspective appear inferior in God's eyes. The sight of the many unconverted appalled him. It was true that the Lord had accomplished great things through him and He had shown His almighty power. However, where was the Bride's adornment? 'How little is there of this divine presence and holy impression in our assemblies. Oh that the little flock in this place were covered with His beauty, filled with His holy joy, and clothed with His garment of praise!' The Saviour is still going around 'to proclaim the acceptable year of the Lord'. 'We have told you that Christ is freely offered to you in your present condition, whatever that may be; that though you have lived in sin, and are now living in sin, and God is angry with you every day, still Christ is freely offered to you every day.' There was no reason to despair, even for the minister. 'Blessed be God, there are some of you who have fled for refuge to the hope set before you; but the most sleep on. Six acceptable years have passed over you. A year of gospel preaching is an acceptable year; a year of revival, when many have been pressing into the kingdom of God, is still more an acceptable year; both these have passed over you. The door has stood open all this time, and any sinner among you might have entered in.' 'But you are still without—Christless, unpardoned, unborn again, unsaved. What can you look for but "the day of vengeance"?'

It seemed as if M'Cheyne delivered his farewell sermon that day. He lived with the constant awareness that his death was close at hand. For this reason, he called attention to the trumpets of eternity which resounded so powerfully. It was for him an absolute reality that 'Man goeth to his long home!' He lived near the portals of eternity. During summer that year, he definitely felt that his physical strength was declining. Besides a few attacks of illness, he also experienced severe ordeals. What form these trials actually took, Bonar doesn't mention. M'Cheyne himself observed on 17 July 1842: 'I am myself much tempted, and have no hope, but as a worm on the arm of Jesus.' One month later, he wrote to Bonar: 'I have been carried through deep waters, bodily and spiritual, since last we met.' An intense struggle raged within his innermost being. Powerful temptations seized him. However, he did not yield, because his Saviour upheld him. If He was nearby, then he was enabled to bear the worst afflictions; then burdens became bearable. How he longed for His love and fellowship. When would the day dawn that he would be forever in His presence? 'Often, often, would I have been glad to depart, and be with Christ. I am now much better in body and mind, having a little of the presence of my Beloved, Whose absence is death to me,' he wrote on 4 August.

**Journey to England**

During these difficult months of testings, he received an invitation to undertake an evangelistic tour. The destination of the journey was north of England. Shortly prior to this, William Burns had made the acquaintance of the dry spiritual climate of this region, and especially Newcastle. He called this city an 'iron-walled citadel of Satan'. His perception of it was: 'The sleep of death is on the city.' Despite the great resistance he had experienced, he managed to come to grips with the masses after some time. As it turned out, it was most inconvenient for M'Cheyne to undertake this journey. He found himself in the midst of the heat of the crucible of misfortune, but he wasn't without hope. Purified, he endured his suffering. 'Some flowers must be broken or bruised before they emit any fragrance. All the wounds of Christ send out sweetness; all the sorrows of Christians do the same,' he wrote to John Purves in Jedburgh. This trying path was not without affect; he was continually drawn into a deeper commitment to Christ. He replied by mail that he was prepared to accompany them. His brothers need not expect anything from him, for the One who commissioned him alone gave him the strength for the task. 'Remember me especially, who am heavy laden oftentimes. My heart is all of sin; but Jesus lives.'

The travel party, besides Purves and M'Cheyne, consisted of three other colleagues: Alexander Cumming from Dumbarney, Alexander Somerville from Glasgow and Horatius Bonar from Kelso. They crossed the border and at last reached Newcastle. They preached in the open air on many occasions. One evening, M'Cheyne spoke to a crowd of approximately a thousand people which had gathered together on a precinct between the Cloth Market and St Nicholas' Church. The topic of his sermon was 'The great White Throne'. It was a beautiful evening, with stars illuminating the sky. An impressive silence reigned over the attentive audience. The services continued until ten o'clock, but no one departed. 'We shall never all meet again,' spoke the obviously moved minister, 'till we meet at the judgment seat. But these glorious heavens over our heads and the bright moon that shines on us, and this venerable church behind, are my witnesses that I have set before you life and death.'

**Conversion of three cousins**

He couldn't omit visiting the small village of Ruthwell on his return journey. He cherished precious memories of this beautiful place in Dumfries where his mother was born. Here he would often spend his school holidays. During those years he used to visit the stately manse of Henry Duncan and would play in the large garden. The picturesque church not only reminded him of the years of his youth, when he had enjoyed life and the beauty of nature in a carefree manner, but also his probationary period, when he had delivered his first sermon to the village inhabitants, who were well-known to him. He now made his way to the hamlet of Clarencefield, which was situated nearby and where his aunt lived. He treasured up many memories of the first house on the right, *Clarence Cottage.* Here he met his three cousins, Mary, Charlotte and Georgiana Dickson. They had matured by this time into flighty girls who displayed a careless attitude to life. They were brought up on the European mainland and thus came into contact, not only with cultured forms of behaviour and a highly refined lifestyle, but also with social circles where neither God nor His commands were considered important. They were attracted to a greater degree by the frivolous way of life than by the Christian faith, and when they returned to their parental home, they revealed their aversion for everything associated with religion. However, they attended the village church, but the gospel proclaimed by Duncan left them unmoved.

Thus, M'Cheyne came into contact with his cousins. They watched as the slender figure in minister's dress strode towards them across their property. 'Mr. Perfection is coming!' they exclaimed, for thus they had nicknamed him. What could Robert teach them? Would he immediately address them in

Clarence Cottage in Ruthwell after an engraving of A.L. Struthers.

Parish Church of Ruthwell.

earnest terms? James Dodds, who was acquainted with him from former days and who more than once visited the cottage, was curious as to the outcome of this meeting. Their cousin to meet his cousins in a friendly disposition. With cautionary demeanour he associated with them. The day after his arrival, Dodds espied him taking a morning walk with his cousins and it was as if their light-heartedness had disappeared. He had touched their hearts. The appearance of their cousin seemed to wield a secret power of attraction over them. His godly conduct of life impressed them. During his short stay they accompanied him on his sick visitations and they helped him in the distribution of tracts. However, this was not all; the Spirit of God began to convict them. While Robert was praying with them, Mary began to sob loudly, and Charlotte was deeply touched. Even Georgiana's proud character was shattered. A friend of Dodds wrote to him: 'She threw herself on me after church last night and burst into tears, saying she saw things in a new light now.' *Clarence Cottage* became a 'house of weeping'. There Robert and his cousins sat having tea. The neighbours too came to meet him. Dodds wrote concerning this: 'The girls were all weeping, and such a scene followed as I cannot describe on paper. Maria and Georgiana fell on our necks and sobbed, crying out about sin, yet exclaiming they had never known happiness before. Charlotte, the other sister, said little, but looked much.'

M'Cheyne's visit to Ruthwell was not in vain. It was as if he 'must needs go through Samaria'. What spoke to the girls when he entered their house? They weren't attracted so much by his words, but by 'the solemn, affectionate compassion' that he radiated. He said little, but the look of love irradiating from his eyes burned like an awl into their hearts. In addition, God's Spirit blew over them in a manner inexplicable. After the unexpected visit of their cousin, Robert, they became pilgrims to the heavenly city. With joy, Robert wrote to his father concerning the remarkable transformation in his cousins: 'You do not know what deep anxieties I have for you all, that it may

dearest Robert is the
prayer of ever your
affectionate Cousin
Charlotte

y God grant that you may
very soon restored to
perfect health –

End of a letter of Charlotte Dickson.

be well with you in eternity. The three young ladies at the Cottage are the first of my kindred to whom I have been savingly useful. Their change is, indeed, very wonderful; and, if they endure to the end, is enough to convince an infidel of the reality of the Holy Spirit's work.'

After the return to his manse at the beginning of September 1842, he received a letter from Mary. Many letters followed during the next seven months, not only from her, but also from the other cousins. God's work continued in them, but their need for teaching was great. Gradually they were drawn towards the Saviour. The light expelled the darkness and *Clarence Cottage* became a place of song. They soon visited their cousin and were received with joy by him and his sister Eliza. When the time drew near to depart, Mary didn't accompany her sisters immediately, but remained hanging about in Dundee. Just like Mary of Bethany, she was in need of personal guidance. She wasn't so inclined to freely appropriate the consolation of the gospel. Doubts and uncertainty continued to gnaw at her heart of hearts. Her critical spirit didn't allow her to assimilate everything immediately. According to Charlotte, this attitude was exaggerated. The latter possessed a natural aversion for a sombre mood and she was afraid that her sister would end up with a similar frame of mind. She knew somewhat more of the freedom that is in Christ, and wrote to her cousin: 'I do not agree in thinking it necessary or pleasing in the eyes of God that this world should be converted into "a living tomb".' Wasn't Mary too preoccupied with self? 'I pray God may open her heart and convince her of sin and make her willing to give up all to follow Jesus,' thus wrote Charlotte.

The struggle to find the acceptable balance was not a foregone conclusion for the intelligent girls. Hadn't their cousin convinced them 'that religion was a galling and enslaving yoke'? All the same, the cheerful life of faith could combine with one's existence in the world, although the struggle between the spirit and the flesh would never cease. It wasn't possible to find an explanation for everything immediately and it took time to guide them into the ways of God's Word. The light of the Sun of Righteousness broke through the haze. In addition to his preaching, M'Cheyne taught them the meaning of the parable about the wise and the foolish builder. Charlotte now saw clearly that her faith should be founded on the Rock, Jesus Christ. Soon afterwards, she asked the St Peter's kirk session to be admitted to holy communion. Lamb wrote with joy in his diary: 'It was gratifying to hear of some of the relatives of the minister—three young ladies—who had for the first time joined the church, giving themselves up openly at the sacramental table to Him who loved them and gave Himself to redeem them from sins and death.'

**Longing for holiness**

Thus M'Cheyne's life alternated between joy and sorrow. His sister Eliza supported him in every way and organized the domestic matters of the manse. After spending six years in

M'Cheyne's manse on Union Place, pulled down in 1907

Strawberry Bank, they moved to a more spacious house. It was a single villa in Union Place, a street not far removed from the church and the previous home. Her brother returned home from his journey to England refreshed and ready to resume his duties. 'I have returned much stronger, indeed quite well. I think I have got some precious souls for my hire on my way home. I earnestly long for more grace and personal holiness, and more usefulness.'

In this frame of mind, he faced the coming autumn. He felt physically stronger, but it turned out to be merely a brief spell of health. He enjoyed the sun-drenched bay nearby his house. The Magdalen Yards formed the shore of the magnificent Bay of Tay. The gentle rays of the autumn sun filtered lazily through the autumn leaves. 'Scarcely a day passed but he gazed upon the glowing west after dinner; and as he gazed he would speak of the Sun of Righteousness, or the joy of angels in His presence, or the blessedness of those whose sun can go no more down till his face shone with gladness as he spoke.' 'And there shall be no night there'; the rays of the eternal Son caused the streets of the heavenly Jerusalem to gleam. How 'he looked for a city which hath foundations'. Did he not have a premonition of his imminent death? The Lord was close by. 'And during the winter he was observed to be peculiarly joyful, being strong in body, and feeling the near presence of Jesus in his soul. He lived in the blessed consciousness that he was a child of God, humble and meek, just because he was fully assured that Jehovah was his God and Father.' Who could better witness to this fact than his best friend, Andrew Bonar, who knew him so well? Wasn't God's fatherly nature in his heart and on his lips? Did he not stand in the liberty with which Christ had set him free? Nothing could separate him from His love.

**In London**

Robert M'Cheyne thirsted after holiness. He desired to live his life in Christ, through Him and to His honour. He lived continually in the innermost sanctuary, where the mysterious reconciling work is revealed. Even during his travels, his delicate physical condition and a sense of his impending death didn't recede. His congregation didn't always understand him. They certainly couldn't make him out when his friend, James Hamilton, invited him to assist in the administration of the Lord's Supper in November 1842. This wasn't next door, because since 1841 Hamilton no longer served as pastor of the Abernyte congregation, but instead he was attached to the Scottish Church of Regent Square, London, where Edward Irving had been the minister before his dismissal. M'Cheyne's elders were not in agreement with his proposed absence from home for ten days. He had an irrepressible desire to evangelize everywhere, which proceeded from a growing conviction that he was more of an evangelist than a pastor. This didn't mean that he would become more emotionally detached from St Peter's. His ministry, however, knew more extensive boundaries than the West End of Dundee.

His visit to London was richly blessed, certainly for his own soul's benefit. He read with great pleasure the Song of Songs, which explained the condition of his heart. The love of Christ filled his soul and he progressed still more in the knowledge of Him who had given His life on his behalf. After Hamilton had brought his friend to the railway station, he looked for an empty carriage in order to be able to meditate and pray; but how disappointed he was when another person entered. Bonar observes that 'this visit was a blessed one; and the growth of his soul in holiness was visible to many'. His letter of 5 November 1842 to Horatius Bonar affords us a glimpse of his heavenly disposition: 'Oh that my soul were new moulded, and I were effectually called a second time and made a vessel full of the Spirit, to tell only of Jesus and His love.'

His holy way of life also meant that he had died to his own sanctity. If the craving after fame and honour were a great snare with which he had struggled, then still more cunning was the temptation to be known as a 'a holy man'. Therefore, he paid attention to his heart to see if he was satisfied with his 'own holiness.' He remained a disciple, despite the fact that he surpassed many in holiness. It was an experience to sit with him at the table. After the midday meal he was accustomed to singing a psalm or song. Often he would choose 'The Lord is my Shepherd,' or songs that inspired one to grow in sanctification. Thus, he sang once more the verse from William Cowper:

O for a closer walk with God,
A calm and heavenly frame;
A light to shine upon the road
That leads me to the Lamb.

This hymn certainly interprets the longing of the heart for a closer fellowship with God. 'The Lamb is the light thereof.' The Lamb is the candle, which irradiates the narrow pathway to heaven. He followed the Lamb along ways where the seed of the Word had been sown and to places where it had not. His eye was steadfastly focused on Him, who declared to His children, 'Abide in Me, and I in you.' This was the secret of

M'Cheyne's. One of his friends observed: 'I have sometimes compared him to the silver and graceful ash, with its pensile branches, and leaves of gentle green, reflecting gleams of happy sunshine. The fall of its leaf, too, is like the fall of his – it is green tonight and gone tomorrow, it does not sere nor wither.'

**'Reformation'**

To M'Cheyne, sanctification was neither a self-regulating nor legalistic display. He despised a slovenly way of life that appealed to Christian liberty. Scrupulous conduct before God and man begins in the inner chamber. He drafted a few short guide lines on paper, concerning a thorough self-examination under the title of *Reformation.* Appealing to Malachi 3:3, 'He shall purify the sons of Levi,' he declared that the duty of all servants of the Word begins with oneself and one's own house-hold 'with confession of past sin, earnest prayer for direction, grace and full purpose of heart'. He posited two chief subdivisions: 'Reformation' and 'Reformation in secret prayer'. Personal sanctification is also of the greatest importance for ministers. 'I am persuaded that I shall obtain the highest amount of present happiness, I shall do most for God's glory and the good of man and I shall have the fullest reward in eternity, by maintaining a conscience always washed in Christ's blood, by being filled with the Holy Spirit at all times, and by attaining the most entire likeness to Christ in mind, will, and heart that is possible for a redeemed sinner to attain to in this world.'

Although the grace which offers man eternal life is no meritorious gift, yet the measure of the glory hereafter shall be dependent on the life of the believer in this world. Without sanctification no one shall see the Lord. How necessary it is then, to confess one's personal sins before God's face! 'I ought to confess often the sins of my youth, like David and Paul, – my sins before conversion; – my sins since conversion: sins against light and knowledge, against love and grace.' Then he continued further with his list of sins, whereupon followed: 'I ought to go to Christ for the forgiveness of each sin. I must never think a sin too small to need immediate application to the blood of Christ.' There is no sanctification without appropriating the suffering and the obedience of Christ. 'I must not only be washed in Christ's blood, but clothed in Christ's obedience. Christ for us is ever new, ever glorious. "Unsearchable riches of Christ" – an infinite object, and the only one for a guilty soul.'

Sanctification concerns conformity with Christ. That can only occur by means of the Holy Spirit. For this purpose, it is necessary to be convinced of ones's own shortcomings. 'I ought to have a number of Scriptures ready to be meditated on, such as Romans 7, John 15, to convince me that I am a helpless worm.' He had an aversion for the idea that he was a confirmed Christian: 'That I have overcome this or that lust so long: that I have got into the habit of the opposite grace, so that there is no fear.... this is a lie of Satan.' How many temptations of Satan were lying in wait to lure him away from Christ and His holiness! Vigilance was commanded under all circumstances, so that one should not once again be caught up in the snares of the devil.

Now there was the necessity of personal prayer. Experience was his teacher, but without the Spirit of prayer he could accomplish nothing. He observed his times of devotion, without exception. The chief points concerning times of quiet prayer were, according to his opinion, 'confession, adoration, thanksgiving, petition, and intercession.' The early morning is still the most appropriate time to be alone with God. The best is "to have at least one hour alone with God." The list which he used for his intercession was considerable: family, friends, congregation, church, etc. including also, the Jewish nation. His daily prayer was the indispensable breath of his soul. 'I ought to spend the best hours of the day in communion with God. It is my noblest and most fruitful employment, and is not to be thrust into any corner. The morning hours, from six to eight, are the most uninterrupted, and should be thus employed, if I can prevent drowsiness. A little time after breakfast might be given to intercession. After tea is my best hour, and that should be solemnly dedicated to God if possible.'

**His life was Christ**

What secret did M'Cheyne possess which made his life different from that of the average minister? Was it perhaps his godliness, his devotion to prayer, his meticulous way of life? No, the secret of M'Cheyne lay not so much in his gifts and graces, with which he had been so richly endowed. His secret lay in the words of the apostle, 'His life is hid with Christ in God.' Hewat observes in the booklet on William Lamb concerning this: 'He thought so much about Christ, and spoke so much about Christ, that the Christlike image was gradually in me.' Subsequent to his death, a letter was discovered in his desk, which he had received from a stranger. The latter had heard him preaching in St Peter's and was edified by his words. However, there was something even more impressive: 'It was not what you said, nor even how you said it, but it was your look – it was so Christlike – the face of one shining from being in the presence of his Lord.' His life was Christ and he radiated this in his ministry and indeed in all his ways. He yielded his talents in service of Him in order to win souls. 'A poet, a musician, an artist, a scholar, an athlete; all these things he counted but loss, as if they existed not – that he might bring souls into the kingdom of his dear Redeemer. Christ Jesus and His saving work for men was the supreme thing – the most intense of realities – for M'Cheyne.'

Before his journey to Palestine, he had made an idol of his congregation and now he was himself afraid of becoming idolized by his congregation. In particular, those who had no personal knowledge of the Lord Jesus were those who thus honoured him. They so esteemed the 'means' more than the Mediator Himself. Often he said, 'Ministers are but the pole; it is to the brazen serpent you are to look.' Surely the reason the brazen snake had to be destroyed in Hezekiah's day was because the nation of Israel had committed idolatry with it. Was it not,

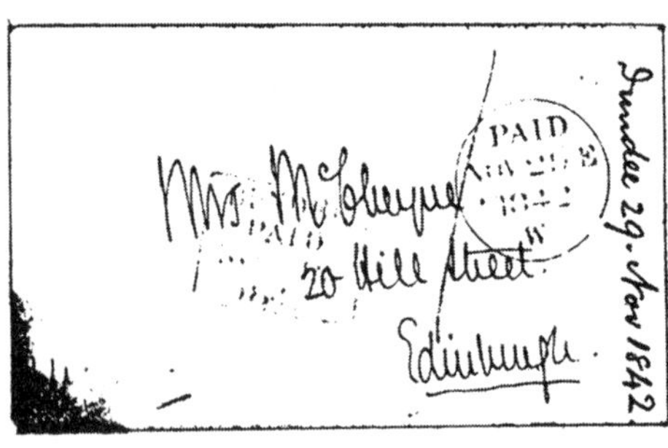
Mrs McCheyne
20 Hill Street
Edinburgh.
PAID
Dundee 29. Nov 1842.

My dear Mamma,

I write you a few lines lest you should be wearying to hear of Eliza. She is doing well. She has been up several hours today in my study. She is allowed to eat mutton chops and to drink a little wine.. so that I hope she will be soon quite restored. She was not so well on Saturday – but yesterday and today she is evidently mending. I find I am too late for this night's post having been called away to see some people so that you will have the benefit of tomorrow's bulletin.

Yesterday was the anniversary of my first Sabbath in St. Peter six years ago a solemn day to me.

Letter from McCheyne to his mother, dated 29th November 1842.

therefore, necessary that he become more and more emotionally detached from St Peter's? His poor health no longer permitted him to make his house-to-house visitations. In the long run, his work as an evangelist suited him better than pastoral ministry. The cares of the congregation pressed down on him as a heavy burden. His church council was sensible enough to take measures to relieve him, and appointed Alexander Gatherer as his assistant minister, who assisted him until the end of his ministry. He had good contact with him. Whenever he was out of the city, Gatherer kept him informed concerning the welfare of his congregation. Thus M'Cheyne wrote to Gatherer from Ellon on 20 February 1843: 'I am glad to hear of your preaching on such precious texts, and hope they were blessed to many. Never forget that the end of a sermon is the salvation of the people. I have had some sweet seasons of communion with an unseen God, which I would not give up for thousands of gold and silver.'

**The beginning of 1843**

Thus began the year 1843. On 1 January there was a celebration of the Lord's Supper at St Peter's. Andrew Bonar and John Milne were requested to assist. In a letter, M'Cheyne asked Milne: 'Pray for me, for I am a poor worm, all guilt and all helplessness, but still able to say, "In the Lord have I righteousness and strength." When shall the day break and the shadows flee away? When that which is perfect is come, then that which is in part shall be done away.' He preached from 1 Timothy 1:16: 'Howbeit for this cause I obtained mercy.' Lamb thought it an excellent sermon, 'showing that if in such as Paul – the persecutor, blasphemer, and impious – Jesus Christ showed forth the longsuffering of His grace, making it sufficient to save any of us, though the chief of sinners.' As M'Cheyne concluded the communion service, he spoke to the careless hearts: 'Or despisest thou the richest of His goodness and forbearance and longsuffering; not knowing that the goodness of God leadeth thee to repentance?'

Shortly afterwards, he spoke on Colossians 1:27: 'To whom God would make known what is the riches of the glory of this mystery among the Gentiles; which is Christ in you the hope of glory.' At the end of his sermon summary, he noted down, 'Very sweet and solemn night.' 'Have you got the legal title to glory?' asked M'Cheyne in his application. 'Christ dwelling in you by faith. You have heard how those who are enlightened by God embrace Christ, and put Him on abidingly for righteousness? Have you done so? Have you put on Christ? This is the only legal title to glory. If you have not this, your hope is in vain. Christ formed in you? Does Christ live in you, and walk in you? "Without holiness no man shall see the Lord."'

'The hope of glory' filled his heart. This glory was the subject he often touched on during the last months of his life. He preached in Newton-on-Ayr, in Ayrshire, on 'the Great White Throne,' from the same text that he had used in Newcastle: 'And I saw a great white throne, and him that sat on it, from whose face the earth and the heaven fled away; and there was found no place for them' (Rev. 20:11). He had also preached from this Scripture in Dundee; not in St Peter's, however, but in the open meadows or city pastures. The rain fell steadily down, but the people remained behind to listen until the end. According to Bonar, this was 'one of his most impressive sermons', a summary of which, unfortunately, is no longer extant. A relative of Roderick Lawson, minister of Maybole, heard this sermon as a young man and later related the following: 'The service did not take place in the church, but in the Newton graveyard, some distance from the building. It was a remarkable open-air service. M'Cheyne's subject was the Great White Throne, and he continued preaching till the sun set behind the mountain tops of Arran, across the sea. As the orb of day went down he took that going down into the darkness as the emblem of the setting of time with all the children of Adam.' The reverse side of the glory, which is the inheritance of God's children, is the judgment of the godless. His greatest longing was focused on the return of Christ, but he was overcome with dismay when he thought what portion would be theirs who do not know Christ.

In January 1843, he visited Collace, where he preached on 1 Corinthians 9:27: 'A Castaway.' It was according to Bonar, 'A sermon so solemn that one said it was like a blast of the trumpet that would awaken the dead.' How his soul craved for the eternal tabernacle! His diary, which he maintained for so many years, had its last entry on 6 January. He knew that from then on his life would find a place in God's memorial book. The Lord had numbered his wanderings. The last notes in his diary didn't concern his own spiritual walk, but mentioned a few conversions which were a sign of hope to him. Certainly many names appeared in his diary and notebook. The rather discouraging beginning to the new year changed when he could write: 'Heard of an awakened soul finding rest – true rest, I trust. Two new cases of awakening; both very deep and touching. At the very time when I was beginning to give up in despair, God gives me tokens of His presence returning.'

What was the reason for his dejection? Was it that God had concealed Himself for a time by revealing no new 'sheaves' which would be gathered one day into His barn? Whenever it was quiet on the frontiers of the church, he was afraid that there were reasons for the Lord's withholding His hand from His heritage, by allowing no 'new births' to be evident. However, was all true fruit always revealed in the open? Wouldn't eternity bring to light much hidden work in God's kingdom? As long as it was day, he continued on with his labours, although his longing to live with the Lord became steadily stronger. 'Often, often, would I have been glad to depart, and be with Christ. I am now much better in body and mind, having a little of the presence of my Beloved whose absence is death to me.'

He was of the opinion that this day would speedily dawn. 'I do not expect to live long. I expect a sudden call some day, perhaps soon, and therefore I speak very plainly.' His congregation, too, noticed something unusual about him, especially when he concluded a sermon with the following words: 'Changes are coming; every eye before me shall soon be dim in death. Another pastor shall feed this flock; another singer lead the psalm; another flock shall fill this fold.'

**On evangelistic tour**

In February 1843, he made his last evangelistic tour to the north of Scotland. Concerning this, Bonar quoted an expression, 'The oil of the lamp in the temple burnt away in giving light; so should we.' The Lord raised him up. It was as if he gave him a cask full of the oil of His love. 'He set out,' says one that saw him leave town, 'as unclouded and happy as the sky that was above his head that bright morning.'

His preaching in the district north of Aberdeen left a deep impression behind. Sometimes people wanted to throw stones at him, but as soon as he began to speak, their hands dropped. He preached also in 'the granite city', where Burns had been not so long ago. He wrote concerning this event on 14 February, to his assistant minister, Gatherer: 'I had a nice opportunity of preaching in Aberdeen; and in Peterhead our meeting was truly successful.' Thus, he proceeded to journey through the land, braving the winter weather and other discomforts. 'Today the snow is beginning to drift. But God is with us, and He will carry us to the very end. I am quite well, though a little fatigued sometimes.'

Never before had he experienced the feeling that the Lord was so nearby as when he undertook this journey. He was full of it when he returned to Dundee on 1 March. The next evening, it was the usual prayer meeting, wherein he reported on his journey. He was visibly tired and exhausted. On 7 March, he wrote to Eliza, who was staying with her parents: 'I am truly happy to be home after all my wanderings. I preached and spoke twenty-seven times in twenty-four different places, and these the darkest spots in rugged Scotland.' He felt like a fish in the water there. What might his sister have thought when she read the words: 'I can almost say, as Wesley did to the Bishop of

London, when he had said, "You would be far better with a parish, Mr. Wesley." "The world is my parish, my Lord." ' His friend, William Burns, could likewise have reiterated what he had said, but then he was not appointed to a flock. From Kirrimuir, Burns wrote a letter to him on 13 March. This spurred him on to surrender his future to the Lord. 'Have you got, or are you really seeking, light on your path? Set apart a day for doing so, with fasting and humiliation. I know not how it is, but it seems more than clear to me that you must without delay give up your charge, and enter on that tempting field in which I am honoured to be. The fields here are white.'

God's ways were quite different from what Burns might have imagined. When M'Cheyne received this letter, it wouldn't be very long before he would be relieved of his post for good. A typhoid epidemic had been prevalent already for a few weeks in the West End of Dundee. Many lay sick on their beds, and the tired pastor tried to assist them in their suffering, as he had the strength. It concerned him not that he ran the risk of becoming infected himself. On 5 March, he preached twice in his own church and, for the time being, looked forward to undertaking no new journeys. He wrote to his father: 'All domestic matters go on like a placid stream – I trust not without its fertilizing influence.' The bond with his own congregation remained as strong as ever.

**Last sermons**

On 5 March, he preached three times and a week later, on 12 March, for the last time to his congregation. The text for his morning sermon was taken from Hebrews 9:15: 'And for this cause He is the Mediator of the new testament,' and in the afternoon, he preached on Romans 9:22-23. They were sermons of comfort as well as announcements of judgment. One of the listeners wrote down the gist of them, but could not reproduce the spirit with which M'Cheyne spoke. In the first sermon he emphasized the eternal heritage which falls to the share of God's children. 'He shall see the face of God without a cloud, and that to all eternity. Here, O believer, you have many clouds to darken your view; but there, there will be none; and then, there is being with Christ, which is another part of the eternal inheritance.'

The afternoon sermon dealt with 'The vessels of wrath fitted to destruction.' He spoke to the unconverted as he was accustomed – plainly and without mincing his words. 'When lately in the north of Scotland, I stood on the seashore, and saw the rocks standing out of the sea. It was very remarkable to stand and see the mighty waves dashing upon the rocks. There are two things remarkable in it: first, the greatness of the rocks on which the waves dashed: second, the rocks remaining unmoved – no force of the waves could move them. Brethren, this scene is an emblem of what will be witnessed another day, when God shall pour out His wrath on the wicked.' Then God's children will no longer weep over the destruction of the impenitent. The period of grace will then be forever past. M'Cheyne concluded this moving sermon with the words: 'O, brethren, till that day come let us weep on; for although God will be glorified in the destruction of the vessels of His wrath, He will be more glorified in making them vessels of mercy. The Lord bless His own Word. Amen.'

For the final time he descended the steps of the pulpit. Did his congregation realize that it was his farewell sermon? That evening he went on to Broughty Ferry, where he preached on Isaiah 60:1: 'Arise, shine ...' This was the last time that he preached the message of reconciliation, or as Bonar observes: 'It was the last time he was to be engaged directly in proclaiming Christ to sinners.' Could he have put it in a more concise manner? After his death, an unopened letter was found, from a woman who couldn't help writing to him that this sermon was a blessing to her. It was not so much the words that had impressed her as his manner of delivery. 'I saw in you a beauty in holiness that I never saw before. You also said something in your prayer that struck me very much. It was, "Thou knowest that we love Thee." Oh, sir, what would I give that I could say to my blessed Saviour, "Thou knowest that I love Thee!" '

**M'Cheyne's final sickbed**

The following evening there was a meeting in St Peter's concerning the church crisis. A schism was now more unavoidable than ever. The government in London remained relentless and would not allow the Church of Scotland more freedom. McGill Crichton informed the congregation concerning the situation as it was and M'Cheyne too spoke with much earnestness on this occasion. When he arrived home, he felt shivery and sick. He began to get a violent headache and could not sleep at all that night. Despite the fact that his condition deteriorated the next day, he travelled to the eastern district of the city to officiate at the wedding of Georgina Anderson and William Stewart. After the ceremony, a little girl came up to him with a flower. 'Will 'oo put this in 'oor coat?' she asked jauntily. 'O yes, my dear,' replied M'Cheyne, 'but you must help me.' Thus the child pinned the flower to a hole in his jacket. 'Now I have done what you wished; will you do what I would like?' 'Yes,' answered the girl. 'Well, I wish you to listen to the story of the Good Shepherd who gave Himself for the sheep.' When he began to narrate the story to her, five or six other children gathered around him. They listened open-mouthed. It was a children's talk from the heart of a pastor who loved the young so much and, just as the Saviour, never wished to send them away.

When M'Cheyne arrived home, he felt deathly sick. A violent fever racked his body. On the way home, he walked by his friend and colleague, Patrick Miller, to ask him if he would stand in for an address to a students' meeting in St Andrews, but he was not at home. Then he walked to Dr Gibson, his doctor, in order to inform him of his condition. Gibson brought him back to the manse. He felt that the fever was striking back, draining all his excess energy. In a few words, the doctor intimated that he was concerned about his physical condition. Seriously ill, he retired to bed that night. However, he couldn't fall asleep and the next morning he said that he thought he wouldn't make it through the day; so ill he felt. He spoke with difficulty and a fever clouded his spirit. However, no complaint came over his lips. 'What? shall we receive good at the hand of God, and shall we not receive evil?' he said. His spiritual condition was directly affected by his physical suffering. He often repeated the words of the psalmist: 'My moisture is turned into the drought of summer,' and 'my bones waxed old'. He could exchange merely a few words with his assistant, Gatherer. When Patrick Miller arrived, M'Cheyne had a terrible headache. After Miller had prayed with him and had read from Matthew 11:28, the sick patient solemnly folded his arms. It was as if he awaited his end.

The next day the congregation came together for their weekly prayer meeting. Constant prayer was made on behalf of their beloved teacher. The church building remained open the following few evenings so that the believers could come together to pray for his recovery. He was not spared spiritual struggle. The evil one attacked him, but didn't overcome him. During the hour of the prayer meeting, he asked to be left alone for an hour. When his servant thereafter entered his room, he called out with a joyful voice: 'The snare is broken, and we are escaped!' Satan had retreated and left him alone. How his feverish face shone with joy! He felt quite happy within himself and was full of peace in his heart. That evening he thanked the Lord. 'For strength in the time of weakness; for light in the time of darkness; for joy in the time of sorrow; for comforting us in all our tribulations, that we may be able to comfort those that are in any trouble, by the comfort wherewith we ourselves are comforted of God.'

It was a pity that his sister was in Edinburgh, resulting in a dearth of nursing care. Elder P.H. Thoms informed his parents on the Thursday of the latest developments concerning the condition of their son. Dr Gibson too wrote a brief note to the Hill Street home. In reality, the latter realized that the situation was perhaps not as sombre as might originally have been thought. He wrote: 'I have no hesitation in writing you a few lines this evening, rejoiced as I am to say that he is, as I hoped he would be, greatly better already so much so that I have now little doubts of his being all right again in a very few days.' The letter arrived on Thursday evening and his father immediately decided to leave for Dundee the next morning with Eliza. They reached Union Place in the course of the afternoon. 'We found Robert in bed and still feverish yet he was perfectly calm.' He dictated a letter to his father for Dr. Bunting of the Wesleyan Missionary Society, the Methodist missionary organization, with whom he had a lecture engagement on 30 April. All appointments were provisionally cancelled. Dr Gibson didn't know whether he had contracted typhus or not, but, after Sunday, when the sickness took a turn for the worse and spots began to appear on M'Cheyne's body, he could diagnose it correctly.

M'Cheyne lay on his bed in an extremely weakened state. Yet, the doctor remained optimistic and hoped for his recovery. Adam M'Cheyne returned home with mixed feelings, and yet not without hope. He permitted his wife to come along and she arrived in the course of Thursday afternoon, 21 March. Andrew Bonar too received news of his sickness. Eliza sent him the following letter on Friday: 'Dear friend, If in your power, do come. It has pleased God to lay my beloved brother on a sickbed from which there is little probability of his rising for many a day, should God spare him to us. The doctor says it is typhus fever, and this is the ninth day. He was perfectly sensible till this time yesterday, but had a bad night. Some hours he seemed to spend in prayer, in a low half-audible voice. Then he began to address his people so urgently that we could not bear to hear his dear voice, it was so moving.' She wrote that her brother was continually inquiring after his best friend. M'Cheyne, thinking that it was he who was sitting in the dining room, called out repeatedly, 'O, send him to me! Send him up! Why will you keep him below?' Actually, he wasn't allowed to receive any visitors at all, and he was perhaps led to believe that his best friend was also prohibited from visiting him. How he was inextricably bound with invisible bonds to Andrew.

**'This Parish...'**

Did he sometimes think about Bonar when, all of a sudden, he spoke about Smyrna? On the return journey from Palestine, when he lay ill with a violent fever on deck as the ship sailed passed the island of Patmos in the direction of Smyrna, the words of Andrew were of great comfort to him. Then, too it seemed as if he wouldn't see the coast again, but after he had gone ashore in Smyrna, he began to recover. Didn't his thoughts then also go out to his congregation? Surely he thought about the lost souls in St Peter's, who as yet had no Surety for their guilt? He carried his congregation close to his heart and during the last days of his earthly career, his thoughts often turned to his flock. Even when his condition deteriorated because of the violent fever, he was heard to have said: 'This parish, Lord; this people, this whole place! Holy Father, keep through Thine own name those whom Thou has given me.' On another occasion, he prayed without ceasing for two hours for his congregation; he upheld especially, the unconverted before the throne of grace. He could not cease to plead for St Peter's and called out, 'Hinder me not; I will pray and praise God while I have a voice.'

His congregation thought about him continually and pleaded with the Lord to spare him. They didn't realize that they would never again hear his voice. When a member of the congregation visited him on Sunday and intimated how much he longed to hear his voice from the pulpit again, he gave the brief yet powerful reply: 'For My thoughts are not your thoughts, neither are your ways My ways.' This was the word of his Master and His counsel would endure. 'I am preaching the sermon that God would have me to do.' He was totally united with God's will and way for him and was acceptable in His pleasure. All that God does is good; He renders no account for His deeds.

On Tuesday, Eliza recited a few hymns to him. He couldn't easily assimilate everything. He seemed, however, to grasp the last line of a verse from William Cowper's hymn:

Sometimes a light surprises
the Christian as he sings:
It is the Lord who rises
with healing in His wings.

How often had his melodious voice resounded through the manse. How often, too, had he not drawn comfort from the Psalms or hymns, which witnessed to the precious blood of the Lord Jesus. Now he could hardly utter a word. Soon he reached a state of unconsciousness. The fever sapped his physical and spiritual strength. His soul was, however, united with his God. Once, in his inert state, he suddenly said to his nurse: 'Mind the text (1 Cor. 15:58): "Be steadfast, unmovable, always abounding in the work of the Lord," ' dwelling with much emphasis on the last clause, 'forasmuch as ye know that your labour is not in vain in the Lord.' His weak voice now became more powerful. He turned to his kirk session and said: 'I don't think much of policy in church courts; no, I hate it; but I'll tell you what I like – faithfulness to God and a holy walk.' The condition of the church in his country touched him deeply even in his subconscious state. How his soul yearned for holiness! How he longed that the garments of King Jesus would be preserved unblemished in the midst of a crooked and perverse generation. It was often as if he climbed the pulpit to address his congregation. 'You must be awakened in everlasting torment, to your eternal confusion. You may soon get me away, but that will not save your souls.'

A great dismay prevailed over the city. Many walked through Union Place in order to learn about the condition of the beloved minister. Everywhere, prayer meetings were held. On the Thursday evening, St Peter's Church was once again full, but also the following evening many gathered to pray for him. The agreement was to use the school building for this purpose, but the overflow was so great that people had to take refuge in the church. It was on Friday night that the news did the rounds, that his condition had deteriorated further. Would they still lose their teacher? Voices were raised, calling for an all-night vigil in the church. The elders and ministers could only, with great difficulty, dissuade the crowd from following this plan. Thus, the grieving people went their way, awaiting the coming course of events.

In Ruthwell too, there was sorrow. The Dickson cousins besought God for the recovery of their beloved Robert, who had become their spiritual father. They were surprised to have received no letters from him for a while. When a note was delivered to the door of *Clarence Cottage*, they understood the reason for his silence. Charlotte replied in a few lines. With a heart full of love, she wrote to him: 'I pray that you have been enabled to draw very near to God; that you have had much sweet communion with your heavenly Father. May the Spirit of love teach you to know more of the love of Jesus—that love which passeth knowledge; to continue in His love and oh, may your joy be full!' She hoped that he might rest 'calmly and peacefully in the bosom of the Good Shepherd'. As P.S had done, she expressed the hope that he would speedily be raised from his sickbed.

**His death**

His cousins' wish remained unfulfilled. Charlotte's letter arrived just after his death. It was Saturday morning, 25 March 1843. The signs of a burgeoning spring were visible everywhere in the gardens along the streets which overlooked the calm reflection of the bay. In the manse at Union Place everything was quiet. Dr Gibson sat next to the bed of his beloved friend. The patient lay unconscious, gasping for breath because of the fever which gripped his body. It was half-past nine when the dying man suddenly raised his hands high in the air. It was as if he wished to pronounce a blessing. Then he sank bank onto the cushions. His lips trembled faintly. Without a sigh or a sob, he passed away. The battle-weary pilgrim took leave of the earthly vale of tears and received a place in the Father's heavenly home. His wish, which he had expressed in poetic form in

January 1837, was fulfilled:

> Do you ask me for pleasure?
> Then lean on His breast,
> For there the sin-laden
> And weary find rest.
> In the valley of death
> You will triumphingly cry-
> 'If this be called dying,
> Tis pleasant to die!'

The news of Robert Murray McCheyne's death soon spread through the city. At five o'clock in the afternoon, Andrew Bonar learned of his friend's death while in the midst of his sermon preparation. 'I hastened down, though scarcely knowing why I went,' he wrote. He would no longer meet his friend here on earth. It was as if a sword had penetrated his soul. 'Never, never yet in all my life have I felt anything like this. It is a blow to myself, to his people, to the Church of Christ in Scotland. O Lord, the godly ceaseth and the faithful fail! My heart is sore. It makes me feel death near myself now. Life has lost half its joys, were it not the hope of saving souls. There was no friend whom I loved like him.'

At nine o'clock that night, Bonar entered the city. It was busy around the house of mourning, and men, women and children stood outside St Peter's, crying with grief. In addition, William Lamb was in the church with his fellow brothers when Bonar walked up. The congregation gathered together in the church building. St Peter's became a 'place of weeping'. 'Such a scene of sorrow has not often been witnessed in Scotland. It was like the weeping for King Josiah. Hundreds were there; the lower part of the church was full, and none among them seemed able to contain their sorrow. Every heart seemed bursting with grief, so that the weeping and the cries could be heard afar off.' 'O, what a night was Saturday!' wrote Bonar in his diary. 'During prayer, the cries and lamentations of the people resounded through the church, as if their hearts were bursting.'

The people didn't wish Bonar to leave, before he had addressed them yet again. He opened the Bible to Revelation 21 and read the first six verses: 'And I saw a new heaven and a new earth ...' He spoke words of encouragement, which had so often rang from the mouth of the deceased pastor: 'And whosoever will, let him take the water of life freely.' William Lamb listened to the words of comfort, which were fulfilled in M'Cheyne: 'I looked often to the pulpit, and thought it is empty tonight. Where is he now, who so often spoke from it, warning the careless and comforting and edifying believers? He is gone before and is near the throne singing the song of Moses and the Lamb.'

Bonar cast one final glance at his dead friend. 'O, it was truly solemn, and when I gazed upon Robert's face, I cannot tell what agony it was to think he was away. His face as he lay, was so calm, so expressive, with the very indentation that it used to make when he spoke. Oh, it is bitter!'

He was nearly thirty years old when he passed away on 25 March 1843. His life was serving and following. It was true for him: 'For ye are dead, and your life is hid with Christ in God.' The love for the Saviour had consumed him. He followed the Lamb everywhere, compelled by the love of Christ. He brought many lost souls into the sheepfold, not by entering another way, but by entering alone through the door of the Great Shepherd. From this same love issued the longing after the heavenly sheepfold, to live with the Lamb for eternity. The desire of his Death-song was fulfilled:

> Even treading the valley, the shadow of death,
> This 'watchword' shall rally my faltering breath;
> For when from life's fever my God sets me free,
> Jehovah Tsidkenu my death-song shall be.

**A Sabbath of mourning**

The following Sabbath, the doors of St Peter's again opened. This time the church people arrived from everywhere. Sorrow was clearly visible on their faces. John Roxburgh, the minister of St John's, described the spectacle: 'On each occasion the church (including the galleries) was crowded in every part; and it was remarked by those who were present that they never before saw so many men in tears. It was truly a weeping congregation.' William Lamb too assumed his place. He wrote in his diary: 'Felt much solemnized this morning, and was enabled to pray with much fullness. At St Peter's Andrew Bonar officiated. In the forenoon he preached from Romans 8:38-39, "For I am persuaded that neither death, nor life, nor angels, nor principalities, nor powers, nor things present, not things to come, nor height, nor depth, nor any other creature, shall be able to separate us from the love of God, which is in Christ Jesus, our Lord." The discourse was most suitable to us in the present afflicting circumstances, showing clearly that all those things could not separate us from the love of God, that is, take away God's love to believers in Christ Jesus. Mr. Bonar said he took these words as a ground of comfort to himself. Whatever changes take place here, God's love remains the same to His people – as the mountains stand round about Jerusalem, and always cast the same shadows on the Temple.'

Bonar preached once more at the afternoon service. Now he chose Romans 8:28-30 as his text: 'And we know that all things work together for good...' He received the strength to preach, despite the deep sorrow that filled his heart. God's work continues, although the Lord may remove His servants. His counsel will stand, also during times of testing. Lamb listened attentively to the words of comfort and recorded the following: 'Among other things, he said that it is consoling to know that there is a Father's hand in all trials – that afflictions are needed to conform the children of God to the image of His Son.' This day a great deal happened in their hearts. Bonar felt inadequate in every way. How little he had actually done in God's honour!

At a Meeting of the Elders & Managers of St Peter's Church & Congregation, Dundee, held within the Session House on Monday the 27th March 1843. —

The Meeting having been opened with prayer, the following resolutions were unanimously adopted by the Meeting.

1. That this Meeting desire to express their sense of the unspeakable loss sustained by the Congregation of St Peters, in the death of their much loved pastor – the Reverend Robert Murray McCheyne and their earnest hope, that as his Ministry was eminently blessed of God in the Conversion of Souls, so this solemn dispensation may be sanctified to the congregation and to the Church at large.

2. That they would also express their heartfelt sympathy with the surviving relations of their Minister, and their trust that the same Almighty Being who in his inscrutable Providence has seen meet to remove one so much & so justly loved, will himself comfort & sustain them under this bereavement.

3. That it would be most gratifying to the feelings of this Meeting, and in accordance with the wishes of the parishioners and congregation, that the remains of their beloved Minister should be

First page of the minutes of the Kirk Session of St Peter's, in which the death of M'Cheyne was mentioned.

How humiliating for him was the holy life that his friend had lived! The thoughts of his heart multiplied when he beheld the congregation of St Peter's before him, at the end of the service. 'The sight of the people coming out at the door, where often we passed out so happily together, his books, and then his body laid that night out of our view for ever!'

That evening, Patrick Miller preached about the future from the beginning of Revelation 7 until the end. 'He spoke of him removed from us in mercy and judgment; in judgment upon us for prizing the man and forgetting the Master; and mercy, in order to bring us more to the Master.' With this Bonar agreed. 'How very unlike Robert am I! 2 Kings 2 much in my mind. O that his mantle would fall upon me! Evil days are begun. He was so reverent toward God, so full also in desire toward Him, whether in family prayer or at the common ordinary meetings. He seemed never unprepared. His lamp was always burning, and his loins always girt.'

That Sunday evening, Lamb was as usual leading the Sabbath School. He deviated from the usual lesson and read a speech instead about 'The Lambs of the Flock', which M'Cheyne had delivered the previous year. 'Many of the children wept, and I could not help mingling tears with my first prayers for these "lambs" of the flock of our dear, departed pastor, who so carefully tended them and loved them.' After Sunday School, Lamb went to Miss C. to lead the family devotions there. Was it perhaps the same Miss Collier from Thompson Street, who had such an intimate bond with the deceased teacher? In many homes in West End, sorrow prevailed. Lamb thus concluded his journal: 'This has been the saddest Sabbath that has yet dawned on St Peter's. Hitherto God seems to have smiled on this part of His vineyard, and blessed His servant's work much. Today many, many entered His courts with "the spirit of heaviness", and felt as if God were hiding His face from them, chastening us sorely, though in love.'

St Peter's Churchyard.

**Letters of condolence**

Many letters of condolence were delivered to the manse during the days that followed. The kirk session, consisting of the elders and managers, met together on Monday, 27 March, under the chairmanship of David Brown. He expressed 'their sense of the unspeakable loss' through the death of 'their much loved pastor'. Their hope was focused on the fact that 'his ministry was eminently blessed of God in the conversion of souls, so this solemn dispensation may be sanctified to the congregation and to the church at large'. As a third point, the kirk session intimated that 'the wishes of the parishioners and the congregation were that the remains of their beloved minister should be interred in the churchyard of St Peter's – the spot to which in the discourses he so often pointed – and the place which will ever remain associated with his name and labours as a minister of Christ.' In conclusion, it was determined that the decisions of the meeting should be conveyed by a delegation to 'Adam M'Cheyne Esquire, the respected father of their deceased pastor'. In reality, the wishes of the church council conflicted with the family's decision. However, Adam M'Cheyne agreed to satisfy the congregation's wish, although he had previously decided that the body of Robert should be placed in the family grave in St Cuthbert's Churchyard in Edinburgh.

After M'Cheyne's death, Mrs Thain wrote a detailed letter to the mother of the deceased on 27 March from *Heath Park*. From the fullness of her grieving heart, she wrote that Robert's death signified a severe blow for their entire family. 'My poor Alexander, he will be feeling deeply, having lost the best friend he had on earth.' Her son, Alexander, lived in Edinburgh and had corresponded regularly with M'Cheyne. How was Jessie, her daughter, faring? She too loved him so much. 'Jessie is quite overpowered. She will write her dear friend Eliza as soon as she is able.' How often did their friend stay under their roof! He was an esteemed guest at *Heath Park*, where he was surrounded by much love and concern. Now it was all in the

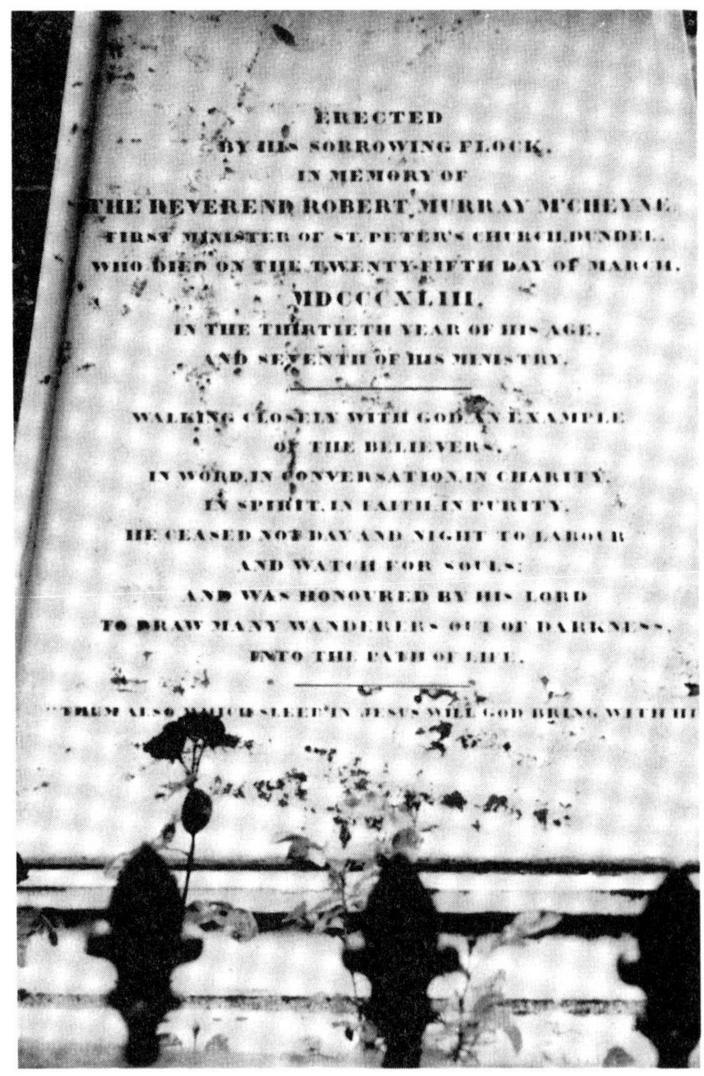


Inscription on the grave monument in St Peter's Churchyard.

past. They would never again see their best friend on earth. He was now beyond all striving and when mother Thain wrote her letter that morning, this line from one of his poems recurred in her thoughts: 'The battle fought, the victory won.'

Mary Wanless, the orphan girl who had frequently visited the manse, heard the news of M'Cheyne's passing away on Sunday. At the time, she happened to be with Mr Nixon, minister of Montrose. 'I was coming out of the church, when a woman stopped me and told me about his death. They said the people prayed in groups for him to recover, but God did not do so.' Margaret Sime was thirteen years old when her minister died. The memory of those bleak days remained with her. 'My feelings through all this was that there was a dark cloud hovering over the west end of Dundee and God speaking through the cloud. It was a long time before the feeling left me.'

**The funeral**

The day dawned when Robert Murray M'Cheyne's body would be entrusted to the bowels of the earth. His grave was dug at the end of the path alongside the church building, at the height of the pulpit. The funeral took place on 30 March. The route from the house of mourning to St Peter's was crowded with people. They stood in rows waiting for the funeral train to pass by. 'Long before the hour arrived, the whole line of road intervening between the dwelling-house and the churchyard was crowded with men, women, and children, principally of the working classes. Every window overlooking the procession, and the church itself, were likewise densely filled with females, almost all attired in deep mourning, and the very walls and housetops were surmounted with anxious onlookers. Altogether, not fewer than six or seven thousand people must have assembled.' The coffin was followed by nearly all the men of the congregation, dressed in appropriate clothing for the occasion, and his colleagues from the city and its surroundings and many other places. Thereafter it was followed also by members of the seceding churches, as well as many elders and people from all ranks and classes of society. The entire churchyard and Perth Road was overcrowded with people. In absolute silence, the coffin containing the mortal remains was lowered into the grave. His friends Andrew Bonar, Robert McDonald, William Burns, John Baxter, Alexander Somerville and Patrick Miller stood there. Roxburgh expressed the feelings of many when he said: 'The grave was dug in the pathway, near the southwest corner of the church, and within a few yards of the pulpit from which he has so often and so faithfully proclaimed the Word of life; and in this his lowly resting-place all that is mortal of him was deposited, amidst the tears and sobs of the crowd. There his flesh rests in that assured hope of a blessed resurrection, of the elevating and purifying influences of which his life and ministry were so beauteous an example. His memory will never perish.'

According to Scottish tradition, speeches were not delivered at the graveside. Silently, many walked past the place where he had been buried. That continued for the next few days, as expressed by Bonar: 'Crowds of people on all sides; but, amidst the weepers, many were hardened too. Strange mixture of both! The grave is at the west corner of the church, at the flat parapet, parallel to the pulpit. It is Mizpah; it will watch till Christ comes between him and his flock.' A prayer meeting was held in the church on Saturday night. After William Burns had opened the gathering, Bonar preached from Acts 20:21. Alexander Somerville, M'Cheyne's friend, also addressed the crowd that had arrived in great numbers. The people wished to remain. Some of them asked the teachers to return again soon.

They were now like sheep without a shepherd. Someone asked, 'What shall we do now?' Margaret, the deceased James Laing's sister, came up to Bonar and told him that a woman was awakened by reading a pamphlet concerning her brother who had recently passed away and she added that 'she was brought to Jesus last Sabbath'. She had tears in her eyes. 'So I hope He is to be with us still.' God's trustworthiness was her only comfort. Jamie and his teacher were no longer; they were jubilant now before the throne, but God's work continued. Before his death, M'Cheyne had prepared the pamphlet for the press concerning Jamie's sickness which resulted in his deathbed. The Lord wished to use it for the conversion of sinners. Thereafter, Bonar went to the manse, where he met the grieving M'Cheyne family. He wrote that he departed in the evening from the house which 'was to me unspeakably melancholy'.

**The mourning in the church**

The following Sunday, Bonar had to conduct the service of worship. Was he still overpowered by melancholy? Should he have ascended the pulpit of his beloved friend whilst in this state? Hadn't the Lord been good to them in years gone by? How he punished himself with the thought that he was so inclined to overlook God's mercy because of his own sadness! The Lord came to his assistance with His sustaining and comforting grace. 'I have felt a sweet, calm rest in God; but never do I think of Robert's calm blessed countenance in death without being overpowered again. The singing of the last psalm on Thursday evening brought so much to my mind, and the look of his congregation also, that I could do nothing but weep as we stood up to sing. I was glad that Alexander Somerville was beside me in the pulpit.' The Lord helped pull his servant through. Bonar preached in the church on Acts 20:25-27 and then on Elijah. The words rang through the building: 'And now, behold, I know that ye all, among whom I have gone ..., that I am pure from the blood of all men ...' And in the evening he spoke on Acts 8:2, 'And devout men carried Stephen to his burial, and made great lamentation over him.'

Alexander Somerville, too, delivered a sermon of mourning. The overflow was so great that he had to speak at the cemetery. His text was from Revelation 15:2 3. William Lamb wrote concerning this: 'Along with many others of the congregation I was outside, and joined in the worship there. Mr. Somerville, standing but a few paces from the new grave of our departed pastor, engaged in the usual way by praise and prayer, which, in the particular place and circumstances, I felt very solemn, more so than had I been inside.' William Burns and John Roxburgh spoke words in memory of their deceased friend. Robert M'Cheyne's sun had set, but the sun of God's faithfulness still continued to rise over the city. God's children were certainly sorrowful, but not in despair. What an appropriate message issued from Somerville's mouth that afternoon. He had chosen Hebrews 4:14-16 as his text, containing the very applicable words of the apostle. It was a sermon full of comfort and encouragement. His finger didn't point to the grave of his friend, but he focused his attention above, to the great High Priest. His work continues: 'Let us hold fast our profession.' Next came the apostle's admonition: 'Let us therefore come boldly unto the throne of grace, that we may obtain mercy...' Grieving and yet, at the same time comforted, the people returned home. Lamb wrote the following concerning this solemn ceremony: 'What a solemn meeting, thought I, surrounding the grave of our dear pastor, who but a few days since conducted our devotions! His voice is now silent on earth, and others fill his place.' In this mood, he went to his Sunday School class. He read the children M'Cheyne's pamphlet, *Reasons why Children should flee to Christ,* and he 'spoke a short time urging that on them'. Alexander Gatherer also addressed the children. What more could he do than awaken the children to seek Jesus?

Robert Murray M'Cheyne's work was over. He had carried out the counsel of God. Bonar wrote: 'He has gone to the "mountain of myrrh and the hill of frankincense, till the day break and the shadows flee away." His work was accomplished! His heavenly Father had no other vine for him to train; and the Saviour who so loved him was waiting to greet him with His own welcome: "Well done, good and faithful servant: enter thou into the joy of thy Lord." The memory remains, as well as the fruit that he had harvested by his labours, until such time as these too would be gathered into the heavenly barns. He was the one who "spent his nights and days in ceaseless breathings after holiness, and the salvation of sinners. Hundreds of souls were his reward from the Lord ere he left us; and in him have we been taught how much one man may do who will only press further into the presence of his God, and handle more skilfully the unsearchable riches of Christ, and speak more boldly for his God.'

His grave witnesses until this day to his relentless zeal in winning souls for Christ. The church council provided a sober monument which would retain the memory of their beloved pastor and teacher. Alexander Somerville observes: 'Our friend Lazarus sleepeth, till Jesus comes to wake him out of sleep.' At the foot of the grave stone were chiselled the following characteristic words that testify to a life lived in the service of his Master, to a heart 'compelled by the love of Christ':

He ceased not
day and night to labour and watch for souls;
and was honoured by his Lord
to draw many wanderers out of darkness
into the path of life.

"Them also that sleep in Jesus will God bring with him."

The gravestone of McCheyne in St Peter's Churchyard.

# Chapter 14

# THEY FOLLOW IN HIS FOOTSTEPS

**To his remembrance**

'The memory of the just is blessed.' Although M'Cheyne had passed away, yet his name certainly would not be forgotten. Subsequent to his death, he not only continued to live on in the minds of many, but his memory was a perpetual blessing as well. Although his spoken words and holy life were no longer present, yet his life story (both spoken and written) would be read by thousands. He left behind a sorrowful and mourning people, but subsequent to his death, his work would continue to yield fruit. The *Dundee Warder* inserted a detailed article on the occasion of his death, in which his significance and life's work were mentioned. The atmosphere of sorrow gave place to feelings of gratitude. 'Let us rejoice, rather,' observed the writer, 'that he was spared so long, and blessed to be the instrument of so much good, and that he has fallen like a good soldier of Christ, faithfully contending to the last under the banner of the Captain of salvation. He has been taken away in the midst of his days and usefulness. But he has left behind him a sweet and fragrant memory that will be cherished for many generations. "The memory of the just is blessed." His name will survive in connection with the revival of vital, spiritual religion, not in this town only but throughout Scotland; and his manifold labours, his eminent graces, and saintly and apostolic spirit, short as his interesting and active course has been, will mark him out in history as the second Willison of Dundee.'

Many contributions were written in his memory. The country as well as church press devoted detailed attention to his death. Speeches were delivered everywhere, making mention of his significance as one of the leaders of the Scottish revival movement. His colleague, John Roxburgh, too, rendered a comprehensive summary of his life and work. 'Whether viewed as a son, a brother, a friend, or as a pastor, often has the remark been made by those who knew him most intimately, that he was the most faultless and attractive exhibition of the true Christian which they had ever seen embodied in a living form. His great study was to be Christlike. He was a man of remarkable singleness of heart. He lived but for one object – the glory of the Redeemer in connection with the salvation of immortal souls.' Everywhere, he earned respect also because people were convinced of 'his perfect integrity'. His great talents of intellect and heart impressed many. 'His spiritual mind had a quick and strong perception of the connection of the great principles for which the church is contending, with the interests of vital godliness in the land.'

James Hamilton from London dedicated a tribute to his deceased friend. He wrote among other things: 'More than any one whom we have ever known, had he learned to do everything in the name of the Lord Jesus. Amidst all his humility – and it was very deep – he had a prevailing consciousness that he was one of those who belong to Jesus; and it was from Him, his living Head, that he sought strength for the discharge of duty, and through Him, his Righteousness, that he sought the acceptance of his performances.' Hamilton thought his passing away to be a great loss to the church. He was an example to many of holy conduct and heavenly fervour, to the humiliation of ministers who showed little faithfulness in their work. 'Hireling shepherds will not regret the brother who is gone. His life and labours were a reproof to them.' Thus was the death of 'this faithful witness a striking call to ministerial disinterestedness and devotedness. "Be thou faithful unto death, and I will give thee a crown of life." And while some are crying mournfully, "Where is the Lord God of Elijah?" we pray that many find the answer in a double portion of Elijah's spirit descending on themselves.' 'Even so, Lord! Amen.'

**'Memoir and Remains'**

'The memory of the just is blessed.' This applied also to the *Memoir and Remains*, the biography and posthumous writings, which Andrew Bonar compiled after the death of his friend. He had informed the father of the deceased in April 1843, that he wished to write a biography. Immediately, Adam M'Cheyne reacted positively and sent him a detailed report of Robert's life. In his opinion, he hadn't discovered much: 'I regret much that I have so little to communicate.' The question that concerned M'Cheyne's father bore reference to the memories of his youth and information on his family relationships and circumstances, including his time as a student, rather than details about his spiritual life, because he supposed that Bonar knew more about the latter than he did. Besides many letters and notes, he also gave him a 'Memorandum' which had been preserved by Robert's mother. The latter included details 'of what took place from the time of her arrival till his death'. This data was a good basis from which to go to work.

On Saturday, 30 April 1843, Andrew Bonar began his compilation of M'Cheyne's *Memoir and Remains*. The Disruption of the Church of Scotland, which took place in May of that year, distracted him from writing until September. His friends too helped him in this extensive task. Alexander Somerville offered his advice concerning the manner in which

MEMOIR AND REMAINS

OF THE

REV. ROBERT MURRAY M'CHEYNE,

MINISTER OF ST PETER'S CHURCH, DUNDEE,

BY THE

REV. ANDREW A. BONAR,

MINISTER OF THE FREE CHURCH OF SCOTLAND, COLLACE.

VOL. I.
MEMOIR, &c.

*SECOND THOUSAND.*

DUNDEE:
WILLIAM MIDDLETON, 64 HIGH STREET.
J. GALL & SON, W. WHYTE & CO., J. JOHNSTONE, W. P. KENNEDY,
W. OLIPHANT & SON, AND R. OGLE, EDINBURGH; D. BRYCE,
AND W. BLACKWOOD, GLASGOW; J. DEWAR, PERTH;
W. M'COMB, BELFAST; HAMILTON, ADAMS, & CO.
AND J. NISBET & CO., LONDON.
[illegible]

Church board at the entrance of the St Peter's Churchyard (November 2002).

Title page of 'Memoirs and Remains', first edition 1844.

Andrew Bonar and his wife Isobella Dickson (Copyright Rev. William M'Knight).

he should compile this biography: 'I think the best way will be for you to draw out your sketch of Robert's early days, and let me get a sight of it afterwards; what little facts I may be able to add may be jotted down and engrossed by you in your work. But really his public life is the most interesting part of his history, the light seeming to have broken in upon him so gradually that there is not any very interesting transition in his soul's history.' Alexander too, knew no clear report of the moment when Robert had embraced Christ. His conversion was visible to everyone, but we are still in the dark with respect to the precise manner in which this took place.

In December, the great task was complete. On Saturday, 23 December 1844, Bonar recorded: 'Finished my *Memoir of Robert M'Cheyne* yesterday morning. Praise, to the Lord. I have been praying, "Guide me with Thine eye." I may soon be gone; but I am glad that the Lord has permitted me to finish this record of His beloved servant. Yet it humbles me. My heart often sinks in me. Just tonight I saw my soul full of nothing but self, and all that comes forth seems a black steam of selfishness.' The book was published the following year. Adjacent to the title page, there appeared a portrait of Robert as he looked at twenty-one years of age. The engraver proceeded from an original self-portrait that he himself had drawn at that age, and that his father obligingly made available for his biography. The first edition contained 648 pages, of which 166 pages constituted the actual *Memoir*. The remainder included letters, sermons and various writings. The work was divided into two sections and initially, the circulation was not so large. Reprints soon followed. In 1892, a more comprehensive work appeared, which was reprinted many times. By the end of the century, hundreds of thousands of copies of the book had found their way into many homes, in Great Britain and America as well as Australia.

In addition, other books from his estate were published. In the year of his death, there appeared a publication of his last two sermons, 'Two last discourses,' which M'Cheyne had delivered on 12 March 1843 in St Peter's. Elder P.H. Thoms wrote a foreword for the latter from his house on the Crescent. The third edition of the *Narrative of a Mission of Inquiry to the Jews* appeared that same year. It constituted a report on the journey to Palestine in 1839. M'Cheyne had co-operated with others in its compilation. Andrew Bonar's foreword is dated 29 March 1843, a few days subsequent to the death of his friend. 'O that the Lord God of Elijah may cause His mantle to fall upon the many souls of the prophets who loved him as their own soul!' he wrote. In the years that followed, other sermons were added to new publications, which enjoyed a wide public interest. Thus, in 1846, the *Additional Remains* was published. The latter was a collection of sermons which had been compiled from M'Cheyne's sermon summaries. Only eternity will reveal the blessing these publications have been to many.

It came to light from time to time, in a wonderful way, how hearts were touched by these writings or by the life of M'Cheyne himself. At a conference in Mildway in June 1876, Andrew Bonar met Constance Bullen, with whom M'Cheyne had been well acquainted when eighteen years of age. His conversion then made little impression on her and neither did the poem which he dedicated to her at that time. Her attention was focused rather on worldly pleasures, and the sad Robert gave expression to his emotions in a poem: 'She chose the world.' She had preserved a lock of hair together with a verse of poetry that he had written for her. Her heart was touched, however, at the news of his death, and shortly afterwards she decided to follow the narrow way. Her former friend could not witness this experience; she was 'as of one born out of due time,' Robert being merely instrumental in leading her to the Lord.

**A retrospective view**

Years later, in 1860, an unknown friend of M'Cheyne's recorded his viewpoint retrospectively in the *Sabbath School Magazine*. He happened to be Thomas Alexander, then minister of the Belgrave Presbyterian Church in London. Before his conversion,

Gravestone of Peter Hunter Thoms, elder of St Peter's, who died on 17th June 1882 at the age of 86 years. He was Provost of Dundee from 1847 till 1853.

he had tried his hand at everything, from violinist to seaman. His father was a teacher in Fowlis, a few miles from Dundee. His memories of M'Cheyne date back to his youth. The *Memoir* of Bonar sharpened the impressions he had preserved of M'Cheyne. Was the impression of him offered by this book not distorted? Was it not a misrepresentation? he was asked. 'I answer,' he wrote, 'his biographer is incapable of colouring; he is not a mere article writer, a bookmaker; he speaks, writes, works under the eye of the great God.' 'The colours of that godly man's life were those of the Holy Ghost; that was a glorious piece of His workmanship.' Was he too not a witness to the labour of the Lord's anointed?

When Tom returned to the place of his birth, the revival in Dundee was in full swing. Every Sunday he would walk with his father and twenty or thirty others to St Peter's. It was winter; on one occasion 'snowflakes, large, white, and thick, slowly fell ...' At the entrance to the church, he caught sight of a man from his youth, 'leaning on the stone pillar, with his shoulder resting quietly on it, a short black pipe in his mouth, and with the blandest smile on his honest face ...' Previously, he had been a hopeless drunkard, but God's Spirit had touched his heart. How much had changed here! He had to think of the times previously when he had attended Sabbath School; when he entered the church here for the first time; then it had snowed too. Now he watched as the people listened with intensity to the penetrating sermon, he heard M'Cheyne's prayer and his pronouncement of two words with holy respect, 'Holy Father.' Earlier, such a sermon would have had little effect on him. The impressions had died away. He then recalled a man saying to him, 'Though God were to make you this offer, and you could win heaven by telling it, you never could get there, for you do not know.' The riches of Christ displayed by the minister passed him by. Now he saw neither parish nor minister; instead he heard the message from heaven. He listened, open-mouthed. It was a powerful sermon which penetrated through to the depths of his soul. 'Then he made me see that God's holiness required a perfect obedience. And how it got it in that of the Lord Jesus ...' M'Cheyne declared Christ's work on behalf of sinners. Thereafter, he repeated the words of Scripture: 'If they do these things in a green tree, what shall be done in the dry?' An arrow went through his soul. 'There was no way of escape, but by fleeing to Him who said, "Him that cometh to me, I will in no wise cast out." '

Never before had he heard anything like this. What was the secret of his preaching? He continues: 'I answer, It ought to be no secret at all. It was simply, "I believed, and therefore have I spoken; we also believe, and therefore speak." God was the secret of his strength. Holiness was the secret of his strength. Prayer was the secret of his strength. I remember a powerful close to one of his sermons. I never saw such an effect produced before or since, and I have heard all the greatest pulpit and other orators of our day. The people bowed down like a bulrush in the blast, lifted up their voice, and wept aloud. He was telling them that God was clear of the blood of their souls; that Christ was; that the Spirit was. And then he added that he also was on God's side, and that he too was clear of their blood. He called God to witness on his soul that he lied not, that he had preached to them in season, out of season ...'

**Jessie Thain's sorrow**

Memories can be reawakened, and these can also be painful. Jessie Thain was overwhelmed by sorrow when her father and friend in Christ passed away. She was overcome with grief every year, on the anniversary of his death. When she visited his grave in the churchyard, she stood in a daze. 'Even the sight of St. Peter's spire, "where the goings of our God were so mightily seen," opened afresh the wells of her grief.' In April 1844, she received a copy of the recently published *Memoir.* During this time, Eliza became her best friend, with whom she could share her grief. She wrote to her that she was disappointed by the book at first: 'I began it the evening it came and, as I could not rest until I had read it, I finished the *Memoir* next day. Although it seemed very, very precious, my first feelings were those of a great regret – that it is so short, and thus the half has not been told. But as I had read it so hurriedly, and had only a confused idea of it, I am reading it over again and enjoying it much more than the first time. It is indeed most savoury; and don't you feel it very quickening, dear Eliza, to see what the dear subject of it attained to? O, to have such a sight of sin as he had, and to prize the blood of sprinkling as he did ...' A year later, Jessie reread the *Memoir* for the third time. Then she recorded: 'O Lord grant that this record of Thy faithful servant's journey through this vale of tears may be greatly and universally blessed of Thee, especially to those who are engaged in the glorious work of the ministry; that by it they may be led to cultivate greater holiness of walk and conversation, and to long more for the glory of Jesus in the salvation of souls.'

Was her parental home in Blairgowrie, the stately Heath Park, not a memorial too, because her friend had visited it so often? On

SONGS OF ZION:

TO

CHEER AND GUIDE PILGRIMS ON THEIR WAY

TO THE HEAVENLY JERUSALEM.

BY THE LATE

REV. R. M. M'CHEYNE,

MINISTER OF ST PETER'S, DUNDEE.

Be filled with the Spirit; speaking to yourselves in psalms, and hymns, and spiritual songs, singing and making melody in your heart to the Lord.—*Eph.* v. 18, 19.

DUNDEE:
WILLIAM MIDDLETON,
HIGH STREET.

MDCCCXLIII.

'Songs of Zion', poems of M'Cheyne, published in 1843. This copy was a present to Mrs. Coutts, 'from her very affectionate Friend, Lockhart Murray M'Cheyne, Edinburgh, 16 June 1843'.

18 January 1844, Jessie wrote in her diary: 'Tuesday last brought some things to my remembrance – being a year that day since our dear friend was here, and whom we then saw for the last time. How ignorant we are of what a day will bring forth, for how little did I then dream that I was not to see his dear face again till the Lord Jesus shall come and all His saints with Him.' Two months later, she stood at his grave: 'I felt so overcome while standing there that I couldn't realize anything; but oh, how applicable are his own words to himself:

> The precious dust beneath that lies,
> Shall at the voice of Jesus rise,
> To meet the Bridegroom in the skies,
> There, there, we'll meet again.

With lingering steps and wistful looks I left the spot and even the outward wall of that dear church touched many a cord in my bosom and told many a tale to my aching heart.'

Life continued. Jessie Thain's diary also came to an end. On 31 July 1845, she celebrated her twenty-fourth birthday: 'This day, twenty-four years, I was born into a world of sin and sorrow. How long have I lived and to how little purpose.' However, the Lord had left his mark on her life. She had friends too with whom she could heartily agree, such as Eliza M'Cheyne, of whom she wrote, 'My affections are entwined around her in no ordinary way.' The last entry in her diary was made in November 1847. Was her death imminent? The words with which the book ended were soon about to be fulfilled: 'We are journeying unto the place of which the Lord said, I will give it you ... (Num. 10:29).' Many trials came her way. Her parents were still alive and her brother, Alexander, was studying for the ministry in Edinburgh. The memory of her friend never left her, but Jesus meant even more to her than he did, and it was her prayer: 'Oh that my precious Saviour would always continue with me, that He would abide with me forever.'

Did Jessie Thain mean more to Robert M'Cheyne than merely a spiritual companion? His thoughts about marriage are enshrouded in haze. Proof of his engagement has never been supplied. It has been asserted with certainty, however, that Robert was engaged to a girl 'Miss M., from a respectable west-country family.' Apparently, her name was Murray, being in fact the sister of the fiancee of Henry Douglas, who later became minister of Kilsyth. Robert's father maintained a stony silence over a possibility of his son having been married. Both his brother William and his sister remained single. Eliza lived until 1888 and William died four years later. Their parents both passed away in 1854 and found their last resting place in the graveyard of St Cuthbert's, at the foot of the old castle of Edinburgh. They left no posterity, but their surname lived on in many hearts, such as that of Mrs Coutts, their family friend, who was so attached to their son. She couldn't read the *Memoir* of Bonar with dry eyes. His death was a tragedy to her and also to her friend, Miss Collier. Mother M'Cheyne gave Mrs Coutts the *Songs of Zion*, a small collection of Robert's poems, which were soon published by William Middleton in Dundee. These songs were as 'a dew from the Lord' to many.

### The Disruption

After M'Cheyne's death, events followed one another in quick succession. Two months later the great 'Exodus' of the Church of Scotland took place. On 18 May 1843, it was unusually busy in the capital city. People thronged in front of St Andrew's Church on broad George Street in New Town, waiting in eager anticipation. The annual General Assembly met in this church, subsequent to the sessions which were solemnly opened in St Giles'. The Commissioner of Queen Victoria came from Holyrood Palace and strode inside to listen to the sermon delivered by Dr Welsh. On this day the company listened to the same doctor, who didn't proceed to the usual deliberations, but instead read a protest. One could hear a pin drop in the stately eighteenth-century church building. The protest was aimed at the state intrusion into church matters, and was an accusation against the government's arbitrariness, as well as a defence of the freedom of the church and of the 'Crown Rights of Christ'. Patronage was, and remained, unacceptable. When Welsh's momentous speech was over, he bowed to the commissioner and left the church building. Dr Chalmers followed him and more than three hundred ministers joined in the long procession, which proceeded across George Street through New Town in the direction of Cannonmills, on the North side of Water of Leith. The Lord Provost of Edinburgh, uniformed and sitting on a horse, dismounted and walked together with the others to the large Tanfield Hall. Thousands followed the company of reverend brothers to the place where the first meeting of the Assembly of the Free Church took place. The Great Separation, or the Disruption, as it became known, became a reality on this day.

How M'Cheyne had longed for this time to arrive, but it was not granted him to experience these events. His friend, William C. Burns, walked in the procession. He wrote concerning this: 'Tuesday to Edinburgh per steam through a great storm on the way to the Assembly. Thursday, I was honoured to join in the solemn procession of ministers etc., from the St. Andrews' Church to the Free Assembly hall, Cannonmills, walking between my father on the one side and uncle George of Tweedsmuir on the other. This was a scene of which I know not what to say! The opening of the Free Assembly was graciously solemn. Surely the Lord was there.' The birth of the Free Church was greeted with joy by many. Besides the struggle which had taken place on the church front, it was the revival which had acted as an undercurrent to make the way for this memorable event. In the background, M'Cheyne and his friends had exerted an unmistakable influence on church life. The Holy Spirit had caused their preaching to be a blessing to many thousands and this fact initially determined the nature of the new church. In the first place, the Free Church didn't consist of a perfect church organization, but rather the living stones of God's house. The revival movement continued thereafter in the new church. At the Assembly of 1844, Dr Charles J. Brown from Edinburgh preached on the 'State of Religion'. This had a tremendous impact on the audience. 'The Spirit of God,' says one who was present, 'seemed to move over ministers and people and bow their souls as the wind bends a field of corn.' The church rose again in the same way that the temple was restored in the days of Ezra and Nehemiah. Horatius Bonar recalls that during the first six years of the Free Church's existence, evangelization was undertaken with much enthusiasm. Although the leaders of the first hour had passed away, namely, David Welsh in 1845 and Thomas Chalmers in 1847, God's work still continued.

The first years of the Free Church were the most difficult. Everything had to be started from scratch. Church buildings had to be erected and new manses furnished. The opposition to the new buildings was great, especially from among the landed nobility. Ministers were forced to abandon their old manses. In due course this happened to Henry Duncan from

Scene of the Disruption, exodus of ministers and elders from St Andrew's Church on 18 May 1843. In the first row: Thomas Chalmers and David Welsh.

Ruthwell too. He was forced to bid farewell to his stately manse, which M'Cheyne had often visited in his youth. This he did with joy. He was almost seventy years old at the time he had to move out of his church and home. When he lay on his deathbed a few years later and people asked him if he regretted his decision, his reply was resolute: 'Regret! what have I to regret? Can a man regret having had grace to act up to his principles?'

Nearly all the church members of Blairgowrie transferred themselves to the new church. Not long afterwards, a large church building was erected. However, for the time being, people had to improvise. When Robert McDonald returned from the unforgettable assembly in Edinburgh, his first task was to look for a provisional shelter. It wasn't easy to find a building, but his elder, John Thain, knew what to do. He happened to be a shipowner and could avail himself of a large sail. Thus, a tent was erected and the new congregation could meet together. The first psalm which resounded across the beautiful landscape, was the 'Old Hundredth', which 'was sung with intense gratitude and thanksgiving. The presence of the Lord was felt throughout the whole service – it seemed, indeed, the house of God and the very gate of heaven.'

### The 'Disruption' in the 'Carse'

It wasn't easy for James Grierson to leave the large church building in Errol. It was made more difficult by the fact that it was packed to capacity when he returned from Edinburgh to take his leave. He suggested that the next time they meet it should be on the green grass in the open air in front of his manse. 'The whole audience was most deeply affected.... The burst of feeling was perfectly overwhelming to myself as well as to others,' he observed sadly. He didn't hold many expectations for the first attendance on 4 June 1843. From his study, he watched a few widows lying down on the grass. However, soon the crowds poured in. The grassy field was surrounded by bushes, especially laurels, with lilac trees and laburnums scattered here and there. The church towers were

Grave of James Grierson on the old Churchyard of Errol.

all that stood out above the natural beauty. Here the first parish of the Free Church found a sheltered place. The pulpit was placed on the grass and Grierson preached from Hebrews 11:24-27: 'Choosing rather to suffer affliction with the people of God.' These words kept him occupied the whole Sunday. During the afternoon service he distributed from his pulpit a copy of the 'Deed of Demission,' containing the signatures of four hundred and fifty-one ministers, to exemplify the significance of this day. The more than six hundred present were deeply impressed. The Lord would also continue with His work in Errol and would provide the new parish with a church and a manse. What must have gone through the mind of M'Cheyne's old friend, when he saw the roads before his manse crowded with especially the common people who had come from near and far to hear the gospel being preached? 'At this sight I burst into tears, thanked God, and took courage.'

Thus, the peaceful landed estates of the Carse of Gowrie were witness to the Disruption, the schism of the church, which despite its dark side yielded so much blessing. A few months before the separation became an accomplished fact, Alexander Beith, minister of Stirling, travelled through the fertile region to encourage the parishes. Thus he came to 'Annat Lodge' in Rait, where he was received by relatives of Alexander Moody Stuart. The summer residence of the gifted St Luke's minister was found here on this country estate, which retained so many memories. From Rait he rode to Errol to encourage Grierson. New parishes sprang up and new church buildings were erected everywhere; in Collace too, where Andrew Bonar worked with much blessing.

Andrew and his brother Horatius had also accompanied the procession from St Andrew's Church in Edinburgh. 'Solemn meeting there. I forgot too much at the time that the eye of Christ was upon us. He was smiling and saying: "I know thy works," ' recorded Andrew. On his arrival back home, he preached in the open air to five hundred people. Having no house in which to worship God, the congregation met together provisionally under a canvas shelter. A 'kind friend in Dundee', the elder, Edward Caird of St Peter's, had arranged this. When, for the first time, the wind blew and the rain began to fall, they were gathered together under the roof of a new church. The Lord does everything well!

### St Peter's after M'Cheyne

St Peter's parish also transferred to the new church. How M'Cheyne had longed for the day of the Disruption! The young assistant minister, Alexander Gatherer, wrote to Andrew Bonar on 24 May 1843: 'The dark days predicted so frequently by our friend seem now at hand. How much he would have enjoyed them! How delighted he would have been with the proceedings of last Thursday! I recollect, in writing from the Convocation with such a prospect in view, he said, "How happy it is to live at such a time!" ' According to Smellie, those were dark days with the stars blazing in the heavens. A new period was ushered in for Dundee also. Most of the ministers joined the Free

Church, and new church buildings arose throughout the city.

How was the church building on Perth Road faring? Just a short while ago so many offerings were collected to make its construction possible. Would the building now have to be ceded to the Auld Kirk? God's providence decided otherwise. It appeared that the church building belonged in name only to the Kirk of Scotland, but on paper it was in the possession of a certain Mr Millar of Rosangle. How this all precisely came about is uncertain; in any case, St Peter's was the first parish, which together with building and manse could be transferred to the Free Church. The congregation bought the church building for twelve hundred pounds. What a windfall for the sorrowing congregation! During this busy time, Gatherer and other ministers tried to the best of their ability to care for the parish, which lacked a pastor. Ultimately, as it turned out, Gatherer didn't become M'Cheyne's successor. He took up a post in 1844 near Kincardine O'Neil instead. Unfortunately, he became an invalid a few years later and had to give up his work for good.

The kirk session took on themselves the task of calling a new minister in April. Two elders walked to Collace to inform Andrew Bonar that he, together with Islay Burns, made a twosome. It was painful for the former, not only because of a great reluctance to occupy the pulpit of his deceased friend, but also because he felt that his place was in Collace. Ultimately, Islay Burns, a brother of the evangelist, became the new pastor and teacher, and was duly confirmed as candidate for the ministry on 7 June 1843. It was the first induction service to take place in the Free Church. The next month communion was held, which was, of course, attended by Bonar. He spoke with 'extraordinary freedom' on the Pearl of great price, and wrote: 'When the people were gone, walked round with Islay Burns to Robert M'Cheyne's tomb, and when I saw the grass growing over it, waving in the shade, while darkness was nearly hiding it from view, I felt most solemnly. The text came powerfully to mind, "His banner over him was love", for that was Robert's experience surely all his days!'

Islay Burns was a man who feared the Lord, but he could not stand in the shadow of his predecessor. In the beginning, he tried to imitate M'Cheyne's preaching techniques, until he realized his mistake. He had surely received his own gifts. What distinguished him from his predecessor? According to a later opinion, 'the work of the one was conversion, the other that of edification.' Some moved to other parishes, but most of them remained under the roof of the church, where so many precious memories were cherished. There were fourteen members in the first kirk session of the Free St Peter's, and the communion roll gives a division of the districts which fell under their oversight. We come across such names as Peter H. Thoms, James Wallace and William Lamb. We read of many who remained, with whom we are acquainted, such as Miss Collier and Mrs Likely and Alexander Laing, Jamie's brother. We follow the streets around St Peter's on foot, such as Hawkhill, Perth Road, Paton's Lane, Miller's Wynd, Magdalen Yards and so many other alleys and streets of West End. Here M'Cheyne trod and here God's work continued even after his death.

The congregation suffered a heavy loss when William Lamb died. He fell off his horse and passed away at thirty-three years of age. 'So tragic an end of a life of such usefulness, and to a career of such promise, produced a profound sensation in the community.' The kirk session composed a memorial note on 8 November 1848 to commemorate his death: 'In the bloom of youthful vigour, in the freshness of early zeal and opening usefulness in the cause of his Lord and Saviour, and at the very moment when, prepared by a season of peculiarly solemn and sanctifying discipline, he promised to be more than ever a comfort to the Church of Christ, of which he was an officebearer, he has been, in the inscrutable providence of God, suddenly snatched away.'

The contemporary elders of M'Cheyne would follow him in their death. Years later, on 23 September 1877, the elderly John Matthewson passed away. John Smith, who knew him so well from his youth, paid him a visit. 'He was lying peacefully on his bed and knew me. I took his hand, saying, "Come, Lord Jesus, come quickly," to which he responded, and he pressed my hand as I repeated to him some of the precious words of God.' Thereupon both of them sang: 'The Lord is my Shepherd,' and after prayer, 'Rock of ages.' Thus Matthewson passed into the next life. Well-known people from church life were mentioned in a newspaper at the beginning of this century by a contemporary of M'Cheyne's days. Men such as the elder and ex-bailiff Ogilvie, bank agent from Lochee, who passed away shortly afterwards, were among the names to appear. Together with Edward Caird, he belonged to the Sabbath School staff. Then there was Patrick Hunter Thoms, who was twice provost of Dundee; he was a bosom friend of M'Cheyne's, who lived not far from the church in the Crescent, a park situated on the Tay. He too was to 'be gathered unto his people', and his gravestone stands next to that of M'Cheyne's.

Islay Burns remained attached to the parish until 1864, after which time he accepted an appointment as principal of the Free Church College, Glasgow. His successor, Duncan McGregor, who was there from 1864 until 1876, ministered with much blessing among the people of West End. He was a man who originated from the Highlands, and seemed well-acquainted with the spiritual climate in those Northern mountainous regions. For many years it was the Highlands which held onto the work of God's Spirit, when, during those days, the stream of spiritual fervour waned in the south of Scotland. In the Free Church, too, the tack was gradually changed and spiritual life languished.

After the departure of McGregor, who was much loved by the people, this process of spiritual decay didn't pass by St Peter's. A superficial service of worship, which was foreign to the profound preaching of men such as M'Cheyne and the Bonars, permeated church life as leaven does in bread, causing irreparable damage. A core of the faithful St Peter's members remained, however, until the end of the century. The number

54

COMMUNION BOOK.

| Name. | Place of Residence. | Occupation, or Profession. | Date of Year. |
|---|---|---|---|
| District No 13 | Mr William Lamb Elder | | |
| A | | | |
| David Adams | Small's Wynd | | |
| Mrs Dd Adams | Small's Wynd | | |
| Ann Adams | Small's Wynd | | |
| Agnes Adams | Small's Wynd | | |
| Jean Adams | Small's Wynd | | |
| Ann Anderson | Mills Buildings | | |
| Janet Anderson | with Miss Whitson | | |
| B | | | |
| Mrs Balfour | Small's Wynd | | |
| Jean Balfour | Small's Wynd | | |

Part of the Communion Book of Free St Peter's, just after the Disruption. District 13 was the section of elder William Lamb.

of church attenders in about 1855 was so great that a mission was formed, which met together in Taylor's Lane. From this originated a new congregation which, in May 1870, opened the doors to M'Cheyne's Memorial Church. This magnificent building was erected not far from St Peter's, at the crossroads between Perth Road and Hawkhill. The well-known Baptist teacher from London, Charles Haddon Spurgeon, was afforded the honour of inaugurating the church, and two years later the first minister, Rev. A.H. Reid, arrived. The population increase in this district necessitated the extension of this church building in 1899.

## Recollections of M'Cheyne

Both church buildings were incorporated into the reunion of the two largest dissenting Presbyterian denominations, which took place in 1900. The new church was called the United Free Church, after the fusion between the Free Church and the

United Presbyterian Church. This last church originated from the Erskines' group amongst others, which separated itself from the established church in 1733. A new era for Dundee was ushered in, but liberal thinking would also wreak havoc here. 'I-chabod, saying, The glory is departed from Israel.' The city expanded, industrialization continued, but God's work went into decline.

M'Cheyne's manse on Union Place had to make way for an extension to a rope factory. Before the house was demolished, the elderly John Smith visited Union Place. Together with Tom Brown, he had led a prayer group. Together they had once visited the first manse on Strawberry Bank. Now it was nearly seventy years later. He set foot in the study 'where he had likely composed those solemn words of warning'. Here Smith bowed his stiff knees in the room where the beloved teacher of his youth had passed away in Christ and 'where he yielded up his immortal spirit to Him who gave it'. Precious memories flashed through his mind. He also had to think of William Burns, who as a missionary, later departed for China to 'be greatly used of God in that distant land'. All this was in the past, however, and would never be repeated. The generation of the St Peter's anointed pastor's acquaintance had passed on.

In M'Cheyne's Memorial Church, a place of honour was afforded a Bible with the following inscription: 'Presented to the Rev. Robert Murray M'Cheyne, minister of St. Peter's Church, Dundee, by the members of his congregation, as a mark of their affection and esteem. January 1837. 2 Thessalonians 1 :11-12.' Until now this Bible contains the memories of M'Cheyne's labours. Certain texts were underlined which had meant so much to him, such as, among others, Song of Songs 2:3: 'I sat down under his shadow with great delight, and his fruit was sweet to my taste.' Chapter 3 verse 4 was also underlined: 'Whom my soul loveth.' By means of this love he was attached to God's children in the parish, and this love transcended the boundaries of death and eternity. Therefore his work wasn't in vain, and his memory was an eternal blessing to so many.

# Communion plate and furniture stolen from closed Dundee church

VALUABLE RELIGIOUS articles and historic pieces of furniture have been stolen from St Peter's Church, St Peter Street, Dundee.

Ironically the theft was discovered when the church—which is not now used for worship—was opened to allow an expert from Sotheby's to carry out a valuation.

Police yesterday estimated the value of the articles taken, including a Communion set, at several thousand pounds.

Mr Bob Munro, the church's joint property convener, said last night, "Sales of the 647-page memoirs of Robert Murray McCheyne are close to a million copies and people from 60 different countries have visited the church so the monetary value of the items stolen is not as important as their historic value.

"A stolen grandfather clock, for example, was presented by pupils of his evening classes to Robert McCheyne in 1838."

Mr Munro said the church was usually kept locked but was opened for the large numbers of visitors from Northern Ireland, Holland and the United States who came to see the church of the renowned preacher.

"It would appear that entrance was gained by severing a heavy steel padlock securing protective steel bars at the entrance at the front of the church," he explained.

"The intruders knew exactly what they were after, taking some valuable items and leaving others.

"There was absolutely no damage to the main building."

The grandfather clock has a circular face with Roman numerals and inscribed plates on the front.

The Communion service, in silver plate, comprises 10 goblets, two tall jugs and four plates.

Antique chairs were also taken, including dining-room chairs, covered chairs and Victorian hall chairs.

"Among them was a Communion chair which was ornately carved," said Mr Munro.

"It was tall and wide and sat in the centre of the pulpit area. It must be well over 100 years old.

"As soon as I opened up the church I realised something was wrong and contacted the police.

"We have photographs of the items and hope this will help in tracking them down."

Because the building was used infrequently it was impossible to say when the theft might have occurred.

The congregation linked with McCheyne Church, in Perth Road, a few years ago to form the combined charge of St Peter's McCheyne.

*The missing Communion plate and some of the stolen furniture.*

Relics kep in St Peter's Church, such as the Communion plates and cups, Communion tokens, some editions of the 'Memoir', letters of M'Cheyne, photographs etc. Some of them which had value were stolen in 1986. The 'Courier and Advertiser', a Dundee newspaper had an account of the unwished visit of the thieves. The rest of the 'relics' were taken to the City Archives and City Museum.

St. Peter's M'Cheyne's Memorial Church, Church of Scotland, in July 1992. The building is closed now.

### The circle of friends after his death

Sorrowful friends were left behind, but they didn't despair. In June 1843, holy communion was celebrated in Collace, and sixty people from St Peter's were present. Bonar's Scripture text was: 'Until the day break, and the shadows flee away.' An eyewitness wrote later as a reminder: 'He referred to Mr. M'Cheyne as standing on the "mountain of myrrh" till the day break; and as he pointed to the bread and wine before him, as shadows that would flee away, there came a great hush over the congregation; and then the sound of sobbing from the Dundee people who were present, at the mention of their beloved minister's name.' The Lord's presence was still here in this hilly landscape of Collace. Elizabeth Morrison witnessed that she had received a faith's view of Jesus such as she had never before experienced.

Brotherly love was a characteristic feature which remained also after M'Cheyne had passed away. On 25 January 1844, George Smeaton, minister of the Free Church of Auchterarder, sent a circular letter to a number of his friends. He himself, during his study years, had been a member of the Exegetical Society, to which M'Cheyne and the Bonar brothers also belonged. His letter was directed to ministers. We read the names of John Milne from Perth, Andrew Bonar from Collace, Patrick L. Miller from Dundee, Robert McDonald from Blairgowrie, Alexander Somerville from Glasgow, James Hamilton from London, John Purves from Jedburgh and Horatius Bonar from Kelso, all well-known names to the deceased pastor of St Peter's circle of friends. His death was recalled to memory and he issued a reminder to devote one day per month to prayer and fasting – a suggestion which had first originated with M'Cheyne.

M'Cheyne was a great advocate of concerted prayer and practised it not only in Dundee, but also in other places. Smeaton's intention was to continue this practice. He proposed that the first Tuesday of every month be set aside for this purpose, and that everyone bring their own needs and those of the church to the throne of grace. It was the urgency of the times which forced him to put this plan of action into practice. Although it wasn't possible to meet together due to the distance that separated one from the other, yet this prevented no one from submitting their collective needs to God in personal prayer. The commotion surrounding the Disruption was over, and now people had the time to take up the task of rebuilding God's parish. How necessary it was to beseech God's Spirit to be poured out over the new flock. How would the Free Church be able to grow spiritually without constant prayer? Wasn't collective prayer not also a 'means of knitting us in love to those who have been upon our hearts in times of near communion with the Lord'? How often weren't they refreshed when returning home after their gathering! The brothers must surely have experienced the worth of the apostle's words: 'Bear ye one another's burdens, and so fulfil the law of Christ.'

**Andrew Bonar's end**

The mutual bond was maintained through the years. 'Let brotherly love continue' was common practice for them. This custom still existed after 1856, when Andrew Bonar delivered his farewell sermon in Collace. He was inducted by Robert McDonald from Blairgowrie as minister of the new mission in the district of Finnieston, in the great city of Glasgow. He worked there with much blessing until his death in 1892. The same Hebrew letters which were inscribed above the entrance to his new church had also adorned his study in Collace. The significant words were: 'He that winneth souls is wise.' This was his life's mission, as it had been the experience of his unforgettable friend. How happy he was for his parish during the years 1859 and 1874 when new revivals left behind a blessing in their wake. He continued to labour on in God's vineyard until he was well advanced in years. His brother, Horatius, who moved from Kelso to Edinburgh, died in 1889.

The memory of the years gone by sometimes revived his spirit. The annual day of M'Cheyne's death was always a day of sadness. He dreamed once about him, and also about Alexander Thain, the promising minister who died at an early age. He would often go to St Luke's to assist his friend, Alexander Moody Stuart, with the administration of communion. 'William Burns was there often, Robert M'Cheyne, Alexander Somerville, my brother Horace, Dr. Duncan, and many others. The God of Elijah lives still.' He was also present at the inauguration of the Memorial Church in Dundee. He preached outside the kirk before a great crowd, while McGregor of St Peter's preached inside. 'Felt deep, deep sorrow at the thought of the past. What gales of the Spirit have blown, and yet my sails have been ill set, and caught little of the breezes in these great awakening times!'

The end of the pilgrimage drew near for Andrew Bonar. He passed away without any visible death-struggle, in absolute peace of mind. 'He was in the dark valley and did not know it. Living or dying, he was the Lord's, and He was with him.' On

Grave of Andrew Bonar in Sighthill Cemetery, Glasgow.

Grave of Adam McCheyne and his wife on St Cuthbert's Churchyard Edinburgh.

Grave of Horatius Bonar in Cannongate Churchyard, Edinburgh.

Grave of David Martin M'Intire D.D. (1859-1938), beside the monument of his father-in-law, Andrew Bonar. Pulled down by vandals.

Wednesday, 4 January 1893, men, women and children trudged through the snow to the graveyard on Sighthill in Glasgow. On the summit of the hill, his body was buried next to that of his wife and son, 'within sight of the great city where so long he lived and laboured.' Here his mortal remains await the Day of Judgment.

His son-in-law, David MacIntyre, who succeeded him and continued in his footsteps, was buried alongside him in 1938. He had heard much from the mouth of his father-in-law concerning M'Cheyne. Some typed letters from the year 1921, which he wrote to his sister-in-law, Marjory Bonar, are still preserved. She breathed the same warmth we come across in Bonar and his friends. One letter concerns the assurance of faith, with which Marjory had some difference of opinion. According to her view a 'close and unbroken communion with Christ is a grace specially bestowed on mature believers'. MacIntyre couldn't agree on this point: 'It is for all believers, for the youngest and the least mature: "He shall gather the lambs with His arm".' Then he observes: 'I have known Christ in personal experience now for more than fifty years, and can only wonder at His goodness and feel how little I know of the unsearchable riches of His grace. I would not willingly be out of communion with Him for five minutes, but this is not an experience which belongs only to recent years.' He spoke with the same spirit that had inspired M'Cheyne. He and his friends surely drew strength from Christ's blood, and lived at the same time close to the Fountain of living water which would never run dry.

**The death of Somerville**

How did Alexander Somerville's life proceed further? He too was an interceder and yearned after the throne of grace.

David MacIntyre, in his book, *The Hidden Life of Prayer*, says of Somerville that, 'in the work of his own congregation, it was his custom to go into the church alone, and go over the pews, and, reading the names of the sitters in them commit

Inscription on the gravetomb of Alexander Moody Stuart in Kilspindie Churchyard.

Parish Church of Kilspindie.

*St Peter's Church*

"We already have churches in England and have been looking for a Scottish base for some time. We believe there is a great need to expand our church and St Peter's would provide us with an ideal opportunity to do just that."

Should Mr Paisley's offer be successful—and his colleagues see no reason to believe that it will not—the F.P.C.U. intend to send missionary graduates to Dundee to help put "roots" down in the area and gather a congregation.

"It will be fairly slow work and initially we intend to start things at a fairly low level and build up," added Mr McIlveen, who agreed that, if successful, Mr Paisley was likely to visit Dundee on an occasional basis to preach.

Mr McIlveen's optimism was, however, offset slightly by the surprise expressed last night by the current minister of the united charge of St Peter's McCheyne, the Rev. J. Harrison Hudson. The two churches were united some years ago and Mr Hudson's congregation are technically responsible for St Peter's Church building.

"This is news to me," he said when told of Mr Paisley's visit by a "Courier" reporter. "As far as I am aware there are no offers in for St Peter's."

Mr Stuart Fair, legal adviser to St Peter's McCheyne, was also unaware of any offers for St Peter's, which has an asking price of £40,000 plus.

"I understand, however, that Mr Paisley intends to do that and has instructed Scottish solicitors," he said.

Should an offer be received for St Peter's it would be up to the congregation of St Peter's McCheyne whether to accept it or not. The earliest such an offer could be considered would be September, the next time the church board meets.

The church was first opened for worship in 1836 and the Rev. Robert Murray McCheyne, soon to become a household name in Dundee, was ordained shortly afterwards. Mr McCheyne, who died at 29 after a brief but spectacular ministry, is buried in the south-west corner of the kirk.

Although it is no longer used for worship St Peter's still attracts large numbers of visitors interested in the work of the renowned preacher.

During last Thursday's trip to Dundee to view the church Mr Paisley also toured the Discovery, arriving unannounced in a large black car accompanied by four detectives.

*The Rev. Ian Paisley*

"He spent over an hour looking round every department of the ship," said the master, Mr Bill McGregor. "We did not talk about politics at all. Mr Paisley came across as a very polite and charming character who was fairly knowledgeable of the history and design of Discovery."

Last night Mr Paisley was in Brussels on E.E.C. business and could not be contacted.

St Peter's Church as it was in July 1992. Rev. Ian Paisley, the Ulster militant minister, tried to buy the building in 1987, which was closed, but the Free Church of Dundee offered more for the building, and became the new proprietor.

After the union of the Free Church and United Presbyerian Church in 1900, it became a United Free Church congregation, which went into the Church of Scotland in 1929. The 'Wee Frees', who continue the old Free Church, have the building now as the meeting place of a small but increasing congregation.

them to God in prayer.' Somerville laboured with much blessing for many years in Glasgow. In addition, he was a far-travelled man, who visited nearly all the continents in order to extend God's kingdom. Mission work was his particular interest. He followed the course of the revival in 1858/1859, not only in his own country, but also in Ireland and America. When D. L. Moody visited Scotland in 1874, he was one of the first to meet him. Moody and Sankey travelled through the land during the revival of 1874. They visited St Peter's too during this time.

Somerville died in 1889, earlier than Andrew Bonar, but shortly after Horatius had passed away. On 5 August 1889, he had attended Horatius' burial in Canongate churchyard in Edinburgh, and a month later he himself was no more. Without a struggle, he passed on to the next life, dying in the arms of his son. His wished to be buried in his usual black suit with minister's collar. A long procession followed the bier to its final resting place. The elderly Bonar walked along in the procession of his friend. The thoughts of days gone by filled his mind. He had developed a close affinity for Somerville and M'Cheyne. Somerville knew Robert already from his youth, as they had attended the same school together. He had also been probationer in Larbert, but since their ways had parted, due to Robert's death, he continued working for many years in His Master's vineyard, until the day arrived for him too to be relieved of his post.

**The last of the 'M'Cheyne Group': Moody Stuart**

William Burns died in far-off China in 1868; James Hamilton in 1867; Robert MacDonald in 1893. The last of the circle of friends to die was Alexander Moody Stuart. After the Disruption, he took over the use of Free St Luke's, a large, new church building on 43 Queen Street. Adam M'Cheyne became the first elder-secretary of the new parish. Moody Stuart also practised a life of intense prayer. He delivered a tender speech during a service: 'O Father, Holy Father, heavenly Father.'

His diary witnessed to a life lived in intimate fellowship with Him, and associated with the God of the covenant. He could say that no matter what mountains or valleys he had experienced in his life, no day passed by without his 'seeing the beauty of the Lord and quickening through His grace.' His longing for an uninterrupted fellowship with his God was fulfilled in July 1898. On his deathbed, the elderly teacher repeated his favourite psalm: 'Bless the Lord, O my soul, and forget not all His benefits.' With joy he cried out, 'I give my body to the grave, that grave in which the holy body of my Saviour lay ...'

His funeral didn't take place in Edinburgh. He wished to be buried in his wife's family grave. He surely cherished many memories of the summer-cottage in Annat, in the village of Rait. The Carse of Gowrie was a complete contrast to Edinburgh. He used to preach here in a small chapel on Sabbath evenings. From his cottage he could view the Firth of Tay and catch a glimpse of the towers of Errol on a clear day. How much he had enjoyed the splendid view across the glowing hills, which enhanced the beauty of the diverse landscape! His friend, Andrew Bonar, had lived not far away. If he should stand on the shore of the bay, he could spy the railway bridge across the Tay, which formed the junction between Fife and Perthshire in the neighbourhood of Perth Road. The construction of this Rail Bridge had taken from 1871 until 1878 to complete. The steam trains would rumble to and from Dundee on Sundays too. Surely it was to M'Cheyne's deep sorrow that God's day was thus desecrated in his city also. On 28 December 1879, whilst the train was in the process of crossing the bridge, the concrete pillars gave way and the locomotive engine, together with its passengers, plunged into the dirty waters of the Tay. One hundred people lost their lives that day and sorrow overcame the city.

The growing industry of Dundee remained hidden from the view of Annat. What a glorious memory was retained of this place in years past, when the friends would meet together in

Moody Stuart's cottage garden, and Andrew Bonar and Robert M'Cheyne sat together on the garden bench and spoke of the wonders of their God. Now it was all over. M'Cheyne was the first to pass away. The rest followed him. Now it was Moody Stuart's turn. His wish too was fulfilled. His work in St Luke's was complete. His funeral took place on 4 August 1898. The beautiful churchyard surrounding the Kilspindie church was overcrowded with people. Dr Douglas Bannerman addressed a few others in the little church, behind which the colossal tomb loomed. It stood ready to contain the lifeless body of the deceased.

The following Sunday, Bannerman led the service of mourning in Moffat Free Church, the parish of Moody Stuart's son. On this occasion he said : 'On Thursday your minister and I stood together at the grave of his father who, like Abraham, "died in a good old age, an old man, and satisfied, and was gathered unto his people." His grave looks onto the broad Carse, with its fields ripening to harvest, and the great river flowing to the sea. The full glory of the summer sunshine was over the hills and woods and waters that he loved so well, and over the trees of Annat. In the church beside the burying-place, under the great trees on the border of the field, we read those Scriptures which tell that "as in Adam all die, even so in Christ shall all be made alive," and how as "one star differeth from another star in glory, so shall it be in the resurrection of the dead." Then there resounded from the Kilspindie graveyard, the song of many to the words of the 65th paraphrase, the rhyming tune of Revelation 5:6 until the end:

Worthy the Lamb that died, they cry,
To be exalted thus;
Worthy the Lamb, let us reply,
For He was slain for us!'

**'Triumphant Burst into a Song!'**

It was the song of the elders, the song of Moses and of the

Lamb: 'Worthy is the Lamb that was slain ...' The waves of the Red Sea had made way for M'Cheyne and his friends, and the way to the heavenly Canaan opened up before their eyes. It was their longing to witness to the Lamb, to magnify Him. The shadow of death had to yield to His full light, who is the Candle of the heavenly sanctuary. 'And there shall be no night there.' The journey through the wilderness was not without struggle, nor without darkness. However, the fiery column preceded them. 'They sing the Song of Moses'; M'Cheyne had written a poem in 1835 about these very words. His poem ran thus: 'Dark was the night, the storm is high,' concerning the narrow way to eternal life. However, his pen didn't stop there. From the next few stanzas, it seemed that he moved up to higher ground. A yearning was expressed from his heart, in the same way the deer pants after the streams of God's comfort and love:

And oh! when life's dark journey's o'er,
And death's enshrouding valley past,
We plant our foot on yonder shore,
And tread yon golden strand at last.

Shall we not see with deep amaze,
How grace hath led us safe along;
And whilst behind – before, we gaze,
Triumphant burst into a song!

# Chapter 15

# WHOSE FAITH FOLLOW

## The significance of M'Cheyne and his circle of friends

Did M'Cheyne and those ministers who belonged to his circle of friends exert any significant influence on the theological trends of thought of their time? M'Cheyne's 'school' tended to be more spiritual than theological. Their influence was evident not so much in the college halls or the study rooms of the theological students; they distinguished themselves not in controversy, when it concerned the fight against error, but their contribution was more effective in spreading the classical teaching on grace to the general public. Their task was especially focused on evangelization and revivals and didn't exist to give substance to theological structures. Hence their strength lay in their preaching, which distinguished itself from the preaching of others 'in demonstration of the Spirit and of power'.

## Characteristic features of his preaching

'M'Cheyne brought into the pulpit all the reverence for Scripture of the Reformation period, all the honour for the

William Garden Blaikie D.D. (1832-1886).

J.H. Merle D'Aubigne (1794-1872).

headship of Christ of the Covenanter struggle, all the freeness of the gospel offer of the Marrow theology, all the bright imagery of Samuel Rutherford, all the delight of the Erskines in the fullness of Christ.' Thus Dr W. G Blaikie characterized the minister from Dundee in his book *The Preachers of Scotland.* It was as if all the talents a servant of the gospel could possess were united in one person. He holds a prominent place in the rich tradition of Scottish preaching. Blaikie mentions him with the ranks of great preachers such as John Welch, Samuel Rutherford and John Livingstone, when it concerns the 'tender tone' from the pulpit, as if he wished to plead with and compel his listeners to receive the truth of God's Word.

Blaikie mentions a new element in his preaching, that of 'winsomeness'. His presentation from the pulpit was prepossessing. He knew how to arrest the attention of his audience and to how secure the most hardened sinner. The breath of God's Spirit caused his heart to tremble and from this originated his strength to preach God's Word. We saw earlier how, with great emphasis, he proclaimed Christ and insisted on his listeners coming to Him. In a discussion concerning his preaching, Dr D.V. Yeaworth, in his thesis about M'Cheyne, came to the following conclusion: 'These aspects of M'Cheyne's style, being genuine parts of his own personality, together with the consistency and openness of his Christian character, give rise to his uncommon success as a preacher. Fired by his own experience with Christ, and his desire for others to have the same, his ministry was nothing more than a sincere presentation of that experience as he found it corroborated in the Scriptures.'

**The Scottish tradition as background**

As we have noticed, M'Cheyne was part of a rich tradition. Practical theology characterized the contents of his preaching. The themes of the Reformation – the teaching on reconciliation by the merits of Christ alone, the teaching on sin and grace, the justification of the ungodly – were central too. What was characteristic of this theology which was of eternal blessing to so many in Scotland? It was especially the teaching on reconciliation which put its stamp on the religious life of this land. Rightly, Dr J.H. Merle d'Aubigne, author and leader of the revival of the previous century, who visited Scotland more than once, observed: 'The Scottish theologian places himself at once in the centre of the Christian doctrine; it is on faith in the reconciliation by the expiatory sacrifice of Christ that he takes his stand. The grand dogma, which tells us at once of the sin of man and the grace of God – this fundamental doctrine which contains, on the one hand, the consciousness of our guilt, and on the other, the assurance of an irrevocable council of mercy and salvation, is the vivifying centre of Scottish theology. Faith in the Lamb of God, who had borne the sins of the world – this the mill with which the Scottish child is fed in the schools of the towns, the mountains, and the plains.'

Theologically speaking, where does M'Cheyne fit into the Protestant tradition of Scotland? It is difficult to place him in a definite corner. The development of Reformed teaching in his country has experienced shifts in emphases as well as aberrations. It is striking that despite his close affinity to the latter tradition, he took up such a substantive place and didn't allow himself to tip the scales of either extreme. He certainly lent a willing ear to the thoughts and ideas of others, but he didn't wish to become a slavish imitator of a certain teaching or author. An example here serves to illuminate or clarify. Edward Irving, who with much fire defended his premillennialistic viewpoint concerning the end times, enthused both Andrew and Horatius Bonar. They had taken up the thread after his death, and both in speech and in writing defended his viewpoint. M'Cheyne sympathized with Irving's viewpoint, and yet he had reservations concerning his vision, and could not become over-enthusiastic about his premillennialism. M'Cheyne wasn't a man of extremes but rather of balance. Biblical harmony characterized his life, preaching and teaching.

**Development of the doctrines of grace**

The renewed interest in the traditional and classical themes of sin and grace, which characterized his time, agreed entirely with M'Cheyne's aspirations and those of his contemporaries. It was their purpose to demolish the last remaining vestiges of the Moderates' stronghold. M'Cheyne and his followers formed a small and notable group within the Evangelicals, but they were no exception when it concerned Christ-centred preaching. Many brought the message of grace, few with as much spirit as they.

M'Cheyne's teaching was out and out Calvinism. The 'Five Points,' which were disputed especially by the Arminians, formed the foundation for his doctrine. He was actually no dogmatist, as were some of his contemporaries. What concerned him most was practical theology, rather than a methodical explanation of the teaching. The Bible was the handbook from which he developed his thoughts. Although M'Cheyne endeavoured in every way to be a Biblical theologian, yet he also took note of both the ancient and the present day sources. He read many theological and homiletical works. He was well-acquainted with the books of Jonathan Edwards, Samuel Rutherford, John Bunyan and Thomas Boston. He read the writings of his contemporaries, and regularly consulted commentaries such as those of Matthew Henry and John Calvin, and Quesnel concerning the Gospels. Although he wasn't a theologian of repute as were Thomas Chalmers and William Cunningham, yet he made a study of old and recent theological works. He considered the Westminster Confession of Faith to be a paraphrase of Christian teaching based on the Scriptures.

Blaikie mentions a few trends in Scottish church history, elements which appeared in his preaching. As has previously been mentioned, the teaching on reconciliation was the heart of Scottish theology. This golden thread still wove its way until the end of the nineteenth century, when Hugh Martin can be reckoned as one of the last exponents of orthodoxy. The teaching on reconciliation was unfolded under the major headings of the law and the gospel. Here, Luther's influence was unmistakable. It was no wonder that his *Commentary on Galatians* greatly appealed to M'Cheyne. The mentality and emphases of the great Reformer had put their stamp on theological thinking. This didn't occur at the expense of the Calvinistic teaching on election, to which John Knox had adhered and which the Westminster Confession later fully explained. It was the first Reformer, Patrick Hamilton, who further elaborated on the Lutheran distinction between the Law and the Gospel in his *Places*. A contemporary of Knox, Henry Balnaves, wrote an exposition of the teaching on justification which entirely concurred with Luther's opinion.

As time passed, the teaching on grace displayed a number of shifts in emphases. The Covenanters of the seventeenth century offered more attention to the 'marks of grace' than did the Reformers. The Westminster Confession derived the assurance of salvation to a greater extent from the marks and evidences of grace than from the promises contained in the gospel and the reconciling work of Christ. The tendency to devote more attention to the inner work of God's Spirit than to the facts of salvation, continued during the course of the seventeenth century. This shift elicited a reaction from the so-called Marrow men in the succeeding century. To their ranks belonged Thomas Boston and the Erskines, men who reverted back to the first Reformers, without criticizing the Westminster Confession. They placed much less emphasis on the teaching of election and defended especially the general offer of grace, by not declaring the gospel to be dependent on characteristics of conviction of sin or of penitence. Thomas Chalmers pursued this course as a reaction to the teaching of the Moderates. He certainly had a tendency to tone down the teaching on election in favour of an unhindered proclamation of the gospel.

## The place of M'Cheyne in the Scottish Reformed tradition

What was M'Cheyne's opinion of these developments? It is

difficult to describe this conclusively. However, Blaikie's observation is true that he made use of all the characteristic elements of the Scottish theological tradition in his preaching. He guarded against partiality; what concerned him was the full counsel of God. In contrast to the proposition of the Marrow men that the promises of the Word are for all, he strictly taught that the unconverted were excluded from the benefits of the promises. Concerning this there is a slight difference in approach. 'The preparing operations by the law' didn't constitute such an emphasis in the preaching of the Erskines as was the case with M'Cheyne; they included the work of 'awakening' and 'conviction' of sin in the full invitation to salvation, so as to avoid every tendency to make the promises conditional. Doesn't Christ promise that the Spirit 'will convince the world of sin'?

The offer of grace was an indisputable element in M'Cheyne's preaching, but he also gave attention to God's sovereignty and His eternal plan. The manner in which he describes 'the awakened sinner' corresponds to a great degree with the *Sum of Saving Knowledge*, the work that made such a great impact on him at the time of his conversion. Some sermons, in which the preparatory function of the law received so much attention, could have awakened the emergence of the so-called hyper-Calvinism, although this never was his intention. What concerned him was the need for a knowledge of man's misery, and not to make the function of the law conditional. In this respect, the entry in his diary made on 22 July 1832 should be understood: 'Had this evening a more complete understanding of that self-emptying and abasement with which it is necessary to come to Christ, a denying of self, trampling it under foot – a recognizing of the complete righteousness and justice of God, that could do nothing else with us but condemn us utterly, and thrust us down to lowest hell, a feeling that, even in hell, we should rejoice in His sovereignty, and say that all was rightly done.' It seems the guidance he received in finding salvation in Christ influenced his preaching, although it was never his intention to propose his own experience as a norm or model for others to follow.

M'Cheyne was apprehensive of a superficial conversion, which missed out 'a deepness because the seed had not root'. Hence, in his preaching, he guarded against going over to a biased emphasis on God's love whilst neglecting to focus attention on God's right and the law. In his consideration of the assurance of faith, he avoided extremes and spoke in clear tones: 'A sense of forgiveness of sins does not proceed from marks seen in yourself.' Yet there is also an assurance which flows from 'what we see in ourselves; the seal of the Spirit, love to the brethren, etc.' Here we find the distinction made by the Marrow men between 'assurance of faith' and 'assurance of sense'. Thus he strove in all things for harmony. To him this meant that there shouldn't be an inner struggle, such as is clearly observed in a contemporary such as John Duncan. Instead this impartiality characterized his entire person and work. His friend, Alexander Moody Stuart, observed that his 'views of divine truth were clear and determined' and were 'free from extremes'.

As already mentioned, Chalmers gave new impulse to a declining Calvinism. His learning methods were more practical than dogmatic. It was precisely his practical theology, interpreted according to the need of the church and national life, that determined the spirit of M'Cheyne and his friends. The dogmas were no pegs of dead orthodoxy, but living truths. Andrew Bonar mentioned succinctly that the hearers needed 'pegs' on which they could hang the truth. Yeaworth observes in this regard: 'The core of M'Cheyne's message was the Person and work of Jesus Christ, and His relation to God and man. This was the major theme of the preachers of the Disruption generation; to M'Cheyne, however, this was not merely a matter of orthodoxy but an experience of utmost importance.' The truths had to become a living reality in the hearts and lives of the listeners. The point was the purpose of God for sinful people, not only according to His pleasure, but also in the proclamation of His deep love for sinners without distinction, along with the threat of His eternal punishment whenever His well-meaning message was spurned through stubborn unbelief.

Were there striking features in M'Cheyne's theology, which indicated originality? Did he preach an exclusive message? The picture we have portrayed of his life shows certain marked characteristics. However, he didn't differ from others in his theological point of view. What then is characteristic of his message, which distinguishes him from ministers of the same tradition? The great secret of his proclamation is 'holiness'. He not only practised, but also emphasized this aspect to a greater degree than most other teachers of the Scottish church. Although he knew that many among God's children were not progressing in holiness, he never neglected to stress the point that holiness should be a reality in the Christian faith and life. Although he had to leave much room in his preaching for addressing the unconverted because of the spiritual condition of his audience, the stress on the need for holiness never fell into the background. This was the characteristic of his theology, even as it characterized his person and life. It was a holiness closely linked to the offices of Christ as Prophet, Priest and King. He avoided every form of fleshly activism and detested every evidence of passivity. A scrupulous use of means, such as meditation and prayer, were not interpreted by him as appropriate for further holiness, but were, according to him, necessary to revive and preserve the workings of God's Spirit in the life of holiness by God's grace.

**Theological climate of his time**

The theological climate of the time in which M'Cheyne lived was determined by a transition from the period of the Moderates to a new revival. The scales tipped from a rigid morality, in which the Person of Christ was pushed into the background, to a fully Biblical interpretation of the salvation truths. The emphasis here fell on the gospel and faith in Christ as Mediator and Substitute. Extremes were unfortunately not unheard of. Chalmers leaned sometimes too far to the other side by not giving the teaching on predestination the place which the Westminster Confession afforded it. He was afraid of a fatalistic look at God's grace. According to him, nothing should detract from human responsibility. His vision held no deviation from the 'Westminster Standards,' but constituted a different approach.

On the edge of the rising evangelical trend, another development emerged that we could characterize as 'hyper-evangelism'. The characteristic of this trend was that reconciliation was placed within a universal framework. John M'Leod Campbell began to criticize the Confession, which he thought was dominated by the teaching on election. He was a minister in Row at the time of his suspension in 1831. He taught that Christ had settled the account for all, that the law was not necessary as a preparatory function to salvation in Christ, and that all people could acknowledge God as their Father. He taught the general Fatherhood of God, with a strong accent on the virtue of God's love. Campbell had great difficulty with the classical teaching of 'reconciliation through satisfaction'. His influence was limited, although the teaching on general reconciliation began to gain more ground. At about the this time, Edward Irving began to come into the spotlight. Besides his premillennialistic viewpoint, he upset the theological climate with his extreme views on the charismatic gifts and on Christ's incarnation. Campbell's and Irving's deviation occurred when M'Cheyne was about to embark on his theological training. It was noticeable that a man such as Chalmers, fully acquainted with them as he was, didn't cross swords with them. He thought their ideas unbiblical, but valued their struggle to emphasize the unhindered proclamation of the unconditional gospel.

M'Cheyne, however, distanced himself from Campbell and Irving and their followers. Election was an important element in his preaching, as was the preparatory function of the law. He depicted in clean-cut manner in nearly every sermon the necessity of 'awakening' from guilt and sin, without which, in his eyes, the preaching of the cross would remain powerless.

Actually, according to him, this conviction of the law was a necessity and no condition. Especially during the time of the revival in his congregation in Dundee, he portrayed the awakened sinner in his perception of hopelessness and in his condition outside of Christ. This is more characteristic of him than of his spiritual contemporaries. His message was not only 'Gospel,' but also 'Law.' It was as if the influence of Luther and Patrick Hamilton resounded through his preaching.

**The 'M'Cheyne Group' after the Disruption**

To a large extent, all members of the M'Cheyne group were of one mind. Yet there were differences in emphases as well as of approach. Horatius Bonar laid great stress on human responsibility. He made the cross of Christ an intimate reality, especially in his book, *God's Way of Peace*, as though the preparatory function of the law might be neglected. Chalmers' influence on him is unmistakable. As such, he followed a somewhat different course from M'Cheyne, although there were between the friends no essential differences of opinion.

After the Disruption, the M'Cheyne group made an important contribution to the establishment of the Free Church. Originally, the new church followed in the footsteps of men such as Chalmers. The theology of her colleges in Edinburgh, Glasgow and Aberdeen was thoroughly Calvinistic. There was no difference between the followers of M'Cheyne and the lecturers who initially occupied the professorial chairs. Theologians such as William Cunningham, John Duncan and George Smeaton continued to uphold the old teaching. Yet there soon came into existence a trend which no longer focused on the classical themes. The Higher Criticism movement, which swept in, especially from Germany, appealed to many students. Intellectualism overran the practical, experiential side of theology. This trend dominated in the long run. A logical consequence was that it smothered the first fires of revival and began to set the tone for a superficial Christianity. It was no wonder that men such as M'Leod Campbell appealed to the followers of this trend. The profound and tested truths of guilt and grace were dismissed as old-fashioned, and had to make way for a liberal interpretation of God's Word and world events. The church tried to conform to the development of new theological thinking and the outcome of scientific research.

How did men such as Andrew and Horatius Bonar react to this new trend in theology? They pursued M'Cheyne's theme on the necessity for revival of spiritual life and the emphasis on holiness. But they were more theological in their thinking than their deceased friend, and their writings give one an impression of their achievements in this field. Did they recognize the trend that was detrimental to original Calvinism? They certainly condemned every form of Higher Criticism, and resisted the continuing secularisation.

From the viewpoint of a positive attitude and love for God's kingdom, the Bonar brothers offered their assistance to every endeavour to extend God's kingdom. Hence they heartily supported the American revival preachers, D.L. Moody and I.D. Sankey, on their journey through Scotland in 1874. Moody's non-theological message was no reason to reject his work. His proclamation of the gospel consisted of some rich elements, but also had its dangerous aspects. The element of law-conviction was largely missing, and no role was given the law as the source of knowledge of man's misery. This was the reason that Dr John Kennedy from Dingwall, among others, strongly objected and labelled their teaching as 'Hyper-evangelism.' Kennedy belonged to the rich religious heritage of the Highlands, where a tight nucleus held fast to time-honoured themes and resisted new developments. Horatius Bonar defended himself against Kennedy's strident condemnation, and pointed to the positive influence which emanated from Moody's work. Kennedy himself was a great champion of revival. He recognized the dangers of superficiality, which were so characteristic of the theological climate at the end of the nineteenth century. The outcome confirmed his fears. The critical developments continued and were disastrous for the spiritual life which had blossomed abundantly in the past.

A totally different trend emerged during the declining years of the nineteenth century. This was the appearance of the Holiness Movement which, especially by means of conferences in Keswick, England, resulted in a furtherance of a 'higher holy life'. The positive aspect of the holiness endeavour was the furtherance of growth in the grace of Christ. The negative aspect of this movement was the way in which indwelling sins in believers were described. It was reasoned too readily that these could be overcome. The *Memoir* and the preaching of M'Cheyne breathed a different spirit. A deep awareness of indwelling sin characterized his life and those of his spiritual contemporaries. Horatius Bonar distanced himself from the Keswick movement, and defended his viewpoint in a letter to Evan Henry Hopkins. His brother, Andrew, however, supported the movement and visited the conferences held in Mildway and Perth, where he preached on more than one occasion. The blessing which he received during these times, when weighed in the balance, influenced him more than the criticism of his brother.

By the grace of God, M'Cheyne and his friends gave new impetus to the spiritual life of the church. What concerned them more than anything else was the extension of God's kingdom. They stimulated many to launch out in dependence on God's Spirit on behalf of the extension of Christ's realm. They served the whole church, and were the means whereby many thousands were brought to Christ. The significance of the Jewish nation played no secondary role in this. They established the basis for the spreading of Christian principles among the Jewish people. On 24 May 1889, during a session of the General Assembly of the Free Church, a service was held to commemorate the first Mission station founded among the Jewish people fifty years previously. Andrew Bonar too spoke on this occasion and mentioned the wonders God had performed among the old Jewish people. The longing for reform within the nation of Israel was again revived.

John Kennedy D.D. (1819-1884).

McCheyne's Bible and walking stick, kept for years in McCheyne's Memorial Church, are in St Peter's now.

It was entirely appropriate that, in their endeavour, there should be an interest in the work of revival. Scotland boasted a rich tradition in this respect. This tradition was maintained when in 1839 a new wave of revival swept across the land. The *Lectures on Revival of Religion*, a book that came off the press in 1840, consisted of contributions by different ministers, illustrating a number of aspects of revival. This book is a good interpretation of the spirit in which the revival took place. It was characterized by a Biblical profundity and was, generally speaking, free of extremes. They wished to build on this foundation, although later revivals such as those of 1859 and 1874 were more superficial than that of 1839. In the first place, there arose among them a longing for the abundant work of God's Spirit and, in this respect, they bore in mind the Biblical promises, such as, for example, Ezekiel 34:26: 'I will cause the shower to come down in his season; there shall be showers of blessing.'

**'Whose faith follow...'**

'Whose faith follow, considering the end of their conversation' (Heb. 13:7). M'Cheyne's conversation, as well as those of his friends, was 'in heaven'. Their work was not in vain, because they had laboured abundantly in God's vineyard. M'Cheyne had preceded them in heavenly glory and they imitated him. His life was a brilliant example of holiness and godliness. The lives of the greats in God's kingdom show that by the grace of God the impossible becomes possible. M'Cheyne was well aware that he was powerless to command a blessing to come down from above. The urgency with which he entreated his listeners accompanied a deep awareness of his own inability, but at the same time of God's omnipotence. The harmony of God's Word resounded throughout his preaching. The adoration of God's sovereignty and the benevolence of God's message formed the pillars for his labour in God's kingdom. Despite the incomprehensible area of tension between God's secret counsel and His revealed will which was caused by limited human reason, he strove towards a harmony which distanced itself from human intrusion into God's pleasure, and which concluded in wonderment and worship of God's grace.

Our 'wanderings' through Robert Murray M'Cheyne's life have been personally enriching. A deep nostalgia fills the heart, when we read of the wonderful and rich harvest in days gone past. What remains of the rich blessing of those days? Has not his memory in the national life of the people largely been forgotten? Our visits to the places where M'Cheyne lived and worked motivated us to transfer ourselves back in time to the life and home environment of one of Scotland's great sons. The stately rows of houses in New Town, Edinburgh, have since then undergone little change. The street plan round about St Peter's in Dundee exists to this day, although many of the buildings have had to make way for modern homes. The spire of St Peter's still stands as a solemn witness to the blessed days of yore, and the monument that adorns his grave is a silent witness to the wonders of God's grace in Dundee. The anonymous stone at the entrance gate displays in one word the contents of the message of one 'dying who spoke to the dying.' That word is *Eternity*. M'Cheyne knew from experience its awesome meaning. From a deep compassion for the eternal lot of the 'flock' which he served, he sought ceaselessly to impress the meaning of that word on the memory of his audience. His grave still preaches the transitoriness of human life, but also the immortality of the Word of God. The following words resound down the ages: 'The voice said, Cry. And he said, What shall I cry? All flesh is grass and all the goodliness thereof is as the flower of the field; the grass withereth, the flower fadeth...but the Word of our God shall stand for ever' (Isaiah 40:6-8).

# BIBLIOGRAPHY

*The New Statistical Account of Scotland*, vol I List of parishes-Edinburgh, Edinburgh 1845.

*Registers of St. Peter's Parish Dundee*, (Minutes of managers, Communion Roll 1843, Seatholders Register), kept in City Archives, Dundee.

*The Confession of Faith (Westminster Confession of Faith incl. The Sum of Saving Knowledge)*, repr. Inverness 1958.

Peter Anton, *Kilsyth, a Parish history*, Glasgow 1893.

William Arnot, *Life of James Hamilton*, London 1870.

J. Baillie, *Een rijke oogst, Alexander Paterson van Kilmany*, Amsterdam 1858.

Peter Bayne, LL.D., *The Free Church of Scotland*, Edinburgh 1894.

Alexander Beith, *Memories of Disruption Times*, London 1877.

William Garden Blaikie, D.D., LL.D., *The Preachers of Scotland*, Edinburgh 1888.

Andrew A. Bonar, D.D., *Diary and Letters*, London 1893.

Andrew A. Bonar, *Sheaves After Harvest*, London z.j.

Andrew A. Bonar, *Memoir and Remains of Robert Murray M'Cheyne*, Edinburgh 1973.

Andrew Bonar, *Narrative of a Mission of Inquiry to the Jews in 1839*, 2 vols., Edinburgh 1848.

Horatius Bonar, *A Memorial*, London 1889.

Horatius Bonar, *The Life of the Rev. John Milne of Perth*, London 1868.

Horatius Bonar, *The Life and Work of the Rev. G. Theophilus Dodds*, Edinbrugh 1883.

Horatius Bonar, *Memories of the Dr. Horatius Bonar*, Edinburgh 1909.

Marjory Bonar, *Reminiscences of Andrew A. Bonar, D.D.*, London 1897.

Thomas Brown, F.R.S.E., *Annals of the Disruption*, Edinburgh 1884.

Dr. J. de Bruijn, *Thomas Chalmers en zijn kerkelijk streven*, Nijkerk 1954.

Islay Burns, D.D., *Memoir of the Rev. Wm. C. Burns, M.A.*, London 1870.

John Cunningham, D.D., *The Church History of Scotland, vol. 2*, Edinburgh 1882.

James Dodds, *Personal Reminiscences and Biographical Sketches*, Edinburgh 1888.

Andrew L. Drummond and James Bulloch, *The Scottish Church 1688-1843*, Edinburgh 1973.

G.T.C. Duncan, *Memoir of Rev. Henry Duncan, D.D.*, 1848.

William Ewing, D.D., *Annals of the Free Church of Scotland 1843-1900*, 2 vols., Edinburgh 1914.

*Dundee Warder*, 1843.

*Dundee Advertiser*, 1836.

G. Fairlie, *The Early Days of St. Peter's Dundee*, 1975.

Fergus Fergusson, D.D., *The Life of the Rev. Dr. Andrew A. Bonar*, Glasgow, n.y.

J.R. Fleming, *A History of the Church in Scotland 1875-1929*, Edinburgh 1933.

J.R. Fleming, D.D., *A History of the Church in Scotland 1843-1874*, Edinburgh 1927.

Janet R. Glover, *The Story of Scotland*, London 1960.

William Hanna, LL.D., *Memoirs of Thomas Chalmers, D.D., LL.D.*, Edinburgh 1854.

J. Harrison Hudson e.a., *Let the Fire Burn*, Dundee 1978.

W.M. Hetherington, LL. D., *Memoir and Correspondence of Mrs. Coutts*, Edinburgh 1854.

P. Hume Brown, M.A., LL.D., F.B.A., *History of Scotland*, vol. III, Cambridge 1911.

Werner Keller, *...En zij werden verstooid onder alle volken*, Zwolle z.j.

William Lamb, *M'Cheyne from the Pew*, Belfast 1987.

Marcus L.Loane, M.A., D.D., *Sons of the Covenant*, Sydney 1963.

Robert Murray M'Cheyne, *Gleanings after the Vintage*, Dundee 1843.

Robert Murray M'Cheyne, *A Basket of Fragments*, Inverness 1979.

Robert Murray M'Cheyne, *Additional Remains*, Edinburgh n.y.

Robert Murray M'Cheyne, *Two Last Discourses*, Dundee 1843.

Robert Murray McCheyne, *The Believer's Joy*, Glasgow 1987.

Robert Murray M'Cheyne, *McCheyne's Helps to Devotion*, Glasgow 1988.

Robert Murray M'Cheyne, *Familiar Letters*, Edinburgh 1848.

Robert Murray M'Cheyne, *Manuscripts van Robert Murray M'Cheyne*, kept in New College Library, Edinburgh. David M/ M'Intire, *The Hidden Life of Prayer*, Tain 1989.

John Macleod, *Scottish Theology in relation to Church History since the Reformation*, Edinburgh reprint 1974.

Kenneth Moody Stuart, M.A., *Alexander Moody Stuart D.D.: a Memoir ...*, London 1900.

A. Moody Stuart, *Recollections of the late John Duncan, LL.D.*, Edinburgh 1872.

John Muir, *St. Peter's Church Dundee*, Dundee 1936.

Ian H. Murray, *The Puritan Hope*, London 1971.

Adam Philip, M.A., *The Evangel in Gowrie*, Edinburgh 1911.

Adam Philip, *The Devotional Litterature of Scotland*, London z.j.

William Reid, M.A., *Revival Truth*, London 1860.

David Roberts R.A., *The Holy Land*, London 1982.

Hew Scott, D.D., *Fasti Ecclesiae Scoticanae*, 7 vols, Edinburgh 1915-1928.

Alexander Smellie, D.D., *Robert Murray McCheyne*, London 1913.

Alexander Smellie, *Evan Henry Hopkins*, London 1920.

George Smith, *A Modern Apostle, Alexander N. Somerville, D.D.*, Edinburgh 1893.

J.C. Smith, *Robert Murray M'Cheyne*, London 1910.

T.C. Smout, *A Century of the Scottish People 1830-1950*, London 1987.

T.C. Smout, *A History of the Scottish People 1560-1830*, London 1990.

A.N. Somerville, *Precious Seed, sown in many lands*, London 1890.

Jessie Thain, *Diary of Jessie Thain*, Dingwall 1955.

L.J. van Valen, *De rotssteen van mijn hart, het leven van "Rabbi" John Duncan*, Kampen 1991.

L.J. van Valen, *Die aan alle wateren zaait*, Ede 1989.

Keith Walker, *Robert Murray M'Cheyne: Saint and Preacher*, Banner of Truth magazine, issue 246 en 247, 1984.

James A. Wylie, *Disruption Worthies*, Edinburgh 1881.

David Victor Yeaworth, *Robert Murray McCheyne (Phil. diss., unpublished)*, 1957.

# Some biographical details of Robert Murray M'Cheyne and a few friends

**Robert Murray M'Cheyne**
Born in Edinburgh on 21 May 1813, a son of Adam M'Cheyne and Lockhart Murray Dickson; a student of the High School and University of Edinburgh, licensed to preach on 1 July 1835, assistant both at Larbert and Dunipace, ordained at St Peter's, Dundee on 24 November 1836, passed away in Dundee on 25 March 1843.

**Andrew Alexander Bonar**
Born in Edinburgh on 29 May 1810, a son of James Bonar and Marjory Pyott or Maitland, studied at the High School and University of Edinburgh, licensed to preach on 1 July 1835, assistant at Jedburgh, ordained in Collace 20 September 1838, became transferred to the Free Church in 1843, ordained in Finnieston Free Church, Glasgow 4 December 1856, Doctor of Divinity (D.D) 22 April 1874, Moderator of Free Church General Assembly 1878, married to Isabella Dickson, passed away on 30 December 1892.

**Horatius Bonar**

Born in Edinburgh on 19 December 1808, a son of James Bonar and Marjory Pyott or Maitland, studied at the High School and University of Edinburgh, licensed to preach on 23 April 1833, assistant at St John's, Leith, ordained in Kelso North Parish 30 November 1837, transferred to the Free Church in 1843, Doctor of Divinity (D.D) 9 April 1853, ordained in Chalmers' Memorial Free Church, Edinburgh 7 June 1866, Moderator of the Free Church General Assembly 1883, married to Jane Catherine Lundie, passed away in Edinburgh 31 July 1889.

**William Chalmers Burns**

Born in Duns 1 April 1815, a son of William Hamilton Burns, studied at the University of Aberdeen (Marischal College) and Glasgow, licensed to preach on 27 March 1839, assistant at St Peter's Dundee 1839, transferred in 1843 to the Free Church, sent out as a missionary to China in 1846, passed away in New-chawang, China 4 April 1868.

**James Grierson**

Born in Ruthwell 1791, studied at the University of Edinburgh, licensed to preach on 22 September 1816, ordained in Errol 12 August 1819, transferred to the Free Church in 1843, Moderator of the Free Church General Assembly 1854, Doctor of Divinity (D.D) 25 March 1854, married to Margaret Moncrieff, passed away in Errol on 22 January 1875.

**James Hamilton**

Born in Paisley 27 November 1814, a son of William Hamilton, studied at the University of Glasgow and Edinburgh, licensed to preach in 1839, assistant at St George's in Edinburgh and in Abernyte, ordained on 21 January 1841, National Scotch Church, Regent Square, London 22 July 1841, Doctor of Divinity (D.D) 1848, married to Anna Hovenden, passed away on 24 November 1867.

**Robert McDonald**

Born in Perth 1813, a son of Alexander McDonald and Charlotte McFarlane, studied at the University of St Andrews and Edinburgh, licensed to preach on 8 June 1836, ordained at Blairgowrie 15 June 1837, transferred to the Free Church in 1843, ordained in North Leith Free Church on 12 March 1857, Doctor of Divinity (D.D) 12 February 1870, Moderator of the Free Church General Assembly 1882, married to Catherine Malcolm, passed away in Leith on 21 August 1893.

**Alexander Moody Stuart**

Born in Paisley 15 June 1809, a son of Andrew Moody and Margaret Fulton McBriar, studied at the University of Glasgow, licensed to preach on 5 October 1831, missionary to Holy Island, Northumberland, 1831-1835, ordained in St Luke's Edinburgh 27 July 1837, transferred to the Free Church in 1843, Moderator of the Free Church General Assembly 1875, Doctor of Divinity (D.D) 1875, married to Jessie Stuart of Annat, which surname was added to his own, passed away in Crieff on 31 July 1898.

**Alexander Neil Somerville**

Born in Edinburgh 30 January 1813, a son of Alexander Somerville and Elizabeth Munro, studied at the High School and University of Edinburgh, licensed to preach on 9 December 1835, assistant in Larbert and Dunipace, ordained in Glasgow, Anderston, 30 November 1837, transferred to the Free Church in 1843, Doctor of Divinity (D.D) 2 May 1877, Moderator of the Free Church General Assembly 1886, married to Isabella Mirrlees, passed away in Glasgow 18 September 1889.

# Other books of interest in the Christian Hertiage imprint

A
BASKET
OF
FRAGMENTS

*The sermons of revival*

R.M. McCHEYNE

## A Basket of Fragments

*R. M. McCheyne*

Robert Murray McCheyne (1813-1843), the pastor of St. Peter's Dundee, died in his thirtieth year and in his seventh of his ministry. His epitaph describes him as a man who "was honoured by his Lird to draw many wanderers out of darkness into the path of life". Dr Baxter of Blairgowrie wrote of McCheyne: "The chief thing about him was the unaction from the Holy One... at times he was awakening... at other times he was melting and moving as he dwelt on the great theme of redeeming love".

This selection of sermons was first published five years after McCheyne's death. They were compiled from notes taken down by hearers "without the least view to publication", they bring before us the extemporaneous pleadings with sinners in which few so greatly excelled as did Robert Murray McCheyne. These sermons are stamped with eternity, they are the expression of one upon whose heart the weight of perishing sinners pressed and who earnestly longed for their conversion.

**ISBN 0-906-731-038**

Large Print Edition
COMFORT
in
SORROW
R.M. McCheyne

## Comfort in Sorrow

*Robert Murray McCheyne*

We have all needed comfort at some time in our lives. People search for comfort in all sorts of places, from the empty psychobabble of the self-help book to the oblivion of alcoholism.

The only completely satisfying source of comfort is found in the Bible – and more particularly knowing Jesus as a friend.

This is shown in the story of the death of Lazarus. Jesus comforted Lazarus' sisters, Mary and Martha, weeping with them, before going on to raise Lazarus back to life after four days in the grave. Robert Murray McCheyne, one of Scotland's greatest preachers who saw great revival in his 30 years of life, looks at this wonderful passage, offering us tremendous encouragement and pointing us to the one true source of comfort – Jesus.

**ISBN 1 85792 012 0**

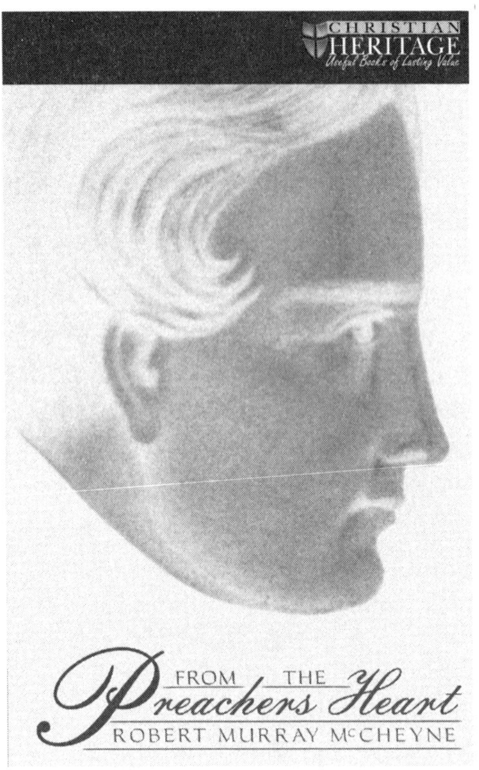
CHRISTIAN
HERITAGE
Useful Books of Lasting Value
FROM THE
Preachers Heart
ROBERT MURRAY McCHEYNE

## From the Preacher's Heart

*Robert Murray McCheyne*

Robert Murray McCheyne has had a tremendous impact not only on the people of his generation but through his writings ever since. He died in his thirtieth year, having taken the charge of St Peters in Dundee as a young man of twenty-three. A church regularly filled to overflowing with 1,100 hearers – from a total population in the area of 4,000.

His sermons were spiritual and forceful – in many ways models for preachers today. They were also attended with wonderful power and fruitfulness when they were first preached. McCheyne was a man who stood out amongst his contemporaries – regarded as one whose grace and gentleness were obvious to all who met him.

He preached with urgency – 'as a dying man to dying men' – sermons as relevant today as when published over 150 years ago.

*'The workmanship of McCheyne, exquisite sermons in miniature, the fruits of a spiritual genius.'*

**Maurice Roberts**

*'When preaching, McCheyne was full of passion, conviction and determination to reach the listener at their point of need, as well as giving them what he considered to be God's message for the day... shows the heart of one who is considered to be amongst the greatest of Scottish Preachers.'*

**Paul Berry**

**ISBN 1-85792-025-2**

CHRISTIAN
HERITAGE
Useful Books of Lasting Value
The Passionate
PREACHER
PREVIOUSLY UNPUBLISHED SERMONS BY
RoBt MURRAY McCHEYNE
EDITED BY DR. MICHAEL M. MCMULLEN

**The Passionate Preacher**
Previously Unpublished Sermons by
Robert Murray McCheyne
*Edited by Dr. Michael M. McMullen*

*The words of McCheyne are of great value today, as the kind of evangelical and spiritual outlook he stood for is badly needed again...*

**Rev T. F. Torrance**
**Professor Emeritus, Edinburgh University**

*We cannot all be McCheynes but we can all learn from... the spiritual goals and methods which characterised his ministry.*

**Geoffrey W. Bromiley**
**Professor Emeritus of Church History and Theology, Fuller Theological Seminary**

*To have McCheyne's unpublished sermons in our hands is, without doubt, a great privilege... at a time when models of biblical and passionate expositions are so desperately needed.*

**Jim Elliff**
**Pre sident, Christian Communicators Worldwide**

Robert Murray McCheyne stands as one of the outstanding preachers of Scottish history. His name is up there alongside Livingstone, Knox, Burns and the Haldane brothers. He had only been licensed a short time when he was given the charge of St Peter's, Dundee – a very challenging position for a young man of 23. Even at his trial sermon as a candidate, two people were saved. In the seven years that followed till his death, St Peter's was regularly filled to overflowing.

McCheyne is a wonderful example of what God calls us to be, holy and committed to Him in all things. McCheyne enjoyed the blessing of God because he enjoyed the holiness of God.

Dr Michael M. McMullen is a lecturer in Church History at Midwestern Baptist Theological Seminary, Kansas City

**ISBN 1-85792-410-X**

ANDREW BONAR AND R.M. MCCHEYNE

# MISSION OF DISCOVERY

## THE BEGINNINGS OF MODERN JEWISH EVANGELISM

The journal of Bonar and McCheyne's Mission of Inquiry

# **Mission of Discovery**

## The Beginning of Modern Jewish Evangelism

*Edited by Allan Harman*

The Beginning of the Modern Jewish Evangelism
The jouranl of Bonar and McCheyne's Mission of Inquiry
– edited by Allan Harman

In Scotland there has been a concern for the Jewish people since the time of the Reformation. In 1838 this led up to the appointment of a Church of Scotland committee 'to collect information respecting the Jews, their numbers, condition and character, – what means have hitherto been employed by the Christian Church for their spiritual good, and with what sucess, whether there are any openings for a mission to their nation, and where these are most promising'.

The committee sent a 'Mission of Inquiry' in 1839 consisting of Dr. Alexander Keith, Dr Alexander Black, Robert Murray McCheyne and Andrew Bonar, Keith and Black did not complete the whole trip, having to return in ill health from the arduous trek around Europe and the Middle East. This book is based on the journal of Bonar and McCheyne.

On their journey they were attacked by robbers, quarantined due to there plague, persecuted by governing authorities and set upon by religious leaders. Through all this, they managed to hand out thousands of tracts, talk to many people and speak in Synagogues. As a result the first Church of Scotland missionary to the Jews was sent out to Hungary in 1814.

This epic chronicle has a fascination that stems from the attention to detail both men had for what they saw. It is part travel book, adventure story and social history. This is an absorbing story of the scattered Jewish people of the mid-19th century and the problems of travel was available.

**ISBN 1-85792-258-1**

## Christian Focus Publications

publishes books for all ages

Our mission statement –

**STAYING FAITHFUL**

In dependence upon God we seek to help make His infallible word, the Bible, relevant. Our aim is to ensure that the Lord Jesus Christ is presented as the only hope to obtain forgiveness of sin, live a useful life and look forward to heaven with Him.

**REACHING OUT**

Christ's last command requires us to reach out to our world with His gospel. We seek to help fulfill that by publishing books that point people towards Jesus and help them to develop a Christ-like maturity. We aim to equip all levels of readers for life, work, ministry and mission.

Books in our adult range are published in three imprints.

*Christian Focus* contains popular works including biographies, commentaries, basic doctrine, and Christian living. Our children's books are also published in this imprint.

*Mentor* focuses on books written at a level suitable for Bible College and seminary students, pastors, and other serious readers. The imprint includes commentaries, doctrinal studies, examination of current issues, and church history.

*Christian Heritage* contains classic writings from the past.

For a free catalogue of all our titles, please write to

Christian Focus Publications, Ltd
Geanies House, Fearn,
Ross-shire, IV20 1TW, Scotland, United Kingdom
info@christianfocus.com

For details of our titles visit us on our website
www.christianfocus.com